RICHARD COBDEN
A Victorian Outsider

RICHARD COBDEN

A Victorian Outsider

Wendy Hinde

Yale University Press
New Haven and London
1987

Set in Linotron Bembo by Best-set Typesetter Limited, Hong Kong, and printed and bound in Great Britain at The Bath Press, Avon.

Library of Congress CIP Data

Hinde, Wendy.
    Richard Cobden: a Victorian outsider.

    Bibliography: p.
    Includes index.
    1. Cobden, Richard, 1804–1865.   2. Legislators —
Great Britain — Biography.   3. Social reformers — Great
Britain — Biography.   4. Great Britain — Politics and
government — 1837–1901.   5. Great Britain. Parliament.
House of Commons — Biography.   I. Title.
DA536.C6H47   1987   941.081′092′4   [B]   86-26661
ISBN 0–300–03880–1

CONTENTS

CONTENTS

LIST OF ILLUSTRATIONS

PREFACE AND ACKNOWLEDGEMENTS

Among the well-known figures in the middle years of Queen Victoria's reign Richard Cobden stands out as a man of contrasts and contradictions. His name is associated with the rising class of middle-class businessmen and manufacturers, but his business career was never more to him than a means of acquiring financial independence. In some aristocratic circles he was regarded as little better than a red revolutionary, but the workers distrusted – and even hated – him because he accepted the factory system (but not its abuses), and to many of his fellow Radicals he was maddeningly cautious about pushing for more political reform. A realist in domestic politics, he proclaimed views on foreign and colonial policy that were too idealistic – even at times too visionary – to make much impact. His campaign to repeal the Corn laws made him a popular hero; his criticism of the Crimean war turned him temporarily into an outcast. He believed that the way to reform at home and peace abroad lay through providing a national education system for the 'people'. But the people rejected his views on peace and were apathetic about political reform. After 1846 his most sympathetic and thoughtful audience was often found in the House of Commons, although its members were largely recruited from the aristocracy whose predominance he abhorred. He never really overcame his difficulty in coming to terms with the age in which he lived. But although he remained – in Bagehot's words – an outsider, there was something about his personality which made his contemporaries willing to listen to him even when they did not agree with him.

This attempt to understand Cobden and his career owes a very great deal to the support of Richard Ollard, who edited the book, and I am most grateful for all his advice and encouragement. I would like to thank the Trustees of Dunford House for their permission to quote from the Cobden Papers deposited in the West Sussex Records Office, and the former Principal of Dunford House, Mr Hayman, for his kindness in giving me such an interesting guided tour of the house. I am most grateful to Mrs Sylvia Lewin for allowing me to make use of some Sturge family papers in her possession, and for showing them to me in the first place. Finally, I would like to express my warm appreciation of the unfailing helpfulness and courtesy of the staff at the Cambridge University Library.

I would like to thank the Manchester Central Library for providing illustrations 3 and 4 and the back of the jacket; *Punch* library for 6, 7, 8, 11, 12 and 13; the National Portrait Gallery for 10 and 14 and the front of the jacket; and the BBC Hulton Picture Library for 1, 2 and 9.

ABBREVIATIONS

BL Add. Mss.   British Library, Additional Manuscripts.

WSRO Add. Mss.   West Sussex Record Office (Chichester),
                      Additional Manuscripts.

CP   Cobden Papers, West Sussex Record Office.

MCL   Manchester Central Library.

UCL   University College, London.

Morley   *The Life of Richard Cobden* by John Morley,
                      1. Vol. 1903 ed.

1 Cobden as a young man.

CHAPTER 1

From Sussex to Manchester (1804–34)

'Our quarters are within a very short walk from the summit of the Downs which commands a glorious view looking down upon the sea with the Isle of Wight in the distance on one side, and upon the wooded parts of Sussex, stretching up towards Surrey on the other ...'. When Cobden wrote this description of the view from the Downs above his birthplace, he was at the height of his fame and popularity and had travelled widely in Europe, the Middle East and the United States. But, he added, 'after seeing so much of the world's scenery, I think there is nothing in nature so beautiful as the *wooded* parts of the South Downs in this neighbourhood'.[1]

Richard Cobden was born there on 3 June, 1804, at Dunford, in the tiny hamlet of Heyshott, near Midhurst, the second son and fourth child of William Cobden and Millicent Amber. His forebears are believed to have been settled in the district since the 17th century, living unremarkable lives as yeomen farmers. Richard's grandfather, his namesake, born in 1737, was a farmer and maltster; for some years he also held the office of bailiff of the borough of Midhurst. When he died in 1809, he left his property to be divided equally between his only son William and his four daughters. The old farm house and land at Dunford had to be sold and William and his family moved to a small farm on the edge of Midhurst.

William Cobden was a kind, affectionate, honest and good man. He was also weak, gullible and thoroughly incompetent at running his own affairs. He allowed himself to be repeatedly cheated until his fortune had gradually ebbed away, and in 1814 he was forced to sell his farm.[2] Fortunately, his wife possessed in full measure the strength of character and good sense which her husband lacked. Twenty years after her death, her son Richard described her as 'an energetically pious woman'.[3] She had eleven children and – in spite

1

of material hardships – she evidently managed to provide them with a happy and secure home. In time she also became the chief bread-winner. When, after several moves, the family finally settled at West Meon, near Petersfield, Mrs Cobden, with the help of friends, opened a village shop which became the family's principal source of income.

For young Richard, the consequences of the move from Midhurst turned out to be little short of disastrous. He and his brother Frederick had to leave their school at Midhurst, and for the next five years without a break Richard was exiled to one of the notorious Yorkshire schools which Dickens was later to expose in *Nicholas Nickleby*. His fees were paid by his mother's brother-in-law, Mr Cole, a London merchant dealing in textiles, who probably read an advertisement for the school in one of the London papers. When Dickens read similar advertisements more than twenty years later, it was beginning to be suspected that the group of private schools in or near Bowes, which offered such a wide syllabus for such moderate fees, and were prepared to keep boys during the holidays into the bargain, were not all that they purported to be. Dickens's worst suspicions were confirmed when he visited Bowes, posing as the friend of a widowed lady who was looking for a school for her two sons.[4] No such reconnoitring was carried out before Richard was despatched to Bowes Hall. No doubt his uncle was too busy and his parents too thankful for the offer of what seemed to be a good education for their son.

When Cobden came to read *Nicholas Nickleby*, he is reported to have said that he himself had been to a school similar to Dotheboys Hall where he had been ill-fed, ill-used and ill-taught. The only first-hand evidence we have is a batch of eight pathetic letters from Richard to his parents, his uncle Cole and his brother Fred. Written in a beautiful copperplate hand, their stilted style and unctuous sentiments betray that, if not actually dictated, they must have been inspired and closely vetted by the school authorities.[5] But enough is left uncensored to reveal, if only by implication, his sense of isolation, even after he was joined by his younger brother Charles. Letters from home, usually accompanied by a few shillings, were far too infrequent to assuage his homesickness and he always wistfully begged for more. In March 1816, he was reduced to asking Fred, then working in London, whether he had heard from their parents lately and, indeed, where they lived, 'as it is now a long time since I heard from them'. A letter from his father eventually turned up early the following December, having taken four months on the way. In March 1817 he told his parents that he had now been separated from them for more than three years 'and I assure you I look back with more pleasure to that period than to any other period of my life which was spent to no effectual purpose, and I beg to return you my most sincere thanks as being the means of my gaining such a sense of learning as will enable me to gain a genteel livelihood ... '. He could not resist also assuring them that 'it gave me some uneasiness not to have the pleasure of hearing from any of my friends in answer to my letter last Christmas, but', he added, dutifully softening the implied reproach, 'I suppose the hurry of business has been the cause of my disappointment.'

In all his letters Richard insisted that he was studying hard and was in good health, except for some unspecified ailment in his feet (perhaps chilblains) which at one stage he reported to be in a 'dangerous state'. Whatever this might have meant, by the time he wrote his last letter to his parents in September 1818, his feet had recovered and he was wondering what situation he was likely to be placed in when he left school.

He left Bowes sooner than he had dared hope. Early the following year an usher at the school wrote privately to William Cobden revealing that Richard's health was not as good as his parents had been led to believe. Richard was immediately removed from the school.[6] This swift and decisive reaction to the usher's letter suggests that Mr and Mrs Cobden had had no inkling of the life their son was leading. What is perhaps more surprising is that Richard should not apparently have been scarred by his five-years' ordeal. Nor does it seem to have cast a shadow over his relations with his parents, although it may unconsciously have contributed to his chequered relations with Mr Cole over the next few years.

Sometime in the autumn of 1819, Richard began work as a clerk in his uncle's warehouse at 45 Old Change*. The work was boring but at least he had a chance to fill in some of the gaps in his education. He bagan a course of miscellaneous reading ranging from Aristotle to *Evelina*. He haunted second-hand bookstalls and saved up for the books he wanted. In the early mornings before breakfast, he studied French in his bedroom. His uncle and aunt, in whose house he lived, thoroughly disapproved of his spare-time activities. How would all that book-learning, they said, help to turn him into a good businessman?[7] There were other complaints, more psychological than practical. To Mr Cole, Richard was not just an employee, but also a dependent relative who owed everything to him and who in return ought to dedicate himself wholeheartedly to his benefactor's interests. There is no reason to suppose that Richard did not

---

* Presumably – because of Cobden's subsequent business career – his uncle dealt in textiles, but this is not explicitly stated.

conscientiously carry out his duties. Nor did he undervalue his obligations to Mr Cole. But he could not see why in return he should have to suffer'a life of continued vexation'.[8] He was a normal, lively teenage lad and he failed to pass his uncle's stringent tests of dedication and deference. By the autumn of 1821, although Richard was considered sufficiently responsible to be temporarily left in sole charge of the warehouse, Mr Cole had become so exasperated with him that he suddenly gave him a month's notice. However, Richard responded with a respectful letter and the trouble blew over.

The following May Richard was again in trouble with his employer, who again gave him notice and, according to Richard, threatened to throw him out of his house into the bargain. By this time he would have been glad to go, as he had found himself a new job with a merchant in Ghent. His parents, however, would not consent to the move. Frederick had gone off to the United States more than five years earlier, and Mrs Cobden did not want to have another son seeking his fortune abroad. Her husband strongly supported her opposition because he was counting on Richard to find jobs in London for his three younger brothers, Charles, Miles and Henry, when they were old enough.[9]

Richard therefore reluctantly abandoned his plan to find a more congenial job and see some more of the world at the same time. Somehow he and Mr Cole patched up their differences, although not without some gloomy forebodings on Richard's part. 'I know well how forlorn are my prospects', he told his father, 'how weak are my resources in this world. Nothing to help me through but my own reputation and the good opinion of my principals . . . Would to God I were in some place where the prejudices of relations and the obligations of benefactors no longer pressed upon me. I am sure I could give satisfaction to strangers, but *here*, as I told Mr P(artridge), I am afraid the obligations I am under to Mr C(ole) are thrown in the scales against me and makes him never satisfied with my endeavours.'[10]

One consolation for Richard during these difficult years was the ending of his agonising isolation from his family. West Meon was not exactly near to London, but it was near enough for him to spend his holidays there, for the carrier to transmit parcels inexpensively in both directions, and even, on summer evenings, for Richard to meet his father somewhere along the road between Alton and Egham. He would send his parents whatever little luxuries he could afford, as well as patterns of materials for them to choose from. He also sent his mother materials to be made up into shirts and night-shirts for himself. His shirts, he wrote on one occasion, should be a size smaller than his father's and must all be cut out by his mother. 'The last shirts I got were made by Emma and do not reflect much credit on her for unless I stick a pin in behind my neck and shorten the collar it falls half way down over my shoulders and that is not comfortable in cold weather.'[11]

There was also correspondence about Charles's wardrobe. He too had been removed from Bowes Hall and, being only eleven, had been found a place at Christ's Hospital. By 1823 he was eagerly looking forward to leaving school, and Richard wrote at length to his father about the wardrobe Charles would need when he started out in the world. He proposed to get enough blue cloth to make him a new best suit and one of his own, which he had outgrown, would do very well for everyday wear. The boy's shirts were to be made at home by his sister Jane who was instructed to make them large enough at wrist and neck – for 'you know Charles has a great dread of appoplexy' (sic).[12] Charles had to wait some months for a job, but in March 1824 Richard was able to report that, with Mr Cole's help, a place had been found for him with a city firm on very advantageous terms.[13]

By this time Richard was no longer looking for a new job for himself. At Christmas 1822, Mr Cole had had a complete change of heart towards his nephew, expressing great satisfaction with his work, giving him extra responsibility and liberally increasing his salary. Richard had more money to spend, not only on presents for his family and books for himself – such as *Childe Harold* and Brougham on *Popular Education* – but also on indulgences like visits to the theatre or Vauxhall Gardens. His life was beginning to have some compensations, but he still found it painfully restricted and, after his summer holiday at West Meon in 1824, he confessed to Fred that he could not resign himself to 'another year's durance in Old Change ... without an inward struggle'.[14]

A year later Richard's mother died. An epidemic of typhoid was sweeping through West Meon. Mrs Cobden went to help nurse a neighbour's child and caught the disease herself. She seemed to be recovering, but had a relapse and died towards the end of July. Her death removed the family's chief prop, and although Frederick had by this time returned from America, having failed to make his fortune there, it was Richard who henceforth had to take his mother's place. It was to him that father, brothers and sisters looked to plan and provide for them.

Fortunately, at this sad moment in his life Richard was released from the tedious and restricted life of a warehouse clerk and promoted to travelling salesman for his firm. Friendly, energetic, gregarious and filled with a consuming curiosity about places and people, Richard was well suited to his new job. His first tour was

formidably long: from Birmingham to Liverpool, across to Dublin
and Belfast, back across the Irish Sea to Glasgow, Edinburgh,
Aberdeen and Perth, then south through Newcastle, York and Hull,
and finally west again to Manchester and the Midlands. Altogether,
he visited forty-one places. 'I am a little anxious', he told his father
on 21 August, 1825, 'about the success of this first attempt at travelling.' But so long as his health did not let him down, he had no
doubt but that he would do well.[15] Five days later he confessed to
Frederick from Shrewsbury that the ordeal he had just been through
(presumably in Birmingham) had destroyed all his romantic
enthusiasm for his travels. He had been greeted with hostile looks
and was convinced that his predecessor had been much preferred and
could have done ten times the amount of business he had achieved.[16]
In a later letter he claimed that at Shrewsbury he had felt so low that
he had been tempted to throw himself into the Severn.[17]

But after this inauspicious beginning matters improved – apart
from a bout of fever at Stockport – and Richard returned home
three months later with his order book full enough for him to be
considered worthy to be sent out on a second tour early the next
year. He had also added considerably to his meagre stock of
experience. He saw with his own eyes the visible effects of the
extraordinarily rapid industrial expansion then taking place in the
Midlands and the North. Travelling through Staffordshire after
dark, he was amazed by the sight of the numerous kiln fires burning
on all sides. 'They glare in the night from the very edge of the
turnpike road to the remotest boundaries of the horizon, and give
an effect the most novel and awful I ever beheld.'[18] In
Shrewsbury, where he had to wait half a day for his coach, his
imagination was fired by the ancient parish church with its beautiful
stained glass. He longed 'to be deep skilled in the mysteries of
mullions and architraves, in lieu of black and purple and pin
grounds. How happy I should be!'[19] In Ireland – 'the land of poverty,
ignorance and misrule' – he travelled from Dublin to Belfast through
a countryside where a collection of huts was called a town, where the
pig ate and slept in the same room as the family, and where both
shoes and stockings were considered luxuries. He was not, he
assured Frederick, exaggerating, but only telling the melancholy
truth.[20]

That journey, however, had its compensations. Richard's companion on the outside of the coach was a young Irish lady travelling
with her mother who was safely stowed inside. The young lady
turned out to be 'a most determined bluestocking', and an animated
discussion developed on Walter Scott, Burns, Cobbett, Voltaire,
Rousseau and all the English dramatists: 'I took care', confided
Richard to his brother, 'to be ignorant of nothing.' When it rained,

he sheltered the young lady under his cloak, and when they arrived at Belfast he was duly introduced to her mother. They stayed at the same hotel in Belfast, crossed to Greenock next day on the same steamboat, again stayed that night in the same hotel – and next morning they parted. 'I lost my heart and a week's sleep, and there's an end to the business.'[21]

There are no hints that he temporarily mislaid his heart on his next (or any subsequent) journey as a commercial traveller. From a literary point of view his second trip was distinguished by a brief glimpse of Sir Walter Scott in the Court of Session in Edinburgh, and a visit to the birth-place of Robert Burns.

'It is' – he wrote afterwards to Frederick – 'a sort of gratification that I am sure you can imagine, but which I cannot describe, to feel conscious of treading upon the same spot of earth, of viewing the same surrounding objects, and of being sheltered by the same roof, as one who equally astonished and delighted the world.'[22] From a business point of view, this journey was a failure. It was not his fault. After nearly two years of exceptional prosperity, with money plentiful, credit cheap and a fever of speculation sweeping the country, the boom had suddenly collapsed. Banks closed their doors, firms went bankrupt, and those that were still solvent could not be persuaded to buy goods that they knew they had no chance of reselling at once. When Richard returned to London in March 1826, he found that his own firm had also collapsed and he he himself was out of a job.

He spent the next few months giving what help and support he could to his father at West Meon, taking his sister Emma, who had been poorly, for a few days holiday on the Isle of Wight, and visiting relatives at Chichester. By the end of August he was back on the road again, this time working for a Mr Partridge, who had married another of Mrs Cobden's sisters. Partridge had been a partner of Cole but, after the collapse of that firm, had managed to start in business again with a Mr Price. During Richard's difficult early years at Old Change, Mr Partridge had befriended him and had acted as a safety valve for his indignation with Cole. This, however, did not prevent him from driving what Richard thought was a hard bargain over his salary. In future, he told his father, he would no longer rely on his new employer's friendship – 'I shall trust entirely to myself'.[23]

How Richard's relations with Partridge developed after this unfriendly start we do not know. For the next two years there is a virtually complete dearth of information about his activities. A brief glimpse of him in a letter to Frederick, written from Lincoln in September 1827, shows that he was just as ready to enjoy himself as any other young man in his early twenties. He had just left Doncaster with regret because he was missing the St Leger, and his appetite had been whetted by a visit to the race course the day before. He had seen

three races, but what really roused his enthusiasm was the splendid
show put on by the local nobs as they processed round the course in
their carriages, led by the Duke of Devonshire in a carriage drawn by
six horses with twelve superbly dressed outriders. There is as yet no
sign of the stern critic of the aristocracy he was later to become. In
the same letter he described one of the jolly evenings passed in an inn
dining-room: 'The wine was good and each visit from the bottle
found us more witty and good-humoured ... I talked higher and
looked larger at every glass ... and when at a bottle each we all cried
hold enough, I believe I had credit from my hearers for three things
of which Heaven and your Worship know I stand grievously in need
– wit – wealth – and independence.'[24]

For independence at any rate he had only another year to wait. In
September 1828, he decided he had had enough of Partridge and
Price – who had not seen fit to give him a single rise in salary – and
set out for Manchester with two friends, determined to set up in
business on his own account.

In the late 1820s Manchester was the obvious goal for any young
man seeking his fortune. Between 1815 and 1840, the cotton
industry, largely concentrated in Lancashire, increased at an annual
rate of six to seven per cent, and between 1815 and 1840, nearly half
the value of all British exports consisted of cotton products. In 1792
about 50,000 people lived in Manchester; forty years later their
number had jumped to 250,000. They had come to make a living in
the huge six-storey factories which, belching black smoke and noisy
with the clatter of machinery, were scattered throughout the town.
They lived in the squalid slum-dwellings hastily thrown together
near the factories. Visitors to the town, faced with such a concentration of human energy, ingenuity and misery, were both impressed
and appalled. De Tocqueville, who visited Manchester in the
summer of 1835, summarised his impressions with stark contrasts
and startling paradoxes.

> Look up and all around this place you will see the huge palaces of
> industry. You will hear the noise of furnaces, the whistle of steam.
> These vast structures keep air and light out of the human
> habitations which they dominate; they envelop them in perpetual
> fog; here is the slave, there the master; there the wealth of some,
> here the poverty of most ... From this foul drain the greatest
> stream of human industry flows out to fertilise the whole world.
> From this filthy sewer pure gold flows. Here humanity attains its
> most complete development and its most brutish; here civilisation
> works its miracles, and civilised man is turned back almost into a
> savage.[25]

2 Young Cobden entering a London warehouse to push his way up in the world – an artist's impression.

But when young Richard Cobden went to Manchester in September 1828 with his friends Sheriff and Gillett, he looked no further then the immediate interests of himself and – equally if not more important – his family. The trio had managed to obtain a small loan to supplement their modest savings and they planned to make an arrangement with one of the calico-printing firms to supply it with designs and then sell the finished product on commission from a warehouse in London. They decided to aim high and approached Fort Brothers, one of the largest and most reputable firms, with a warehouse in Manchester and works at Oakenshaw, near Accrington. After several days' suspense and 'a little eloquence' on the part of Richard their offer was accepted. Richard reported with gratification to Frederick that Lawrence Fort and his brother trusted them sufficiently not to bother to take up their references, and he reckoned that his own share of the profits should amount to £800 a year. 'Our anxiety for the success of this undertaking will be intense – all now depends on ourselves.'[26]

The spring of 1829 was a time of acute commercial distress, with serious rioting in Manchester and elsewhere. But the little firm not only weathered the depression but began to prosper. Richard's relief must have been all the greater because at about the same time he found himself grappling with a new crisis in the Cobden family's fortunes. Early in 1827 William Cobden had moved to Farnham where he thought he had a better chance of prospering. Two years later his hopes had collapsed and his small business had failed. Richard decided that the best plan would be for his father to join Frederick, who had recently gone to work with a timber merchant in Barnet, while his five unmarried sisters (Emma had married and settled at Droxford in Hampshire) should join Richard and his three younger brothers in London. He pointed out to his father that the 'dear girls', who had no society in Farnham, would be sure to find some in London.[27] He did not apparently mention the financial burden, most of which would presumably fall on his own shoulders.

Within a year two members of the London household – Miles and Jane – had died. Miles, born in 1812, had done well at school. The rest of the family agreed that he was the cleverest and hoped he would become a doctor or scholar. But there was no money to finance his further education and he was forced, like his elder brothers before him, to take a clerkship in a London warehouse. He hated the work, but he did not have to put up with it for long. By the winter of 1829 he was dying of consumption. In a desperate attempt to save his brother, Richard arranged for him to stay at Torquay. But after a few weeks Miles insisted on returning to his family. He died early one January morning after 'one of the most extraordinary and beautiful death-bed scenes' which Richard described in a letter to

Frederick at Barnet. 'Without', he concluded, 'possessing the slightest taint of superstition or even enthusiasm in my religion, I must say it is my conviction, and ever will be so, that this dear boy was assisted last night by an especial interposition of the divine spirit.'[28] A few months later, in May 1830, Jane, two years younger than Richard, died of the same disease. She spent her last weeks at Barnet where the air was purer, and every evening Richard went to see her, taking with him a bunch of flowers from Covent Garden.

In the meantime, the firm of Cobden, Sheriff and Gillett continued to prosper, and in August 1831 Richard and his partners felt sufficiently sure of themselves to set up in the business of calico-printing on their own account. They went up to Manchester determined to persuade the Forts to sell them a calico-printing factory which they owned at Sabden, a small village some thirty miles from Manchester and eight miles from Blackburn. The factory had had to be closed down during the economic blizzard of 1825–26 but had later been reopened, with a Mr George Foster acting as manager for the Forts. Richard had thought that the Forts would be glad to get rid of Sabden, and was surprised to find they were not. 'We have had', he told his father, 'fifty thousand times more difficulty in this business than I expected and if we have succeeded it is only owing to my invincible *jaw*.' He had no fears that they would not make a success of the new venture. 'I am sure from what I have seen', he assured his father, 'that if you were to strip me naked and turn me into Lancashire with only my *experience* for a capital I should make a large fortune – ay and my family shall have a large fortune too if I live.'[29]

Calico-printing was in fact one of the more risky branches of the textile industry. It required a greater initial outlay of capital, and it was necessary to keep stocks of raw, semi-finished and finished materials for a long time. It was also particularly vulnerable to the vagaries of fashion – Cobden later described the print trade as 'one peculiarly of fancy and invention from year to year'. There were many more failures than successes, but those who succeeded could make magnificent profits. Perhaps Richard was inspired by the example of John Grant (whose sons, Daniel and William, were the originals of Dickens's Cheeryble brothers) who had failed as a farmer, come to Manchester from the Scottish Lowlands, learned calico printing and eventually bought the first Sir Robert Peel's printworks at Ramsbottom.[30]

The three partners had enough capital of their own to start them off in their new venture and, although trade in general was still severely depressed, the prospects for calico-printing were greatly improved in the spring of 1831 by the removal, after years of agitation by the Lancashire calico printers, of the excise duty on calicoes. Printed calicoes soon became very much cheaper, thus placing – in the sententious words of a Victorian local historian – 'a becoming dress within the reach of thousands of females in the humbler ranks of life'.[31]

By the end of January 1832, Richard had completed his move from London to Manchester. At the house in London where he had lived with his sisters and younger brothers, he gave a farewell dinner for his uncles and aunts ('those that can face one another') followed by a party, complete with fiddler, for his younger friends.[32] His two partners remained in charge of their London warehouse at 94 Watling Street, and George Foster was kept on to manage the Sabden works*. Richard himself rented a warehouse in a central position in Manchester and found some temporary lodgings in George Street. If all went well, he hoped to be able to associate his elder brother with him in managing the Manchester end of the business.

Frederick was both Richard's favourite confidant and his most vexing problem. When he came back from the United States in 1824, Richard had confidently assured his father that his brother was sure to succeed wherever he went: 'he carries in his head [the] wherewithal to make him valuable to any man'.[33] He attributed Frederick's failure to succeed over the next few years to bad luck, and when he himself embarked on his first independent venture in 1828, he assured his brother that 'I have not one ambitious view or hope from which you stand separated. I feel that Fortune with her usual caprice, has in dealing with us turned her face to the least deserving, but we will correct her mistake for once, and I must insist that you from henceforth consider yourself as by right my associate in all her favours.'[34]

Richard never went back on this promise. But it must have gradually become clear to him that Fortune alone could not be blamed for his brother's troubles. Fred, in fact, took too much after their father; he was much better at losing money than making it. He was also prone to despondency and lacked energy and enterprise. Richard was always trying both to cheer and stir him up – 'Activity is the sole chance for those who have a fortune to seek.'[35] But by the time Richard was ready to move to Manchester, it was plain that there was no fortune for Frederick in the timber trade at Barnet. Richard assured him that he would do better if he came north. 'Manchester is

---

* The exact size of the Sabden works in 1832 is not known. But six years later Cobden told a parliamentary committee that he had 600 employees and his annual wage bill was between £20,000 and £25,000. (Select Committee on Postage. 2nd Report. Parliamentary Papers, Vol XX, Part II, 1837–78)

the place for money-making business. It is there that every one of *us* must sooner or later go.'[36] Sometime during the winter of 1832–33 Frederick finished winding up, as best he could, his affairs at Barnet, took his father to live with his sisters in London, and joined his brother in Manchester.

By now William Cobden was in failing health, although Richard seems to have thought that there was nothing wrong with him that a change of scene, country air and good nourishment could not put right. He had established himself in a house in Quay Street, with his youngest sister Mary to keep him company, and in May 1833 he was trying to entice his father to join them. He offered 'a trip by the railroad to Liverpool' (opened less than three years earlier), or 'a sail by steam to Wales', or quiet rides on a horse that he would have brought up from Sabden. Repeatedly, with copious under-linings, he urged his father not to bother about expense. '*Do not mind the expense* necessary to restore you to health. Wherever you go *be sure to get the best port wine and the very best brandy* and never mind the cost. Leave that to me . . . I wish you were here. We have some of the best wine and brandy in the world in the cellar and we would give you no other physic.'[37]

Within a month of receiving this appeal William Cobden died at his daughter Emma's house in Droxford. Richard at once formally assumed the responsibility that, in practice, he had been carrying for the past six years. He assured the three girls, Millicent, Priscilla and Sarah, still living in London, that he would 'fulfill to the utmost of my ability the duties of a father to you. Whilst I possess the means you shall not want a protector. I will devote myself to the support of my dear girls.'[38] Shortly afterwards the three girls joined their brother and sister in the house in Quay Street.

Unfortunately, very little information has survived about Richard Cobden's first years in Manchester, but what there is suggests a steady progress towards prosperity. Less than three months after moving, he complacently reported to Fred that he was 'dropping into a general connexion here both business and private that more than meets my anticipations'.[39] This satisfactory state of affairs was largely due to Mr George Wilson, the corn merchant and starch manufacturer who was later to play such a key role in the anti-Corn law campaign. When Richard moved into his George Street lodgings, Wilson gave him a cordial welcome, invited him to a large evening party and furnished him with introductions to the leading members of Manchester's business community.

Soon after his arrival Richard decided to invest in a house in Mosley Street, a fine street of residential houses with a row of trees down each side, running through the centre of the town. When he got possession the following September, he planned to take out the five-windowed front of the house and turn it into a warehouse. This struck him as good business, not an act of vandalism. He saw that the demand for commodious premises in the centre of the town was bound to increase, while well-to-do private residents would become increasinly anxious to escape to the cleaner and quieter suburbs. By the time Richard took over his Mosley Street property his example was already being followed and his house had, as he had foreseen, doubled in value. All the world, he told Fred, was talking of his bargain, 'and there being but one opinion or criterion of a man's ability – *the making of money* – I am already thought a clever fellow'.[40]

He showed the same buoyant self-confidence about his calico-printing business. He realised that the secret of success was to choose patterns that would appeal to the public and, if a contemporary biographer is to be believed, 'Cobden's prints' did indeed become very fashionable.[41] He searched far and wide for suitable patterns. In London, in the spring of 1833, he went to inspect the new stock in one of the smart West end stores. 'Their muslins', he told Fred, 'are very large and more outré in style than usual. I have begged some patterns.'[42] A few months later he visited Paris – his first trip abroad – and ordered about fifty patterns to be copied for him. He was determined to be 'up with the best of them if possible next year'.[43] He had managed to make a start during the years of slump and was now well set to take advantage of the return of prosperity. Gradually he became known, in the words of a contemporary, as 'a calico printer, of good taste and good business ability, beginning to produce articles of a superior quality, competing with the best London prints'.[44]

Cobden can hardly have had time for any active involvement in the turbulent politics of these years. He must have followed in the press the long-drawn-out drama of the passage of the Reform Bill at Westminster; he must have listened to the reformers among his middle-class acquaintances discussing how far they could or should go with the more extreme working-class reformers in agitating for the bill; and he must have been stimulated by the public manifestations of the struggle in a town where radical sentiments had always run high. But he still preferred to spend his scanty spare time on filling the gaps in his own education.

Might we not – he asked Fred in September 1832, when his brother was still in London – in the winter instruct ourselves a little in Mathematics? If you will call at Longmans and look over their catalogue, I daresay you might find some popular elementary publication that would assist us. I have a great disposition, too, to know a little Latin, and six months would suffice if I had a few books. Can you trust your perseverance to stick to them? I think I can.[45]

Whether or not he did stick to his Latin grammar that winter, he had to confess to Bright some twenty-five years later that he knew little Latin.

But his omnivorous general reading in history, literature and economics was stored away in his mind to provide a foundation for his thinking and illustrations for what he spoke and wrote. He was in fact a compulsive reader, partly because of an intense curiosity about the world around him and all that it contained, and partly as an antidote to the life he had set himself to lead. The collapse of the family's fortunes when he was a small boy and the subsequent struggle to make both ends meet had undoubtedly made a deep impression on him. Because of the inadequacies of his father and elder brother he had as a very young man learnt to regard himself as chiefly responsible for his family's welfare. They had always suffered from lack of money and he was determined to put that right. He was young, vigorous and self-confident. He cultivated what he called 'that *Bonapartian* feeling ... that spurs me on with the conviction that all the obstacles to fortune with which I am impeded, will (nay *shall*) yield if assailed with energy'.[46] He enjoyed the challenge to a considerable extent – but not altogether. Commercial life, with its grind, materialism and tedium, was not really congenial to him, and occasionally the strain showed and overflowed into exasperation with Fred's gloom and pessimism. '... to tell you the truth', he wrote after nearly a year in Manchester, 'the world has hardened me into such stern stuff that I can on longer sympathize with those morbid sensibilities – up and be *doing* is my motto'.[47]

By the end of 1834, however, he was beginning to feel sufficiently secure financially to spend more of his time on outside pursuits. In the autumn of that year he paid a brief visit to France and Switzerland which seems to have been entirely devoted to his own instruction and amusement. The following year, he began to contribute fortnightly articles on current affairs, signed 'Libra', to the *Manchester Times*.[48] He started to play a larger part in local affairs and to develop views on local issues like municipal reform and the education of Manchester's rapidly expanding infant population. He was already sure that making money was not what he wanted to be up and doing all the time and all his life.

CHAPTER 2

Discovering America (1835–37)

Early in 1835, Cobden completed his first pamphlet, called it comprehensively *England, Ireland and America*, and asked the well-known London publisher and bookseller, James Ridgway, to publish it under the pseudonym 'A Manchester Manufacturer'. Ridgway agreed, although he told the young author that no one ought to publish a pamphlet unless he had something more than just publication in view. Cobden thought he had, although he was unwilling – or unable – to be more specific. He assured Frederick: 'I have another object in distant and dim perspective.'[1] What seems to have been clear to him at that moment was that he must try to persuade other people of the truth of the convictions he had reached about the international scene and Britain's place in it.

Cobden's pamphlet amounted to a root and branch condemnation of British foreign policy over the past fifty years. It was stimulated by the strong current of anti-Russian feeling that had been provoked by the brutal suppression of the Polish revolt in 1830–31. In the press and at public meetings all over the country the cause of the patriot Poles (often linked with the cause of reform at home) was fervently championed, while societies of Friends of Poland sprang up to raise funds for the refugee Poles who had fled to England. Among the torrent of violently anti-Russian diatribes, a pamphlet published by David Urquhart in 1834 particularly incensed Cobden. Urquhart, a year younger than Cobden, was still at the start of his colourful and eccentric career, but – unlike Cobden – he already had considerable practical experience of Europe and the Near East. He had fought in the Greek War of Independence and later gone to Constantinople. Here he had learned Turkish and achieved a highly unusual *rapport* with influential Turks which had left him with the fervent conviction that the Ottoman empire could be reformed and

16

regenerated – if only the Russians would let it alone. And he vehemently urged that England should make sure they did.

To Cobden, this was nonsense. He denied that the Ottoman empire was capable of regeneration and argued that if it were taken over by any other European power the whole civilised world would stand to gain. The fear that a Russian occupation of Turkey would threaten India was dismissed on the grounds that the British people would in any case be better off without either India or any other of their colonial possessions. Cobden described them as 'gorgeous and ponderous appendages to swell our ostensible grandeur', whose defence was a wholly unnecessary burden on the British exchequer.[2] In his opinion, the colonies should be released from all commercial restraints and allowed to go their own way.

He argued that no British interests were involved in the defence of Turkey; it was simply that Russia had taken the place of France as the 'chimera' that haunted the British. He was convinced that their attempts over the centuries to maintain a balance of power in Europe were vain and futile. He accepted without question the traditional Foxite argument that the wars against revolutionary and Napoleonic France had been as unnecessary as they were wicked. The Europeans should be left to settle their differences as best they could, while the excitable British public – which, admittedly, was prone to agitate for intervention in every faraway quarrel – must be educated to understand that its only genuine foreign interest was the preservation of peace. 'The middle and industrious classes of England can have no interest apart from the preservation of peace. The honours, the fame, the emoluments of war belong not to them; the battle-plain is the harvest-field of the aristocracy, watered with the blood of the people.'[3]

Cobden reinforced his attack on the constant preoccupation of the British with the plight of foreigners – Poles, Turks, Greeks, Belgians and so on – by contrasting it with their shocking disregard of the plight of their fellow subjects in Ireland – that 'appalling monument of our neglect and misgovernment'.[4] He was writing at a time when the Irish problem seemed more than usually intractable. Daniel O'Connell was campaigning for repeal of the Union against a background of the peasants' endemic warfare against tithes. At Westminster, three ministries had collapsed within a year because of differences over the treatment of the established (Anglican) Church of Ireland and over the control of disorder. Cobden had no slick remedies to suggest. Like most of those who tried to think objectively about Ireland, he realised that religious differences were at the heart of the country's troubles. So long as the Irish people were forced to support a state church that six-sevenths of them violently repudiated, there could be no tranquillity in Ireland and consequently

no possibility of effectively tackling the dreadful poverty in which
most of the Irish peasants lived. In the meantime more and more of
them were fleeing to England where they contaminated the working
classes with their squalid habits and depressed British living
standards through their competition. In his own 'otherwise civilized
and wealthy town', Cobden wrote, the Irish immigrants had
congregated in one district, known as Little Ireland, which exhibited
all the 'filth, depravity and barbarism' of their native land.[5] In
Ireland, the Irish were more sinned against than sinning – but not, it
seems, when they fled to England in a deluded search for a better
life.

If the British neglected Ireland, they also failed to understand the
significance of what was happening across the Atlantic. Britain's
supremacy was threatened, Cobden believed, not by the 'barbarian
force' of Russia, but by the commercial rivalry, developing
industries and peaceful policies of the United States. The Americans
had limitless natural resources to be developed; their initiative was
not stifled by the heavy taxation that in England was necessary to
service the national debt and support a large army and navy; and they
enjoyed – as the British did not – the inestimable advantages of
universal education and a cheap and unfettered press. 'If knowledge
be power, and if education give knowledge, then must the
Americans inevitably become the most powerful people in the
world.'[6]

Cobden denied that he was advocating republican institutions for
his country – they would not in his opinion suit the English
temperament. But he believed that the government of the United
States was 'at this moment the best in the world', and the Americans
the best people, individually, because 'the people that are the best
educated must, morally and religiously speaking, be the best', and
nationally, because they were the only great community that had
never waged war except in self-defence.[7] Thus it seemed to him to
be crystal clear that 'our only chance of national prosperity lies in
the timely remodelling of our system, so as to put it as nearly as possible upon an equality with the improved management of the
Americans'.[8]

Cobden's primary aim was to persuade the British government
and people to adopt a passive rather than an active foreign policy. He
argued that Britain should make itself felt in the world through the
example of its economic and political progress, not through its
armed might; and that if it would 'purify' its institutions, free its
commerce and remove the crippling burden of taxation from its
press, it would do more for political progress throughout Europe
than it could ever do by actively intervening in the continent's
affairs. The only really effective and beneficial way of spreading

British influence abroad was through 'the great panacea' – commerce.

> Not a bale of merchandise leaves our shores, but it bears the seeds of intelligence and fruitful thought to the members of some less enlightened community; not a merchant visits our seats of manufacturing industry, but he returns to his own country the missionary of freedom, peace and good government – whilst our steam boats, that now visit every port of Europe, and our miraculous railroads, that are the talk of all nations, are the advertisements and vouchers for the value of our enlightened institutions.[9]

The writer of this effusion was typical of his age, class and background. He was equally typical in making a passing reference to the factory system as an inevitable and irremoveable outcome of mechanical discoveries; but he was more enlightened than some in adding that its evils must be mitigated and if possible removed.[10] Many of the foreign visitors – including de Tocqueville – who were drawn to England at this time by its astonishing material progress would not have thought that Cobden's picture of Britain's proper role in the world was altogether fanciful. He himself believed in his vision, and he presumably hoped that it would help to cure the British of their itch to meddle in other countries' affairs.

In *England, Ireland and America* Cobden referred to himself as one who was 'fond of digging deep into the foundations of causes', and the pamphlet was the product of his indefatigable efforts at self-education. His arguments were buttressed with the contents of heavy statistical works, reinforced by Adam Smith and Burke, and embellished by references to his lighter reading – Spenser, Cervantes, Le Fanu. The essentially academic foundation of his thinking was sometimes reflected, especially when discussing European affairs, in an imperfect grasp of political realities, while his radical preconceptions led to a distinctly blinkered view of recent history. On the whole, however, as a first attempt at pamphleteering by someone with no experience of public affairs, it was a remarkable effort*. It dealt with issues which were to remain important to Cobden all his life, although (curiously) the reform which made him famous, and for which he fought most successfully, does not seem to

---

* Twelve years later Cobden told a friend that he was 'much in advance of the times' when he wrote this pamphlet and a second one, called *Russia*, published the following year. 'There was much in the style and detail of those pamphlets which, owing to my being a young writer and politician, was defective, but the *principles* were sound.' (to Joshua Walmsley. *Life of Sir Joshua Walmsley*, by H. M. Walmsley, p. 190)

have been at the forefront of his mind. The repeal of the Corn Laws is introduced at the end of the pamphlet almost as an addendum, and although Cobden stresses the tremendous importance of the Corn Laws as an obstacle to the expansion of British commerce, he had not yet thought the issue through to the radical solution he was soon to adopt.[11] Ireland, perhaps the most pressing problem and the one to which he devoted most space in his pamphlet, was the one he did not afterwards actively pursue. He fell into the error for which he had reproved his countrymen and perhaps for the same reason – Ireland filled the outsider, whether sympathetic or hostile, with despair. After a brief visit there in 1836, Cobden told a friend that the remedy for its troubles did not lie in new law: 'no direct act of the legislature can materially raise that country – the evil has been the growth of centuries. You and I shall not live to rejoice over its cure.'[12] Naturally enough, he preferred to devote his energies to problems that offered a reasonable chance of solution.

When it was first published in London – at 3/6d a copy – Cobden's pamphlet did not attract very much interest, although subsequently 10,000 copies of a cheap sixpenny edition were sold by the Edinburgh publisher, William Tait. In Manchester, however, Cobden was pleased by its reception. 'The work', he told Mr Cole, on April 30, 1835, 'has hit the taste of our practical minded readers to a nicety and I have had some complimentary callers to solicit my acquaintance from amongst the *cotton lords* in my neighbourhood.' He asked Cole's help to get the pamphlet noticed in the London papers. 'My object is to get the principles advocated in the pamphlet known in the quickest possible time. They are sure to be known and acknowledged eventually, because they are founded in truth.'[13] Clearly, if he failed to get on in the world, it would not be for lack of self-confidence.

Next day he set out for Liverpool to begin his journey to the United States.

In the early nineteenth century the British had not yet quite come to terms with the transformation of their thirteen American colonies into the Republic of the United States. Economically, it is true, the two countries were close and getting closer, each being the other's most important trading partner. But at the diplomatic level, relations tended to be either frosty or fractious, while at the popular level they were characterised, on the British side, by an immense curiosity, sometimes baleful, sometimes hopeful. Those unable to visit the United States themselves eagerly read the published accounts of those who had been there; more than 300 such books appeared between 1824 and 1870.[14] There were a good many critical ones, like

Mrs Trollope's *Domestic Manners of the Americans,* which fed lurking prejudices on one side of the Atlantic and caused great indignation on the other. But among those in Britain who were out of sympathy with the prevailing Whig/Tory aristocratic establishment there was a great fund of sober enthusiasm for the United States, its democratic political institutions, disestablished religion, cheap press and educational system. In the radical press, whether the middle-class *Westminster Review,* or the working-class *Poor Man's Guardian,* the American example was constantly held out as the one to emulate.

As his pamphlet showed, Cobden had made up his mind where he stood on America before ever he had set foot on the quay at New York. Like many other transatlantic travellers, he went primarily as a tourist, to satisfy his curiosity. In terms of time spent and distance covered he could hardly have expected to probe very deep. He landed in New York on 7 June 1835 and sailed for home on 16 July. He went from New York to Philadelphia, Baltimore and Washington, then west to Pittsburgh, north to Lake Erie and the Niagara Falls, east through Utica and Albany to Boston, then back to New York by way of Providence. The whole trip took just over five weeks. He spent his last week visiting and sightseeing in New York and making a weekend excursion up the Hudson to the Catskills. For most of his journey he was accompanied by his brother Henry, then living in the United States; he was armed with letters of introduction and had various friends and acquaintances along the way. But his most valuable asset was his friendly and gregarious nature, which made it easy for him to win the confidence and loosen the tongues of his fellow travellers.

After the years spent on the road in Britain, working for his employers in London, Cobden was a hardy and philosophic traveller. Marathon coach journeys – one of forty, another of more than fifty hours – were taken in his stride; only once, after a three-hour wait to change coaches in the middle of the night, did he confess to having lost his temper.[15] His fortitude must have been more severely tried by his experience of the American railways whose development he had enthused about in his pamphlet. On the short journey from Boston to Providence, the train was late starting; then the passengers had to get out and walk because part of the track had not been properly completed, and finally Cobden's carriage caught fire and the passengers were doused with water. The steamboats, whose size and speed greatly impressed him, were a much happier experience.

Throughout his journey, Cobden took every opportunity he could to visit American institutions: factories, schools, prisons, law courts. But what most deeply absorbed his attention was the size, potential and beauty of the country and the characteristics of the people who lived in it. After crossing the Alleghanies (thanking God he was no longer in 'the country of slaves') and looking down on the vast plain stretching westwards, he told his brother: 'Here will one day be the headquarters of agricultural and manufacturing industry; here will one day centre the civilisation, the wealth, the power of the entire world'.[16] After first setting eyes on Lake Erie, he soliloquised:

> what could have been the feelings of those first explorers of this continent who after traversing five hundred miles of uninterrupted forests found themselves on the shore of this fresh water ocean! – what a sublime idea would it convey of the magnitude of that continent which contained within its bounds such a lake, and what food for the imagination in the unknown regions beyond it![17]

But it was the Niagara Falls which stirred him most profoundly. 'Thank God that has bestowed on me health, time and means for reaching this spot, and the spirit to kindle at the spectacle before me!' He gazed on the Falls from both the American and the Canadian side, and from every angle; from below, from above – a 'fearful position' – and from behind, which was not at all dangerous, but a 'severe adventure'.[18] Three days passed – a longer stop than in any other place except Boston and New York – before he reluctantly tore himself away from 'this greatest of all nature's works'.

'No one', Cobden assured Fred, 'has yet done justice to the splendid scenery of America.'[19] About the appearance of the inhabitants, especially the women, he was much less complimentary. His first impression of New York women was extremely un-favourable, and by the time he had got to Boston he had still not set eyes on a single wholesome, blooming, pretty woman. After a few days however, he decided that Boston's females were 'decidedly prettier than those of New York but still deficient in *preface and postscript*'.[20]

Contrary to his expectations, Cobden's estimate of the American character, as opposed to the American physique, rose as a result of his journey.

> Great as was my esteem for the qualities of this people, I find myself in love with their intelligence, their sincerity, and the decorous self-respect that actuates all classes ... They have not, 'tis true, the force of Englishmen in personal weight or strength, but they have compensated for this deficiency by quickening the momentum of their enterprises. All is in favour of celerity of action and the saving of time. Speed, speed, speed, is the motto that is stamped in the form of their ships and steam-boats, in the breed of their horses, and the light construction of their waggons and carts; and in the ten thousand contrivances that are met with

here, whether for the abridging of the labour of months or minutes, whether a high-pressure engine or a patent boot-jack. All is done in pursuit of one common object, the economy of time.[21]

After his experience on the railway between Boston and Providence, he lost a little of his enthusiasm for American speed, confiding to his diary the tart comment: 'The Yankees are too much in a hurry to finish things properly before they "go ahead"'.[22] The Americans' conceit also tried him sorely from time to time. He called it an 'unfortunate peculiarity' which could only grow worse as the United States grew stronger and more prosperous. The people he met were always trying to get him to make comparisons between England and America which they confidently assumed would be to the advantage of the latter. Cobden would try to parry these inquiries, but occasionally, 'finding my British blood up', he would pay the United States an extravagant compliment on the astonishing progress it had made in only fifty years, but add that this was too short a period in which to test a nation's worth; seven centuries hence, would they be able to claim as much for their country as he could now claim for his country's steady advance in liberty, wealth and refinement?[23] (In his pamphlet this is a point that one looks for but never finds.)

But the abiding impression that Cobden carried home with him was one of pleasure. He had enjoyed every minute of his visit, the United States had exceeded his expectations and, contrary to his feelings before setting out, he now felt that no reasonable person could fail to settle down happily there for good, provided he had no personal ties to draw him back across the Atlantic. The United States was the favourite refuge of English radicals who found the pace of reform at home unbearably slow. But there is no evidence that Cobden ever thought seriously of adding to their number.

Arriving back in Liverpool on 16 August, 1835, after a long and excessively tedious voyage, Cobden returned to his business, which had continued to thrive in his absence, and to all the public duties and spare time activities competing for the attention of a public-spirited and intellectually inquiring Manchester manufacturer.

There was plenty of choice. Manchester men were not, as was commonly supposed, interested only in making money. Some were also keen on self-improvement, and a variety of learned societies existed to help them stretch their minds and widen their intellectual experience. Cobden was an active member of the Literary and Philosophical Society; when the Society held its annual dinner in March 1836, he attended as vice-president. Shortly after returning from America, he joined the Statistical Society, founded two years earlier by some leading Manchester Unitarian manufacturers in collaboration with Dr James Phillips Kay (Shuttleworth), who had already published a searing pamphlet on the appalling living and working conditions of the Manchester cotton operatives. The Society reflected the concern of the more educated and intelligent manufacturers over the human suffering upon which their own prosperity rested. Unable themselves to perceive any far-reaching remedies, they sought to lighten their consciences by providing some precise information, instead of vague generalisation, for the investigation of the problem. When Cobden joined the society, it was in the middle of a detailed house-to-house inquiry into the living conditions, wages, religion, school attendance and so on of the working classes of Manchester and five neighbouring towns. Cobden attended the society's meetings regularly, but does not seem to have played a more prominent role.

Cobden was more actively concerned with the Manchester Athenaeum, which he helped to set up and in which he played a leading part during its early years. In his first speech before a large assembly on 28 October, 1835, he supported the establishment of an Athenaeum where a library, newsroom and lecture courses could all be found under the same roof. He told his audience that it would be a shame if Manchester, while erecting mills in every direction for the manufacture of cotton, should not set up even one mill to produce some valuable mental manufacture.[24] The membership aimed at was middle class – there was already a thriving Mechanics' Institution to provide the same facilities for the artisan class. The Athenaeum opened the following January in temporary quarters and – with typical municipal panache – one of the leading architects of the day, Mr Charles Barry, was commissioned to design its permanent home. His impressive Greek-porticoed building was opened in 1839. For several years its cost gave the managing committee some severe financial headaches, but did not impede the institute's steady development. In 1844, the proceeds of a 'Great Literary Soirée', with Dickens presiding, helped it to achieve financial stability.

Another society in which Cobden was greatly interested was the Manchester Phrenological Society. Among otherwise level-headed people the pseudo-science of phrenology enjoyed a considerable vogue at this time. The theory that the external examination of a person's head could reveal much about his mental abilities had originally been expounded by two continental scientists, Gall and Spurzheim. Their ideas had been enthusiastically taken up by George Combe, a writer to the signet in Edinburgh, who spent much time and energy propagating them through his lectures and writings. He was a persuasive, opinionated man who carried his belief in

phrenology to the length of examining the head of his future wife –
the daughter of the famous actress, Mrs Sarah Siddons – to make
sure that her 'higher faculties' would agree with his own.[25] He was
regarded as a dangerous infidel by many religious people, especially
evangelicals, but although his book, *The Constitution of Man*, had a
very mixed reception at first, it came to be one of the most widely
read books of the day. Later, when Prince Albert met Combe, he
was sufficiently impressed to invite him to examine the heads of the
royal children and advise on their education. On the other hand,
when Macaulay found himself listening to two phrenologists in a
railway carriage, he could hardly keep a straight face.

Cobden had his fair share of scepticism and it is hard to see why he
was as attracted to phrenology as for a time he clearly was.
According to Combe, Cobden told him that *The Constitution of Man*
seemed 'like a transcript of his own familiar thoughts'.[26] He was
certainly at a restless, unsettled stage of his life, full of intellectual
curiosity, full of concern for the world's injustices and perhaps not as
sure as he liked to appear that he knew all the answers. Phrenology
may have seemed to offer some new insights on how to make the
world a better place.

Anxious to spread Combe's ideas, in August 1836 Cobden invited
him to give a course of lectures in Manchester. The local phrenological society, founded a few years earlier, had failed to flourish, in
spite of having equipped itself with a splendid set of 210 casts of
heads, masks and skulls. Although Cobden felt obliged to admit that
'Manchester is not phrenological at present', he assured Combe that
his lectures would fall on receptive ears.[27] How long his illusions
lasted is not clear. But when they had faded, he was left with some
phrenological turns of speech and – much more important – a good
friend.

'We are', declared Cobden on 12 April, 1836, 'as mad as in the
worst days of tory misrule upon the subject of foreign intervention.'
His attack on British foreign policy in his first pamphlet had entirely
failed to get the subject out of his mind. This time, it was Spain – 'a
nation of bigots, beggars and cut-throats, with a government of
wh–res and rogues' – that set him off in a letter to the Edinburgh
publisher William Tait. Spain was in the middle of a particularly
bloody civil war in which both sides were almost equally worthless,
and Palmerston's refusal to refrain from meddling, largely through
the Royal Navy, was hard to justify. Cobden was all the more
disgusted because his indignation at the debased state of the Irish
peasants had just been stirred up again by a brief visit to Tipperary. It
made his blood curdle, he told Tait, to reflect that money which

might have helped 'our miserable fellow citizens' was being thrown away on 'barbarians beyond the Bay of Biscay'. And he added, with his customary emphatic underlining: '*There is more wisdom in the management of any thriving chandler's shop in Edinburgh than in our foreign office at this reformed epoch.* We are overgoverned, what we want is (sic) ministers that will be quiet and not plunge us into ruinous engagements.'[28]

His object in writing to Tait was to tell him that he proposed to give public vent to his indignation in an article that he intended to offer to *Tait's Edinburgh Magazine.* The article would not be on Spain, but would be a renewed attempt to cure the British of their rampant Russophobia. Urquhart and his friends had been organising a steady stream of anti-Russian propaganda in periodicals and pamphlets, and Urquhart himself had published a reply to *England, Ireland and America.* Six weeks later, Cobden told Tait that his article had grown into another pamphlet which he wanted to be published in exactly the same form as the first one. He enclosed some of the manuscript and promised to finish it as quickly as he could. He was going abroad early in July for ten weeks and wanted the whole pamphlet to be in type and revised before then.[29] He successfully met the deadline he had set himself but, by the beginning of July was so absorbed in the congenial task of 'pushing' his pamphlet, that he postponed his trip abroad until October. He stirred up friends in London to make the pamphlet known to local booksellers and newsvendors. He arranged for copies to be sent to all the London papers, and he despatched copies to many local papers in the Midlands and the North. He pointed out to Tait that the success of the new pamphlet would help the sales of the first, which in any case he was sure would go on selling for years, because he had had so many unsolicited testimonials that it met with the approval of intelligent and thinking people in Manchester. 'The other day', he wrote on 6 June, 'a remarkably tall and venerable quaker, with a brim of more than the orthodox width, called to introduce himself by saying "Richard Cobden, I call to say I have read thy book and aprove thy sentiments and think thou ought to be *encouraged.*"!' This impressive visitor, it transpired, had emigrated to Philadelphia twenty-five years earlier.[30]

Encouragement was, in fact, the last thing Cobden needed; he spontaneously generated it out of his unquenchable self-confidence. Wide and deep though his reading had been, he still viewed the world from the point of view of a Manchester manufacturer, who held that the same rules of common sense and 'homely wisdom' by which men managed their private concerns should also govern affairs of state. He was convinced that any honest and intelligent person had only to understand his views to be converted to them, and his sole desire, he said, was to be extensively read. Ideas for further pamphlets – 'Our Colonies', 'Standing Armies', 'The National Debt' – flitted through his brain. When the new pamphlet, called simply *Russia* and published in mid-July, was ignored by the London papers, it was entirely the papers' fault, not the pamphlet's, and before going abroad in October, he defiantly sent Tait £25 to cover the cost of advertising the pamphlet – giving it 'a good puffing' – in half a dozen London papers and periodicals. Needless to say, he also included the text of the advertisements.[31]

In an attempt to disarm opposition, Cobden began his pamphlet by insisting that he was thoroughly hostile to the St Petersburg government . His point was that by comparison the government of the Sublime Porte was infinitely worse. He attempted to show that the Ottoman regime was in such an irreversible state of decay that the Turks, no less than the rest of the world, could only benefit if the Tsar were to become the ruler of Constantinople. He did not, he insisted, wish to palliate or justify any Russian aggrandisment, whether against Circassians, Persians, Finns, Poles or Turks, although he claimed that those subjugated were, or would be, better off under their new masters. He merely wanted to point out that the British people, with their 'passion' for colonial conquests, were in no position to cast stones at the Russians. More important, he wanted to persuade them that it was entirely against their own best interests to get involved in these remote quarrels; 'we are not called upon to preserve the peace and good order of the entire world'.[32] This argument applied strongly to Poland, 'upon which has been lavished more false sentiment, deluded sympathy, and amiable ignorance, than on any other subject of the present age'.[33] He condemned the Partitions, he said, as strongly as anyone, but what mattered now was not whether the Poles were ruled by this dynasty or that, but whether they were well-governed, with sufficient food and shelter and adequate protection for life and property. The recent revolt had not been a genuine national rising; it had been engineered by the Polish aristocracy under whom the peasants had been much less well off than they now were under the Russians.

For the British to fear Russia, Cobden argued, was ridiculous. It might be a giant in size, but its resources were undeveloped, its people backward and its government impoverished. It had been able to take over its neighbours not because of its own strength but because of their weakness, disunity and barbarism. Its geographical position made it dependent on the goodwill of other maritime powers who could enforce a blockade of both the Baltic and the Black Sea with less than a dozen warships. Moreover, however high Russia stood in the scale of civilisation by comparison with Turkey, it was vastly inferior to the progressive, liberal countries of western Europe –

and, of course, to Britain most of all. The true source of national greatness, argued Cobden, lay in the arts of peace, not in the evanescent triumphs of war. And he hammered again at the point he had been making in his first pamphlet. 'If we look into futurity ... may we not with safety predict that the steam engine ... will at no distant day produce moral and physical changes, all over the world, of a magnitude and permanency, surpassing the effects of all the wars and conquests which have convulsed mankind since the beginning of time!'[34] Russia had little to show the world but an example of violence. But

> England's industrious classes, through the energy of their commercial enterprise, are at this moment, influencing the civilization of the whole world, by stimulating the labour, exciting the curiosity, and promoting the taste for refinement of barbarous communities, and, above all, by acquiring and teaching to surrounding nations, the beneficent attachment to peace.[35]

In the year before Queen Victoria ascended the throne, Cobden spoke for all her future subjects who believed they had within their grasp the key to a brave new world in which aristocratic power and privilege would wither away and the hard-working, God-fearing middle classes would come into their own. But few could ever go all the way with him in the sheer idealism of his vision.

The last two chapters of *Russia* are devoted to demolishing the two stock arguments used to justify British intervention in the affairs of Europe: the maintenance of the balance of power and the protection of commerce. He demolished the balance of power to his own complete satisfaction, concluding that it was merely a chimera – 'an undescribed, indescribable, incomprehensible nothing'.[36] But while his arguments bear impressive tribute to his reading, they are too theoretical, too divorced from the reality of international politics, to carry much conviction. His final chapter – which he himself thought the best – is much more effective, perhaps because the recent announcement of an increase in the naval estimates gave him an ideal opportunity to expatiate on a theme that lay at the heart of his thinking. The government claimed that more ships were needed to protect the country's extended commerce. Cobden argued that they were at best irrelevant and at worst positively damaging. What really mattered was that British goods should be the cheapest in the market. To increase armaments involved increasing taxes on essential imports to pay for them, which in turn put up the cost of manufactures and thus handicapped commerce. Cobden illustrated his argument with a personal anecdote. He had been one of the directors of the Manchester Chamber of Commerce chosen to compare samples of European textiles, submitted by the Board of

Trade, with their British equivalents. He and his colleagues had had 'the disagreeable duty' of reporting that the Swiss Turkey-red chintz prints and the mixed cotton and linen drills from Saxony were both superior in cheapness and quality to similar articles produced in Britain. The reason for the comparative dearness of the British goods was the heavy duties levied on essential imports and the greater cost of the workers' food. The obvious remedy, the directors stated, was a reduction of the duties on corn, oil, soap, and so on. If, Cobden added, they had said the foreign goods were cheaper because the British Navy was not sufficiently strong and the remedy was to add half a million pounds to the naval estimates, they would have immediately – and rightly – been certified as lunatics.[37]

Cobden reinforced his argument by comparing trade across the Atlantic and in the Mediterranean. One third of all British exports consisted of cotton textiles sent to the United States. More than a million British textile workers depended for the raw material of their industry – and hence for their livelihood – on cotton imported from the United States. Yet this precious transatlantic commerce received virtually no naval protection – nor did it need any. On the other hand, the impregnable fortress of Gibraltar, with its triple line of batteries and thirty-six defending warships, was quite incapable of preventing the Gibraltarians from buying the cheaper Swiss and Saxon textiles rather than the dearer British ones.

Britain's naval superiority, Cobden argued, was not merely useless as a means of promoting and protecting trade. By stirring up envy and suspicion in other countries, it positively hampered the development of those friendly relations that were so essential to promoting commercial ties. The more Britain became linked to other countries by the 'amicable bonds' of trade, the less likely did any armed conflict become and the less necessary would it be to undermine the competitiveness of British manufacturers by raising taxes to pay for armaments.

> Were our army and navy reduced to one half of their present forces, and the amount saved applied to the abolition of the duties upon cotton, wool, glass, paper, oil, soap, drugs, and the thousand other ingredients of our manufactures, such a step would do more towards protecting and extending the commerce of Great Britain, than an augmentation of the naval armaments to fifty times their present strength ...[38]

Within six years Cobden's arguments for freeing trade were to be accepted in principle and a beginning made to put them into practice. But not so his pleas for naval reductions and a different approach to the European powers. The fear of Russia was not confined to a credulous public stirred up by alarmist press reports. To Melbourne,

Palmerston and other members of the government, Russia's conduct
in Persia, Poland and Turkey over the past ten years seemed to
suggest a deliberate policy of expansion which would ultimately be
harmful to British interests. In fact, a few years earlier, Tsar Nicholas
I had accepted the advice of his ministers that, for the time being at
any rate, it would better serve Russian interests to preserve a weak
Ottoman empire amenable to Russian influence and control.
Nicholas had confided his decision to the Austrians, but not to the
British. Palmerston continued to suspect Russia's intentions in spite
of the assurances of Lord Durham, his ambassador in St Petersburg,
that he had nothing to fear. Durham, popularly known as Radical
Jack because of his unabashed radical views, had first gone to St
Petersburg in 1832 on a special mission, full of mistrust for the Tsar
and sympathy for the Poles. Nicholas, however, had disarmed him
by making a personal friend of him, and-to the disgust of English
radicals – Durham returned home declaring that although Russia had
wronged Poland politically, the Poles were better off under Russian
rule than they had been under their own aristocracy.

Although susceptible to the Tsar's flattery, Durham saw clearly
enough that Russia's power was limited, and he thought it highly
unlikely that Nicholas would try to seize Constantinople so long as
Britain made clear that it would oppose such a move. In a report sent
to the Foreign Office in March 1836, during his second mission to St
Petersburg, Durham wrote that while Russia's defensive power was
invincible, it lacked the military, financial and economic means to
wage an aggressive war.[39] His argument on Russian capabilities ran
very much along the same lines as Cobden's, so it is not surprising
that when a copy of *Russia* reached the ambassador the following
August, he should have pronounced it to be excellent. (He can,
however, hardly have agreed with Cobden's views on the virtues of
non–intervention.) He was indeed so impressed that he wrote to
Joseph Parkes, the radical parliamentary agent and lawyer, to ask
him to find out more about the author. 'If he is a political writer, and
not really engaged in trade, he should be encouraged, for his powers
are great. If he really is a silk manufacturer, all I can say is – he has
more of the statesman in him than most Cabinet Ministers.' Parkes's
reply suggested that he knew Cobden personally, although there is
no record of where and when they had met. He described Cobden as
'well to do, self-instructed with a powerful reflecting intellect, thinks
for himself, and is equally above imposing on the world as on
himself'.[40]

The excuse for Cobden's excursion through the Mediterranean in
1836–37 was his poor health. He had never been very robust,
although no evidence survives as to any specific complaint. During

the winter of 1835–36 he had a serious illness, made worse, as so often in those days, by his doctor's inept ministrations. He had many calls on his time and energy and he did not allow himself a proper convalescence. Apart from his business and literary activities, he was a director of the Chamber of Commerce, an overseer of the poor, a police (municipal) commissioner, a sidesman of his parish church and an active member of several local societies. He continually overtaxed his strength, and by midsummer his friends were urging him to go away for a really long holiday. The lure of foreign travel was great and he probably did not need much persuading. He hoped to return in the spring, he told Tait on August 28, 'as hearty as a fox-hunter. At present though the spirit is willing, I find the flesh too weak to enable me to accomplish all that I would'.[41]

His horizons were expanding, and so were the things he wanted to do. He planned to make his brother Henry responsible for all the details of the calico-printing so as to give himself more time for public affairs and politics. He had made up his mind to try to get into the House of Commons where, he told Fraderick, he believed he could be more useful than anywhere else.[42] A general election had been held only the year before, but Melbourne's Whig government had fallen into such a state of paralysis that the Cabinet was believed to feel that its only hope of a new lease of life lay in a dissolution, if the King could be persuaded to grant one. Cobden was in touch with some leading Stockport radicals who had consulted Joseph Parkes about his suitability. Parkes had told them roundly that Cobden would be an honour to them, not they to him.[43] By way of making himself known, he sent a thousand copies of *Russia* to Stockport for distribution and sale, and before departing he composed an election address which his friends would find some pretext to publish at the end of the year.

Frederick's chronic fears for the future were greatly stimulated by his brother's increasing preoccupation with public affairs, and while waiting for his ship to sail from Falmouth on October 21, Richard composed a long screed of advice, admonition and encouragement to his elder brother. In it he incidentally revealed a good deal about himself. Frederick, he wrote, must not worry about the business or try to plan too far ahead. 'I am of a sanguine temperament and hope tells me that the next two years will not prove less advantageous to me and to you than the last.' But he felt that in the past he had some-times been too precipitate, and he advised both his brothers to proceed calmly and carefully without trying to be over-ambitious. Moreover, their style of doing business left something to be desired.

> I would impress upon you both the necessity of conversational and temperate intercourse upon matters of business. Avoid that extremity of tone in your communications which you, my dear

Fred, are apt to fall into. This is not a superlative world, either for good or evil, and therefore *that degree* of speech is rarely applicable to the affairs of life. Learn to suggest without appearing to advise – to advise without censure – and to censure without passion.

This advice Cobden tried hard to follow himself and if, in the heat and passion of the campaign against the Corn Laws he did not always succeed, he always regretted it afterwards. When he wrote this letter he did not yet perceive what public battles he should feel called upon to fight, but he knew he had come far and he meant to go further.

I am as anxious as you are to make a large income because I agree with you that it will be necessary to my happiness and that of others. But let us not tolerate a morbid anxiety, nor encourage groundless apprehensions about the future. What has been done by me has been done without capital and with only a youthful experience. You know that I do not live except to learn; and of course our capital must accumulate unavoidably. Now believe me there is something still in the womb of time for us, and we shall not live without profiting from the favours of fortune whose favourites we certainly have been.

And he ended by assuring his brother that he did not intend to turn his back upon the business, and when it required a 'main spring' – which it did not at present – he would be there to provide it.[44]

Although in theory Cobden was travelling for his health, he was far too determined a seeker after knowledge to be content with a rest cure. He filled his notebooks with facts and figures, learned mostly from the English merchants he sought out in Alexandria, Constantinople, Smyrna and elsewhere; and he filled his letters home with amusing accounts of the vicissitudes of travel and lively descriptions of antiquities, people and places.

On the way to Gibraltar the ship stopped briefly at Lisbon, where Cobden was digusted by the filthiness of the streets,[45] and Cadiz, where he was enraptured 'by the loveliest female costume in the world – the Spanish mantilla'.[46] In Gibraltar he spent hours leaning out of his hotel window, fascinated by the market place beneath, where various races bawled and jostled, argued and bartered.[47] At Malta he disapprovingly noted nine of the Royal Navy's line-of-battle ships lying in the harbour, and wondered what was the use of hanging on to a volcanic rock whose importance had disappeared now that it was no longer needed as a religious sanctuary against Turkish hostility. He decided that Bonaparte's anxiety to keep the island had given the British an exaggerated idea of its importance.[48]

In Alexandria Cobden greatly admired the date palms surrounding his hotel, which combined utility with elegance.[49] On the other hand, the ruined catacombs, baths and other antiquities aroused little enthusiasm. On the contrary, they provoked some censorious comments on modern man. He deplored the decline 'in one of the most useful habits, that of personal cleanliness'. Where once there had been 4000 public baths, now not a single one remained intact – 'why are the moderns less solicitous – even the more affluent classes – than in ancient times about the luxuries of the bath?'.[50] When he went to inspect Cleopatra's Needles, he found that only one was upright; the other had been thrown down in an attempt to carry it off to England. Cobden condemned 'the folly and injustice of carrying these remains from the site where they were originally placed, and from the associations which gave them all their interest, to London or Paris, where they become merely objects of vulgar wonderment, and besides are subjected to the destroying effects of our humid climate.'[51]

In Cairo, Cobden was one of a small group of English travellers granted an audience by the ruler of Egypt. Mehemet Ali was an Albanian military adventurer who by force of arms, murders, massacres and intrigues had risen to be Pasha of Egypt, Syria and Crete. Nominally the Sultan's vassal, to all the great European powers he represented a standing threat to Ottoman stability. Mehemet Ali, however, liked to pose as an enlightened and progressive ruler, who devoted his energies to turning Egypt into a modern state. Through extortionate taxation and the granting of monopolies, he had succeeded in channelling the whole wealth of the country into his own hands. He spent lavishly on dams, bridges and other public works as well as on his army and his court. Many European visitors were impressed by what they saw and, when they met the Pasha, disarmed by his friendly and agreeable manners.

Cobden, however, had briefed himself well on Mehemet Ali's history, and as he entered the citadel he was painfully aware that he was crossing the very place where, only ten years earlier, the Pasha had ordered several hundred of his Mameluke guests to be treacherously massacred.[52] When he met the Pasha he was neither disarmed by his smiling bonhomie – which he suspected to be false – nor impressed by his glowing account of the wealth and prosperity brought to Egyptian villagers through the cultivation of cotton, which he knew to be false. It was, he wrote afterwards, 'the most audacious puff ever practised upon the credulity of an audience'.[53]

Cobden remained in Egypt for nearly seven weeks – quite long enough to confirm his belief that the Pasha was sucking the country dry and to be appalled by the degrading poverty in which most of the people lived. Far from being a reformer, Mehemet Ali was 'a rapacious tyrant', who had imported the products of western civilisation to exalt himself, not to benefit the people. Nearly thirty cotton factories, for example, had been set up – magnificent buildings filled with the most costly machinery from England and France. Cobden visited as many as he could and he discovered that a few years of mismanagement had reduced most of them to a shocking state of dilapidation. The expensive machinery had been abandoned and shoddy goods were being produced by primitive and uneconomic methods. At the same time, the surrounding country-side, with its fertile soil, was turning into a desert because those who should have been cultivating it had been forced into the factories.

Before leaving Cairo Cobden had a second interview with Mehemet Ali, who had been told that he was a manufacturer from the chief cotton town in England. This time they had much more of a genuine exchange of views, although Cobden refrained from mentioning, as he would dearly have liked to do, the utter wretchedness in which most of the Egyptians lived. He could not help being impressed by the Pasha's 'love of facts and quickness of calculation', and when he made his farewells he could almost have persuaded himself that he was leaving a cotton merchant or broker; 'but in turning towards the door I passed the three black eunuchs who still guarded the entrance to the dwelling apartments of the palace. I felt I was at the court of a Turkish satrap where notwithstanding commerce had for the first time asserted its supremacy, yet where all the worst evils and vices of Mahometanism still prevailed.'[54]

Constantinople in the depths of winter was almost more than Cobden could bear. 'Do not expect a long or rhapsodical letter from me', he told his family, 'for I am at the moment of writing both cold and cross.' The only source of heat, a copper pan of charcoal, gave him a headache, melted snow leaked through the roof on to his bed, and his landlady's large brood of children kept up a loud and continuous din. If he went out, the streets were choked with water and snow and even filthier than usual, and to complete the dreary scene, every person he met dodged away from him as far as possible in case he was carrying the plague. The city had just had a more than usually lethal bout of it, but fortunately – Cobden assured his family – a cold north wind which had set in on the very day of his arrival had now driven it away. (He had apparently decided not to let the plague deter him from visiting Constantinople.) When the weather improved he made an excursion up the Bosphorus to see what was reputed to be the most beautiful scenery in Europe. But even there he was haunted by 'the misery, the dirt, the plague and all the other disagreeables of Constantinople'. He could not look on the palaces, kiosks and wooden houses crowding the beautiful banks without remembering 'the poverty, vice and tyranny of their possessors'. It was only the kindness and hospitality of the English merchants that made his stay in the Ottoman capital tolerable.[55]

In Smyrna, where the weather was too bad for him to go out much, he was again heavily indebted to the English community. Their hospitality made it one of the most comfortable stages of his journey and their conversation turned it into one of the most useful. He stayed there until early March 1837 and arrived in Athens a fortnight later. His voyage through the Greek islands was interrupted by five thoroughtly unpleasant days in quarantine on Syra (Siros), the chief port of the Cyclades. He and his companions were put in a shed resembling a second-rate English cow house, with no ceiling, plaster falling off the walls, the floor strewn with large stones and the only bed a wooden platform reached by three steps. Here he had one of his worst encounters with the ubiquitous flea. 'I am literally eaten up with fleas and bugs', he confided to his journal; 'and the rats chase each other through the room as though they were its legitimate lodgers.' On their last evening they were visited by a doctor, who made them strike their armpits and groins, and by this simple test satisfied himself that they were free of the plague.[56]

Athens aroused mixed feelings in Cobden. He had not of course had a classical education himself, and he was inclined to mock gently those who had. Characteristically, he thought they should have devoted less attention to 'the ancient affairs of these Lilliputian states' and more to the history, politics and geography of the Americas. However, when he visited the Acropolis, the ancient Greeks had him under their spell. 'I am satisfied', he told Frederick, 'that there is nothing now in existence which for beauty of design, masterly workmanship, and choice of situation, can compare with that spectacle of grandeur and sublimity which the public temples of ancient Athens presented two thousand years ago. What a genius and what a taste had those people! *And, mind the genius is still there.* All the best deeds of ancient times will be again rivalled by the Greeks of a future age.'[57]

But that future age was very far distant. The Greeks, who had only recovered their independence six years previously, would, Cobden believed, have first to recover from the deadening effects of centuries of slavery. They would also have to overthrow – as they no doubt soon would – the 'little trumpery monarchy' foisted on them by England, France and Russia three years earlier. King Otho, the son of the King of Bavaria, was in fact turning out to be a determined autocrat and an incorrigible spendthrift. All Cobden's contempt for Palmerstonian diplomacy boiled up as he walked round Athens and saw the cafés filled with flashily-dressed Bavarian soldiers, and a grand palace, a barracks, a military hospital, a royal mint, all going up apace, while two thirds of the town's ordinary dwelling-houses remained in the ruinous state to which they had been reduced by the war against the Turks.[58] What Cobden did not know was that no one regretted more keenly than Palmerston himself that he had agreed to place Otho on the Greek throne; no one was trying harder than the English foreign minister to persuade Otho to mend his ways; and no one was doing more to confirm him in them than Tsar Nicholas, whose aim was to establish Russian influence in Greece.[59]

CHAPTER 3

The Radical Reformer (1837–38)

'Thank God I am once more in old England', wrote Cobden immediately after landing at Falmouth on 21 April, 1837. 'I feel glad to be again on dry ground, for although I have long ago got rid of sea-sickness, I am right heartily sick of the sea.'[1] Although a few months earlier he had assured the ever-anxious Frederick that he was not 'author-mad',[2] he had only been back in Manchester a few days before he was writing to Tait with ideas for articles based on his travels: '. . . let me know if I could make readable stuff of it for your Mag.'[3] But political journalism was soon overtaken by the real thing – by exploring the wider world of radical politics in London.

It was not an auspicious time for a young enthusiast to do so. The parliamentary Radicals, whose political prospects had seemed so rosy in the heady days of the first reformed parliament, were such an amorphous and heterogenous group that contemporaries found it hard to agree on their strength. But in addition to the Irish members, led by Daniel O'Connell, there was another more or less cohesive group known as the Philosophic Radicals, about twenty strong. The cement that held them together was their desire to translate Benthamite principles into practical politics. Their leading members were sincere, distinguished, sometimes brilliant men. But as a party they were fatally flawed by their disunity. Harriet Martineau described them sadly as 'single subject men' about whom 'nothing was more remarkable . . . than their individuality'.[4] George Grote, the historian of Greece, pinned his colours to the secret ballot; the veteran Joseph Hume hammered away doggedly at financial reform; Sir William Molesworth made himself an expert on the colonies; and so on. None of them possessed – nor may they have even wanted – the qualities of leadership. 'We have all', wrote Joseph Parkes to Lord Durham in January 1837, 'the Radical section, been quarrelling

very heartily, but no real *split* among us. Only as to our policy.'[5] By
which he really meant their tactics, for what they quarrelled about to
the point of paralysis was whether they should support the Whigs,
who were such feeble reformers, or oppose them and risk bringing in
the Tories who were not (they assumed) reformers at all.

Cobden gravitated naturally towards the Philosophic Radicals, but
on the whole he was not greatly impressed by them. George Grote,
although 'a mild and philosophical man, possessing the highest order
of moral and intellectual endowments', lacked what, for want of a
better phrase, Cobden called the necessary *'devil'* to be an effective
politician. He referred to the Grotes as 'Mrs and Mr' because it was
so obvious that she was the better politician of the two.[6] His
judgment of the young Molesworth, who had the disadvantage of
being a baronet but impeccable credentials as a reformer, was less
shrewd. He described him as 'a youthful, florid-looking man of
foppish and conceited air', and dismissed him as being – whatever he
might *say* – without any democratic principles.[7] John Roebuck,
whose jingoism was to prove so alien to Cobden, he conceded to be a
clever fellow – 'but I find that his mind is more active than powerful.
He is apt to take lawyer-like views of questions, and . . . is given to
cavilling and special pleading'.[8] Only Parkes seems to have met with
Cobden's unqualified approval, no doubt partly because Parkes so
clearly approved of him, but also because he was 'not only profound
in his profession but skilled in political economy and quite up to the
spirit of the age in practical and popular acquirements'.[9] In other
words, Parkes, who was not a Member of Parliament, appealed to
Cobden because he had more than mere talk to his credit; he had
been a leading member of the Birmingham Political Union during
the Reform Bill crisis, and secretary of the commission responsible
for preparing the great reform of municipal corporations two years
earlier.

Unfortunately, apart from Parkes, we do not know what the men
Cobden met in London thought of him. He must already have
acquired something of a reputation in London radical circles, for he
was evidently made very welcome, and by his own complacent
account would not have lacked for invitations if he had stayed in
London for a year. He postponed his return home for a few days
because of a pressing invitation from the editor of the radical *Morning
Chronicle*, Mr Easthope, to a dinner above the paper's office in the
Strand. Easthope tried hard to persuade him to meet Palmerston,
whom he described as open to conviction and a cleverer man than
most of his colleagues. But Cobden refused; he had, he said, made up
his mind that Palmerston was 'an incurable block-head'.[10]

Cobden had not been back in Manchester more than a few days
before, on 20 June, the old King died and the general election, about

which everyone had been speculating for so long, became a certainty
before the summer was out. Cobden had already presented himself
to the voters of Stockport as a thoroughgoing radical reformer. He
had privately described his election address, composed the previous
October, as touching 'upon every subject that a candidate in our time
can, could, may, might, would or should refer to', and he claimed
that upon every issue he had 'gone the *whole hog*'.[11] The Chartists,
who in the spring of 1837 were campaigning for annual parliaments
and universal suffrage, would not have agreed, since Cobden
demanded only triennial parliaments and household suffrage. Nor
would the prominence given to Ireland's troubles, which reflected
Cobden's concern, have aroused much, if any, interest in the voters
of Stockport. But the most assiduously reforming voter could hardly
have complained of a programme that included the disestablishment
of the Church of England as well as of the Church of Ireland, the
ballot, the repeal of the Corn Laws, withdrawal from the colonies, a
cut in the army, an isolationist foreign policy and the reform of the
House of Lords through the admission of representatives of the
manufacturing interest. He forgot to mention factory reform – a
rather odd omission in view of the government's unsuccessful
attempt during the previous summer to dilute the provisions of the
1833 Factory Act limiting the hours of work for children. Cobden
repaired this omission in a letter to the chairman of his election
committee in which he stated that if he had been in Parliament, he
would have strongly opposed the government's amending legislation.[12]

The other important issue omitted from Cobden's election
address was the new Poor Law passed in 1834 – by far the most
controversial piece of legislation between the Reform Bill and the
repeal of the Corn Laws. In the autumn of 1836, the Poor Law
commissioners had not yet introduced the hated new system of no
relief outside the workhouse in the factory districts of Lancashire and
Yorkshire. In January 1837 the first (unsuccessful) attempt to set up
the new machinery in the North was made at Huddersfield, and by
the summer the anti-Poor Law agitation was in full swing, with
organising committees, public meetings and huge outdoor rallies. It
was fanned by the onset of a severe economic depression, bringing
with it the fear – and the reality – of unemployment for the workers,
and it also had strong middle-class support from those who realised
how much suffering the strict application of the law would cause.
Cobden's only comment on it that seems to have survived from this
period was a passing remark in his first pamphlet to the effect that the
new Poor Law would effectually check the further increase of the
pauper population.[13] In other words, he accepted the distinction,
which the reformers wanted to reinforce, between the independent

'deserving' poor and the idle paupers who deliberately sponged off the rest of the community through the swollen poor rates. Presumably, he regarded the new Poor Law as a solution for a grave social problem, based on common sense and the laws of political economy. It was an accomplished fact, which would not concern him if he got into Parliament unless it revealed serious flaws, and he apparently preferred to ignore the current controversy.

Cobden approached the task of getting into Parliament with characteristic energy and self-confidence. When the time came, he told Tait early in May, 'I will throw myself amongst the people, and go to work with a determination not to be beaten. I have all my life from choice been fighting uphill battles, and never found perseverance and industry yet to fail of success, and it shall go hard but the same instruments will *lick* the tories of Stockport.'[14]

His first meeting with his election committee went off 'right well' and filled him with even greater enthusiasm and confidence. 'Now, after having seen a little and heard a good deal about the Stockport chaps', he wrote to a friend in Manchester, '*I am of a decided conviction I shall get in. Nothing but winning will satisfy me.*'[15]

There were three candidates at Stockport for two seats. The other two were a Tory and another reformer, Henry Marsland. Cobden met his fellow reformer at a dinner party in London in June, and described him, with mingled complacency and contempt, as 'a poor creature – narrow and timid minded'. He could not believe that the electors would prefer Henry Marsland to him, but if they did, 'then good-bye to politics, for I'll never run the risk of so great a humiliation again.'[16]

He was humiliated. When the poll was declared, Cobden, with 418 votes, was far behind Henry Marsland with 480 and the Tory candidate with 471. But of course he did not give up politics. He believed that the Tories must have indulged in bribery. He was certain that his own supporters had been far too confident of victory – he did after all suffer under the grave disadvantage of being a stranger to the borough. He claimed that the millowners to a man had opposed him – perhaps because he had proclaimed his belief that the factory workers ought to be able to bargain with their employers for shorter hours without the intervention of Parliament.[17] He was consoled with a piece of plate for which 17,000 of his supporters had subscribed one penny each, and by an open-air rally at which the star attraction was the great Irish politician Daniel O'Connell.[18] The rally was followed by a dinner for 2500 guests crammed into a huge tent pitched in a field. According to one of the guests: 'A tolerable cold dinner was eaten with much difficulty and crowding. There was singing, speaking and shouting in abundance, and we did not leave till one in the morning.'[19]

If Cobden was disappointed by his failure to get elected, the Radicals as a whole were – to use Mrs Grote's expressive word – 'consternated' at their losses throughout the country. Many of their leaders, including Hume and Roebuck, were defeated, and their total strength was reduced to about sixty. Grote ascribed the Radicals' unpopularity to the surge of loyalty for the young Queen, and daily lamented the death of William IV.[20] But neither did the Whigs do as well as they had expected, in spite of the Queen's open support, and Cobden hoped that with the two main parties more nearly balanced, the Whigs might feel obliged to treat their Radical allies – upon whom they were now more dependent – with more consideration. It was a reasonable hope, but Melbourne did not see it that way. 'To approach nearer the Rads', he wrote to Lord John Russell, 'is not a cure for evils which have come upon us because we were already too close to them.'[21] Russell accepted his reasoning, and when the new Parliament met in November 1837 and the Radicals persistently probed him on the government's intentions with regard to the ballot and the further widening of the franchise, he was provoked into slapping them down with a finality highly embarrassing to his prime minister and, in retrospect, to himself as well. Henceforward, Lord John was burdened with the unfortunate nickname of 'Finality Jack'.

A secret ballot had been seriously considered by the Whigs when they were drawing up the Reform Bill. They had dropped the idea but it continued to arouse strong feelings. As the Radicals gradually realised how little difference the Reform Act made to who was actually sent to the House of Commons, they became increasingly keen to sweep away the traditional system of voting under which all the world, including a man's landlord or employer, knew how he cast his vote. They assumed that a secret vote would greatly undermine the political power of the landed aristocracy in the counties. It would of course also work the other way at the opposite end of the social scale by preventing the non-voters in the towns from exercising an indirect influence on the voters' choice by their vociferous presence at the poll; and when the privilege of the vote still only belonged to one in seven of the male population, this was by no means an unimportant consideration. A more frivolous argument against the ballot (though not to those who made it) was that it was unmanly and unEnglish. 'What pitiful figures we should cut', wrote Lord William Russell, 'sneaking up to the ballot box, looking with fear to the right and the left and dropping in our paper, the contents of which we are afraid or ashamed to acknowledge.'[22] But to both supporters and opponents of the ballot, the core of the argument was that it would help to shift political power away from those who had monopolised it in the past. Every year, thousands of people signed petitions asking Parliament to grant the ballot. Every year George Grote introduced a motion in favour of it, which every year the Commons rejected.

To Cobden, mulling over the recent elections, the ballot seemed to be 'the most important principle to establish',[23] and he decided to do his best to make sure it was. At a public dinner at Salford on 6 September, held to celebrate the re-election of the Radical MP Joseph Brotherton, Cobden showed how different the election results might have been if the voters had been able to exercise their right without fear or favour, mentioning as an example a Mr Trafford who had brought a hundred tenants to vote, like cattle to a market.[24] Believing that the English could never be got to work up enthusiasm for more than one cause at a time, Cobden urged that associations be set up to promote the ballot instead of the Radicals' more usual rallying cry, electoral reform. He wrote to Grote and Molesworth, suggesting that they should promote ballot associations in London, as he was trying to do in Manchester. He also suggested to Grote that a lecturer should be sent out to publicise the importance of the ballot and to collect evidence of its necessity.[25]

But the campaign never got off the ground. Inside Parliament, the steady increase in the number of ministerial supporters – not only Radicals – voting for Grote's annual motion, forced Melbourne to make the ballot an open question in 1839. But outside Parliament, the great mass of non-voters could see no point in supporting an agitation to strengthen a civic right which they themselves did not enjoy. To the majority of reformers, the most important aim was to extend the suffrage, whether moderately, as the parliamentary Radicals wished, or all the way to universal (male) suffrage, as the Chartists, who were just emerging into prominence, insisted.

Cobden's feelings on this issue were mixed. The depressing outcome of the 1837 election provoked him into wondering privately whether there was not already too much liberty for the intelligence of the people.[26] On the other hand, at the 1838 new year supper for his workpeople at Sabden, he assured them, according to a local newspaper report, that if they were determined to have both the franchise and the ballot, 'he would go with them to the attainment of their object'.[27] To that audience and on such a festive occasion, he might have been a little carried away. But he wrote in a private letter: 'I have unbounded faith in the people, and would risk universal suffrage tomorrow in preference to the present franchise.'[28] Unlike many reformers, he felt that it would be a risk. There was little point in enlarging the electorate unless the new voters knew how to use their votes intelligently – that is, to support the reformers – and not let themselves become mere voting fodder for the opponents of change. In other words, all political reform must have a sound foundation in the education of the people. Without education, Cobden told Tait, he had no hope of any extensive political change. 'The Americans understand this point better than we ... *education, education, education* is the motto of every enlightened democrat in America'.[29] There was a school at Sabden and the factory walls displayed slogans announcing that education was the birthright of man.[30]

In the England of the 1830s such a slogan had a hollow ring. In industrial development the British led the world, but in providing a basic education for the rapidly expanding army of industrial workers they shamefully lagged behind several West European countries, to say nothing of the United States. There was a wide variety of Sunday, parish, charity, Catholic and dame schools. Two rival societies, one Anglican and one non-denominational, had been founded some twenty years earlier with the aim of establishing more schools and, within the limits set by their subscribers' generosity and their own religious prejudices, they had done useful work. Under the 1833 Factory Act, manufacturers were obliged to provide two hours schooling daily for the children they employed, and four inspectors were appointed to make at least some check that the law was being obeyed. But all these put together were very far from closing the gap between what was needed and what was available. And the quality of the education provided – especially in the dame schools – was often so bad that it was a mockery to call it education at all.

Many, however, doubted the prudence of conferring the benefits of literacy on those who had so much to complain about. And many of those who agreed that education was a suitable object of reform, if only because a better-educated work force would be a more efficient one, denied that there was any urgency about it. The Radicals and progressive Whigs in Parliament who insisted that the problem was urgent, realised that it was too big to be solved without the intervention of the state, however anxious they were in principle to minimise state intervention. In 1833 their arguments persuaded the government to make a modest grant of £20,000 for educational purposes. It was used for building schools and disbursed through the two voluntary societies, but as it was laid down that any grant had to be matched by locally raised funds, no help reached those communities who were too poor to help themselves. Moreover the Catholics received nothing, and the Dissenters were convinced that the Anglicans received more than their fair share. The annual grants were continued in 1834 and 1835, while Commons committees inquired into the state of education throughout the country. But what would clearly hold up progress towards legislation to set up a comprehensive state-supported system was the religious issue: every school's curriculum, it was assumed, must include religious teaching, but how was this to be arranged to the satisfaction of both the Anglicans and the Nonconformists?

Like most Radicals, Cobden would have solved this problem by banishing sectarian teaching altogether from the schools, as was the case in Ireland and the United States. The bible might be read to the children in class, but religious instruction should be the business of the Anglican priest or the Dissenting minister outside school hours. He had become an enthusiastic convert to the Massachusetts system of free, non-sectarian, education financed by a local rate, during his stay in the United States. His visit to an infant school had greatly moved him and he dedicated himself in his journal to campaigning for infant schools in England 'where they may become an instrument for ameliorating the fate of the children working in the factories whose case I fear is beyond the reach of all other remedies'.[31]

Manchester was not unpromising ground for an educational campaign. Reformers like Dr Kay, who had an intimate knowledge of the poor of Manchester, had for some years been asking for more schools, and the forthright reports of the Manchester Statistical Society on the existing facilities had stirred many consciences. Yet, when sometime during 1836 Cobden invited clergymen of every denomination to his Mosley Street counting-house, and asked them to try to work out some agreed system of education, they failed completely.[32] In the autumn of 1837, with his convictions about the importance of educational reform reinforced by the election results, Cobden made a determined effort to rally public opinion behind a practical scheme. Towards the end of September, he and some friends organised a meeting on education in Salford Town Hall. The principal outside speaker was Thomas Wyse, an Irish Catholic MP, who had been deeply involved in organising the non-sectarian, system of elementary education in Ireland, and who was a leading member of the new radical pressure group, the central Society for Education, set up the previous year. Cobden, the principal local speaker, appealed for a system of education 'based on liberal principles, untinged by sectarian prejudices'.[33] A month later a much grander affair, described by Cobden in advance as 'a public entertainment on a very large scale', was held in the Theatre Royal, Manchester. The pit was boarded over to accomodate the male guests, the boxes were reserved for the ladies, and the upper boxes and gallery were allotted to the members of the Mechanics' Institution.[34] A packed audience, including no less than nine MPs, sat through more than five hours of speeches, and the meeting did not break up till after midnight.[35] There was no lack of interest in education among the citizens of Manchester.

The following month the Manchester Society for Promoting National Education was set up, with Cobden a member of the committee. He and some friends did manage to set up a few new schools in Manchester, but only one survived for more than a year. They relied on voluntary donations, and at a time of severe economic depression these inevitably ceased. The new national education society did not last for much longer. It also suffered from lack of funds but, more important, its leading members were swept up in the campaign against the Corn laws.

The meagre results of his efforts did not discourage Cobden from taking up the educational challenge again nearly fifteen years later. Perhaps the most important outcome for him of this early campaign was that it led to him making the acquaintance of John Bright, who was to become his most valued personal and political friend. In October 1837 Cobden wrote to Bright's father, Jacob, a well-known cotton manufacturer of Rochdale, asking him to spread the word about the forthcoming education meeting in Manchester among his neighbours.[36] The following December the Brights invited Cobden to speak at an education meeting in the schoolroom of the Baptist Chapel in West Street, Rochdale. According to John's recollection forty years later, he went over to Manchester, introduced himself to Cobden in his Mosley Street counting-house, and gave the invitation.[37] Cobden accepted and spoke at Rochdale on December 21, afterwards staying the night with Jacob Bright and his family.[38]

In September 1837 the British Association held its annual meeting in Liverpool. The Association had been founded in 1831 as a forum to enable the different scientific societies to exchange ideas. Harriet Martineau complained that 'a great deal of mere talk, and boast, and quackery' had to be endured at these meetings.[39] But to Cobden, who went over to Liverpool for the occasion, it was an excellent opportunity to meet distinguished political economists like the statistician and Board of Trade official, G. R. Porter, and to listen to their discussions on protection, monopoly and the Corn laws, the great obstacles, they believed, to economic progress. He also at last met his old sparring partner, David Urquhart, whom he had tried without success to see when he was in Constantinople. He found him 'quite wild as ever for the Turks', but liked him well enough to invite him to breakfast when Urquhart later visited Manchester.[40] By this time Urquhart had been dismissed from the British embassy at Constantinople, after the ambassador had repeatedly complained of his insubordination, so that if he and Cobden disagreed as stoutly as ever about the Turks, they could at any rate unite in denouncing Palmerston.

At the end of the year Cobden published a short pamphlet entitled *Incorporate Your Borough*, by a Radical Reformer.[41] It was a stirring call to his fellow citizens to take advantage of the Municipal Reform Act, passed two years previously. It aimed to sweep away the archaic charade of lord of the manor, court leet and borough-reeve, and replace them with a democratically elected council and mayor. Manchester's remaining manorial links were just the kind of feudal remnant most calculated to rouse Cobden's contemptuous scorn, and it boiled over in October 1837 when he found himself caught up in the charade. He was picked as a juror by the agent of the lord of the manor (Sir Oswald Mosley) and after reluctantly attending a meeting of the court leet held in a bare, musty room underneath a dancing academy, he angrily spurned a ticket entitling him to attend an official dinner given on behalf of the lord of the manor.

> Well, what in the world does all this mean? Is it that in this great town of Manchester we are still living under the feudal system? Does Sir Oswald Mosley, living up in Derbyshire, send his mandate down here for us to come into this dingy hole to elect a government for Manchester and then go and get a ticket for soup at his expense? Why, now I will put an end to this thing.[42]

Genuine indignation betrayed Cobden into expressing himself with an arrogance that in later years he would have deplored. But what was really important to him, as to so many radical reformers, was the opportunity provided by the Municipal Reform Act to introduce democratic self-government into the town, not only as a desirable end in itself, but also as preparation for a wider participation in the electoral process at the national level. The new Act gave the vote to every male ratepayer of three years' standing and required one third of the councillors to retire each year. 'Every man's vote', pointed out Cobden in his pamphlet, 'however humble his circumstances may be, is of equal value with his wealthiest neighbour's.'[43] He appealed not only to the working class radicals, who in Manchester were both vociferous and assertive, but also to all those who today would be called lower middle class but were then known as the 'shopocracy' after their largest sector.[44] He did not offer them better government, although presumably it was assumed that this would follow. He offered what seemed at the time more important: participation in government.

Although most people agreed that Manchester could and should be better governed, not everyone felt that a thoroughgoing municipal reform on the lines laid down in the Act was either necessary or desirable. The court leet was regarded as an archaic irrelevance of no practical importance which would have to be abolished eventually, but it did not much matter when. The pre-1835 municipal corporations in the older towns had dealt mainly with the administration of justice and corporate charities, and from time to time had provided some picturesque pageantry. The practical tasks of sanitation, lighting, police and so on had been dealt with by *ad hoc* bodies. For more than forty years Manchester had been administered by 'police commissioners', who in recent years had not, by the standards of the day, made a bad job of it. They had the great attraction, unlike municipal councils, of being limited in the amount of rates they could levy, and some people felt that measures to make the police commissioners more efficient was all that was needed. A municipal charter would clearly be a greater burden on the ratepayers; it was less clear what advantages it would bring.[45]

The largely Anglican Tory oligarchy which had ruled the roost in Manchester for many years were opposed to incorporation because it was a Whig measure, because they feared additional expense, and – most important – because it would probably transfer their dominance over local affairs to the rival, predominantly Dissenting, Whigs, who differed less in social class and occupation than in religion. But the most lively opposition to municipal reform came from the working class radicals. They too suspected that the rates would go up. They simply did not want an efficient 'Bourbon' police force that would restrain their natural inclination to riot whenever they had a grievance. (A contemporary local guide-book regretfully noted that 'Manchester has, by some means, obtained at a distance, an unenviable notoriety on account of its rioting propensities.'[46] They saw no advantage to themselves in having justice administered by local magistrates familiar with local people and problems rather than county JPs, as at present. They feared that the new Poor Law, with its workhouse 'bastilles', not yet introduced into Manchester, would be brought in to oppress the poor. At a meeting of the police commissioners early in 1838, James Wroe, the radical leader, mocked at a pamphlet 'supposed to be written by Mr Cobden', claimed that no other town's affairs were better managed and asked what benefit he himself would gain if the respected chairman of the commissioners 'was seated there with a great big horsehair wig on his head, a stuff gown upon his back, and a tawdry thing called a mace at his side, with a fellow-in-waiting, dressed up like a play actor, to carry it away.'[47]

So it was against what he called an unholy alliance of Tories and radicals that Cobden, supported by the Whigs, led the struggle for Manchester's incorporation. In an attempt to win over the radicals, he circulated 5000 copies of a letter in which he emphasised all the popular features of the municipal reform. But instead of being impressed, the radicals plastered the walls of Manchester with posters warning working men to beware of the Whigs who were up to their 'dirty tricks' again. The reformers were faced with a real prospect of defeat at the public meeting that was to decide for or against incorporation. All they could do was to appeal individually to every one of the £10 voters of known liberal views to turn up at the meeting.

When it was held, on 9 February, 1838, some 2000 people crowded into the Town Hall. In accordance with the procedure laid down in the Act, Cobden introduced a motion that the Queen in Council should be petitioned for a Charter. He admitted that the new law was not perfect. He deplored the property qualifications for councillors and aldermen and hoped he would see the day when the poorest mechanic would be qualified by his talents and integrity for a seat on the bench of justices. He pointed out the advantages of having one third of the councillors retiring each year; '. . . every year there will be that delightful agitation which I love to see, an election of one common councilman for every ward; just enough to remind the other two that, if they don't behave themselves, their turn is coming.' He ridiculed the idea that the radicals or Chartists could hope for any political advance from the existing institutions, and tried hard to dispel the widespread fears that incorporation would be too costly. Such 'corporation baubles as maces, cloaks and chains . . . were gone by, and would never be tolerated in Manchester'.[48] (He was wrong there; they were introduced, much to his disgust, in 1849.)

But even the doses of demagogy with which Cobden liberally laced his speech failed to impress his radical opponents. One of them called the speech a bundle of fallacies; a second described Cobden as 'a man without thought, a mere spouter to gain applause'; and a third called upon 'the men of Manchester to resist the tyranny of the bloated rich, and to trust not to the truckling, vile, base, bloody and brutal Whigs'.[49] The speeches, cheers and counter-cheers went on for more than four rowdy hours. In the end, the pro-Charter votes, swelled by the 'shopocracy', who had responded to Cobden's appeal to attend, carried the day. After three cheers had been given for Mr Cobden, it was suggested that Mr Wroe, the vituperative radical leader, should be treated to three groans; but Cobden and his friends managed to quash such an undignified exhibition.[50]

The anti-Charter faction, however, had by no means thrown in the sponge. While Cobden and his supporters were busy collecting signatures for the petition, they were even more busily collecting signatures for a counter-petition. The petition praying for incorporation was transported to London by train and taken to the Privy Council office by a delegation, including Cobden, on 12 March. It was nearly 100 yards long and contained 11,830 signatures. The counter-petition which followed had 31,947 signatures. This grand total had been achieved by employing professional canvassers, who were paid 3/– a day plus a bonus of 3/– for every sheet of 42 signatures. It was an open invitation to forgery which was enthusiastically taken up, but apparently not very skilfully. When Cobden inspected the counter-petition in the Privy Council office, he saw that on some sheets the signatures had clearly all been written in the same hand; on others the signatures had been written in the same hand but with different pens; while on others again the writing had been ingeniously varied, but the effect spoilt by the repetition of the same spelling idiosyncrasies. Cobden called it 'a dirty odious business', but he had to admit that his own side had not been entirely guiltless of skulduggery – if not of forgery, at least of greasing palms. He reluctantly justified it on the ground that if their opponents would not play fair, neither could they.[51]

Towards the end of May the Privy Council sent two commissioners, Captain Jebb and Mr Alexander Gordon, to Manchester to test the validity of the rival petitions. They carried out their scrutiny in the Town Hall and in private, except for one representative from each side. For three weeks, Cobden, representing the reformers, had very little time for anything else. Eventually, the commissioners accepted 7984 (67.5 per cent) of the pro-Charter signatures, and 8694 (27.2 per cent) of those against. The latter still had a slight edge over their opponents but, in view of the indecently wholesale scale of their forgeries, the Privy Council was inclined to grant a Charter. In the middle of September, however, Captain Jebb reappeared with two assistants, and spent ten days making door-to-door inquiries among the rate-payers. The day after Captain Jebb returned to London, Manchester heard that it had joined the ranks of the new municipal boroughs.

The first meeting of the new municipal council was held on 15 December, 1838. Cobden was among the sixteen aldermen chosen, and he in turn proposed Thomas Potter as Manchester's first mayor. There were no Tories on the council because none had stood for election. Instead, they tried to sabotage the new regime. The county coroner began an action for trespass against the new municipal coroner, and hundreds of corpses received duplicate inquests from the rival coroners. A rival body of overseers of the poor was elected. The newly recruited municipal police constables were locked out of their police stations by their Tory-inclined officers. And so on. It was several years before the last embers of resistance had died, and by that time one suspects that Cobden was no longer greatly interested. At Stockport in 1837, he had been fighting a political battle on his own behalf. In Manchester a year later he was fighting for a cause. It had been an exhilarating, exhausting and to some extent – since he had been forced to look closely at the seamy side of politics –

a depressing experience. But when it was over, he was ready for
more. Henceforward, Manchester was principally important to him
as the power house of a campaign fought on a larger, national stage –
the campaign to repeal the Corn Laws.

While in London during the summer of 1838, Cobden appeared
before a Commons select committee to support a reform which he
later believed had played a significant part in securing the repeal of
the Corn Laws – Roland Hill's penny postage. Hill, nearly ten years
older than Cobden, had a good deal in common with him, although
he had not been so successful in making his way in the world. He
was largely self-educated, had had a poor and feckless father, was
very interested in education and had a great desire to do good in the
world. He had drawn up a plan for the reform of the postal services
and, after failing to interest the government in it, had published his
ideas in a pamphlet. The response was immediate. Hill had touched
on a grievance that affected every literate person in the country
except the very rich and those who enjoyed free franking facilities.
Hill reckoned that the actual cost to the Post Office of carrying a
letter from London to Edinburgh was 1/36th of a penny, but the cost
to the recipient (not the sender) was over a shilling. This was expensive even for the wealthy; for the poor it was prohibitive. Consequently, extraordinary ingenuity was exercised in bypassing the Post
Office. Carriers and commercial travellers acted as unofficial post-
men. Businessmen squeezed several letters on to one sheet of paper
which, when it reached its destination, was cut up and distributed.
Bundles of letters were included in parcels of books, to be passed on
by the local bookseller. But however widespread and ingenious the
letter-smuggling, it was no substitute for a cheap official postal
service.

So strong was the feeling aroused by Hill's pamphlet that even
Melbourne's lethargic government had to appoint a Commons
committee to study Hill's proposals for a pre-paid penny postage for
letters weighing half an ounce or less. Cobden appeared before the
committee on 7 May as spokesman for the Manchester Chamber of
Commerce.[52] He painted a vivid picture of the various ways in
which people avoided using the post, claiming that only one in six
letters sent from Manchester to London went through the official
channel. (When he got back to Manchester he was told that one in
ten would have been more accurate.) He naturally emphasised the
importance to trade of a cheaper post, but equally he stressed how
much it would help to preserve family and personal ties. The 50,000
Irish people living in Manchester, he said, might as well be living in
New South Wales for all the opportunity they had of keeping in

touch with their relatives in Ireland. The committee was inclined to be sceptical about whether many of the working class either could or would want to write letters. Cobden assured them they were mistaken, claiming that most of his own work people at Sabden could write and no young person was taken on who could not. When the committee suggested that it would simply be impracticable for the Post Office to deliver a much larger number of letters, Cobden declared that with the new railways the weight of the mails was no longer of any consequence. The letters could be taken to the various provincial centres by rail, and there sorted and distributed in the usual way. He pointed out that an elephant had recently been taken from London to Manchester (where it was to be exhibited) by rail at 20 miles per hour without the slightest difficulty.

He gave equally short shrift to a compromise plan, much mooted at the time, for a twopenny post. Only a reduction to one penny, he assured the committee, would be enough to persuade people to use the post. Francis Place, the veteran Radical, who was an ardent champion of the penny post, wrote that only those who had been really poor understood the psychological difference between one penny and two, 'how unwilling careful people are of spending twopence, how careless they are of spending a penny'.[53] Cobden had grown up in a very poor household and he did understand. Finally, he strongly supported Hill's revolutionary proposal that the postage should be paid by the sender, not the recipient. The advantages of the proposal were not hard to grasp, but the use of the postage stamp to carry it into effect did not seem as simple and obvious as it does today. Cobden, drawing on Hill's ideas, suggested the use of 'small vignettes, something similar to the stamp on patent medicines; something to be affixed by the party with gum on the envelope', and then stamped by the post office.[54]

Roland Hill was delighted with Cobden's evidence which, he wrote, confirmed his own views and threw much new light on the subject. Cobden, who never lost an opportunity to distribute his own pamphlets – he had already sent copies to Hill – urged him to get out a cheap edition of his postal reform pamphlet. If it could be slightly abbreviated and brought out at sixpence it would be widely bought, and he himself was willing to bear half the cost of the reprinting. He urged Hill to have the cheap edition widely advertised in the provincial press and offered to contribute £10 to an advertising fund. He invited Hill to give a lecture in Manchester and offered to put him up. He urged him to organise an agitation for the penny postage during the forthcoming parliamentary recess. 'Nothing can be done without agitation in all its varieties of form, whether by newspapers, pamphlets or public meetings.'[55]

At this time Cobden was heavily involved in the struggle for

Manchester's Charter, but his imagination had been fired by the thought of how much cheap postage might do to widen the horizons and improve the lot of working people. Hill was an older man with whom Cobden had had only one brief meeting, but that did not stop the flow of his advice. It was a tribute to the charm that lay behind Cobden's sometimes rather brash and overbearing self-confidence that Hill, far from being affronted, found himself apologising for telling Cobden about the private difficulties that prevented him from giving all his time to the reform of the Post Office; '. . . your conversation, evidence and letters have created a feeling in my mind so like that which one entertains towards an old friend, that I am apt to forget I have met you but once.'[56]

The penny postage was finally introduced on 10 January, 1840, and there followed several months of doubt and confusion over how the new system should be operated. There was, in Harriet Martineau's words, 'a great fertility of invention about envelopes, stamps, paper that could not be imitated, and gums that were warranted harmless and seemly'.[57] Hill sent a copy of the proposed stamped envelope to Cobden, who suggested that instead of 'max', which three quarters of penny letter writers would not understand, it would be better to put 'weight under $\frac{1}{2}$oz'. He thought that the words 'under' or 'below' would be more likely to make people keep below the limit than 'not exceeding'. And he added the advice which succeeding generations of civil servants have all too clearly ignored: 'You can't be too nice in the selection of plain terms for giving directions to the multitude.'[58] In the end, the envelope was abandoned and everyone settled down happily to using the famous penny black stamp (and the twopenny blue).

When the Penny Post Bill passed the House of Lords Cobden is said to have exclaimed: 'There go the Corn laws'. Eight years later, when the Corn laws had at last gone, he saw no reason to think differently; '. . . without the penny postage', he told Roland Hill, 'we might have had more years of agitation and anxiety'.[59] But only three years later, when answering a questionnaire on the new postal system, he admitted that all the witnesses before the Commons committee, himself included, had overrated the immediate advantage of the change to the working classes. Too many of them could not write, or only with difficulty and reluctantly. In his own household, his servants wrote and received very few more letters than before, while his wife and sisters and their friends wrote and received four times as many.[60]

On 25 August, 1838, Cobden sailed from London for a six-week tour of central Europe. If he had had time, he told a friend, he would have liked to stay long enough in each country to learn all about it for himself. But as it was, he could only find out enough to enable him to read the accounts of others with more advantage. 'My plan is to get the outline of the principal features, and like the painters, leave other hands to fill up the details for me.'[61]

He began his tour in Hamburg and Berlin, and then made his way to Vienna and Salzburg by was of Leipzig, Chemnitz, Dresden and Prague. He inspected factories, especially textile factories, cotton mills, iron works, technical schools, infants' schools and workers' houses. He visited museums, art galleries, palaces, churches and theatres. Indefatigably, he filled his journal with facts and figures about production, trade, wages, hours and prices. He thought it worth while to record such items as the curious carvings outside a church in Chemnitz. He was also interested in manners and social customs, confiding to his diary the odd (to him) fact that Prussian married couples occupied separate beds in the same room, while at evening parties in Dresden the gentlemen were 'rather more disposed than in England to be separate from the sex'.[62]

In Protestant Berlin he discovered, rather to his surprise, what an enjoyable day Sunday could be. After attending church at nine, he spent the rest of the morning visiting the king's country palace at Charlottenburg. In the mausoleum he took a rather critical view of the huge reclining statue of the late Queen Sophia, reputedly a masterpiece, concluding judiciously that the effect was striking, not equal to the work of Chantry or Thorwaldsen, but inferior only to them. Among the Sunday strollers in the palace grounds he approvingly noted 'the frequent absence of the odious bonnet which seems a part of the Englishwoman's nature'. After dinner he hired a horse and joined the crowds of people making their way to the Tivoli gardens. On the way he was suprised to see ladies knitting and sewing at their windows – *this being Sunday*'. But by the time he got to the gardens he was prepared to enjoy the lively scene without surprise, let alone censure.

> Hundreds of well-dressed and still better behaved people were lounging or sitting in the large gardens, or several buildings of this gay retreat: in the midst were many little tables at which groups were sitting. The ladies had their work-bags, and were knitting, or sewing, or chatting, or sipping coffee or lemonade; the gentlemen often smoking, or perhaps flirting with their party.'

There was a little railway and other amusements; there was music and there were fireworks; there was no rowdiness, rudeness or drunkenness.

On his way back to his hotel, Cobden looked in at two theatres, both of which were crammed. He evidently thought it was all as it should be. But after describing his Sunday in Berlin in a letter to one of his sisters, he felt obliged to end on a slightly defensive note: 'If you think this is an improper picture of a Protestant Sunday, on the other hand, the sober and orderly German thinks the drunkenness, the filthy public houses, the miserable and moping mechanic that pines in his dark alley in our English cities on the Sabbath-day, are infinitely worse features of a Protestant community, than his Tivoli Gardens. Are both wrong?'[63]

He discovered that Berlin was lit by gas made from British coal, and the owner of a textile factory just outside the city told him that two boilers, which it would have taken six months to obtain in Berlin, had been procured from Manchester in six weeks. At Leipzig he was taken for a ride on a new 15-mile stretch of railway – it took about 40 minutes – and went over a works where railway carriages were being manufactured under the supervision of two Englishmen. (Most of the locomotives came from England.) In Saxony he was greatly impressed – and alarmed – by the rapidly developing textile industry and the formidable competition it would represent for British industry. But one calico-printing firm in Chemnitz impressed him unfavourably. The children employed there had to work from six in the morning to six in the evening, after which they had two hours schooling. Cobden was shocked. 'This is too much for the welfare of society - the race must deteriorate: *we do not put colts to work thus prematurely!* Still it is wonderful to say the children looked healthy. But the delicate must soon perish in such an ordeal.'[64] Presumably he was as concerned for the children as for society.

At Dresden he visited some public gardens and salons near the river. There was a band as big as the Covent Garden orchestra and admission cost only 1½d. Cobden found the place full of 'genteel persons', sipping coffee and listening to the music, the men with their pipes, the women with their knitting. 'These resorts', he noted, 'much wanted in England. There is no rendezvous but the public house or the beer-shop for the poor – none but the costly assembly for the middle class.'[65] Prague had the best-dressed people he had seen, as well as the greatest number of palaces, spires and public buildings in any town of similar size that he had visited. It also had by far the best infants' school he had come across; he gave it a very long and enthusiastic entry in his diary.

As these glimpses of his travels show, Cobden found much more to approve than disapprove. He praised the simplicity, moderation and kindly good nature of the German people. He was greatly impressed by German roads, railway development and – above all – the attention given to education. He had been told, he reported approvingly, that a German village lad enters the army an uncultivated boor and comes out of it an educated man. (An educated man was also a much better fighting man, but that does not seem to have occurred to Cobden.) Saxony he described as 'a little beehive', its people as perhaps the most industrious and frugal in the world,[66] and its king – with rather less enthusiasm – as 'a man of the utmost simplicity of character and still not wanting in intellect'.[67] (He had met Frederick Augustus several times when visiting factories and railways.)

But when it came to governments, his highest praise was reserved for Prussia's, which he suspected was the best in Europe. So impressed was he that the democratic aspirations which he had so recently been expounding to the citizens of Manchester flew straight out of the window, 'I would', he confided to Frederick, 'gladly give up my taste for talking politics to secure such a state of things in England.' He compared Prussia's 'simple and economical government, so deeply imbued with justice to all and aiming so constantly to elevate mentally and morally its population', with that great juggle of the "*English Constitution*" – a thing of monopolies, and Church-craft, and sinecures, armorial hocus-pocus, primogeniture, and pageantry', and he concluded that the British people would be much better off with the first than they were now with the second. He described the King of Prussia as 'a good and just man', who had destroyed his own despotism by educating his people.[68] This verdict on Frederick William III was not merely a transient flight of fancy. He repeated it three weeks later in another letter. 'The King, who is one of the best of men, has voluntarily broken the sceptre of absolutism ... by raising up an enlightened public opinion to control the policy of his government.'[69] But he could hardly have written it ten years later, when the King's son, with the army whose educational training he had admired so much, stamped on Prussia's first representative assembly.

Throughout his life Cobden was convinced that education was the key to political progress; at this time he was deeply depressed by the obstacles that religious bigotry was placing in the path of educational reform in England; and he felt overwhelmed by what he called 'the *opaque ignorance* in which the great bulk of the people of England are wrapt'.[70] It was perhaps not so surprising that he should have been dazzled by what he saw and heard in Prussia.

Before starting for home early in October, he looked at England again and saw it more clearly. The country was sliding into a deep economic depression. In the North there was much distress and consequently much unrest. Frederick had written to his brother full of fears for the future and lamentations over the futility of political endeavour. Richard would have none of it. 'We must choose between the party which governs upon an exclusive or monopoly principle, and the people who seek, though blindly perhaps, the good of the vast majority. If they be in error we must try to put them right, if rash to moderate; but *never, never* talk of giving up the ship . . .'. He wrote with all the more assurance because he believed he had found an issue on which the scattered ranks of radical reformers could unite – the repeal of the Corn laws. '*It appears to me*', he told his brother, '*that a moral and even a religious spirit may be infused into that topic, and if agitated in the same manner that the question of slavery had been, it will be irresistible.*'[71] It took more than seven years, but in the end it was.

CHAPTER 4

The Birth of the League (1838–40)

For centuries the trade in corn, the raw material of the Englishman's basic food, was considered a proper object for regulation by the state. The practical effect of the long series of Corn laws might be unsatisfactory or negligible, but the need to go on trying was taken for granted. In mediaeval times, when England was normally a corn-exporting country, the primary aim was to supply the consumer with a steady supply at reasonable prices by regulating the internal trade in corn and restricting or banning exports in times of scarcity. After the Restoration of 1660, legislation showed a greater concern to protect the interests of the producer. But until towards the end of the eighteenth century, the landed gentry, who predominated in Parliament, did not seriously attempt to advance their own interests at the expense of those of the consumer. When supplies of wheat were scarce or excessively expensive, popular anger fastened not on the landlords, but on the corn dealers who manipulated the internal corn trade to make the maximum profits for themselves.

During the last decades of the eighteenth century the rapid growth of the industrial towns of the North and Midlands enormously increased the demand for wheat and turned Britain decisively from a corn-exporting to a corn-importing country. The landlords responded with enclosures, principally of common pasture and waste land, and by improved farming methods. Their efforts to increase production were greatly stimulated by twenty years of warfare against Revolutionary and Napoleonic France. By the last years of the war, when Napoleon's Continental System had reduced imports to a trickle, and a series of poor harvests pushed up the price of wheat still further, the farmers were making huge profits and the landlords were consequently able to charge high rents. In 1814 the return of peace and the ending of the blockade, together with an exceptionally abundant harvest the previous autumn, caused the price of wheat to plummet. The agricultural interest, which had put so much effort and capital into increasing production and had done so well out of wartime conditions, took fright and demanded that Parliament should take steps to preserve the prosperity to which it had become accustomed. More convincingly, it argued that Britain should not be more dependent than it could help on foreign sources for its basic foodstuffs. The plight of the landowners and their tenants was part of the general economic depression that afflicted the whole country in the postwar years and was beyond the wit of legislators to control. But a Parliament in which landowners greatly predominated did its best for its own. In 1815 it passed a Corn law unequivocally designed to protect the producer, whatever the cost to the consumer. The new law prohibited the import of foreign wheat altogether until the domestic price had risen to 80/– a quarter. When the price rose above that level, wheat could be imported, or released from bonded warehouses, free of duty. The bill provoked tremendous opposition from the manufacturing, commercial and working classes. The press fulminated against it, public protest meetings were held, petitions were signed, the London mob rioted. But a Parliament of landowners shaken out of their traditional complacency by the revolutionary upheavals across the Channel, was determined to put the interests of its own class first. It was as impervious to reasoned argument as to the menace of the window-breaking mob.

The new Corn law, however, did not satisfy even the landlords and farmers. It kept foreign corn out but, when domestic supplies were plentiful, it could not prevent prices from falling. After a run of excellent harvests, the price of wheat fell as low as 38/10d a quarter in November 1822. The farmers complained because they could not pay the high rents, fixed on the assumption that wheat would fetch around 80/– a quarter. The landlords complained because their incomes were declining. Both were inclined to put the blame for their difficulties as much on heavy taxation and the government's deflationary currency policy as on the 1815 Corn law. Neither they, nor the government, nor the innumerable armchair critics really knew how to cushion agriculture's inevitably painful transition from wartime to peacetime conditions. Nor could they see how to resolve the tragic paradox that one section of the community could apparently only prosper at the expense of the rest.

Among the working classes in the industrial towns agitation against the Corn law waxed and waned according to the price of bread. The manufacturers, whose hostility to the law was largely based on their assumption that cheap bread would allow them to pay lower wages and thus make their products more competitive abroad, were at first muted in their opposition because of the high protection they themselves enjoyed. But during the 1820s their criticism became much less inhibited as the general intellectual movement towards free trade gathered strength, while at the Board of Trade William Huskisson began to dismantle the trade barriers which, instead of protecting British industry, were hindering its expansion into foreign markets. Moreover, British manufacturers were becoming increasingly aware that foreign countries, which could not afford to buy the products of British industry because Britain would not buy their surplus corn, were beginning to set up their own industries to satisfy their own needs. In the mid-1820s a severe economic recession, bringing with it unemployment and social distress, stimulated a new wave of radical agitation against the 'bread tax'. In newspapers, journals and pamphlets the campaign against the Corn laws grew steadily more vigorous and vituperative. So far as the script was concerned, it was a full dress rehearsal for the performance that the Anti-Corn Law League was to put on nearly twenty years later.

Inside Parliament the Corn law and the problems of agriculture provided a chronic source of discord and perplexity. In 1828 it was decided to repeal the total ban on foreign corn until the domestic price had risen to 80/– a quarter, and introduce a sliding scale of duties which rose as the domestic price fell, and decreased as the domestic price increased; when the domestic price rose above 72/–, only a nominal duty of one shilling was imposed. Unfortunately, the new law encouraged speculation and excessive variations in price. But at least it did not keep out much-needed supplies during the four subsequent years when the harvests were particularly bad.

The reformers seem to have felt that no more could be expected from a Parliament that was so overwhelmingly the preserve of the landed gentry, although publicists like Colonel Perronet Thompson and Ebenezer Elliott* made sure that the issue was not forgotten as political attention concentrated on the struggle for the reform of Parliament. After the passage of the Reform Bill in 1832, four excellent harvests prevented any significant revival of the Corn law

---

* Colonel (later General) T. Perronet Thompson (1783–1869) first published his *Catechism on the Corn Laws* in 1827. A second edition appeared within a fortnight and about twenty editions within a few years. It became the popular bible of the anti-Corn law movement and Thompson himself became a very active and highly respected member of the Anti-Corn Law League. When he stood at a by-election at Sunderland in August 1845, Cobden told an election rally that he would walk 200 miles barefoot to help return Thompson to Parliament. He was in fact defeated, but was elected for Bradford two years later. (see L. G. Johnson. *General T. Perronet Thompson.* (1957))

Ebenezer Elliott (1781–1849), known as the 'Corn Law Rhymer', was an eccentric character and a bad poet, who was obsessed with the Corn laws. His *Corn Law Rhymes*, published between 1831 and 1846, were immensely popular.

controversy outside Parliament, although in the House of Commons much time and mental energy was spent on investigating the financial problems of the landed gentry.

How important were the Corn laws in reality? The 1815 law had failed to maintain prices when domestic supplies were plentiful and the 1828 law did not keep out foreign corn when domestic supplies were seriously inadequate. As protection for the producer, the laws only made sense on the assumption that a plentiful supply of cheap foreign corn was available for import. Supporters of the laws claimed this was the case, and that without restrictions on imports domestic producers would be ruined by a flood of cheap corn from Poland and elsewhere in northern Europe. On the other hand, William Jacob, sent by the government to Europe in 1826 to investigate European grain supplies, concluded that as a rule Europe had no large surplus of grain for export. Most modern historians have accepted Jacob's conclusions more readily than many of his contemporaries did, and have argued that the Corn laws cannot have had any appreciable effect on the price of bread. The latest research, however, suggests that for nearly twenty years after 1815 large supplies of European grain were available for import, and that domestic prices were kept up by their exclusion.[1]

Whatever the truth, there is no doubt that during the early decades of the nineteenth century the population was growing more rapidly than the average annual harvest of home-grown wheat. The pressure for foreign imports was bound to increase and contemporaries had no doubt at all about the importance of the Corn laws. To the farmers and landowners, they were an indispensable protection in an increasingly unfriendly world. To factory workers, manufacturers, and all town dwellers, they were examples of blatant class legislation, designed to benefit one section of the community at the expense of the rest. They were a symbol of privilege at a time when privilege was increasingly being called into question. They were a demonstration of where political power lay at a time when other classes – in particular the middle class – were demanding a greater share in running the country. The sense of indignant outrage provoked by the Corn laws was well summarised by one of their most moderate critics when arguing against the proposed Corn law of 1815:

> To increase the rent roll of proprietors, by compelling all other members of the community to pay more for their corn than they otherwise need to do, would be as gross a violation of natural justice, as it is possible for the mind to conceive. It would be tantamount to laying a tax upon bread, for the purpose of pensioning off the landed aristocracy. It would be nothing better

than legalized robbery, taking money out of the pockets of the poor and of the industrious, in order to lavish it on the idle and the rich.[2]

When Richard Cobden first began to take an interest in public affairs in the early 1830s, there was a temporary lull in the agitation against the Corn laws and he himself, determined to widen his horizons, showed more interest in foreign than in domestic affairs. In his first pamphlet, published in 1835, he suggested a modification of the Corn law (a fixed duty of 2/– a quarter), while in his second, published a year later, he advocated free trade in general without mentioning the Corn laws. In October 1836, Cobden told a correspondent that he did not think the issue of the 'suicidally selfish' Corn laws would be satisfactorily settled in their day.

It will only be done by a mighty effort of the irresistible masses – probably a commercial crisis or a famine harvest will after all decide the matter. I confess this a very unphilosophical and unstatesmanlike solution of a difficulty in legislation; but it has long presented itself to me as the most probable. *The Corn laws are only part of a system in which the Whig and Tory aristocracy have about an equal interest. The Colonies, the Army, Navy and Church, are, with the Corn laws, merely accessories to our aristocratic government.* John Bull has his work cut out for fifty years to come to purge his house of these impurities.[3]

A year later, stimulated by the economic discussions at the British Association meeting in Liverpool, Cobden began to change his mind. Walking away one evening at midnight from a soirée in the town hall with a Manchester friend, Henry Ashworth, he suddenly stopped and said; 'I'll tell you what we will do, we'll use the Chamber of Commerce for an agitation to repeal the Corn law.' When Ashworth pointed out the snags in this proposal, Cobden seemed disappointed, but although he declared that he was determined to use his own resources for an anti-Corn law campaign, he let the matter drop for nearly another year.[4]

In 1838 the worst harvest for more than thirty years coincided with a new economic depression, and opposition to the Corn law revived both inside and outside Parliament. Cobden, as we have seen, was absorbed in the struggle for Manchester's Charter but, even before the issue was finally decided, he was making plans for a visit to central Europe with the primary intention of collecting evidence to demonstrate the stifling effect of the Corn laws on international trade. 'When I return', he wrote on 23 August, 'if nobody else will stir, I'll give a lecture in Manchester to show up the iniquitous system and excite the people here to resistance.'[5] He returned with plenty of useful material. But he had no need to stir people up with a lecture.

A small group of seven men, meeting in the York Hotel, Manchester, on 24 September, had already given the first impetus to an anti-Corn law campaign. By the time Cobden got back to Manchester, the provisional committee of an Anti-Corn Law Association had been announced*, subscriptions were beginning to come in and the first lecture under the auspices of the association had been given in the Corn Exchange.

On the same day that the anti-Corn law campaign was being inaugurated in a Manchester hotel, outside the town, on Kersal Moor, the Chartists were holding a huge rally, perhaps as large as the gathering at Peterloo and certainly displaying some of the banners that had appeared on that famous occasion nearby twenty years earlier. The Chartist movement was on the crest of a wave. Its famous six-point Charter had been published four months earlier; it was not yet fatally weakened by internal divisions over aims and tactics, and men made desperate by unemployment and hunger provided it with an eager audience. By the middle of September the price of wheat had risen above 73s and although large quantities of bonded wheat were released on to the market the price continued to rise at an alarming rate. The Chartists' demands for political reforms meant different things to different people at different times and places. But most of those assembled on Kersal moor that day would probably have agreed with the speaker who declared that the 'question of universal suffrage is a knife-and-fork question, a bread-and-cheese question.'[6]

It was against this sombre background of economic depression and human distress that the fight against the Corn laws began. Cobden joined the council of the new association as soon as he got back to Manchester, but for the rest of the year the Chamber of Commerce was the repealers' main public preoccupation. It was a conservative and slow-moving body, since not all manufacturers were convinced of the wisdom of making further inroads into the protective system that had sheltered them so well. But by December 1838 there was growing concern about the state of the economy and a special meeting of the Chamber was held to discuss a petition to Parliament on the Corn laws. There was a record attendance, but the petition pro-

---

* In 1836, an Anti-Corn Law Association had been set up in London with the support of most of the leading radical MPs. But it had never come to anything.

posed by the president, George Wood, MP for Kendal, was a very timid document, tentatively suggesting a modification of the existing law. The opposition to this was led by Cobden and J. B. Smith, a Manchester cotton merchant who was such a persistent critic of the Corn laws that he had been nicknamed 'Corn Law Smith'. Eventually, after a long debate, the meeting was adjourned for a week.

When the Chamber reassembled, Manchester's first municipal elections had been held, a large majority of the new councillors were free traders and Cobden had been elected an alderman. But the directors of the Chamber were not to be moved very far. They submitted their original draft petition, unchanged except for a more positively worded conclusion. Cobden scornfully declared that it would have no more weight than a thesis drawn up by some tyro in political economy at a university. He produced an alternative draft which analysed the threat of foreign competition to the cotton trade and pointed out that the factory workers depended for their very subsistence on its prosperity. The draft ended with a comprehensive plea for 'the true and peaceful principles of *free trade*', the repeal of all laws restricting the importation of corn and other foreign foodstuffs and the removal of 'all existing obstacles to the unrestricted employment of industry and capital'. After the rival petitions had been debated for more than five hours, Cobden's draft was adopted by an overwhelming majority.[7]

But the president and most of the directors of the Chamber remained unconverted, and Cobden set to work 'to effect a revolution in the government of that hitherto worse than useless body'[8] at the forthcoming annual general meeting in February 1839. He and his friends energetically canvassed for new members whose votes would help to get rid of the existing directors. John Bright was among those who received an urgent request from Cobden to join the Chamber and to send him by return of post his authorisation for Cobden to pay his annual guinea subscription.[9] The campaign was entirely successful. There was a clean sweep of the old directors at the annual general meeting, and J. B. Smith was appointed president instead of George Wood.

But by the time the free traders gained firm control of the Chamber of Commerce they no longer really needed it. The Anti-Corn Law Association was developing into a more effective instrument. Funds had been raised and an administrative framework set up (Cobden was on the finance and executive committees as well as on the council). A modest lecture tour had been mounted (admittedly with mixed results), and links established with similar associations in Leeds, Liverpool, Glasgow and other manufacturing towns. Towards the end of January 1839 delegations from other associations were treated to a huge public dinner in the Manchester Corn Exchange. It was attended by 800 guests, including a number of sympathetic MPs. Next day it was decided that representatives from all the local associations should assemble in London for the meeting of Parliament on 5 February to act as a pressure group for the repeal of the Corn law.

Neither Parliament nor the government was likely to be sympathetic. Lord Melbourne's Whig ministry had run out of steam. It had no more reforms to propose (apart from Lord John Russell's attempt at educational reform) and was fast losing the grudging support of the Radicals upon whom it depended for its majority in the House of Commons. The Cabinet was preoccupied with the aftermath of a rebellion in Canada, the endemic problem of controlling Ireland, and its own disagreements and mutual dissatis- faction. It was, as the diarist, Charles Greville, remarked, 'a rickety concern'.[10] Moreover, although the growing agitation in the northern towns and in the press had forced the Corn law on the ministers' attention, most of them, especially the prime minister, understood little or nothing about the difficulties of northern manufacturers or the plight of unemployed factory workers. Melbourne blamed the unrest on the manufacturers who were taking advantage of the high price of corn to demand cheaper bread so that they could pay lower wages. But since the Cabinet was divided on whether the 1828 Corn law should be amended – and if so, how – he determined to make the question an open one and himself adopt a policy of wait and see.[11] To the fury of the free traders both inside and outside Parliament, there was not a word about the Corn laws in the Queen's Speech.

The politicans at Westminster, however, were not allowed to forget the feelings of the rest of the country. Enthusiasm for the Chartists had grown and spread far and wide during the winter, and on the day that Parliament met, a Chartist convention opened at the British Hotel in Charing Cross. The delegates called themselves the Peoples' Parliament and with a great deal of flamboyant and sometimes alarming oratory they set about drawing up a petition to be presented at Westminster. It took them a long time because they agreed on very little apart from their implacable distrust of the Corn law repealers whose motives they (like Lord Melbourne) believed to be purely selfish.

At the same time, the anti-Corn law delegates, with J. B. Smith at their head, assembled at Brown's Hotel in Palace Yard. They could hardly have stationed themselves closer to the citadel they intended to storm, but their attempts to interview prominent politicians were either spurned or ineffectual. Inside the House their cause fared no better. Charles Villiers, Whig MP for Wolverhampton and a dedicated opponent of the Corn laws*, made two attempts to persuade the House to consider the numerous anti-Corn law petitions before it. Neither was successful and the delegates were obliged to disperse to their home towns with nothing achieved.

Cobden, who had remained in Manchester, was not unduly discouraged by the setback. He did not believe that anything could really be expected from the present House of Commons and he was convinced that Manchester, where business habits prevailed and cash was readily available, was a much better place from which to launch an agitation than London, where their efforts might be hampered by incompetent enthusiasts. '*My hopes of agitation are anchored upon Manchester*', he emphatically assured Smith.[12]

The Chartists, however, were determined to disrupt the Corn law repealers' activities, whether in Manchester, Leeds, Liverpool or anywhere else, and on 28 February they successfully took over a meeting called in the Manchester Corn Exchange to hear a report on the recent London conference. According to Cobden, who two days earlier had confidently claimed that the Chartists would not upset them, there was 'an irruption of ragamuffins', which involved less than a quarter of those present, but more than enough, when they started to hurl chairs at the platform and smash the lamps, to create complete confusion and force the repealers to abandon the field. Several gentlemen were seriously hurt and Cobden, whose head was nearly split open by a chair leg, was lucky to get away with only the loss of his hat.[13] Although the most peaceable of men, he seems to have regretted afterwards that the repealers had not put up a better fight when their opponents were in such a minority. But, as he explained, 'our friends were timid and dispersed and the ragamuffins were concentrated and resolute'.[14]

A few days later, the repealers convened another meeting in the Corn Exchange. This time admission was by ticket only, and there was virtually no disturbance, despite Cobden's robust condemnation of the 'lawless men' who 'feloniously broke in upon this room, which we had paid for, and violently took possession of property which we were pledged to preserve or to pay for; and then, having driven out those who had paid for the use of the room, took upon themselves to conduct the riotous proceedings you have heard of.'[15] As a good business man, the loss of money evidently riled him as much as the loss of dignity. Privately, however, he was not

---

* Charles Villiers, born in 1802, was the younger brother of the Earl of Clarendon. According to a contemporary, who met him often in her father's house, he was thoroughly aristocratic in appearance and manner. He was also 'decidedly untidy. His letters were untidy, his hair was untidy, his collar was untidy'. (E. I. Barrington, *Servant of All*, I, p. 18.)

discouraged by the Chartists' violence which, he claimed, had made the best of them ashamed and increased working-class support for the repealers.[16] After the Corn Exchange fracas, some Manchester working men were in fact moved to set up an Operative Anti-Corn Law Association, and their example was gradually followed in a number of other towns.

Meanwhile the repealers were preparing another descent on Parliament. In March 1838 Charles Villiers had unsuccessfully moved for a parliamentary inquiry into the Corn laws. On March 12, 1839, with the anti-Corn law delegates reassembled in Brown's Hotel, he tried again. The debate continued over five nights and ended with a majority of 147 against Villiers's motion. The anti-Corn law delegates were forced to realise that they had a long haul ahead of them. The following day they decided to set up a permanent organisation to which all the local associations would adhere. It was to be called the Anti-Corn Law League, with headquarters in Manchester, and it was to concentrate on the single aim of repealing the Corn law.

The headquarters of the League was in a large house called Newall's Buildings, in Market Street, right in the centre of the town. The first meetings were held in a small, narrow, chilly room, with a dingy red blanket draped to ward off the draughts. Later, as the League's activities grew in size and complexity, it took over the whole house except the basement. The Council, which occupied 'a really handsome chamber', usually met once every day and sometimes more often, and anyone who had contributed £50 or more was entitled to attend. Many did so when they had occasion to come to Manchester. But inevitably, the practical, day-to-day running of the organisation was left to a small group of local men, mostly manufacturers and merchants, who had the time and enthusiasm for a close involvement in the League's work. Henry Ashworth, to take one example, a prominent Lancashire cotton spinner, devoted at least a quarter of his time to League business throughout the campaign, seriously neglecting his mills in the process.[17] But the three leading spirits, especially in the League's early years, were J. B. Smith, George Wilson and Cobden. After about two years, Smith was forced by ill-health and business difficulties to play a much less prominent role. George Wilson, a Manchester starch and gum manufacturer who succeeded Smith as president, was – in modern slang – the indispensable anchor man. Unassuming and conciliatory in manner, he was a born administrator and a superb chairman. Cobden, who had first worked with him in the struggle for Manchester's Charter, thought very highly of

him. He used to say that Wilson could always see the end of anything from the beginning, and after the fight was over he told him in
a letter: 'You and I made the League, and the League made others.'[18]

The influence of Cobden himself – his energy, enthusiasm, drive –
was all-pervasive at Newall Buildings, and his authority was seldom
seriously questioned. After August 1841, his parliamentary duties
and lecture tours restricted his physical presence, but he always kept
closely in touch by letter. A visitor to the League's rooms in January
1843 was able to observe Cobden taking part in the Council's daily
deliberations: 'in a gentleman who sat leaning on his left arm, the
arm of the top rail of his chair, listening to the letters the chairman
read, calm, reflective and pale – I at once recognised ... Richard
Cobden; and when he spoke, so mild was his voice, so unassuming
his style of giving an opinion, so clearly was the opinion given, that I
at once saw the source of much of that importance he has acquired.'[19]

The anti-Corn law campaign was a hard, uphill struggle, but
under its dedicated and highly businesslike management the League
machine grew steadily larger and more effective. It was built on the
example of several previous pressure groups, in particular the anti-
slavery movement, but with more money than previous movements
at its disposal, it was eventually able to make an unprecedented
impact. At Newall Buildings, the activities of local associations were
encouraged and, so far as was possible and tactful, controlled; a vast
correspondence was carried on with both supporters and opponents;
numerous propaganda and fund-raising activities were organised
(including huge tea parties, that very Victorian institution, which
Cobden thought was the 'only way to reach the family firesides');[20]
paid lecturers were appointed and supervised; a fortnightly (later
weekly) paper was produced; and a huge flood of propaganda poured
forth – tracts, speeches, handbills, posters, wafers (for envelopes),
each bearing an appropriate slogan. At the height of the campaign,
some 300 people were employed at Newall's Buildings in producing
the various types of propaganda. A German visitor described how he
was taken through the various rooms where this work was being
carried on 'until I came at last to the great League Depôt, where
books, pamphlets, letters, newspapers, speeches, reports, tracts and
wafers, were all piled in neat packets of every possible size and
appearance, like the packets of muslin and calico, in the great
warehouses of Manchester. Beyond this was a refreshment room, in
which tea was offered us by several, hospitable ladies with whom we
engaged in conversation for a little while.'[21]

Some years after the anti-Corn law campaign had been successfully concluded, Cobden decided to go through his accumulated

correspondence for that period. He was amazed to discover how exclusively his thoughts and actions had been concentrated on the struggle. 'I really was not aware', he wrote to a friend, 'till I took this view of the period from 1838 to 1846 how completely I had isolated my mind upon the one topic.'[22] Inevitably, his business suffered, and probably more than it would have done if he had not already decided that he would prefer not to devote the whole of his life to private gain.

As soon as he returned from Germany in October 1838, he agreed on a friendly separation from his original partners, Sherriff and Gillett, leaving them the Sabden works and the London warehouse. He himself intended to take Frederick into partnership and, with the help of their younger brothers, Henry and Charles, start a new business based on a printing works at Crosse Hall, near Chorley, which he had already leased, and the Manchester warehouse. Why he took this hazardous step is not clear, but probably he wanted to provide for his brothers. He told Frederick, who as usual was full of misgivings, that he was willing to give 'a few years of entire exertion' towards making the new venture a success. But at the end of about five years he was determined to hand the business over entirely to his brothers. His health had never been very robust and he doubted whether he would live more than another twenty years; he wanted to give at least part of his life to 'more rational and worthy exertions' than 'heaping up money'.[23]

Increasingly preoccupied though he was with the Corn laws, Cobden clearly did not envisage in the autumn of 1838 how quickly and completely he would get swept up into the campaign to repeal them. Nor could he have foreseen that a year later Henry would secretly elope to South Australia with a wife whom Richard described as coming from 'a very low and disreputable station'. Whether or not she really was a prostitute, as this description seems to suggest, Richard, who had always taken his family responsibilities tremendously seriously, was furiously, and rather priggishly, angry. Henry, he told a business friend, had 'committed suicide morally for ever'. His own conscience, he added, was clear, except that he had done too much for his brother and spent too much money on him.[24] Had he been less hurt, he might have been more tolerant.

In spite of Henry's defection, Richard gave an optimistic account in the same letter of the new firm's progress. They had arranged to be sent the 'Parisian novelties' at least a month in advance of their rivals, which will 'give us a great advantage in taste over our neighbours ... We are making very bold preparations for the spring and hope to make some money'. Cobden's business career so far had been remarkably successful, and what little evidence there is suggests that its success was due as much to his own efforts as to those of his partners. (His investment in building land in Manchester, on the other hand, was a disaster.) But the new family firm was launched at the beginning of a deep and prolonged economic crisis, when Richard's attention was being increasingly absorbed by public affairs, and with only the unsatisfactory Frederick at the helm when Richard was absent. He may have continued to give more time and attention to the business than the surviving evidence suggests. But he is reported to have once remarked to a friend that he was never bothered about private problems when engaged on public affairs,[25] and his letters to Frederick were more concerned with the progress of the anti-Corn law campaign than with their business affairs.

'On some terms or other', wrote Cobden a few days after the Chartists had disrupted the meeting in the Manchester Corn Exchange, 'the masses must co-operate with the middle class or there is no hope for us.'[26] He believed that the Chartists' hostility arose from their ignorance and for that he blamed aristocratic misrule. 'Every instance of violence or turbulence in the great multitude of work-people ought to be laid to the charge of the aristocracy, who have drawn the utmost from their labour to spend in wars and extravagance abroad and at home, and neglected to return any portion for the expense of educating them.'[27]

Unfortunately, most workers thought as badly of the middle classes as Cobden did of the aristocracy. Some Chartists did approve of free trade; others were in favour of Corn law repeal, but wanted political reforms first. But most felt a profound suspicion of the League because it was primarily a middle-class manufacturers' organisation. They had been taught by the unstamped* radical press that the middle classes were, in the words of the *Poor Man's Guardian*, 'the destroyers of liberty and happiness in all countries'.[28] They believed that the middle classes had duped them over the Reform Bill in 1831–32 and they suspected they would suffer the same treatment over the Corn law. Only radical political reforms, they argued, could ensure them regular employment at a decent wage. 'Never, never, never', wrote the Chartist newspaper, the *Northern Star*, 'will the repeal of any bad law guarantee you against the re-enaction of as bad a one until you get Universal Suffrage.'[29]

As Cobden realised, the arguments of the repealers were not particularly easy for uneducated men to grasp. As they understood it, the free import of corn would lead to a cheaper loaf, which would allow the bosses to pay lower wages. It would also, by throwing

---

* So-called because they were published illegally, without paying the newspaper stamp of one penny which made them too dear for many workers.

large tracts of land out of cultivation, drive thousands of farm
workers into the towns, where they would force down wages by
competing for work in the cotton and woollen mills. Only the
employers stood to gain, with the help of their degrading factory
system – a system which moved Sir Charles Napier, the army
commander of the northern district, to exclaim in the privacy of his
journal: 'Hell may be paved with good intentions, but is assuredly
hung with Manchester cottons.'[30] It seemed inconceivable that those
who were content to profit from that system could be genuinely
interested in helping the workers. Some verses in the *Northern Star*
said it all.

> Who are that blustering, canting crew,
> Who keep the cheap loaf in our view,
> And would from us more profit screw?
> > The League.
>
> Who cry 'Repeal the curs'd Corn Law',
> And would their workmen feed with straw,
> That they may filthy lucre paw?
> > The League.
>
> Who wish to gull the working man,
> And *burk* the Charter, *if they can*,
> With their self-aggrandising plan?
> > The League.[31]

It was not selfish self-interest that moved Cobden to dedicate himself
so wholeheartedly to the repeal of the Corn law. As we have seen, he
was interested in making money only to the extent that it would
enable him to discharge his family responsibilities and eventually
give him leisure to spend on pursuits that interested him much more.
He denied that a cheaper loaf would mean lower wages. He argued,
on the contrary, that the free import of corn would benefit workers
as well as employers because it would create a greater foreign
demand for British manufactures, which would increase the demand
for labour and thus raise wages. To him the Corn laws were a
bastion of aristocratic dominance which he was determined to overthrow, while free trade was a means not only to economic prosperity
but to international co-operation and peace. Few manufacturers
shared Cobden's idealism. Most were mainly concerned with the
threat of foreign competition to their own businesses. Many probably hoped that repeal *would* reduce the cost of labour, and the
League was always vulnerable to attack on the effect of repeal on
wages because of the uncertain voice with which it spoke on this issue.
    Cobden was not typical of his class and there was a good deal of
mutual dissatisfaction between him and his fellow manufacturers.

The *Manchester Guardian*, the paper most widely read by Manchester business men, approved of free trade in principle, but deplored the League's crusading fervour. Cobden's radicalism was too strong for some to swallow, while he thought the prosperous middle classes were far too pusillanimous and compromising about reform and was extremely scornful of their failure – as he saw it – to shake off their traditional deference to those above them in the social scale.

Cobden's patience with the Chartists soon wore thin. Early in April 1839 he was complaining about their 'insane ravings and their continuous appeal to brute force' which frightened off potential sympathisers.[32] But the Chartists had plenty of excuses. The deepening economic recession was throwing more and more people out of work, leaving them with only the hated new Poor Law between themselves, their families and starvation. In May General Napier, a kind-hearted man with radical sympathies, feared that 'Tory injustice and Whig imbecility' would precipitate an insurrection. 'The doctrine of slowly reforming', he confided to his journal, 'when men are starving, is of all silly things the most silly; famishing men cannot wait.'[33]

Largely owing to Napier's firm but moderate and humane handling of the crisis, the threat of an armed rising gradually petered out. The Chartists' petition, with 1,200,000 signatures, was finally rejected by the Commons on 12 July 1839. By then the Chartist convention, which was much too preoccupied with the rival merits of moral and physical force to achieve its goals, had moved from London to the more congenial atmosphere of Birmingham, where its activities precipitated violent rioting that had to be suppressed with troops and police brought from London. The heavy hand of the authorities, together with a widespread revulsion against Chartist violence, inflicted a grave setback on the movement. In November, the failure of an attempted rising at Newport, south Wales, where some people were shot down by soldiers, set the seal on its temporary eclipse.

By the end of 1839, the League's efforts to channel popular discontent into its own movement had also largely ground to a halt. The League's lecturers – some sent from Manchester and others organised by local associations – met with much hostility, even violence, and made few converts. Cobden's attempt to set up a big conference at Lincoln at which speakers from Manchester would enlighten the local farmers and landowners, came to nothing. The League's only substantial success was the establishment of its own fortnightly newspaper, the *Anti-Corn Law Circular*, which first appeared on 16 April, 1839. It was filled with ammunition for Corn law repealers and accounts of their meetings and other activities, all presented in as morale-boosting a way as possible. Everything in the paper was directed against the Corn laws, although sometimes the message was indirect. One issue, for example, carried an article entitled 'Nicholas Nickleby', which praised Dickens as 'a sort of moral alchemist ... scenes that the great cannot even imagine, he carries straight into their drawing-room ... He makes the cries of the poor to be heard in the palace and gets the miserable an entrance into the great man's house.' The article ended by asking whether the great ones could calmly read Dickens's book without some mis-givings that all was not right.[34]

By its third issue, the *Circular* had a circulation of 15,000, but a great many copies were given away – to anyone who contributed at least one pound to League funds, to sympathetic newspapers, reading rooms, clubs and so on. Two months after the paper was launched, Cobden told a supporter in London that a copy was sent to all the clubs and to some as many as half-a-dozen. 'Can you learn if they are put upon the tables of any of the clubs to which we send them?'[35] It was important to find out if the League's promotion efforts were well directed because they cost money, which was in short supply. The *Circular* was run at a loss – not surprisingly when so many copies were given away – and could not pay its way even when it began to take advertisements. Considerable sums were spent on buying the support of other papers, either for cash or by promises to buy large numbers of those issues which contained articles favourable to the League. The expenses of the lecture tours proved much larger than had been anticipated and were sometimes only very tardily met – one lecturer was stranded in Arundel because he could not pay for his lodgings and eventually had to slip away secretly, leaving his luggage as security.[36]

When the League was first set up, it was authorised to raise a fund of £5000. There were plenty of promises, but many of the local associations failed to redeem them. (Manchester, which pledged itself to raise £2000, was a notable exception.) At a time of severe economic depression this was very understandable, but it was a bitter disappointment all the same. 'People won't part with a penny', grumbled Cobden, 'to save myriads from misery, and that's the reason why we're pretty nearly bankrupt.' He added that the League was supposed to be a rich and powerful body, and they were reluctant to reveal their weakness by making a public appeal for money.[37] By the end of the year the League's chances of survival could not be rated very high.

But far from advertising its weakness, let alone collapsing altogether, the League managed to inaugurate the new year of 1840 with an impressive demonstration that it was still in business. Some 200 delegates from nearly 80 local associations were summoned to a conference in Manchester. The proceedings were designed to make them aware of the League's financial difficulties while at the same time rekindling their enthusiasm for a glorious cause that sooner or later could not fail to succeed. The culmination of the conference was a huge banquet held in a temporary wooden pavilion built in eleven days on a site in St Peter's Fields donated by Cobden. The walls and roof were covered with white and pink calico, while from the front of the galleries which ran all round the hall hung deep crimson draperies on which appropriate mottoes were inscribed in large letters.

The party on the platform included local dignitaries from Manchester and other towns, as well as 26 MPs, including Charles Villiers and – the star attraction – the great Irish leader, Daniel O'Connell, who, we are told, produced a great impression with'a speech of mingled power, humour and pathos'. Cobden was among the other 12 speakers, but he spoke for only about 10 minutes, with a collecting box and a subscription book in each hand. He was still very much a hard-working back-room organiser for the League and little known to the general public. Fortunately, however, a contemporary account of the banquet described in some detail his platform style.

... On he goes, with head immoveable and straight, and you can see a settled purpose, and a well-digested design in his very manner. Words come on him with the simplest and most natural facility. There is no effort. Every sentence is clear and intelligible; the diction unambitious but precisely correct; the utterance lively, continuous, and singular for the expression of good sense, sincerity and manliness. From the passions you see he draws but little assistance; but the intellect is steady in its work, and the moral sentiments throw over all the graceful drapery of high principle and exalted philanthropy. His manner and matter are eminently calculated to inspire confidence among men of business serious reflection and sincerity. We never saw any man who, from the beginning to the termination of his speech, keeps the end he has in view so steadily and continuously before him.[38]

The following evening a second banquet was held for 5000 working men. The galleries were occupied by their wives, female relatives and friends; the chair was taken by the president of the Operatives' Anti-Corn Law Association; and the speeches were provided by some of the MPs and local dignitaries on the platform. It was a triumphant occasion for the League, which had been suffering so much abuse from the Chartists. The fulsome – to modern ears insufferably condescending – surprise with which the middle-class chroniclers of the scene described the sobriety, intelligence and good manners of the guests, is perhaps an indication of the social tensions of the day.

The Manchester conference was undoubtedly a success. It helped the committed repealers in the scattered local associations to feel part of a nation-wide movement. Outsiders were impressed by the stir it created in Manchester: the special trains, the changed coach times, the special pavilion, the to-ing and fro-ing of the delegates in the streets, the presence of so many important people. (The railings in front of the house where O'Connell was staying were flattened by the press of people anxious to catch a glimpse of 'the Liberator'.) Above all, the rally restored the League's finances. George Wilson's frank admission that the League was £1,200 in debt met with an immediate response from the local associations, as well as inspiring what Cobden called 'a compact body of zealous repealers' to pledge themselves to set aside a part of their incomes for the League.[39]

In Cobden the conference induced a mood of euphoric confidence which at times bubbled over into self-delusion. 'Every day we are mounting higher in public favour', he told Villiers on 7 February. 'Give us a couple of months more, and we will have sole possession of the mind of the country.'[40] Ten days later, he was fairly carried away. *'We shall radicalise the country in the process of carrying the repeal of the Corn law.'* The penny postage was just coming into operation and he foresaw great things from it – 'we shall by and by be able to carry any measure by a coup de *billet*'.[41]

What in sober fact they did, now that the League was again in funds, was to redouble their efforts to convert the country to repeal. Cobden and his northern colleagues realised that a lead given by London was much more likely to be followed than one given by Manchester. So a small deputation, including two of the League's most experienced lecturers, Sidney Smith and A. W. Paulton, was sent to London to resuscitate the moribund anti-Corn law association formed there in 1836. The veteran reformer, Francis Place, was reluctantly persuaded to give his active support, and an office for the new Metropolitan Association was set up in the Strand.

At the same time a new series of lecture tours was organised in response to what Cobden claimed were the 'pressing calls' for lectures received daily from all parts of the kingdom, including the agricultural districts.[42] His letters assumed an almost biblical fervour. 'Our lecturers', he assured Villiers, 'shall continue to haunt them [the landlords] in their agricultural fastnesses, and our circulars shall proclaim their legislative robbery to the ends of the earth. There shall be no peace for the landlords but in their return to the ways of justice.'[43] The lecturers employed included two working men, Murray and Finigan, who, it was hoped, would be able to deal

3 The Anti-Corn law banquet in Manchester 13 Jan. 1840.

effectively with the ubiquitous Chartist hecklers. Early in March, Cobden wrote to Mr Beadon, a supporter in Taunton, introducing Finigan as a handloom weaver who was 'well adapted for lecturing in small places'; but care must be taken to prevent him from getting trapped into some illegal scrape. '*He must have no private meetings with the disaffected working men.*'[44] Finigan's tendency to use inflammatory language did in fact cause considerable embarrassment to the League later on.[45]

Local supporters sometimes volunteered to give lectures in their own districts, and when they did they were warmly encouraged. 'I anticipate', wrote Cobden to Beadon, 'the very best results from your hoisting the repeal banner in Somerset.' He sent a mass of background material and instructed him carefully on how he was to make it up into lectures. He must always adapt his lecture to his audience and remember that his object was to convince farmers and labourers that they did not benefit from the Corn laws.

The best way is to appeal to experience and go over a series of dear and cheap years ... Ascertain in short whether a labourer has more left to spend on clothes etc after buying bread in dear years than cheap. If it can be proved (as it can) that the labourer has less left in dear years, then it must be clear that he has less left to spend with the tailor, shoemaker, grocer, etc, and this brings you to the shopkeepers' case and enables you to prove that they are injured by the high price of food.

Cobden could be counted on to make the most of any keen supporter. Beadon was asked to send him the names of any 'active-minded men' to whom free copies of the *Circular* might be sent, as well as any small reading rooms or societies where the paper might usefully be displayed. Above all, he urged Beadon to organise anti-Corn law petitions for presentation by sympathetic MPs to the House of Commons.[46] The League was determined to renew its pressure on the politicians, and Cobden asked Villiers to delay his annual anti-Corn law motion at least until the end of March, so that it might be supported by as many petitions as possible.[47] He was especially anxious to get petitions from country districts in order to disabuse the landowners in Parliament of their notion that those who worked on the land benefited from protection. 'I consider one petition from the rural districts to be worth as much as a dozen from our part of the kingdom.'[48] But the petitions made little or no impact; nor did the delegates' efforts to lobby ministers. More than 200 of them, led by J. B. Smith and Cobden, were received by Lord Melbourne on 27 March. He listened to them politely, but told them that total and immediate repeal was impracticable. They came away with the depressing impression that the prime minister had only an imperfect grasp of the question at issue, and they were disgusted by the air of smiling incredulity with which he listened to their accounts of severe distress in the northern towns. At another meeting, with the Chancellor of the Exchequer and the President of the Board of Trade, some of the delegates described the unhappy state of the workers in their own district. Mr John Brooks of Manchester was so affected by his own account of the miserable poverty of one family he knew that he broke down and wept. His emotion was contagious and soon most of the delegates were also in tears, while the ministers – in the words of an eyewitness – 'looked with perfect astonishment at a scene so unusual to statesmen and courtiers'. The meeting was ended by Cobden who boldly told the ministers that their decision 'would stamp their character as either representatives merely of class interests, or the promoters of an enlightened commercial policy.'[49] But the ministers were not impressed – they were perhaps more preoccupied with Palmerston's handling of the latest crisis in the Near East – and when Villiers eventually managed to bring his motion to a vote in the Commons at the end of May, it was decisively rejected.

For Cobden, however, there was some personal satisfaction to be gleaned from his appearance before a Commons committee investigating the vexed question of how best to regulate the issue of paper currency. It was a highly complicated and technical problem, and he was at first slightly unnerved by the examination of J. B. Smith, who had preceded him to the committee room. Cobden described it as 'a tissue of definitions and hair splittings', and he felt he really needed to be armed with Johnson's folio dictionary when he had to face the committee.[50] On his first appearance he was indeed blinded by science, for on reading through the transcript of the proceedings afterwards, he found he could not understand some of the questions, and his own answers were so unintelligible to him that he thought they must be incomprehensible to everyone else.[51] At his second appearance before the committee, he persuaded it to strike out the unintelligible part of his evidence and then declared that he would not let himself be puzzled with riddles and definitions a second time: 'I told them plainly' – he reported to his brother – 'that I came there as a merchant and manufacturer to give them information connected with my pursuits, and that I was not there as a scientific man to define the terms of banking and currency, and that I should be obliged to decline answering questions unless I could see their *practical bearing* . This gave me my own way for the rest of the examination.'[52]

Unfortunately, we do not know how the committee reacted to being so firmly handled by the mild-mannered northern manufacturer.

As the spring and summer of 1840 passed, the League's fortunes looked increasingly gloomy. Most of the lecturers whom Cobden had sent forth with such high hopes seem to have made little, if any, impression in the rural areas, and some were lucky to escape without serious injury at the hands of their opponents. By midsummer the money to finance their travels was running low at headquarters in Manchester, and the local associations were proving broken reeds as fund-raisers.

In London, the new Metropolitan Association, after an initial burst of enthusiastic activity, failed to flourish. Most Londoners were usually too immersed in their own activities to bother much about public affairs, and those who did tended to lack crusading fervour. In the City, the source of wealth and influence, there was a good deal of protectionist sentiment and disapproval of the League's uncompromising stand. Matters were not helped by tension between the London repealers and the Manchester men, both of whom thought they knew best. Worst of all, the Londoners were poor fund-raisers.

At the end of September, Place had to confess to Cobden that the association had less than £10 in the kitty, and when a meeting of the general committee was summoned, only one member turned up, the rest not even bothering to send apologies. He ended his letter by asking for £250.[53] Cobden described this request as 'really too bad', and it was ignored.[54] The League had already decided to abandon any serious effort in London, at least until the end of the year, but Cobden was anxious to keep the movement at least *nominally* alive in the capital, and he asked Place to find out the cost of placing some appropriate articles in the cheap London press.[55] He had not yet given up hope of winning over the working classes.

CHAPTER 5

MP and Married Man (1840–42)

Somehow, in spite of his preoccupation with the League during the spring and summer of 1840, Cobden managed to find time to get engaged and married and then enjoy a two-month honeymoon in France and Switzerland. His bride was Catherine Anne Williams, the youngest daughter of Hugh and Ellinor Williams of Machynlleth, Montgomeryshire. Kate, as Cobden always called her, was a school friend of his youngest sister, Sarah. A few weeks after their engagement on 26 March, 1840, he sent her a little pocket-book with a bead cover which he had bought during his visit to Berlin 'for my *intended* long before I knew the object'.[1] This seems to suggest that by his 35th year he was anxious in principle to get married if he could find the right person, and that his courtship of Kate took little more than a year and perhaps a good deal less. He described her to a friend as 'amiable in disposition, with a good share of common sense, excellent health, and *I think* very pretty'.[2] Mrs Gaskell thought the same when she met Kate Cobden in Manchester some 18 months later. She described her as a 'very pretty woman, pearls and white lace and jet black hair and eyes, and an exquisitely clear olive complexion without a particle of colour'.[3]

Cobden was happily and ebulliently in love, and when he returned to Manchester early in May he shared his overflowing happiness with his sisters in Quay Street. 'How can I tell you', he wrote to Kate,

all the pleasant little chat that has passed between Mary and me? We have talked about you incessantly. I have heard all the news about the dresses, and I have seen the patterns of the silks – need I say how highly I approve of your taste? I have ordered a dress of the enclosed [material] to be finished for you – tell me my Kate if you like it. The same pattern in blue and green would have been better, but neither colour becomes you so well as pink . . .[4]

They were married before the end of May and began their honeymoon in Paris. Cobden found the city 'vastly improved' since his last visit some six years previously – more gaslights, more paint and better scavenging. Kate, he reported, was in love with everything – 'though I believe she would have seen even Lapland in *couleur de rose* just now'. They travelled on to Geneva by way of Dijon and Lyons. Cobden described his wife as impervious to fatigue and 'a superlative travelling companion'. He was probably more impressed by her stamina than a more physically robust man would have been. She also had a mind of her own and insisted on spending a night in a monastery. This ambition was duly fulfilled after getting caught in a snow storm on the Simplon pass, where Kate's fame as 'a perfect heroine' was slightly marred by a temporary loss of nerve when her mule went too close to the edge of the path.[5]

They arrived back in London on 29 July, with Cobden's free trade susceptibilities still smarting from several hours' detention by the Customs – 'which ordeal of prying into clothes bags by Her Majesty's servants never fails to make me ill, as a witness and victim of such deplorable measures'.[6] But he did not need this encounter to remind him of the overriding preoccupation of his life; even on his honeymoon he had been unable to shake it off. From Paris he sent J. B. Smith down-to-earth advice on the contents of the *Circular*: 'Don't let any twaddling long articles be inserted. It would be better to give less of leading articles and more of narrative and accounts of lectures etc – unless the leading matter be terse and effective in style and substance.'[7] At Dijon, after an all-night journey, he drafted an article for the *Circular*, and sent it off to Wilson with instructions to cut it up or cut it down in any way necessary. From Lyons he wrote to him at length about the finances of the League.[8] Above all, he brooded on the future of the movement to which he had dedicated himself. And, considering the cheerful optimism with which he usually commented on the League's activities, and the unprecedented personal happiness he was enjoying, his cogitations were surprisingly gloomy. He did not share the complacent belief of many of his countrymen that they had managed their political evolution much better than the Europeans. Whenever he visited the continent, it seemed to him that the French, the Swiss and the Germans had been much more successful than the British in breaking their aristocracy's monopoly of political power. He believed the landed aristocracy in his own country to be entirely selfish – 'they are impervious to all other sensations than fear for their rent-rolls'; and in his most pessimistic moments he thought much the same of the British –

being 'not without my misgivings whether the people of England possess virtue and intelligence enough to throw off the power of an aristocracy, the strongest because the richest that ever bestrode a nation'.[9] And since he was committed to peaceful persuasion, he was forced to the gloomy conclusion that years would probably pass before anything could be done.[10]

How much, if at all, Cobden let his pen run away with thoughts, it is hard to say. At any rate he did not allow his gloomy prognosis to curtail his and Kate's wedding junketings. After less than a month in Manchester, they set off on a tour of the Lakes and Scotland, this time taking with them Cobden's sister, Mary. Cobden was rather condescending about Windermere and Ullswater, regretting that he had not seen them before the Swiss lakes. 'The taste is spoilt for their miniature charms by the splendours of Geneva and Constance.'[11] On their way north from the Lakes they stopped at Gretna Green to go through a marriage ceremony, as the custom then was, before making a detour to Ayr, so that Cobden could show Kate the birthplace of his favourite poet, Robert Burns, which he himself had first visited in his travelling salesman days 14 years earlier.

Cobden was by this time becoming quite well known as a campaigner against the Corn laws, and when he and Kate arrived in Glasgow they found a score of repealers assembled in their hotel, determined to give him a banquet. It was a very noisy affair and Cobden got a headache. But he rose to the occasion and 'gingered' his companions so well that they there and then decided that the next big anti-Corn law banquet must be held in Glasgow. To Cobden this was a most welcome offer. It spared Manchester the expense of the banquet, and 'coming from Scotland, where people are generally believed to be in earnest when they do move, it will have a good moral effect'.[12]

After visiting Edinburgh, the Cobdens finished their Scottish holiday with a week's tour by way of Stirling to Lock Katrine, then back to Glasgow and home by steamer to Liverpool. For Cobden, it was something of a busman's holiday because he tried to meet as many members of the League as possible. He found that the prevailing view on future tactics favoured a fresh flood of petitions to Parliament. Cobden had nothing against this time-honoured method of advertising popular grievances, except that with the existing House of Commons he felt it would be useless. Eighteen months earlier he had assured J. B. Smith: '*That House must be changed before we can get justice.*' He had suggested that the electors of Manchester should be persuaded to pledge themselves to vote only for a parliamentary candidate who promised to vote for total and immediate repeal of the Corn law.[13] He had hoped that Manchester's example would be taken up elsewhere. But his suggestion was not adopted. Too many repealers feared it would push them dangerously close to the murky waters of politics; they preferred to stick to educating the country and petitioning Parliament. Cobden, however, remained convinced that these activities, important though they were, were not enough. Shortly after his return from Scotland in September 1840, he persuaded the League council to adopt a policy of appealing directly to the electors in the manufacturing towns to vote only for committed repealers.

Soon afterwards a by-election at Walsall gave the League an opportunity to practise, in the glare of national publicity, its own version of what might be called politics without party. The local Whigs chose as their candidate a young cornet in the Guards with impeccable aristocratic connections. A three-man deputation from the League went to Walsall to inspect him and found him wanting, not least because he would not commit himself to more than an inquiry into the Corn laws. The young man was apparently so unnerved by his inquisition at the hands of three formidable Mancunians that he decided to stand down. A local free trader agreed to take his place, but immediately changed his mind for fear of a row with his father, a fervent Tory.

To Cobden, it seemed a golden opportunity to put forward a League candidate whose campaign could concentrate exclusively on the Corn laws. He felt that for two years they had been educating the public and now they must seize the chance to test their teaching on the hustings. By no means all the members of the League council agreed. Such a step, they argued, would be too expensive and it might divide the anti-Tory vote. The dissidents were supported by the Whig press in London and the provinces, which waxed extremely scornful over the possibility of a League candidate at Walsall. The *Manchester Guardian* was particularly scathing with its reference to 'a number of gentlemen who call themselves philosophical reformers, and who profess to regulate all their political conduct by a strict adherence to certain dogmas which they call principles, without paying the slightest regard to expediency, or accepting the slightest compromise with persons of different opinions.'[14] The matter was finally fought out on 5 January, 1841 at a series of council meetings attended by many members who normally did little more than pay their subscriptions. In the end, the victory went to the interventionists. Cobden himself happened to be ill, and only made his way in a coach to Newall's Buildings when he thought (wrongly, as it turned out) that an attempt was afoot to overturn his supporters' victory.[15]

The way was clear for the League to campaign in Walsall, but it had neither a suitable candidate nor anything like adequate funds. Cobden had recently confessed to a supporter that the League had scarcely enough cash to cover its current expenses,[16] but little more than a week later this did not stop him from exclaiming to an anxious Smith: 'Damn the money at such a crisis.'[17] The excitement of the crisis did in fact inspire enough supporters to dig into their pockets for a special election fund; Cobden himself contributed at least £100.[18] The problem of finding a candidate proved more difficult. The League's interference had not been well received at Walsall, and no one there would agree to carry its banner. Cobden, moreover, was determined not to take on anyone who might let the League down. In the end, the eminently reliable J. B. Smith was persuaded to stand. His only opponent was the Tory candidate, Captain John Gladstone, the elder brother of William Ewart Gladstone, who loyally came to Walsall to support his brother.

The campaign was fought with all the bad old-fashioned abandon which the Reform Act had done so little to eradicate. Most of the leading members of the League went to Walsall to lend their support and some – George Wilson, for instance, and Smith himself – had doubts about the way the campaign was being fought. Cobden, so far as is known, had none. He had a streak of tough common sense, which prompted him to assure Smith: 'If we lose it will be because we won't take the usual way to win.'[19] So the usual way was taken, by the high-minded Leaguers as well as by the down-to-earth Tories, and there was probably not much to choose between them. The Tories paid the rates of 70 men so as to entitle them to a vote. For £200 Cobden hired two experts in the shady art of manufacturing votes. The Tories bribed Chartists to break up League meetings (although the Chartists hardly needed much encouragement), while the League's bully-boys obliged the Tories to hold their meetings in private. In Cobden's view, such tactics simply had to be accepted in a struggle that was 'life and death to the cause'.[20]

Victory, however, eluded the League. Smith lost by 27 votes in a poll of 699. But his defeat was widely acknowledged to be a glorious one, and he returned to Manchester more like a conquering hero than a defeated candidate.* Cobden, who seldom failed to make the best of setbacks, could on this occasion feel real satisfaction. He had wanted the people to be told that 'the country's salvation must be worked out at the hustings and the polling-booths'[21] and that had now been done. During his campaign, Smith had ignored party politics and concentrated exclusively on the Corn laws; everyone had accepted this and no one had asked if he was a Whig or a Tory. The pro-government *Morning Chronicle* had changed its mind half-way through the campaign and declared that 'the Corn laws are, and must

---

* Gladstone only held the seat until the general election that summer when he was defeated by a free trader.

henceforth be, throughout England, a hustings question'.[22] More-over, the League had demonstrated its ability to fight an election – and almost win – against the hostility of Whigs as well as Tories; it had emerged as an independent political force.

If Cobden was so anxious to increase the number of committed repealers in the House of Commons, why, it might be asked, did he not stand for Parliament himself? After all, less than five years earlier, that was where he felt he could be most useful. One reason was Frederick's opposition to a step that would inevitably divert his brother's attention still more from his business commitments. But the basic reason seems to have been that, as so often with odd men out, he felt a rooted aversion to a political system in which he could not perceive his own niche. In May 1839 he told a correspondent who had urged him to stand for Parliament whenever the opportunity arose, that he was firmly convinced Parliament was not the place for him at present.

> You say I ought to go to that bad House. Do you wish to kill me? Assuredly it would be the death of me, to be obliged to listen night after night to a couple of factions squabbling over appropriative clauses, and such matters, whilst the best interests of the country, the trade, the education, the entire well-being of the nation goes to perdition. No, I'll do my share to improve things out of doors, and to help the people to send a better lot to represent them. I can do no more.[23]

A year later, he told George Wilson that he was quite sincere in his determination not to stand for Parliament at the next general election. If, he added, he really wanted to air his views there, he could always buy a seat – one had been offered to him for £1000 or £1500 – although he realised that that would hardly be a suitable course for a reformer.[24] In September 1840, he turned down an invitation from the Manchester reform association to stand for Parliament with its backing because the reformers had abandoned their independence and because of his conviction – as reported in *Tait's Edinburgh Magazine* –

> ... that to this fatal policy of making political principle subser-vient to the expediency of keeping the Whigs in, and Tories out, of office, he attributed at once the backsliding of the party in power from their former patriotic professions, the degeneracy of leading politicians in an age not otherwise marked by mental or moral inferiority; and, more than all, that destruction of confidence in public men in the minds of the great mass of the People, which had

caused disunion in the Liberal ranks, and threatened destruction to
the Reformers as a party.[25]

After this uncompromising – and perhaps unnecessarily offensive –
declaration of his convictions, Cobden added that, as he had no
reason to think that the Manchester reformers shared them, he did
not intend to offer himself as their candidate. To Francis Place, who
strongly approved of his refusal to join such a 'degraded' assembly,[26]
he expressed himself in less elevated terms: 'Nothing on earth would
induce me to go into Parliament to recognise Stanley [Tory] for
whipper-in. I would rather break stones on the highway than be
counted in and out as *Whig* by Lord John [Russell] & Co.'[27]

The Manchester reformers promptly chose as their candidate
T. Milner Gibson, a young Suffolk squire, who had resigned his
Ipswich seat – which he held as a Tory – in order to join the
reformers. When he stood for the same seat again under his new
colours, he was rejected. At the League's Manchester conference in
January 1840 he had appeared on the platform and had delighted his
audience with his lively wit and the sense of humour with which he
ridiculed his own class. Cobden, however, was disgusted at the
Mancunians' failure to choose one of their own. 'What wonder that
we are scorned by the landed aristocracy when we take such pains
to show our contempt of ourselves? We save our enemies the trouble
of trampling on us, by very industriously kicking our own
backsides.'[28] On this issue the Manchester reformers showed better
judgment than Cobden. Milner Gibson became one of his staunchest
and most useful allies in Parliament. Later, he rose to be President of
the Board of Trade in Palmerston's second Cabinet.

For both humanitarian and practical reasons Cobden was convinced
of the paramount importance of concentrating exclusively on the
'bread tax', but to his great exasperation, not only the Chartists but
men of his own kind whom in general he greatly respected, insisted
on wasting – as he saw it – their time and talents on other objectives.
Parliament's refusal to consider the Corn laws in 1840, which to
Cobden was a spur to campaign still harder on this issue, was to
other reformers an indication that they had better devote their
energies to some less stony object. The Leeds Household Suffrage
Association was set up in the late summer of 1840 by several
distinguished Leeds reformers, including Samuel Smiles, the author
of the famous Victorian bestseller *Self-Help*, who at this time was
editor of the *Leeds Times*. The association's aim was to campaign for
such measures as Corn law repeal, national education, an inquiry
into the condition of the working classes and, above all, parlia-

mentary reform – just the kind of widely-diffused programme that Cobden deplored. In January 1841, he refused to attend a 'Suffrage Festival' organised by the Leeds association, with the pointed excuse that his League engagements left him not a moment's leisure. The festival was held in a new mill, built in the style of an Egyptian temple and not yet filled with machinery. The organisers hoped to have a friendly conference with working people, whose leaders were invited, about extending the suffrage. But the champions of universal suffrage had no use for the advocates of more limited reform, and the proceedings were, in Smiles's words, 'very confused', because of 'the heterogenous audience and the frequent howlings of the Chartists'.[29]

The Leeds Household Suffrage Association did not give up after this débâcle. A working men's club was started in Leeds, lectures were given and discussions held. But this well-meaning attempt to build a bridge between the classes never really got started. 'It was', wrote Smiles many years later, 'like flogging a dead horse to make it rise and go. It would neither rise nor go.'[30] To Cobden, it was all a sorry waste of effort.

Joseph Sturge, Quaker corn merchant and leader of the Birmingham radicals, was another distinguished reformer whose zeal Cobden tried in vain to keep concentrated on the repeal of the Corn law. Sturge was a man with an outsize conscience whose dictates he uncompromisingly obeyed. He regarded the Corn law as an immoral obstacle to the poor man's cheap loaf and was an enthusiastic early member of the original Manchester Anti-Corn Law Association. In Cobden's recollection many years later, it was a few words from Sturge that, more than anything else, persuaded the first anti-Corn law conference in Manchester in January 1839 to stick to an uncompromising demand for total and immediate repeal.[31] But Sturge was interested in many other good causes – parliamentary reform, education, peace, temperance, and above all, the fight against slavery. He had played a prominent part in the campaign to emancipate the West Indian negroes. But he still felt his task was incomplete, and in 1839 he helped to set up the British and Foreign Anti-Slavery Society to work for the abolition of slavery throughout the world. Cobden wished – he told Sturge – that he could direct his energies towards fighting the evils of aristocratic misgovernment at home; 'England then, and the people of England, are in a situation to demand your first aid; the rest should have the crumbs only that fall from the table. But you are giving the entire feast to the natives of Africa, and the people here are in a fair way of starving.'[32]

Early in 1840, Sturge did play an eloquent role in the League delegations that tried to covert members of the government to repeal. But shortly afterwards he diverted his energies into organising a World Anti-Slavery Convention, which was held in London in June and attended by more than 500 delegates. Early next year, Sturge decided to go and study the problem of slavery where it was most intractable – the United States. Cobden tried hard to convince Sturge that his persuasive powers could not be spared from the League even for a few months.[33] Sturge still went, but he doubled his annual subscription to the League to £200, to make up for the practical help he might have given had he stayed at home.

Other members of the anti-slavery movement were more amenable. George Thompson was an exuberant campaigner against the evils of slavery. In 1835 he had crossed the Atlantic to enlighten the Americans. But his tactless oratory had so infuriated a Boston mob that in order to avoid being tarred and feathered he had had to escape in a rowing boat to a departing brig. In 1839 he helped to found the British–India Society with the aim of encouraging the cultivation of Indian cotton as an alternative to slave-grown American cotton. In the summer of 1841, Cobden and his colleagues managed to persuade the Society that it ought temporarily to transfer its energies to fighting the evil on its doorstep, and it was agreed that Thompson should work as a lecturer entirely for the League while the Society continued to pay his salary.[34] The possibility of a general election in the not so distant future made such experienced and dedicated recruits all the more welcome.

The approaching election also injected fresh enthusiasm into the League's propaganda activities, but it did not make them any easier. 'There is nothing', Cobden confessed to a Somerset supporter, 'that we feel more at a loss upon than to find the right arguments to touch the farmer and labourer.'[35] In the towns, where the unemployment figures were steadily rising, the League increasingly hammered away at the argument that the Corn laws pushed up the price of food. In April, the title of the *Anti-Corn Law Circular* was changed to *Anti-Bread Tax Circular*, to emphasise the movement's humanitarian aim. Among working-class audiences the League's arguments were beginning to have some appeal, although a strong suspicion remained that a campaign run by middle-class manufacturers could really only be aimed at bringing down wages. And at many meetings those prepared to listen sympathetically to the League's case were prevented from doing so by the disruptive activities of Chartist thugs. For more than two years after it was formed, the League was unable to hold public meetings in Manchester without attempts at violent disruption, and the same was true of London, Edinburgh, Leeds and many other towns. A meeting at Bristol in January 1841, for instance, at which one of the League's best lecturers, A. W.

Paulton, was speaking, had to be abandoned because it was quite impossible for six policemen to arrest all the Chartists who were demonstrating throughout the hall. There, as elsewhere, the local forces of law and order could not cope.[36]

In Manchester, the League dealt with Chartist violence in the only effective way – by meeting force with its own superior force. Young members of the Operative Anti-Corn Law Association were armed with stout sticks and trained to deal with Chartist disrupters. With Daniel O'Connell's blessing, members of the Irish community – known ironically as the 'Irish lambs' – gave them invaluable support. It was a tough struggle: at one meeting the disrupters had to be driven out four times before the Leaguers could pass their resolutions, but gradually the Chartists were forced into retreat.

A major victory for the League was won at a huge open air meeting in Stevenson Square on 2 June, 1841, called at the request of local working men who asked Cobden to take the chair. After the meeting was announced, posters appeared on walls in Manchester and surrounding towns calling on the Chartists in their 'countless thousands' to put down the 'humbug claptrap of the League.' When the day came, about 20 trade and temperance societies marched into the square. The Chartists were also there in force, their banners nearly obscuring the speakers' platform. But when they started laying about them with their staves, the 'A. C. L. police' responded with such vigour that the Chartists were ignominiously driven out of the square. After the meeting had almost unanimously approved a petition for total and immediate repeal of the Corn law, a procession set out, led by the mayor, Sir Thomas Potter and several other gentlemen on horseback. Cobden marched on foot near the head of the procession. According to an eyewitness,

> The long line of flags and banners, principally with devices and inscriptions on a pure white ground, produced a most imposing effect as they waved in the rays of a brilliant sun . . . Market Street presented one dense mass of spectators, loudly cheering as the procession passed, and the windows were crowded with ladies. On passing the rooms of the League, in Newall Buildings, from the windows of which large banners were waving, each district division gave three hearty cheers. The various bodies congregated in St Ann's Square, where, after a few words from Sir Thomas Potter, the great multitude quietly dispersed.[37]

At Westminster during the early months of 1841, neither government nor Opposition seemed greatly concerned with the worsening economic and social distress in the manufacturing districts.

Palmerston's individualistic, pro-Turkish handling of the long-running Levant crisis over Mehemet Ali's ambitions was pre-occupying many, especially those who feared it would lead to a war with France. (Cobden followed the crisis with furious disapproval, which found vent in a letter to William Tait, which was duly published in *Tait's Edinburgh Magazine*.) Ireland, where O'Connell was makingly disturbingly nationalistic speeches, was also – as usual – causing concern. The Cabinet was depressed by several by-election defeats, and the Prime Minister himself was heard to opine, in a resigned sort of way, that the government could not possibly carry on much longer.[38] How much longer would largely depend on how well the Chancellor of the Exchequer, Sir Francis Baring, could handle the looming crisis in the country's finances. He decided to do so by a very modest dose of tariff reform.

To those who understood the subject, including some senior officials at the Board of Trade, it was obvious that the cumbersome, complicated British tariff system was urgently in need of a radical overhaul. This had become more widely known in 1840 with the publication of a Commons select committee report on import duties. The committee had been heavily weighted with free traders, led by the indefatigable veteran Radical, Joseph Hume, and its report uncompromisingly emphasised the absurdity of the existing tariff system. It pointed out that although there were nearly 900 kinds of article subject to duty, 94.5 per cent of the total customs revenue in 1838–39 had been produced by the duties on only 17 of them. The committee pointed out that lower duties would increase consumption and hence yields, and recommended that modest duties should be concentrated on a small number of widely-used articles.

For the League the report provided welcome ammunition. But in Cobden's opinion it also had the unfortunate effect of encouraging some Corn-law repealers to widen their agitation to include other heavily taxed imports. He was convinced that this would disastrously blunt the attack on the Corn laws. It would also be contrary to the League's constitution which restricted members to the single aim of Corn-law repeal. 'If we wander from the ground we have made our own', he told Villiers, 'we are lost. No agitation for an *alteration of the import duties* will serve us. There is nothing but "*no bread tax*" that will avail us at the hustings.'[39] When, early in May 1841, the Leeds Anti-Corn Law Association voted to enlarge its agitation to include sugar, timber and other duties, Cobden sent Smiles an unequivocal warning that if they went ahead they would in effect be seceding from the League, 'and wherever a branch association drops off from us, we will do our best to rear up another in its place'.[40] The Leeds repealers did not go ahead.

By this time any urge to stray from the League's straight and narrow path could fairly be blamed on the Chancellor of the Exchequer's budget proposals. For the fourth year running Sir Francis Baring was faced with a budget deficit despite the extra taxation he had imposed the previous year. He decided, therefore, to take a leaf out of the select committee's book and try to raise more revenue without increasing taxation. On 30 April, 1841, he told the Commons that he proposed to meet most of the anticipated budget deficit by lowering the duty on foreign (as opposed to colonial) sugar and timber. On the same day Lord John Russell, the Home Secretary, who had already made known his own conversion to a revision of the Corn law, announced that a month hence the House would be invited to adopt a moderate fixed duty on corn imports instead of the existing sliding scale.

The Whig ministers did not see themselves as initiating a great change of policy; they were merely seeking a painless way of balancing their budget. But for the Leaguers it was exhilarating to see the Corn laws at last transformed into a live political issue. Cobden publicly welcomed the tariff concessions as pioneers clearing the road to total repeal.[41] He thought privately that people ought now to be more ready to contribute to the League's depleted funds. 'Money', he wrote to Smith, 'may now I hope be had by applying for it. Can you pick the pockets of any of the members?'[42] Circulars were immediately sent to all the local associations, urging them to step up their fund-raising and other activities during the next month, and deputations were despatched to three or four large towns to stir up the local leaders. (Cobden went to Birmingham with Smith and Ashworth.) Some Leaguers, including Sturge, were so outraged that the League did not denounce the Whig tariff proposals for not going far enough, that they threatened to withdraw their financial support. But on the whole, Cobden was probably justified in claiming 'a sudden accession to our strength both in men and money'.[43]

In the event, the Melbourne government's tariff proposals were the rock on which it finally foundered. Sir Robert Peel decided to attack the reduced duty on foreign (slave-grown) sugar – an issue on which he could count on the enthusiastic support of the anti-slavery lobby which was outraged that the West Indian colonies, where slavery had been abolished less than 10 years earlier, should be given less protection. After a debate extending over eight sittings, the government was defeated by 36 votes. On 27 May, Peel moved a vote of no confidence. After a debate lasting for five nights the government was defeated – by only one vote; but it was enough. By the time Parliament was formally dissolved on 22 June, the country was in the throes of a general election.

In early June, the *Anti-Bread Tax Circular* announced that Richard Cobden had agreed to stand for Stockport which, in the paper's opinion, would achieve immortal honour by electing him. But it added, 'if, as we fear, the brunt of the battle has yet to come, the movement out of doors will sustain severe loss by the removal of Mr Cobden from his indefatigable labour among the people to the less congenial atmosphere of St Stephen's.'

Cobden certainly did not expect to enjoy the atmosphere of St Stephen's. By his own account, his reluctance to enter Parliament was still strong. He rejected overtures from the radicals in both Bolton and Stockport. In fact, he offered to donate £100 towards the expenses of another reform candidate in Stockport and to canvass for him for a week. But he had become a much bigger catch as a candidate in the four years since he first stood for the town and the Stockport electors could not agree on a smaller fish. They assured Cobden they could not turn out the Tory candidate without him, and promised not to make any stipulations about his attendance at Westminster. So he agreed to stand. He wrote apologetically to Frederick, who had just returned from a business trip to New York to be greeted with this unwelcome news: 'You must not vex yourself, for I am quite resolved that it shall not be the cause of imposing either additional expense on my mode of living, or any increased call upon my time for public objects. I did not dream of this, as you very well know.'[44] Perhaps he exaggerated his reluctance in order to conciliate his brother. Frederick, for his part, may well have wondered whether he really did know all Richard's dreams.

The election itself, according to Cobden, 'was carried with unexpected éclat. We drubbed the Major [the Tory candidate] so soundly that at one o'clock he resigned.'[45] Whether the Stockport electors' change of heart was due more to Cobden's views or to his personality – or to some other cause altogether – is not clear. Nor is it easy to gauge how much importance was attached to the Corn laws and free trade generally in the country as a whole. It would probably be true to say that many people did not grasp the connection, which the League had been trying desperately to explain, between the Corn laws and the prevailing economic and social distress, and were thus not greatly interested in repeal. The Whig conversion to Corn-law revision was either regarded as insincere – a death-bed vow, as Gladstone put it – or if taken seriously, as by the farmers, helped to increase the Tory vote in the rural areas. The argument that cheap bread meant lower wages helped the Tories in the towns, where the hostility of many of their candidates to the new Poor Law and the factory system also gained them votes. So did the support of the Chartists and those radicals whose attitude was determined by hatred of the Whigs and distrust of the League.

After a good deal of disagreement, the League reluctantly decided to support Whig candidates wherever it did not have a candidate of its own. Cobden, who had at first argued so strongly that they should support only committed repealers, came to realise that in politics, as in much else, it is a mistake to spurn those whose views do not coincide entirely with one's own. In the event, the League did quite well, J. B. Smith being the only prominent League candidate who failed to win a seat. But nothing could save the Whigs from a decisive defeat, which they themselves seemed almost to expect and even welcome (Macaulay took a comfortable suite in the Albany and looked forward to 'college life in the West end of London' and getting down to his history.[46]) Peel had a comfortable majority of about eighty, and, moreover, he had managed to preserve an entirely free hand for dealing with the country's problems – economic, fiscal and social.

For Cobden, the House of Commons was simply the crucial battlefield for the destruction of the Corn laws, and one Sunday evening in July 1841 he sat down to tell Charles Villiers how he thought the battle should be fought. 'I can now', he wrote, 'think of nothing but the tactics of the opposition in the House.' The Radicals as a whole had done badly in the elections, and the Philosophic Radicals, disillusioned with politics, were either turning to more intellectual pursuits like writing history, or retreating quietly into the ranks of the Whigs. (Mrs Grote now even condescended to accept invitations to that centre of Whig social life, Holland House.) The Whigs' conversion to tariff reform and the League's support of Whig candidates in the election had brought the two groups closer together. But to Cobden the gap between them was still too wide to be bridged.

> It is quite clear there must be an independent Free Trade party who will make it their business to press corn, sugar, etc, etc. at all times . . . Have you begun to *take stock* of the men who will form such a party and of which you will be the acknowledged leader? . . . I have a notion that such a party ought to have a couple of rooms and a secretary or clerk and a messenger as a place of meeting, and for the purpose of giving us a local habitation and a name. A Free Trade club has crossed my mind but that appears to be too am-bitious in the present state of our party . . . We must occupy the ground and give notice that we will not give way for Toryism, Whiggism, Radicalism or Chartism. The people's daily bread must be our daily business with an occasional addition of *sugar, coffee and wood* . . . much will depend on *yourself* to give a right direction to our party at the outset.

He then came down to earth, admitting that he hardly knew two men in the House whose spontaneous efforts to 'work' the free trade question could be relied on, and he urged Villiers to start finding and training 'the pack'.

> But there are not a few on whom I have my eye, who if led aright and *whipped a little from without*, will do anything that is necessary. The League will find the whip and spur – you must *lead* the pack. Count on my incessant aid. Out of the House I can do some service in keeping men up to the mark, but within doors I shall use the privilege of a young member and learn my lesson instead of talking.[47]

In fact he had not sat in the House for much more than a week before he succumbed to the temptation to talk. Melbourne had chosen not to resign before the new Parliament met, and Cobden made his maiden speech during a four-day debate on a Tory motion of no confidence. His speech was a series of variations on the theme that the only issue worth debating was the repeal of the Corn law. He pointed out how much more heavily the 'bread tax' weighed on the poorer classes than on the rich, and emphasised the appalling poverty caused by the current economic depression. He denied that the manufacturers wanted repeal so that they could cut wages; 'the rate of wages has no more connection with the price of food than with the moon's changes'. Free trade would increase the demand for British goods, and the consequent increased demand for labour would cause wages to rise. He ended his speech with an assurance that he had not spoken in a party spirit; he called himself neither Whig nor Tory, but a free trader, and opposed to monopoly wherever he found it.[48]

Soon after Macaulay had entered the House of Commons, he described it as a 'most peculiar audience', in which a man's previous success as a debater or barrister or mob orator was 'rather a reason for expecting him to fail than for expecting him to succeed'.[49] Cobden was apparently not heard with the indulgent courtesy customarily accorded to a new member. Northern manufacturers were a rare and unwelcome species in the House of Commons, and Cobden himself later remarked that he was clearly regarded as a Gothic invader.[50] But his friends told him he had done well, while in Stockport his speech was very favourably received, and in Newall's Buildings Wilson read it out loud to encourage his colleagues 'fagging away at the correspondence'.[51]

On 28 August, the government lost the no confidence motion by 91 votes. Two days later, Peel was on his way to Windsor for his first audience with the Queen as Prime Minister. He had many things to think about – armed hostilities with China and Afghanistan as well as domestic problems – but he had given a remarkably frank assurance that the Corn laws would not be forgotten. He had told the Commons two days earlier that if he could be persuaded that a change in the Corn law would be an effective remedy for the social distress 'I would earnestly advise a relaxation, an alteration, nay, if necessary, a repeal of the Corn laws'.[52] Cobden immediately recognised and accepted the challenge.

Parliament met briefly in mid-September to pass some necessary supply and other bills, and was then prorogued until February – so that, Cobden commented bitterly, 'the members may go to their sports and the people to – the grave'.[53] He listened in disgust as the House voted money for militia in Canada, lighthouses in Jamaica, bishops all over the world, feeling 'vastly edified and scandalised at the way in which the poor devils of taxpayers are robbed'.[54] He held his tongue with difficulty, but on 17 September could not refrain from launching a scathing attack on Peel's decision to postpone any discussion of the Corn laws until the New Year. He told his listeners roundly that they were profoundly ignorant about the state of the country. In his own constituency, Stockport, one fifth of the houses were empty, half of those occupied were not paying rent, nearly half the mills were closed and thousands of working people were wandering the streets looking for work. In Manchester there were great fears of unrest during the coming winter because men could not be expected to sit quiet and see their children starve.[55]

A week later, ignoring impatient protests from the government benches, he again tried to spell out how much trade barriers were responsible for the economic and social distress. He went on to appeal to his listeners' humanity.

> When I go down to the manufacturing districts ... I know that starvation is stalking through the land, and that men are perishing for lack of the barest necessaries of life. When I witness this, and recollect that there is a law which especially provides for keeping our population in absolute want, I cannot help attributing murder to the Legislature of this country; and wherever I stand, whether here or out of doors, I will denounce that system of legislative murder which denies to the people of the land food in exchange for the produce of their industry.

Turning to look directly at two members known for their concern with various philanthropic causes, he went on:

> When I see in some quarters a disposition to trade upon a reputation for humanity ... I will not question your motives, I will not deny that it is really meant; but this I tell you, that if you would give force and grace to your professions of humanity, it must not be confined to the negro at the Antipodes, nor to the

building of churches, nor the extension of the Church Establishment, nor to occasional visits to factories to talk sentiment over factory children – you must untax the peoples' bread.[56]

Some of those listening to Cobden may have felt that a northern manufacturer was ill-qualified to demand sympathy for the sufferings of the workers. (A few days later he was violently attacked by a Tory MP as a cotton lord every farthing of whose profits was dyed in the blood of the poor.[57]) In any case, it was wasted effort. Peel was far from ignoring the problems of the manufacturing districts. He was carrying out a comprehensive review of the whole fiscal system, trying to work out how best to reconcile the legitimate interests of the countryside with the needs of the new industrial classes. But he was determined not to produce any remedies until he was quite sure of his ground.

Cobden's first close acquaintance with the House of Commons had not made him think any better of it. Nor could he perceive the right parliamentary tactics to pursue, although he felt sure the free traders should keep their distance from the Whigs and not fall for any compromise that Lord John Russell might propose. Perhaps inevitably, he was soon dissatisfied with Charles Villiers's low-key, if thoroughly sincere, style of leadership. He did his best to stir him up, writing to him with extraordinary freedom – and cheek – during the brief recess while Peel was Cabinet-making: '... you must be prepared for leading us into action. Get up your steam – nurse your *physique* – keep your *stomach* in order ... by abstinence. The hour is coming and you must be the man. If you will go boldly amongst the enemy, your crew can bring them to action, and maul them in argument.'[58] But by early December Cobden was complaining to J. B. Smith that 'we are sadly off for a leader. Villiers appears to me to shrink from the responsibility of leading us apart from Lord John'.[59]

Outside Parliament, however, Cobden had the satisfaction of enlisting the man who was to become his most famous lieutenant. John Bright and Cobden had known each other for four years without becoming particularly friendly. Bright was an enthusiastic and energetic supporter of the League until his wife's illness forced him to stay increasingly by her side. She died at Leamington Spa in September 1841. Cobden happened to be visiting relatives in the town at the same time, and a few days later he called on Bright to offer his sympathy. According to the account Bright gave many years later, after a while Cobden looked up and said: 'There are thousands of houses in England at this moment where wives, mothers and children are dying of hunger. Now, when the first paroxysm of your grief is past, I would advise you to come with me, and we will never rest till the Corn law is repealed.'[60] Whether or not Bright remembered Cobden's exact words, he certainly remembered their gist and their spirit. For a man in his situation and with his temperament it was the best possible advice, and he followed it valiantly for more than four years. In the process he became Cobden's most valued and intimate friend, although they did not always see eye to eye. A year later, when the League had settled down to the long, hard grind of converting public opinion, Cobden and Bright began their famous partnership on public platforms all over the country in which the cool, persuasive reasonableness of the one was stamped on men's minds by the powerful oratory of the other.

Shortly before he took his seat at Westminster, Cobden attended what was perhaps the League's most impressive and fruitful propaganda effort that year. It took the form of a four-day meeting in Manchester of nearly 700 nonconformist clergy. Ostensibly organised by local ministers, it was in fact entirely run by the League, which arranged accomodation, provided administrative back-up and in effect masterminded the proceedings. The great merit of this and the similar ministers' meetings that followed elsewhere, notably in Edinburgh, was that through them the League's gospel, which to many critics seemed almost entirely Manchester-inspired, was proclaimed, with the authority of the pulpit, all over the country.[61] The narrowness of the League's base was a constant worry to Cobden. He was anxious to make its campaign more general 'and so take away the stigma of its being a millowners' question'.[62] He was scathing about other large towns whose failure to rally to the cause had emphasised Manchester's leading role: '. . . – Leeds ran away after a political *ignis fatuus* – Glasgow deserted us for tariff reform – Birmingham has never had a lucid interval yet.'[63] (After a brief visit to Birmingham in October, he reported in disgust that 'they were drivelling mad about Church rates'.[64])

Early in September, Cobden confided to Bright that the League was 'over head and ears' in debt.[65] Its various propaganda activities were very expensive, and many of its supporters were in such financial difficulties themselves, because of the economic depression, that they could contribute little or nothing to the League's funds. Cobden was greatly agitated lest the League should fail at what he believed to be a crucial moment for lack of money. 'It is', he assured Wilson, 'absolutely a life or death struggle for the League – to get money at once . . .' It was useless, he added, to wait for the fund-raising bazaar that a committee (headed by Mrs Cobden) was preparing to hold in January.[66] His urgency was caused by the impression he had carried

4 The Anti-Corn law Bazaar in Manchester, 31 Jan. 1842.

away from Westminster that Peel was prepared at least to revise the Corn law provided he could carry his party with him. It was therefore up to the League to find – if it could – the means and the methods that would generate the necessary pressure on Peel's supporters.

Instead of finding them, however, the League temporarily lost its way. The council was deeply divided over tactics, and Cobden was hard put to it to control the extremists and prevent a permanent split between them and the moderate majority. He himself – as he freely confessed – had run out of new ideas and for once was unable to give a clear lead.[67] To attack Peel while still ignorant of what measures he intended to take would, he felt, weaken the League's moral influence. But he had no objection in principle to withholding the payment of taxes – as had been suggested during the struggle for the Reform Bill – provided they could be sure of sufficient support for such a drastic step. And they could not. Manchester and its neighbourhood might be ready for a 'fiscal revolt', but they were not typical of the rest of the country.[68] So the idea of a 'middle-class *coup*' remained an enticing dream, and the Leaguers were forced to go on feeding their enthusiasm on a rather stale diet of lectures, tracts, petitions and so on.

But at least the League did not go bankrupt. Somehow, enough money was found to enable it to carry on until the bazaar – a spectacular ten-day affair held in the Theatre Royal, Manchester – raised nearly £10,000 for the cause. It was a welcome boost to morale.

As in the previous year, frustration over the Corn law tempted some free traders to divert their energies to political reforms and the possibility of co-operating with the moderate 'moral force' Chartists. Their sense of the urgency of closing the growing gap between the middle and working classes was expressed by Edward Miall, a Dissenting minister with strong radical views, in a series of articles published in his recently-founded periodical *The Nonconformist* between October and December 1841. Miall proposed a form of suffrage very similar to the Chartists' universal manhood suffrage, but he called it 'complete suffrage' to avoid any alarming Chartist associations.

The indefatigable Joseph Sturge, apparently doubtful of the League's chances of success, decided to make complete suffrage the basis of a new movement. His initiative was well-timed. On the one hand, the League was in the doldrums, and on the other, the 'moral force' Chartists, like Henry Vincent and William Lovett, were anxious to distance themselves from the violent tactics of Feargus O'Connor and his 'physical force' men. A declaration on complete suffrage, drawn up by Sturge, was widely supported, and enthusiastic meetings were held in Birmingham, Edinburgh, London, Glasgow and elsewhere.

By March 1842, more than fifty towns had formed Complete Suffrage Unions, and in April a general conference was held in Birmingham. Although Sturge was in the chair, and the middle class was strongly represented (by Bright, among others) the proceedings were dominated by the Chartists who managed to incorporate all six points of their Charter into the final resolution. They failed to persuade the conference to adopt the Charter by name – Sturge insisted that this would frighten off too many middle-class recruits – but they indicated that they would insist on reopening the question at a further conference to be held at the end of the year.[69] The CSU, they realised, could only help them against O'Connor if it was un-equivocally linked with the Charter. O'Connor, for his part, denounced Complete Suffrage as Complete Humbug.[70]

Many Leaguers joined the CSU. Cobden did not, but he thought too highly of Sturge not to make the best of his new initiative. He was determined that the League in its corporate capacity should have no connection with the CSU, but he did not object to members joining as individuals. On the contrary, he hoped that the CSU might indirectly reinforce the League. 'The more I think of your plan', he told Sturge, 'even as auxiliary to Corn law repeal, the more I like it, for I do think it will be viewed by aristocrats on both sides as a gathering cloud behind *us*.'[71]

Where Cobden differed from Sturge – and from all those Leaguers who were tending in the same direction – was over the 'moral force' Chartists. Sturge saw them as potentially valuable allies. Some of their leaders saw the League, as well as the CSU, in the same light. But Cobden had no use for them at all. Through Sturge he had met several of them in Birmingham and had found them no better than O'Connorites in their 'gross ignorance of our question'[72] – which, unlike Sturge, was all he thought about – and their refusal to grasp that it was 'a working man's question *primarily and finally*'.[73] Once it was settled, the middle-class reformers in the League would be free to concentrate on securing the rights of the unenfranchised. Since neither wing of the Chartist movement could grasp this, it would be better, Cobden thought, to leave them to their feuding and set up a new workers' party independent of both. It was a fantasy, but in considering who might lead the new party, Cobden made some perceptive comments about himself.

> I have not the physical force, and the tone of my mind is opposed to such an undertaking. I know exactly my own field of usefulness – it lies in the advocacy of practical questions, apart from mere questions of theoretical reforms. My exertions are calculated to bring out the middle class, and that will pave the way for a junction with the masses, if they can be brought to act under a rational and honest leader.[74]

Throughout the dreadful winter of 1841–42, the League and the Chartists pursued parallel courses of agitation against the prevailing economic and social distress. Cobden established himself for the winter with Kate and their baby son Richard at Leamington, where they shared a house with two of his mother's relations. By now his dominant position in the League was fast becoming established, and his temporary move to Leamington was to escape the 'anti-Corn law press-gangs' in Manchester who would give him no peace. He made occasional forays: to consult Sturge in Birmingham; to attend a public meeting on the distress in Stockport, or a meeting of manufacturers in Derby on the same problem in the Midlands; or to visit Manchester for the great League bazaar. This, being held on market day, caused such a stir that the doors had to be closed several times and Cobden himself made two unsuccessful attempts to get inside. But he was determined to conserve his health and strength for the parliamentary campaign that would open in February, and he remained as much as possible quietly in Leamington, where it rained incessantly – the sportsmen, he commented sardonically, would need 'a stud of *steamers* to negotiate the waters' – and where he could concentrate on keeping up 'an incessant fire of letters upon all parts of the kingdom to stir them up to action'.[75]

CHAPTER 6

The League Plays with Fire (1842)

On 3 February, 1842, the Queen opened the new session of Parliament. Cobden, having travelled overnight from Manchester, was among the MPs crowding into the House of Lords to hear her refer to the country's finances, tariffs, the Corn law and the 'continued distress in the manufacturing districts of the country . . . borne with exemplary patience and fortitude'. Outside, nearly six hundred League delegates from all over the country assembled in Brown's Hotel for their usual eve-of-session rally. This year, they met with heightened expectations because of the new government. But it was another six days before Peel unveiled his plans.

A huge crowd collected outside Parliament on 9 February. As soon as the doors were opened, there was a rush for the strangers' gallery which, it was estimated, could have been filled six times over by all those who had obtained passes from MPs. Outside, the League delegates, who had been refused a private interview by Peel, decided to make a public demonstration instead. Arm in arm, these staid, respectable manufacturers marched through the streets up to the entrance to the House of Commons and tried to make their way into the Lobby. The police refused to let more than 100 in, and after – in the words of *The Times* – 'a considerable exchange of ammunition in the shape of abusive epithets', the rest retired to the pavement outside where they hailed the MPs hurrying into the House with cries of 'Total Repeal', 'Cheap Food', and 'Down with the Monopoly'. Similar cries greeted Sir Robert Peel, who had the misfortune to meet the angry Leaguers on their return march while he was being driven to the House. According to a (hostile) eyewitness, Sir Robert 'leaned back in his carriage, grave and pale'.[1]

Peel and the Leaguers were not at this stage capable of understanding each other. Peel found them intemperate and obsessional;

101

the Leaguers found him rigid in his economic views and insensitive
to the plight of the poor. They also assumed that he was in the
pocket of the aristocratic landlords – which he was not, although he
had to take account of the fact that any legislative change must be
acceptable to a Parliament dominated by landowners. He felt that the
Corn law could not be blamed for the prevailing industrial depression and that to abolish it completely would simply extend the
distress in the towns to the rural population. But by the New Year
he had managed to persuade his Cabinet colleagues to agree in
principle that it ought to be revised. The actual changes which he
proposed to the Commons were designed, first, to reduce the protection given to domestic corn without impairing the security of the
producer, and second to improve the technical operation of the law
so as to eliminate as far as possible fraudulent speculation and wild
price fluctuations. The changes did not go as far as he himself would
have liked if the political realities had been more favourable. (Only
the ultra-protectionist Duke of Buckingham resigned from the
Cabinet.) But although a compromise between the politically feasible and the ideally desirable, Peel's new scale of duties still made
considerable reductions. For example, the existing duty of 27s 8d
when domestic corn was between 59s and 60s a quarter was cut by
more than half to 13s.[2]

Charles Greville thought that the long speech of nearly three
hours during which Peel calmly and dryly expounded his views on
the Corn law 'bored everybody very much'.[3] Cobden was not bored
but disgusted. According to *The Times* reporter, 'looking exceedingly lachrymose, [he] rose from his seat for the purpose, as it was
generally thought, of inflicting on the House one of his stereotyped
Corn law speeches'. Instead, he made a brief, vehement statement
denouncing Peel's measure 'as an insult to the suffering people ...
whose patience deserved very different treatment from the landed
aristocracy, and from the Cabinet which was the instrument of that
aristocracy ...'[4] Cobden's condemnation was echoed at meetings
throughout the country, the Prime Minister's effigy was burnt in
public, and petitions of protest poured into the House of Commons.
But the Commons were not moved, and by 9 March the Corn Bill
had had its second reading. Three alternative proposals were rejected
– Lord John Russell's for a fixed duty, a Tory MP's for slightly
higher protective duties, and Villiers's for total repeal, which was
defeated by a huge majority of 303.

On 24 February, the fifth and last night of the debate on Villiers's
motion, Cobden made his major contribution to the Corn law
discussions. He told the House that the question to be decided was
simply whether it was just, honest or expedient to lay any tax at all
on the food of the people. He challenged Peel to agree that it was

5 Cobden addressing the League Council.

impossible to fix the price of food by law and when, across the floor of the House, the Prime Minister conceded that it was, Cobden asked what then were they legislating for? If it was to keep up the price of food, would Peel also try to legislate to keep up the price of cottons, woollens, silks and so on? After throwing out this second challenge, to the cheers and laughter of his own side, Cobden folded his arms and waited for Peel's reply. And when it did not come, he declared that 'here is the simple, open avowal that we are met here to legislate for a class against the people'. He pointed out that the prices of the goods produced by the ironmonger and the cotton manufacturer had both fallen by 30 per cent over the past 10 years. Was it fair that they should have to exchange them for the produce of the land kept at its present high price?[5]

No sooner had Cobden sat down than a young Tory squire from Yorkshire, William Ferrand, jumped up and launched a violent attack on him.[6] Ferrand was a 'Church and King' Tory and an enthusiastic farmer who believed that agriculture was the foundation of the nation's greatness and that the rapacity and oppression of the mill-owners, not the Corn law, were responsible for the distress. He had become an enthusiastic factory reformer after rescuing an exhausted factory child from dying in the snow early one morning when he had gone out to shoot wild fowl. His Dantonesque appearance and stentorian voice assured him of the House's attention and, although it was his third attack in 10 days on Cobden, the Tory MPs were, according to the *Morning Chronicle,* 'absolutely frantic with joy'. According to another press report, 'this very extraordinary scene' entirely upset the decorum of the House for the rest of the evening. Ferrand alleged, among other things, that Cobden ran his 'mill' (i.e. print-works) night and day and had made half a million pounds over the past 12 years. He went on to denounce the whole race of northern manufacturers for various cruelties and illegalities, including forcing the truck system of payment (instead of money) on their workers. The whole tirade, its rapturous reception by a majority of the Commons, and the favourable reports in *The Times* and other papers, were all a devastating demonstration of the unpopularity of the northern manufacturers. Cobden commented later that among Tory MPs 'nothing seems to be considered so decided a stigma as to brand a man as a mill-owner'.[7]

Ten days later, Cobden made a personal statement in the House of Commons on Ferrand's allegations. He said he had been told that at Crosse Hall, over the past 18 months, 20 men had been employed at night – but not during the day as well – to complete some work. They were unemployed and only too glad to get the work, as hundreds of others would have been. He also insisted that his firm paid all wages in cash.[8] Ferrand, however, persisted with his efforts to convict Cobden's firm of making truck payments, and eventually a Commons select committee was set up to inquire into the truck system.

In the course of its hearings, the select committee was told by one of Ferrand's witnesses, a solicitor's clerk from Chorley called Isaac Oldfield, that the Cobdens' firm was one of the very few in the neighbourhood that did not either have a truck shop, which the employees had to use in lieu of wages, or let out cottages to them. Four cows, which the firm kept because their dung was used in some dye-making processes, were let to employees who looked after them and sold the milk. It was an entirely voluntary arrangement, beneficial to both sides, and no one complained about it. The only complaint that Oldfield had heard against the Cobdens was that they employed too many Scotsmen.[9] Cobden's satisfaction at his firm's vindication was marred by fears that revelations about other manufacturers' truck practices would damage the credit of the anti-Corn law party as a whole.[10]

The vehement persistence of Cobden's opposition to Peel's Corn Bill is not easy to understand. He told Wilson that as it was after all a mitigation of the present law, he did not see any use in opposing its final passage.[11] But oppose it he did, passionately. Before the bill was read for a third time on 7 April, he moved an amendment to the effect that since the House had repeatedly declared its inability to regulate wages, it was inexpedient and unjust to pass a law to regulate the price of food with a view to raising it 'unnaturally'. He wound up his speech with an emotional outburst against the landlords,[12] and after his amendment had been rejected and the bill passed a third time, he insisted on denouncing it as a robbery of the poor without compensation.[13] Yet only three days earlier he had written to a supporter, 'Peel is doing our work gloriously. He has scattered the "agricultural party" to the four winds and left them without pilot or compass. They will not know their "friends" from their foes. He has acknowleged *our* principle of Free Trade and done some pecuniary hurt but far greater *moral* damage to the monopolists.'[14] If he was grateful to Peel, he chose a strange way to show it. In fact, he probably was not. As so often with people in the grip of a strong emotion, his feelings were not always consistent. But his predominant emotion, swamping any more rational assessment, seems to have been a fear that Peel's cautious revision of the Corn law would paralyse any further pressure for total abolition which he believed was essential to feed the poor, stimulate trade and break the dominance of the landed aristocracy. In December 1841, he told J. B. Smith that 'the greatest evil that could befall us would be a *bona fide* concession. The middle classes are a compromising set',[15] and when this 'evil' actually materialised, his reactions were extreme. He feared that half a loaf was not better, but worse than none, and he almost seemed to welcome the continuance of the distress in the belief that it was the quickest way of gaining the whole loaf. Throughout the rest of the session he never missed an opportunity to denounce the new Corn law.

Meanwhile, on 11 March, Peel revealed the rest of his budget proposals. The highly unpopular income tax was to be brought back at a rate of 7d in the pound, with incomes below £150 exempted. There was also to be a sweeping revision of the archaic tariff system, removing all prohibitory duties and reducing import duties on about 750 articles. Peel reckoned that the yield from the income and other taxes would be sufficient to wipe out the budget deficit inherited from the Whigs and still leave enough to cover the reduction (temporary, it was hoped) in revenue from customs duties. Altogether, the budget came as a great surprise, but for many it was not an unwelcome one, and it established Peel's position as a strong and respected prime minister. After listening to his speech, one Whig MP, who had been amongst his most scornful critics, was moved to exclaim in the seclusion of the Travellers' Club: 'Thank God, Peel is minister'.[16]

The same feeling may have encouraged the resigned acceptance of the income tax outside Parliament. In 1816, the Commons had rejected the renewal of the wartime income tax by a huge majority, and the Whigs had assumed that Peel would never dare to reintroduce it in time of peace. Harriet Martineau was reflecting, without much exaggeration, a widespread feeling when she wrote that there was 'something transcendently disgusting in an Income tax, which not only takes a substantial sum immediately out of a man's pocket, but compels him to confide his affairs to a party whom he would by no means choose for a confidant'.[17] But as part of a general move towards free trade, even northern manufacturers (with the emphatic exception of John Bright) and the *Manchester Guardian* were prepared to accept the reintroduction of the tax. The Chartists too welcomed it as a step towards greater social equality.

There was no welcome, however, from the Opposition in the Commons. As soon as they had recovered from their initial surprise and confusion, and party feeling had had a chance to reassert itself, Whigs and Radicals decided on a policy of outright opposition. Throughout the Income Tax Bill's passage (with Bright an en-thralled observer in the gallery), Opposition speakers denounced it as wrong in principle, unnecessary, excessive, unfair and inquisitorial. Every possible procedural device was employed to impede its passage, with Cobden playing a prominent part in these obstructionist tactics. The government found them tiresomely effective, but to Cobden the Opposition was not nearly aggressive enough. 'We are a parcel of dunghill cocks good at nothing but crowing ...'[18] He declared openly that he did not disapprove in principle of an income tax, but believed this was not the time to introduce it.[19] Yet he opposed it with a persistence and vehemence more appropriate to an issue of principle than one of timing. The reason, it seems, was that he calculated – or miscalculated – that relentless attacks by the Opposition on the unpopular income tax would win them more middle-class support over the Corn law.[20]

It was more difficult for the Whigs and their Radical allies to mount convincing attacks on Peel's tariff reforms, although they could – and did – criticise them in detail. When the Prime Minister introduced the Customs Duty Bill on 10 May, he admitted that there was now no great difference of opinion between government and Opposition on the general principle of free trade. Joseph Hume promptly welcomed the Cabinet's conversion. Cobden said nothing, but privately he belittled Peel's package and derided those who were pleased with it.[21] Those who were emphatically not pleased were Peel's supporters, the Tory agriculturists. They had managed to swallow his Corn Bill, but they could not stomach the reductions in duty on a wide variety of imported foodstuffs. (These did win some private praise from Cobden.) At the end of the debate about the reduced duty on live cattle, a hostile amendment – which expressed in what would now be called coded language the agriculturists' bitter disapproval – was easily defeated, but 85 of Peel's usual supporters voted for it. It was a warning foretaste of what was to happen four years later. But Peel refused to make any concessions, and when the protracted debates came to an end, the Prime Minister's private fear was not that he had gone too far, but that he had not gone far enough to revive industry and commerce and help the starving thousands in the manufacturing towns.[22]

In terms of human suffering, the spring and summer of 1842 were probably the most dreadful period in what came to be called the 'hungry 'forties'. The remorseless increase in destitution and distress spurred the Chartist factions into temporarily shelving their differences in order to organise another mammoth petition. Six miles long, bearing more than 3,300,000 signatures and mounted on a huge bobbin-like frame, it was carried by 30 bearers through the streets of London before being broken up into bundles and dumped on the floor of the House of Commons. But however much the Commons sympathised with the petitioners' distress, there was not the remotest chance that they would consider the Chartists' political demands. Only some 50 Radicals, including Cobden, were prepared even to listen to the petitioners at the bar of the House.

It was left to the League outside Parliament and the small band of Radicals inside to try to make the authorities understand that what they had been content to do for the economic and social crisis was too little and might be too late. The League's propaganda was intensified and meetings were organised all over the country. The Manchester Anti-Corn Law Association sent its MPs a memorial with nearly 64,000 signatures, begging that all supplies to the government should be stopped as the country seemed to be on the verge of revolution. (The Tory press denounced this as treasonable.) Early in July, League delegates from the industrial towns assembled in London and took it in turns to read out detailed reports on the situation in their own localities. It was a tale of mills and blast furnaces standing idle, sharply reduced wages, private relief funds exhausted, shopkeepers ruined, enormous increases in the poor rates, furniture and wedding rings sold to buy food. The meetings were kept up until the beginning of August, with relays of delegates coming up from the provinces to make their contributions to the record of misery and destitution, which was reported in column after column of minute type in the *Morning Chronicle* and other sympathetic London papers. In addition, groups of delegates interviewed Peel and other ministers, repeating the same sad tales, and insisting that only the total abolition of the Corn law could revive trade and set the wheels of industry moving again. When Peel pointed out how much he had already done to reduce the protection to agriculture,

Henry Ashworth replied that six feet of water might drown a man as well as six yards.[23]

Inside the House of Commons, Cobden, Villiers, Milner Gibson and others insisted again and again on bringing up the plight of the industrial districts. Cobden was determined to pin the blame fairly and squarely on the government, and at the end of the session Joseph Parkes reported that he had made 'two or three remarkable and telling speeches'.[24] Peel repeated his arguments that over-investment and over-production should be blamed as much as the Corn law for the economic slump. There were exchanges between him and Cobden about the effect on employment of introducing new, improved machinery. The Prime Minister insisted that, in the short term at any rate, this must mean fewer jobs. Cobden conceded that this might be true in isolated cases, but new machinery could not be responsible for the 29 mills lying completely idle in Stockport.[25] Peel strongly attacked the 'wicked men' who were trying to inflame the minds of the people by exaggerating their sufferings.[26] Cobden repeatedly denied that he was threatening popular violence, but 'I say you are drifting on to confusion without rudder or compass ... Will you tell me ... that the 60,000 people in Stockport are to lie down and die?' He added that he did not believe that the people would break out 'unless they are absolutely deprived of food; if you are not prepared with a remedy, they will be justified in taking food for themselves and their families.'[27]

On 11 July, during a debate on Villiers's (unsuccessful) motion for a committee on the Corn laws, Peel said that if he were convinced that they were the main cause of the distress he would at once give them up.[28] For some time Cobden had felt that Peel was at heart a free trader, and in the last big debate of the session on the economic crisis he made a direct appeal to him to cut loose from 'that bigoted section of his followers who acted as a drag-chain upon him'. He promised the Prime Minister the support of the free traders 'without any reference to politics or party', and urged him to change sides at once 'and if he were taunted for so doing, this would be his answer – that he had found a country in distress, and had given to it prosperity'.[29] It was four more years before Peel was able to give such an answer.

Cobden always insisted that the pressure on the government inside Parliament must be matched by pressure from without, and how far the League could or should go in creating this external pressure was his constant preoccupation. Early in March 1842, he asked Duncan McLaren the leading tree trader in Edinburgh: 'What is to be our future course? All sorts of violent remedies are suggested. Tell me what your cooler judgment recommends ... *in* and *out* of Parliament'.[30] On the same day he told Bright that he really did not know what to suggest in the way of 'ulterior measures', since he still doubted whether a 'fiscal strike' would be successful.[31] In reply Bright took up an idea which some extreme Radicals had been toying with, and suggested that the manufacturers of Lancashire and Yorkshire should threaten the government with a simultaneous closure of their works unless the Corn law was immediately repealed.[32] Cobden dismissed this plan on the grounds that they would never get all the manufacturers to agree, and it would greatly antagonise the workers who would be thrown out of work.[33]

On 21 June Cobden told Bright that some people, including Villiers, were always saying in private that the 'landlords will only yield to fear and after the people have begun to burn and destroy again as they did in 1829. But this is a course which no Christian or good citizen can look at with hope of advantage'. Once again, he reverted to the idea of withholding taxes. Would not 'moral resistance', he asked Bright, be more effective? He pointed out that there were other frustrated reformers besides the Leaguers – those campaigning against the new Poor Law, or for extending the suffrage, or for a 10-hour day – who might be combined into a powerful weapon of passive resistance if they all refused to pay their taxes. 'Depend on it, a widespread and determined "fiscal rebellion" would terrify the enemy far more than pikes or pistols.' And he tentatively suggested that the withheld taxes should be paid into a fund to be used for the purchase of flour in bond which would afterwards be sold free of duty to the poor.[34] No more was heard of this enterprising–too enterprising–idea.

To encourage passive resistance, Cobden urged doing everything possible to discredit the government and the House of Commons, and he put his precept into the most uncompromising practice. He told the delegates at one of the League meetings in London in July that they must do whatever they could, within the letter of the law, to embarrass the government, which 'was based on corruption, and the offspring of vice, corruption, violence, intimidation and bribery. The majority of the House of Commons was supported by the violation of morality and religion.' He added that 'for such a government they should entertain no respect whatever.' He repeated his injunction to keep within the law three times in the closing part of this speech,[35] and it would have been entirely alien to his whole outlook if he had not meant it. But at the same time he was very willing to frighten the authorities with the possibility of violence. On 22 June, he wrote to a supporter in Manchester: 'The Government is very much alarmed at the present state of the country, and any disturbance in the country would, I think, force the aristocracy to do something to conciliate the people. We are doing all we can to increase the uneasiness of the rascals.'[36] Cobden's speeches in the Commons at this time were certainly designed to create uneasiness in the authorities. If they had not been, he would have been failing in his duty to his constituents at Stockport which was one of the most disastrously afflicted towns in the kingdom. Whether he was giving timely warnings or uttering manacing threats depended on the point of view of the listener. But while it was one thing to emphasise what should have been a self-evident fact – that starving men might become violent – it was another to adopt, at a time of widespread popular unrest, a deliberate policy of discrediting the government. Cobden's aim was to encourage passive resistance among the tax-paying middle class as an alternative to popular violence. But his words, repeated, distorted and exaggerated by the League's propagandists and lecturers (who were of mixed quality) might equally well have been taken by the unemployed as an incitement to take matters into their own hands. He seems to have been too distraught to realise what a dangerous path he was treading. When serious violence did break out, he belatedly realised that it was no time for the League to be spreading its propaganda abroad.[37]

The simmering unrest became serious early in July, when colliers at Longton in Staffordshire, faced with a sudden cut in wages, stopped work and began marching from colliery to colliery throughout the Potteries, enforcing closure by raking out boiler fires and drawing boiler plugs. (Hence the name 'Plug Plot' given to these disturbances.) About the same time, attempts by cotton manufacturers east of Manchester to cut wages sparked off similar enforced closures of cotton mills, beginning at Stalybridge and moving on to Ashton-under-Lyne, Dukinfield, Stockport and neighbouring towns. By the second week in August, large bands of men armed with bludgeons, pikes and whatever else they could lay hands on were marching from town to town, forcibly closing down mines and mills, helping themselves to food and money, sometimes attacking public buildings, and meeting with very little resistance, except in Manchester, where the most dramatic confrontation between strikers and authorities took place.

The crisis in Manchester began on 9 August, with the arrival of 5000 to 6000 strikers, and lasted for a week. There were the usual closures of mills and factories and looting of food shops. At a huge open-air meeting on 11 August local Chartists urged the crowd not to give up; the Riot Act was read; and when troops appeared, with two six-pound field guns, the crowd dispersed. Later that day there were street skirmishes between soldiers and strikers, arrests and casualties.

Next day Absalom Watkin, a prominent Leaguer who had been busy swearing in special constables, noted in his diary that the coalman had told his wife there would be no more deliveries, they were now going to have the Charter, the soldiers dared not fire, and Manchester would be attacked from all quarters on the 16th.[38] But early on Sunday, the 14th, 500 Grenadiers arrived by train from London and marched through the town with fixed bayonets; later that day 700 more troops arrived from Dublin by way of Liverpool. On the 15th a conference of delegates representing 85 different trades met to extend and co-ordinate the general strike. But Manchester had become an armed camp, and on the 16th, the anniversary of Peterloo, the Chartists abandoned the procession they had planned to celebrate the occasion. Huge crowds flocked into the town, but the day passed off quietly. For the rest of the week the trade delegates continued to try to organise strike action, and Chartist national delegates, meeting in Manchester, issued a stirring proclamation in support of the strike. But the authorities' show of strength, together with the arrest of many leading Chartists and trade delegates, effectively destroyed the momentum of the strikers, both in Manchester and elsewhere. At their height in mid-August the disorders affected 15 counties in England and Wales and eight in Scotland.[39] From the last week in August to the end of September there was a steady drift back to work, and those who stayed out did so in the hope of wage increases, not for the sake of the Charter.

The role of the League before and during this turbulent time has caused much controversy, both at the time and since. Feargus O'Connor and other Chartists accused the Leaguers of deliberately plotting to provoke a breach of the peace by simultaneous lock-outs. In mid-July, a meeting of Chartists in Manchester sent Peel a memorial spelling out this accusation.[40] (This did not deter the government from suspecting Cobden of being in collusion with the Chartists, and authorising the opening of his letters.) But although prominent Leaguers – and not only Cobden and Bright – discussed privately the possibility of lock-outs, and on at least two occasions it was mentioned publicly, neither the investigations of hostile propagandists at the time, nor the researches of historians since, have uncovered any evidence to suggest that the League deliberately plotted to provoke the unrest. Tory as well as League manufacturers tried to reduce the wages they paid. Both the colliery at Longton and the cotton mill at Stalybridge, which initiated the series of wage cuts, were owned by Tories.

Once the disturbances had broken out, there was much debate in Newall Buildings on how the League should react to them. A special council meeting on 11 August decided – rather late in the day – that 'in the present excited state of the country' the League's lecturers should be withdrawn from all the manufacturing and disturbed districts.[41] At several subsequent meetings there were lively disagreements between those (like Bright) who wanted the League to show some public sympathy with the strikers, and those who felt it would be wiser to stand aloof. After Parliament rose on 12 August, Cobden – for reasons that are not clear – remained in London, although after two meetings on the 15th Wilson told him that his presence would have conduced much to their cordiality.[42] He was particularly requested to be present at the next meeting. He did not go, but he sent very emphatic advice by letter that the League should stay quiet,[43] and his views presumably helped to tip the scales in favour of caution.

But in spite of the League's refusal to make capital out of the disorders, in the eyes of many people – including members of the government – it was already at least morally guilty of fomenting unrest. It was not difficult to find evidence to support this charge. Some of the League's representatives, principally travelling lecturers, but even respectable businessmen, had spoken in ways likely to inflame their ill-educated audiences, many of them made too distraught by hunger and hardship – and even more by the sufferings of their families – to take a cool view of what they heard. The fervent and repeated denials of any mischevious intention, made by the *Anti-Bread Tax Circular* and prominent Leaguers, including Cobden, suggest a guilty feeling that the League had gone too far.

It is clear that Cobden was indeed terribly afraid that the League had suffered a damaging blow to its credit and reputation. When he told Duncan McLaren on 23 August that the 'spark fell upon a train ready for an explosion, and it might have come from any other quarter', he seems to have been implying that the spark had come from the League whose conduct, earlier in the letter, he had been less than completely honest in defending.[44] He had denied, on his honour, 'that the members of the League, or any one of them, ever contemplated – far less abetted – a turn out for the purpose of carrying the repeal.' They had not abetted such a step, but they had contemplated it. Two days later, he repeated this untruth at a crowded meeting of the League in Manchester[45] – so desperate was he, as he had told McLaren on the 23rd, to 'try to set ourselves right with the moral and religious part of the community', without whose support the League would surely fail.

To Cobden, the League had always been fighting for the workers as well as for their employers. But the paramount necessity of rebutting the charge that the League had been co-operating with the Chartists to promote violence forced him to identify the movement, publicly and unequivocally, with the middle class and its peaceful ways. 'I will admit', he declared to his Manchester audience, 'that so far as the fervor and efficiency of our agitation has gone, it has eminently been a middle-class agitation.' Meetings of nonconformist ministers, tea parties, 'obtaining the co-operation of the ladies' – these, he said, were the pacific, middle-class means they had used to spread their views.[46]

Peel was not impressed. On 26 August, he asked Sir James Graham to set up an inquiry into the League's activities. 'I cannot tell you how strongly I feel the advantages of a *thorough* exposure, *founded on proof*, of the Anti-Corn Law League.'[47] It was not difficult to compile a fat and damaging dossier from the speeches and activities of League members. It was written up into a long article by John Croker, the Tory politician and, after a final revision by Peel himself, was published in the December issue of the *Quarterly Review*. The article would have been more effective if it had been more coolly judicious and less violently polemical. In any case, by that time the excitement over the summer's disturbances had died down, and the indignation of the political world had been largely transferred to the activities of the Governor-General of India, Lord Ellenborough, in Afghanistan. But for the members of the League, the article must have been a timely reminder that in trying to walk a tightrope between passive and active reform, they had had a great fall. As a class, the manufacturers were not esteemed, by those either above or below them in the social scale; and when they apparently encouraged the workers to break the law, and then in their capacity as magistrates, arrested them for having done so, they appeared in a particularly inglorious light. It is fair to say that many of them, including Cobden, lost their balance because their faculties were clouded by the dreadful suffering they saw around them. But they knew that their cause had been lucky to escape any permanent damage, and they took care not to run such risks again.

Throughout this tumultuous year Cobden had very little time for either his family or his business. On 26 June, Kate produced a daughter, also called Kate. 'The nurse', reported Cobden to his brother, 'says it is a very fine baby – as usual.'[48] The knowledge that he now had two children to support as well as his wife must have increased his anxiety about the ability of the family firm to ride out the economic storm with only Frederick's indecisive hand on the tiller. 'I am exceedingly anxious', he wrote to his brother on 11 April, 'at your accounts of the state of the business. I see no other hope but in forcing down our stocks so as to have no money locked up unproductively.' He went on to discuss the problem of finding work for their employees and urged Frederick to try to get orders from Germany, Italy or Greece. As for the large family house in

Quay Street, he said it worried him night and day, and he would be glad to let it for an annual rent of £100 or even less.[49] Three months later, at the height of his parliamentary assaults on the government, he found time to go window-shopping in the West End, and afterwards exhorted Frederick to get hold of the muslin styles that were selling best at the very end of the season, 'as a cue for next season, for we seem to be thrown out rather – judging by the fashionable shop windows'.[50] A fortnight later, in a further letter discussing their business difficulties he complained flatly that everyone was wearing a particular sort of muslin, but they had none to offer.[51] The fact of course was that the firm needed Richard's constant supervision and he was far too involved in his public life to give it.

The events of the summer of 1842 strongly reinforced Cobden's disapproval of the Chartists. (They also greatly strengthened the Chartists' hostility to the League, whose members had been in the forefront of the forces of law and order.) When the crisis was still at a comparatively early stage, Cobden told Sturge that he had read an account of a meeting at Coventry where the 'fiendish spirit' of the Chartist speakers reminded him of Robespierre.

> Such scenes as that will drive the middle class and every man who has a shilling left into the arms of the aristocracy for protection. The Chartists don't seem to understand their real position. They direct all their attacks against capital, machinery, manufactures, and trade, which are the only materials of democracy, but they never assail the feudal aristocracy and the State Church which are the materials of the oligarchical despotism under which they are suffering. Fergus and his demoniacal followers seem bent on destroying manufacturers in order to restore the age of gothic feudalism.[52]

This forthright warning failed to make Sturge distance himself from the only other force which wholeheartedly pursued his political aims. Although Cobden continued to write to him with guarded encouragement, he had abandoned his earlier hopes that the Complete Suffrage Union might benefit the League's campaign. By mid-November he was telling Villiers it was quite clear 'that the Free-trade party has nothing to hope [for] from the suffrage people in any form, whether Chartists or "complete men"'. He suspected that the Chartists believed in socialism, and he had been told that Lovett, one of the more moderate Chartists, was opposed to the competitive principle. 'Poor Sturge', he concluded, 'will find himself acquainted with strange bedfellows.'[53]

It was indeed 'poor Sturge'. Presumably chastened by his close brush with the law in the summer, O'Connor* decided to recruit his movement's strength by the safer tactic of taking over the CSU (which a few months earlier he had been busily deriding) at its second conference in Birmingham at the end of December. O'Connor's superior skill in manipulating the composition and proceedings of the conference, combined with Sturge's tactless handling of the moderate Chartists, gave the temporarily united Chartist forces a complete victory. After he had been outvoted on the profoundly emotive issue of adopting the Charter by name, Sturge and his followers withdrew to another meeting place and tried to put their movement together again. But the CSU never recovered from this fiasco and within two years had entirely faded away.

Meanwhile, George Wilson and the other stalwarts of the League in Manchester, undeterred by the bad press they had recently received, organised fresh and, they hoped, more effective onslaughts on public opinion. The League's premises in Newall Buildings were enlarged. The division of the whole country into 12 regions, each with its own full-time League agent, was completed. From 1 December, the *Anti-Bread Tax Circular* was brought out weekly instead of every fortnight. A carefully organised scheme to deliver a a packet of League tracts to every parliamentary elector in the country was set up under the control of the new regional organisers. A new membership drive was started with the help of local members. A special effort was made in London, where the Metropolitan Anti-Corn Law Association was neither efficient at raising money nor amenable to advice from Manchester on how to do better. Cobden was not deterred by their touchiness. He sent their leader advice, instructions and encouragement – 'Your plan of agitating the railway passengers is admirable' – while assuring him that 'in invading the metropolis in *Manchr fashion*' the League headquarters only wanted to strengthen, not interfere with, the existing organisation.[54]

Finally, to finance its activities during the coming year, the League launched an appeal for £50,000. This was a startlingly large sum for those days, and for both practical and psychological reasons Cobden set the greatest store on reaching, and possibly surpassing, this target. Nothing, he felt, could more forcibly convince the monopolists that they must prepare to strike their flag.[55] To stir up enthusiasm, large committees of men and women met every evening in Newall Buildings to maintain a correspondence with supporters all over the country. On 31 October Cobden reported that they intended to keep it up without a holiday until Christmas. 'The steam

* O'Connor was among those arrested and brought to trial, but he was released on a legal technicality.

is fairly rising everywhere, and Manchester will heave up the moral strength of the country before Parl[iamen]t meets.'[56]

To encourage this desirable process, Cobden, Bright, Colonel Thompson and other prominent Leaguers spoke at meetings in northern and Midland manufacturing towns. These well-respected figures were much better able to draw the money out of men's pockets than were the ordinary League lecturers, and the League's finances profited accordingly. At the end of November, Cobden was getting ten invitations for every one he could accept, and wherever he went, several hundred pounds were raised for the League besides the instruction he was able to give.[57]

Cobden was not a very robust man and the pace at which he was living took a great deal out of him. 'I am leading a dog's life', he wrote on 2 December, 'being dragged about from place to place to be exhibited to all idle folks who choose to come and stare at me. I am in a vortex, whirled about at the will of others'.[58] By the end of the year he was feeling worn out from the effects of over-heated rooms and too much talking. He only hoped, he told George Combe, 'that the mainspring will keep the machine in motion till the meeting of Parliament, which' – he added ironcially – 'I look for as a season of relaxation.' Fatigue sapped his self-confidence, and he confided to his friend: 'In truth, circumstances, more of accident than design, have forced me into a position for which I feel myself neither physically nor mentally qualified.'[59] He may have been right to fear that he lacked the necessary physical stamina for his task. But that he possessed the necessary mental attributes was clearly demonstrated by his growing popularity on public platforms, his increasing ascendancy in the counsels of the League, and the combination of indefatigable enthusiasm and practical common sense with which he tried to guide its course.

By the beginning of 1843, the League had made a surprisingly successful recovery from the discomfitures of the previous summer, and Joseph Parkes, who had earlier thought that Cobden would never be able to 'keep up the balloon', gladly admitted that he had been mistaken. 'You are a most extraordinary agitator', he wrote; 'and you have the great quality of a leader of a public question, of sticking exclusively to your object.'[60] Parkes would probably have been surprised to learn that Cobden would have to stick to his last for three more years before his task was accomplished.

CHAPTER 7

Wooing the Farmers (1843–44)

Cobden began the new year of 1843 with a tour of Scotland, most of it in the company of Bright. Before setting out he warned Duncan McLaren in Edinburgh, that 'I have a great aversion to "scenes" got up for my own personal glorification; I am a very bad actor on such occasions, and I would much prefer to avoid a public exhibition of myself as the receiver of a compliment, which after all, is hardly due to me.'[1] But however much he tried to discourage personal compliments, he had by now become the well-known symbol of free-trade principles, and Edinburgh, Glasgow, Kirkcaldy, Dundee, Perth and Stirling all insisted on presenting him with the freedom of their burgh. After crossing the Firth of Forth by steamboat from Edinburgh to Kirkcaldy, Cobden reported to Kate that 'we were met by a crowd of people with a band of music and we walked up the beach in regal state between a couple of rows of people who cheered the Free Trade party heartily'. After holding a meeting and spending the night at Dundee, they arrived next morning at Perth. The Lord Provost had been given too little notice of their arrival to arrange a full-scale meeting, but he immediately improvised a ceremony in the council chamber at which Cobden was presented with the freedom of the burgh. Then on to Stirling in time for 'a splendid meeting', with a great landowner in the chair and plenty of farmers in the audience of about 1500.[2]

They set themselves to carry out a tight and tough schedule in severe winter weather, and not surprisingly both Cobden and Bright had to contend with heavy colds. In Edinburgh, Cobden was obliged to cancel a visit to Leith in order to stay indoors and cosset his cold with a hot bath. The more robust Bright kept going, but he described his cold as 'rather unfavourable to intellectual exertions', and himself as suffering from his incessant labours and lack of sleep.[3] However, it was worth the effort. Their reception was on the whole warmly encouraging, and although at the beginning of the tour Cobden had privately complained that the Glaswegians 'don't understand how to hold a business meeting for collecting cash, and care too much for speeches by mere politicians and Whig aristocrats',[4] by the end Scottish purses had made a very satisfactory contribution to the League's funds.

At the end of January, the League held a week of meetings and banquets to celebrate the opening of the first brick-built Free-Trade Hall, erected in St Peter's Fields on the site of the temporary wooden pavilion put up three years earlier.* The League had come a long way in little more than four years, but it had not been altogether successful in transforming itself from a provincial into a national movement; and for this reason it was decided during this week of celebrations that, since Manchester had the League's official conference hall, London should have its headquarters. But the prestigious new offices which were opened that spring at 67 Fleet Street with the maximum of publicity, were never much more than a facade.† The council stayed in Manchester, and Newall Buildings remained the real power house of the League.

Cobden made no public appearance during the celebrations in Manchester because of the sudden death of his baby daughter. For the same reason he was not in his place in the House of Commons when the new session was opened on 2 February. The occasion was overshadowed by the recent murder of Peel's private secretary, Edward Drummond, who was shot in Whitehall by a mentally deranged mechanic called Daniel Macnaghten, evidently in mistake for the prime minister. Drummond had been a family friend of the Peels, and Peel and his wife were profoundly distressed by his tragic death.[5] Political terrorism was only a vague, alarming possibility, not yet a fact of life. Like Spencer Perceval's assassin just over thirty years earlier, Macnaghten seems to have been moved solely by a personal grudge. But after all the wild talk and smouldering violence of the previous summer, it was easy enough to read sinister implications into Drummond's death.

---

* According to the historian of the League, Archibald Prentice, it was the largest hall in the kingdom apart from Westminster Hall. It was replaced in 1853 by a second Free Trade Hall.
† Many of the London free traders resented the arrival of the League. 'The League office', wrote one of them, 'is become perfectly horrible since the main body of the Goths and Vandals came down from Manchester; it is worse than living in a factory'. But after some bickering, the two groups of Leaguers managed to combine to carry out a successful fund-raising exercise in London. (see McCord, *The Anti-Corn Law League*, pp. 140–1)

Having arranged for Kate and their son to stay with friends, Cobden came up to London on 13 February and established himself in rooms at 8 Connaught Terrace. 'The lodgings are small', he told Kate, 'but the *landlady makes up in size for the rooms!*'[6] Almost immediately a severe inflammation of his right eye (apparently a chronic complaint) forced him to stay indoors. The Commons were debating a motion of Lord Howick's on the economic slump and social distress, which Cobden was extremely anxious to attend. On 16 February, he sent word to Villiers to fetch him down to the House if the 'distress' debate, then in its fourth day, were not adjourned. 'They sadly want *spunk* in their debates', he complained. 'I shall go right at Peel and Gladstone – the latter is open to a worrying.'*[7]

The following day Cobden was fit enough to attend the last instalment of the debate. He rose late in the evening and launched into a spirited demolition of the arguments that had been marshalled in support of the Corn laws. He then turned towards Peel and, in a speech that was to reverberate throughout the country for weeks, he embarked on a passionate denunciation of the Prime Minister. He told him unequivocally that he was responsible for the revision of the Corn law. 'You acted on your own judgment, and would follow no other, and you are responsible for the consequences of your act ... You passed the law, you refused to listen to the manufacturers, and I throw on you all the responsibility of your own measure ...' It was, Cobden went on, folly or ignorance to reduce the duty on drugs and such things while retaining a duty on sugar and corn. The Prime Minister said it was his duty to make an independent judgment.

> ... I must tell the right hon. Baronet that it is the duty of every honest and independent member to hold him individually responsible for the present position of the country ... I tell him that the whole responsibility of the lamentable and dangerous state of the country rests with him ... I say there never has been violence, tumult or confusion, except at periods when there has been an excessive want of employment, and a scarcity of the necessaries of life. The right hon. Baronet has the power in his hands to do as he pleases.

As soon as Cobden sat down, Peel jumped up and, without a trace of his usual remote calm, declared that Cobden 'has stated here very emphatically ... that he holds me individually responsible for the

---

* In his efforts to make a balanced reply to Howick on the first evening of the debate, Gladstone had allowed his burgeoning free-trade views to obtrude too obviously for the peace of mind of the Tory agriculturists. (Gash, *Sir Robert Peel,* p. 370)

distress and suffering in the country; that he holds me personally responsible; but … never will I be influenced by menaces … to adopt a course which I consider – '. By then the House was in an uproar and the rest of Peel's sentence was lost in the hubbub. Cobden tried to explain that he did not mean responsible personally but by virtue of his office. There were cries of dissent and Peel flatly contradicted him. Cobden gave up the attempt to make himself heard, while Peel conceded that he was not certain that the word 'personally' had been used.[8]

Although Lord John Russell declared that he and most of those who sat round him did not agree with Peel's interpretation of the member for Stockport's words, before the House adjourned Cobden insisted on explaining what he had meant. He had, he said, used the word 'individually' in the same way that the Prime Minister himself used the personal pronoun when he said, 'I passed the tariff'. 'I treat him as the government', Cobden added, 'as he is in the habit of treating himself.' Peel coldly accepted this scathing explanation, adding that he thought Cobden's words 'might have an effect, which I think many other gentlemen who heard them might anticipate'.[9]

For it was not really any blurring of the fine distinctions of parliamentary language that made Peel react so violently to Cobden's words. It was because he jumped to the conclusion that they amounted to an incitement to assassinate him. Only great personal strain, grief and loss, combined with the public atmosphere of unrest and incipient violence, would have led Peel to make the presumption. It was of course totally mistaken. Cobden was not afraid to bring the accusation into the open, expressing his astonishment at a public meeting that he, a member of the Peace Society and an opponent of capital punishment even for murder, should be accused of instigating assassination.[10] He was deeply angry, and Peel's inadequate withdrawal – as he saw it – continued to rankle for years.*

In his anger and agitation Cobden was guilty, in the privacy of a letter to his brother, of some unworthy gibes at the Prime Minister.[11] His considered justification for his attack on Peel was given in a letter to the mayor of Manchester, Sir Thomas Potter. He was, he wrote, convinced that the Prime Minister, who 'individualizes in his own person the powers of government', could do more than anyone else to destroy the system of monopoly which, in

---

* When Cobden sat down, the Dorset landowner, George Bankes, whom Cobden had roundly attacked for his treatment of his labourers, also jumped to his feet. The loud cries of 'Bankes' suggests that the House thought he had more to answer than Peel, and until it was alerted by Peel's extreme indignation, did not jump to the same conclusion as he had. (Prentice, *History of the Anti-Corn Law League*, II, p. 40.)

A PLEASANT POSITION.
SKETCHED IN THE HOUSE OF COMMONS, FRIDAY, FEBRUARY 17TH, 1843.

Cobden's view, was responsible for the country's economic and social ills. 'I should have been an unworthy representative of the people, and a traitor to the suffering interests of my constituents, had I failed in my duty of reminding him of his accountability for the proper exercise of his powers.'[12] It was in a way a backhanded compliment to the Prime Minister.

The unhappy affair received enormous publicity. The pro-government London press castigated Cobden for the alleged implications of his speech. *The Times* of 25 February, accused him of 'a reckless effort to fix and concentrate popular odium on the individual to whom he had ... reason for supposing such odium might prove fatal'. On the other hand, the responsible, law-abiding members of the League expressed their outrage at the nature of the attacks on their leader in meetings, addresses and personal letters to him. Cobden was pleased that everyone, whatever their political opinion, was reading his speech with great care in order to discover exactly what he had said.[13] But although he cheerfully told Frederick that 'my gossips at the Reform Club' complained that they could find nothing in the papers but 'biographies of R. Cobden',[14] he really very much disliked the personal notoriety that the affair had brought him.

> I dislike this *personal* matter for many good reasons public and private. We must avoid any of this individual glorification in future. *My* forte is – simplicity of action, hard working behind the scenes, and common sense in counsel, but I have neither taste nor aptitude for these public displays, nor to be 'starred' as a leader. The only good that I see arising out of the fracas of the 17th is that it has excited the Londoners a good deal who require something personal to rouse them.[15]

The enthusiasm of the Londoners was demonstrated a few days after the row in the Commons when they irrupted into a meeting of League deputies at the Crown and Anchor. Cobden described it to Kate as the most extraordinary scene he had ever seen.

> Not only was the large room crammed, but the entrance hall, stairs and passages also and thousands were unable to get in at all. As the people who were inside would not leave, we sent a detachment of lecturers into the entrance hall, who mounted a table and lectured the audience who crowded the hall, passages and stairs. There were two speeches going on at the same time, and the cheers of one meeting were occasionally heard by the other. My reception was very warm indeed ...[16]

A second meeting a week later again demonstrated that a larger meeting place than the Crown and Anchor could provide was urgently needed. Exeter Hall in the Strand, where appeals for many worthy causes were made, was refused to the League, so it was decided to hire Drury Lane Theatre for five nights in March and April for the sum of £300. Cobden and Bright both spoke on the first of these occasions on 15 March. Cobden described it as a 'most glorious meeting'. He told Kate that when he walked on to the stage, 'old hack as I am, I really felt *awed* at the assembly. From the floor to the roof it was one vast map of human heads. It seems as if the house were wainscoted (sic) with human faces.'[17]

How much the Londoners went to be entertained rather than instructed it is impossible to say. Cobden got no personal gratification out of speaking to huge public audiences, and his own preference was always to instruct rather than harangue or entertain. But he realised that if he was to keep his audiences year after year while hammering away at the same themes, he would also have to amuse and entertain them. When the long campaign was in sight of victory nearly three years later, he sent George Combe an apologetic explanation of the uncharacteristically rumbustious style he often felt obliged to adopt at large public meetings.

> You must not judge me by what I say at these tumultuous public meetings. I constantly regret the *necessity* of violating good taste and kind feeling in my public harangues. I say advisedly *necessity,* for I defy anyone to keep the ear of the public for seven years upon one question, without studying to amuse as well as instruct. People do not attend public meetings to be taught, but to be excited, flattered and pleased ... I have been obliged to amuse them, not by standing on my head or eating fire, but by kindred feats of jugglery, such as appeals to their self-esteem, their combativeness, or their humour. You know how easily in touching these feelings one degenerates into flattery, vindictiveness, and grossness.[18]

The process of instruction was continued in the House of Commons whenever the free traders could contrive an opportunity. The most important was provided by Villiers's annual motion for the immediate repeal of the Corn law. There was little new to say on the subject and, after four nights of debate, most of the House had had enough. Not so the free traders, some of whom, including Cobden, had not yet had their say. They knew that speeches made very late at night were inadequately reported and they insisted on another adjournment. The astonishing uproar which ensued reminded the reporter of the *Sun* of feeding time at a menagerie; although the example he gave came (more appropriately) from a farmyard: 'There was cock-crowing in its highest perfection, the bleat of the calf, the bray of the ass, the hiss of the goose, together with divers supplemental sounds, to which Mr Cobden did no more than strict and impartial justice, when he described them as being "the most extraordinary and inhuman noises" that he had ever heard.'

After the Prime Minister and Lord John Russell had left the House, 'the belligerents became fiercer than ever ... for nearly two hours, declamation roared while reason slept, and ... the voice of the Speaker was little more regarded than a whisper amidst a storm'. Numerous motions for adjournment were made and defeated, until at last the exhausted majority gave way and accepted an adjournment.[19] Such were the passions aroused inside Parliament by the threat to the Corn law, symbol of aristocratic, landowning dominance in a rapidly changing world.

The speech which Cobden delivered the following day was wide-ranging but designed especially to drive a wedge between landowners, on the one side, and tenant farmers and farm labourers, on the other. He argued that where the Corn laws did raise profits, the increase went into the landlord's pocket in the form of higher rent. The farmer had a right to ask what benefits he himself was supposed to get, and by how much the landlord had increased his rentals. When Colonel Wyndham laughed at this daring suggestion, Cobden continued:

> The hon. member for Sussex laughs, and truly it would be laughable enough were he to come to me to inquire into the profits of my business; but, then, he should remember that I do not ask for a law to enhance the profits of my business. He, on the contrary, is the strenuous supporter of a law which, in its effect – whatever may be its intention – benefits his own class and no other class whatever. This language, I dare say, is new to the House ... but it is the language I am accustomed to use on this subject out of doors, and I do not wish to say anything behind your backs that I am not prepared to say before your faces.[20]

He did not let them off lightly, and his speech (which was later widely circulated as a short pamphlet) aroused a good deal of comment. *The Times,* condescendingly making allowances for a man who had a repeat a tale 'for the nine hundred and ninety-ninth time', thought it was clever and pointed. The *Morning Post* thought it was full of 'miserable fallacies', described its author as a 'Manchester money-grubber', and castigated the spineless behaviour of his audience who 'listened in speechless terror to his denunciations'.[21] Cobden himself described his speech as 'like Cayenne rubbed in with vinegar. They would not have stood such a dressing a year ago'.[22]

When Villiers's motion was at last put to the vote, the number of its supporters rose from 90 (in 1842) to 125. Cobden was pleased. So also must Villiers have been, especially as he seems – the evidence is very exiguous – to have been going through a crisis of confidence, caused, presumably, by Cobden's growing reputation outside Parliament. Cobden may, as we have seen, have had some private doubts about Villiers as a parliamentary leader, but he had no intention of deliberately supplanting him. Before the opening of Parliament, he wrote to Villiers as if trying to end a tiresome discussion: 'Let it be once for all I entreat fully understood that I do not intend taking the initiative in any main question or motion upon the Corn laws. That rests with you.'[23] After Villiers had introduced his annual motion, Cobden defended its wording against Duncan McLaren's criticism. 'It could not have been stronger, and if you knew the clamor raised by the Whigs against it, you would not scold him.'[24] Yet in March Villiers complained bitterly to Joseph Parkes that his advice had been ignored and everything was being done to freeze him out.[25] The fact was that Villiers was going through the unpleasant experience of being replaced by an abler man, and no one could shield him from it. But to his credit he did not withdraw from the very active role in the anti–Corn law campaign that he had always played, both inside and outside Parliament.

The 1843 parliamentary session ended with Peel still unconvinced that the Corn law ought to go. In any case, it had begun to seem a less urgent issue. The run of bad harvests had been ended by a particularly good one the previous year, and it seemed likely that it would be followed by one almost as good. The protracted economic slump was at last ending and fewer men were out of work. Instead of the 'condition of England' problem, the government was faced with yet another recrudescence of what Peel called 'that great standing evil, which counterbalances all good, the state of Ireland'.[26] O'Connell's campaign to repeal the union was sweeping the country at an alarming rate, and although he kept his huge meetings on a tight rein and refrained from explicit threats, it was clear that the situation might easily slip out of control. Peel was firm but unprovocative, pouring in troops, but not banning the Repeal Association. Eventually, in October, O'Connell backed down from an open confrontation with the government, and was himself arrested. Yet another Irish crisis was safely surmounted.

While O'Connell was agitating Ireland, in England the League's best speakers were carrying their campaign to win over the farmers into county and market towns all over the country. Cobden began with a foray into the heart of the corn-growing county of Norfolk. Accompanied by Colonel Thompson and another League lecturer, Mr R. R. Moore, he arrived in Norwich on 31 March, and two days later sent Kate an ebullient account of their proceedings. He described their first meeting as 'a bumper' with

> about 4000 people in a large and magnificent Gothic Hall. For a long time the Chartists had prevented any public meetings from being held. They had upset bible, missionary, slavery and charity meetings, and driven the bishop and the sheriff from the Hall. They tried the same game with us under the guidance of a fellow from London, but we very soon put them down, and we left off with an unanimous and uproarious expression of approbation. Yesterday we met the farmers in the same place at 11. About 1200 persons were present, a large proportion of them real *live* farmers, some of them were pointed out to me from 28 miles off – I tickled them to a nicety, and never had a more gratifying meeting ... In the evening we had a second meeting with the working class to talk about machinery and wages, and it went off even better than the night before.[27]

At that time, Norwich had the choice of two weekly papers, one (the *Norfolk Chronicle*) strongly protectionist, and the other (the *Norwich Mercury*) equally strongly free trade. Both reported the speeches at all three of the League's meetings at enormous length, and reflected their political sympathies in their comments. According to the *Chronicle's* estimate, there were about 3000 at the first meeting, of whom fully one third were hostile. But it very fairly added that the speakers were listened to 'with considerable attention, being frequently interrupted with loud bursts of applause and occasional marks of disapprobation'. The *Chronicle's* report of the farmers' meeting next day was a classic exercise in damning with faint praise.

> The farmers present, with few exceptions, seemed convinced by the plausible assertions and the specious sophistry of the speakers, who ... tried to divest themselves of that violence by which they have been characterised in other places; and although we have much to offer in opposition to their opinions, we feel bound to say, that, if they had always clothed those opinions in language as moderate as that which they addressed to the meetings in Norwich, they would have stood freer from the imputation which now rests upon them, and which their assumed moderation will not enable them to shake off – of not being merely commercial and social reformers, but democratic revolutionists and political incendiaries.[28]

No such sinister suggestion appeared in the columns of the *Norwich Mercury*, whose reporter's description of Cobden's speaking style may be taken as typical of a basically sympathetic listener.

> It is impossible to converse with him [Cobden] for five minutes and not perceive the strength of his will and his just reliance on that sufficiency to his subject, which is so irresistibly impressive in his public addresses. The short, terse sentences into which he condenses his matter, ... carries conviction at once home to the hearer ... all that he said has been said months and years ago in this and every other liberal journal in the kingdom. But his power of selecting and concentrating the most striking parts with a conversational strength, brings every word within the easy comprehension of the most careless listener, and compels even the most unwilling to attend. To hear is to be convinced.[29]

When Cobden moved on to Yarmouth, huge crowds assembled both inside and outside the town hall and there was a move to adjourn the meeting out of doors. But when the mayor assured the uncomfortably crammed audience in the hall that the state of Mr Cobden's health would not allow him to address them outside, they agreed to stay where they were.

This was exceptional. The usual practice, whenever the crowd was too large for the local town hall, shire hall or assembly rooms, was to adjourn to the nearest suitable open space – field or market place – and improvise hustings out of farm wagons. Sometimes the protectionists displayed placards and advertisements urging the farmers to attend in order to witness the discomfiture of the Leaguers. Sometimes they told the farmers to boycott a meeting. Some landowners preferred to stay on the sidelines, sitting on their horses on the outskirts of the crowd and listening to the speeches. Others preferred to mount the hustings and debate with the League speakers. There was very little rowdiness or violence; much serious discussion and earnest questioning. The League, it was widely recognised, could no longer be expelled from the countryside by abuse and strong-arm tactics, but only by rational argument.

Cobden could not have too much of this. At Rye, where placards had warned farmers not to be misled by the fact that he was the son of a Sussex farmer, the meeting had to be moved from the town hall to the cattle market, but was described by Cobden as 'a very tame affair for want of any open spirit of opposition. The audience was almost as quiet as a flock of their own Southdowns'. But at dinner afterwards, he met some 'very large and intelligent farmers' and his discussion with them was by far the best part of the day's proceedings.[30]

By the end of the summer of 1843, Cobden and Bright and their colleagues, sometimes alone, sometimes in twos or threes, had between them covered a large part of the country. For much of the time Cobden's parliamentary duties restricted the range of his excursions from London, but with the help of the new railways (which did as much for the League's lecturers as the penny post did for its written propaganda) he made his way to Bristol, Lincoln, Lewes, Salisbury, Bedford, Winchester, Hereford, Colchester and many other towns.* Bright was able to range further afield, to the West country and Northumberland and Scotland, until towards the end of July he successfully fought a by-election at Durham, and took his seat in the House of Commons, where Cobden had always wanted him to be.

At this length of time one can only make a very rough guess at the impact of all this itinerant speech-making. It was not the unbroken series of triumphs that contemporary League historians claimed. There were some poorly-attended meetings, some audiences remained hostile, and debating discomfitures were not unknown. It would have been surprising had it been otherwise. Without any help from the League, the farmers had been made nervous about the future of the Corn law by the government's decision to reduce the duty on Canadian wheat. There were angry protest meetings and indignant letters in local papers.† Moreover, not all landlords were the selfish tyrants that League propaganda liked to portray. Some farmers enjoyed a relationship of mutual trust and respect with their landlords, and those who did not tended to be so deeply conservative by nature that they were not easily impressed by teaching that ran counter to their traditional ways of looking at things. On the whole it is probably safe to say that the League lecturers' successes outnumbered their failures, and in the circumstances this was a remarkable achievement.

For Cobden, the personal cost of his campaigning, in terms of family separation and neglected business, was high. He was by nature fond

---

* All classes were beginning to benefit from the railways. On 9 June, 1843, Cobden wrote to Kate from London: 'The Railways are bringing up the people from Manchester during the holidays at a cheap rate – 30/– here and back and allowing them 1½ days in the metropolis. One can't walk the streets without meeting the Lancashire chaps gazing about at the wonders ...' (BL Add. Mss, 50748)

† On 5 May, 1843, the *Lincolnshire Chronicle* published a letter from a Lincolnshire farmer to the 'Farmers of England', which declared that 'the stream of our fortune is careering away in an impetuous torrent towards the open gulf of Free Trade; we must stem it quickly, and with energy, or we are lost. We must stem it by our unaided efforts, as we have been deserted by out natural leaders ...' (Crosby, *English Farmers and the Politics of Protection 1815–52*, 129.)

of children.* However preoccupied with League affairs, the progress and upbringing of his own children (or child) was never far from his thoughts, and he did not let his wife lack good advice when he was away from home. From Edinburgh in mid-January he told her he was pleased to have such good accounts of the children. 'But the time is at hand when we must exercise great self-control in treating them. Our affection must be shown rather by wise management than exhibitions of transports of love. The little things will very soon begin to have their characters formed and we must take care that it (sic) is not spoiled by an exhibition of unreasoning kindness.'[31] A month later, when Kate was staying with the Ashworths after the death of her daughter, Cobden told her to take 'a lesson from Mrs Ashworth how to feed the little man and never let any more sweets enter his mouth'.[32] He also had views on his two-year-old son's intellectual nourishment, telling Kate that he had sent the boy a book, 'but I am by no means an advocate for his beginning too early to learn his letters. After all a learned child is nothing better than a learned prig. It is only when the intellect is tolerably matured that learning is of much use'.[33]

The long separations from his family fretted him so much that he sometimes imagined himself to be neglected and wondered whether Kate really told him everything she had been doing. He taxed her with failing to mention a visit which Bright said she had paid him in Rochdale. 'However', he added, to soften the implied rebuke, 'I suppose it is all my own fault, and it is therefore no use to complain.'[34] But a few days later he declared: 'It is quite impossible we can continue to live apart in this way. I would rather give up Parl[iamen]t than submit to an entire separation from *the boy* – to say nothing of a third party.' The trouble was that his lodgings in London were too small for wife, child and nurse, and he could not afford a house in London while still keeping up the large house in Quay Street, Manchester. He realised that as things were, he had much to excite and interest him, while she had the boy all to herself. 'But I am not satisfied with our mode of life, and I cannot settle into any plan which separates us for half the year.'[35] As a temporary expedient, early in June Kate moved into lodgings in Tunbridge Wells, where Cobden could more easily spend any spare time he could snatch from Parliament and his speaking engagements.

His business affairs came a poor third in his list of priorities,

---

* In May 1842, Cobden briefly visited Manchester, while Kate remained at Leamington. He and Frederick went to the theatre 'to see a pantomime and enjoy the treat of witnessing the glee of the school children who were in the seventh Heaven of delight at the wonderful tricks of harlequins and the roguery of the clowns'. (B.L. Add. Mss. 50748. to Kate, 1 May, 1842)

although it is clear they required more attention than sending his brother the occasional letter of advice and encouragement, or a report on the latest eccentricities of the London fashions. 'Your account is surely enough a bad turn up', he wrote on 17 August. 'There must be something radically fallacious in our mode of calculating cost or fixing prices ... We must have a rigid over-hauling of expenses, and see if they can be reduced; and if not, we must at all events fix our prices to cover all charges. I rather suspect we made a blunder in fixing them too low last spring.'[36] It may be doubted whether Cobden had given as much attention as he should have done to fixing the firm's prices. But he accepted his share of the responsibility, refused to fall into Frederick's state of despair, and insisted that in the improved economic climate they still had a chance of righting themselves.

By the autumn of 1843 the League was faced with a new problem: how to maintain interest in the issue of Corn law repeal when the steady improvement in industry and trade, together with another excellent harvest, made it seem less important. Cobden argued that the economic revival demonstrated the truth of the League's principles; the demand for clothes and other consumer goods had risen because food had been plentiful and therefore cheaper, and so people had more money in their pockets to spend on other things.[37] But with the appeal to men's compassion diminishing, it was all the more important to make a renewed appeal to their reason.

In the brief holiday that he allowed himself after Parliament had risen, Cobden, 'cogitating alone', worked out a new plan of campaign. 'I have a strong opinion', he wrote to Villiers on 2 September, 'in which I know you join, that we must now direct the whole efforts of the League to a thorough organisation of the electoral body.' Disillusioned with the existing House of Commons, he had determined that the League must set its sights on the composition of the next one. It was not enough just to distribute League propaganda to the 300,000 parliamentary electors; with the help of the penny post, a regular correspondence must be established with all of them. He also suggested that a new fund of £100,000 – twice as much as the previous one – should be raised and that the new propaganda campaign should be launched in London, not Manchester, so as to improve the League's image as a national organisation.[38]

The Drury Lane theatre was no longer available (the committee of shareholders had banned its further use for political purposes), but at the cost of £3000 the Covent Garden theatre was booked for 50 nights. On 28 September, the League's opening night, at least 5000 people packed into the huge theatre, to be instructed, edified and moved by a succession of speakers amongst whom, as usual on big League occasions, Cobden and Bright provided the star turns. When Cobden said that the League did not intend to recommend any further petitioning of Parliament, the entire audience rose to its feet, waving hats and handkerchiefs and cheering for several minutes. The *Morning Advertiser,* which published an enthusiastic account of the proceedings, wished that every member of 'the corrupt Commons' had been present to observe what the country thought of them.

In October, a by-election in the City provided an ideal focus for the League's campaigning operations in London, although that astute observer, Joseph Parkes, suspected that its battle-cry of 'total repeal' may have lost the free-trade candidate, Mr Pattison, as many votes as it gained him. However that may be, in the excitement of the contest several prominent City men were moved to declare themselves supporters of the League. Cobden took part in a mammoth rally for Pattison at Covent Garden, but by polling day he was wooing the farmers of Cumberland, Northumberland and East Lothian with Bright and Henry Ashworth. On 22 October, the day after the election, he arrived at Carlisle from Newcastle at 12 o'clock, and then waited on tenter-hooks until at three o'clock he heard the horn of the London mail carrying the welcome news that Pattison had come top of the poll.[39]

A few weeks later, Cobden and his friends had the satisfaction of reading *The Times's* condescending acknowledgment that 'the League is a great fact. It would be foolish, nay rash, to deny its importance'.[40]

It is very rare to find Cobden expressing anything but complete satisfaction with any public meeting organised by the League. But he regularly lamented its failure to make more of an impact in the other great medium of instruction – the public prints. 'The people up here', he wrote to Bright from Manchester 'think we are mere *snobs,* for want of literary champions.*'[41] The *Anti-Bread Tax Circular* was in effect the League's house magazine; it had little or no appeal for a wider audience. In the summer of 1843, when Cobden and his colleagues were discussing how to improve the *Circular,* James Wilson, George Wilson's elder brother, announced that he was thinking of starting a weekly free-trade journal himself. Wilson, who had already published an influential pamphlet in favour of repealing the Corn laws, believed that his paper would do more good if it

* Cobden is here using 'snob' in the now obsolete sense of belonging to the lower classes of society and having no pretensions to rank or gentility.

gave the League independent support without being avowedly its organ. But he did not want to proceed without the League's support or at least its acquiescence.[42] Cobden's initial fears that this venture might clash with the League's plans for an improved *Circular* were dispelled after a talk with Wilson, who made it clear that he was aiming at a different readership – 'the higher circles of the landed and monied interests' was Cobden's impression.[43] So the League Council, after a good deal of prodding from Cobden, gave Wilson its blessing and support. The first issue of *The Economist* appeared on 2 September, 1843, and towards the end of August the League Council unanimously decided to take 20,000 copies of the paper for distribution to leading Tories in Manchester and other Lancashire towns.[44] It was an ideal way of reaching, and perhaps influencing, those who would not dream of looking at any of the League's publications.

Meanwhile, the League's official paper duly underwent its facelift. From a small fortnightly journal, it became a large-size weekly paper. It was given a less provocative name, *The League,* and was published in London instead of Manchester. The first issue appeared on 30 September, but Cobden's comments three weeks later indicate that he was not entirely satisfied with the transformation. Two pages, he suggested, should be set aside for literature, and the reports of League meetings 'kept within bounds or the publication lacks variety'. Like all good journalists, he understood the importance of readability.

Early in the New Year of 1844, a League delegation descended on Scotland. After meetings in Glasgow and Edinburgh it divided, with Bright and Colonel Thompson proceeding westward, while Cobden and Moore made their way north to Perth and Aberdeen. League meetings were usually well advertised and organised in advance. But on the way to Aberdeen Cobden and Moore found themselves making an entirely unscheduled appearance.

> . . . in passing through Forfar we found all the inhabitants at their doors or in the streets. They had heard of our intended passage through their town, and a large crowd was assembled at the inn where the coach stopped, which gave us three cheers; and nothing would do but we must stop to give them an address. We consented, and immediately the temperance band struck up, and paraded through the town, and the parish church bells were set a-ringing, in fact the whole town was set in a commotion. We spoke to about two thousand persons in the parish church . . . It was the first time we ever addressed an Anti-Corn Law audience in a parish church.[45]

What the other coach passengers thought about their involuntary stay in Forfar, Cobden does not say. Nor can we tell whether the townspeople were aroused more by the man or the cause. But the incident illustrates the interest which either, or both, could now arouse.

Cobden and his companion set themselves a gruelling schedule of one-night stands, sometimes with a midday meeting thrown in as well. After holding two meetings in Aberdeen, for example, they were up at four next morning, travelled 35 miles (through a hard frost) to Montrose, held a meeting and continued a further 35 miles to Dundee where they held another meeting that evening. The financial reward for their exertions, although larger than on previous Scottish tours, was disappointing. On his way south through Edinburgh on 19 January, Cobden reported to his brother that 'we have had much cry and little wool – lots of enthusiasm and little money'.[46] He was back in Manchester eight days later, having finished his tour by a rather circuitous route south of the border through Sunderland, Sheffield, York and Hull. Not surprisingly, after nearly three weeks on the road he felt he had had 'a terrible fagging'.[47] But after barely two days rest, he was off to a meeting at Blackburn, then to another at Stockport, and finally, on 31 January, to a huge West Riding rally at Wakefield before catching the night train south for the opening of Parliament the following day.

The 1844 session of Parliament was a frustrating one for the Corn law repealers. As had been forecast, the previous year's harvest was excellent, and since September the price of wheat had fluctuated between 50s and 52s a quarter – lower than in all but seven of the previous 50 years. Trade and industry continued to revive, helped by the beneficial effects of the 1842 tariff reforms. Moreover, Peel's revised Corn law seemed to be working well, and in the debate on the Address he declared firmly that he was not contemplating any change in it.

In these circumstances, it was not easy for Cobden and Villiers to work up any interest in Corn law repeal in the House of Commons. But they did their best, and Cobden made one of his best parliamentary speeches when proposing an inquiry into the effects of protective duties on tenant farmers and farm labourers. His speech was distinguished for its quiet good sense, its methodical exposition of what was wrong with the present agricultural system, its firm insistence that the farmer's prosperity depended on that of the rest of the community who were his customers. He could not, he told the House, imagine anything more demoralising for the farmers than to be told they could not compete with foreigners without protection.

'You do not want acts of Parliament to protect the farmer – you want improvements, outlays, bargains, leases, fresh terms ...' If the farmer was encouraged to look to his own energies and capabilities he would be equal – perhaps superior – to any farmer in the world. (Peel, an enthusiastic advocate of more efficient and scientific farming, must have approved of this.) Turning to the plight of the farm labourers, Cobden claimed that he could not be accused of 'invidious feelings' towards agriculturists because he had always tried to expose, rather than hush up, the wretched conditions of many industrial workers. Quoting from the report of a Poor Law commissioner on rural living conditions in Dorset, Somerset, Devon and Wiltshire, which he said were typical of the whole of the British Isles, Cobden painted a harrowing picture of rural degradation and destitution. The landlords, he said, could not be blamed for the low rate of wages in their districts, but they were responsible for the gross overcrowding, the beastly hovels – 'worse than the wigwams of the American Indians' – on their estates.[48] The specific cases of hardship which he quoted were harrowing, but he spoke with a mildness and moderation that drew approving comments from several subsequent speakers. Gladstone, who had to answer Cobden's speech for the government, said privately later that he would have been glad to have made five sixths of it.[49]

Another listener to Cobden's speech, who could not help but approve of much of it, was Lord Ashley, dedicated factory reformer and an opponent (at first) of Corn law repeal. He had cancelled a public engagement that evening after Cobden warned him that he meant to attack agricultural conditions in Dorset where Ashley's father, the Earl of Shaftesbury, had large estates. As he listened, he could not resist raising a solitary cheer at Cobden's measured condemnation of Dorset landowners, and afterwards conceded privately that Cobden's speech was 'temperate and often true'.[50]

Cobden had developed an oddly ambivalent attitude towards Ashley. At first, like other northern manufacturers, he had felt little but contempt for the young southern aristocrat who was officiously meddling in matters about which he knew nothing. But after he had had a chance of observing him in the House of Commons, he realised that his philanthropy was completely genuine. This, however, did not incline him to overlook Ashley's failure to extend his philanthropy to the farm workers on his family estates, and in December 1843 he had asked Henry Ashworth to go down to Dorset for a week to collect 'a battery of facts which will enable us to turn the tables completely on Lord Ashley and Co. in the next session'.[51] Poor Lord Ashley knew perfectly well that Lord Shaftesbury was a thoroughly bad landlord, but as his father treated him with unrelenting hostility, there was absolutely nothing he could do about it. He was well aware of his apparent inconsistency and, at a dinner of the Sturminster Agricultural Society, he read the guests a mild lecture on the duties of landowners to their dependents. 'I ought not', he explained disarmingly, 'to be lynx-eyed to the misconduct of manufacturers and blind to the faults of landowners.'[52] The chief outcome of his speech was a row with his father which left their relations even worse than they had been. 'I am', he confided sadly to his diary, 'awfully posted between two forces: the Anti-Corn Law League on one side; my father on the other.'[53]

Throughout its long course, the Corn law controversy was regularly punctuated by tit-for-tat exchanges between landowners and manufacturers over the living and working conditions of their respective employees. It was an indirect way of discrediting an opponent's arguments through his alleged inhumanity. Conditions in the textile factories, whose owners were particularly well represented in the League, had for years been a target for philanthropic reformers, and Parliament had made several attempts to regulate the employment of children in them.* In 1843, Sir James Graham tried again. Unfortunately, he stirred up the ever-smouldering religious passions of the day by proposing to set up factory schools under predominantly Anglican control, but with provision for the teaching of other creeds. To Graham, it seemed obvious that the state Church should have general control over state schools, but to the Nonconformists the clause was part of a sinister plot to get the whole country's education into the hands of the Anglican Church. With meetings and petitions, they stirred up a tremendous outcry throughout the country. Lord Clarendon, Charles Villiers's elder brother, thought that with sixpenny-worth of sincerity and good faith the question could be settled in five minutes.[54] But he was too reasonable a man. The amendments which Graham made to the education clause after the bill's second reading, upset the Church without conciliating the Nonconformists. Eventually he withdrew the bill altogether.

Nonconformists were strongly represented in the League, and they joined enthusiastically in the outcry against Graham's education clause. Cobden, on the other hand, supported it, in spite of Bright's warning that he would lose every Dissenter's vote at the next

---

* The most effective, passed in 1833, banned the employment of children under nine, limited the hours of children under 13 to nine, and those under 18 to 12. For the first time, factory inspectors were appointed. Children under 13 were to attend school for at least two hours daily, but this provision was largely a dead letter.

election.[55] He did so, not because he himself was an Anglican, but because of his lifelong commitment to education. Although the bill was limited to children in textile factories and the education clause had defects, it was, he felt, a small step in the right direction, and he had hoped to improve it in committee if it ever got that far.[56]

When the Home Secretary reintroduced his Factory bill in March 1844, battle was joined, not over the education clause, which had been dropped, but over an amendment introduced by Lord Ashley which would have had the effect of introducing a 10, instead of a 12, hour day for workers between the ages of 13 and 18 years. Graham strongly opposed the amendment on the grounds – accepted by all parties to the controversy – that it would also inevitably shorten the hours of adult workers. He argued that the consequent reduction in wages would not be popular with the workers. Peel also opposed the amendment, arguing that it would cripple the country's economic expansion upon which its prosperity and social harmony depended. Ashley's amendment was, nevertheless, carried by 179 votes to 170.

Eventually, nearly two months later, the Factory bill was forced through Parliament without the 10-hour clause, but only after Peel had threatened to resign if it were lost. In the interval between the initial vote for Ashley's amendment and the passage of the bill without it, the Short Time Committee, which for more than a dozen years had been periodically agitating for a 10-hour day, mounted an impressive campaign for Ashley's amendment, while manufacturers' delegates met in Manchester to oppose it. At Westminster the parties were sharply divided on the issue. Charles Greville could not remember 'a more curious political state of things, such intermingling of parties, such a confusion of opposition'.[57] Some Whigs and Radicals – for example Bright, who savagely attacked Ashley – supported the government, while a good many Tory gentlemen opposed it, partly out of genuine humanitarian motives, but also partly out of hostility to the manufacturers as a class, and to their organisation, the Anti-Corn Law League. Peel and Graham, indeed, feared that a successful 10-hour amendment would have gravely weakened the relations between the two classes, and led to a renewed onslaught on that symbol of the landowners' dominance, the Corn law. Graham went so far as to say it would not survive another 12 months if Ashley was successful.[58]

During all the debates on the Factory bill Cobden spoke only once, to oppose Ashley's amendment. He argued that the only practical way to reduce hours without reducing wages was a policy of free trade which would lead to increased production and higher wages. Notwithstanding all the evidence to the contrary produced by the Short Time Committees, he insisted that the workers did not want shorter hours.[59] However misguidedly, both Cobden and Peel were genuinely concerned with the interests of the factory worker, as they saw them. Peel had been told by an experienced factory inspector that wages would drop by a quarter if hours were reduced to 10, and he told the Commons that there was no simple choice between mammon and mercy.[60] Two years later, in 1846, when Ashley tried again (unsuccessfully) to make 10 hours compulsory, Cobden told the reformers that they should introduce a little head as well as heart when dealing with this question and not assume that their opponents had no compassion.*[61]

Where factory reform was concerned, Cobden himself did not find it easy to follow the dictates of his head – which may have been partly why he did not take as prominent a part in the debates on this subject as a Manchester manufacturer might have been expected to do. In 1842 the government published a startling report, reinforced with harrowing illustrations, of an inquiry into conditions in the coal-mines. Shortly afterwards, Ashley introduced a bill to ban the employment underground in the mines of women, girls, and boys under 10 years old. When he had finished his speech, Cobden crossed the floor, sat down by him, and after wringing his hand, said: 'You know how opposed I have been to your views; but I don't think I have ever been put into such a frame of mind in the whole course of my life, as I have been by your speech.'[62] He compromised between his principles and his feelings by abstaining on the bill.

In 1845, Ashley turned his attention to calico printing, which was not yet regulated at all and where, according to a government report, young children were sometimes required to work up to 18 hours a day. This was of course getting very near the bone for Cobden. By the standards of the day, he was a model employer, but more than a quarter of the work force at the Crosse Hall print works in February 1845 were children between the ages of eight and 13, and there were even a very few who were only seven.[63] When Ashley introduced a bill to regulate the employment of children in calico print works, Cobden complained that the public would be led to think that there was 'something peculiarly demoralised about the printers of calico'. He could not resist pointing out that whereas in print works children worked in a mild climate, under cover, for 3/– a week, in agriculture, he believed, they worked for only 1/6d and were exposed to all weathers.[64] But he did not, as Ashley had anticipated, launch a

---

* A bill to limit the hours of women and young persons to ten was at last passed in May 1847. Cobden was abroad at the time, but he was still against it because it would also limit men's freedom to work as long as they liked. In fact, employers were able to get round the Act by introducing a relay svstem. This was banned in 1850.

'dreadful onslaught' on the bill,[65] partly because the Home Secretary, who was distinctly unenthusiastic, had left him little to say, and
partly because – as he put it in a letter to his brother – 'I thought it
best not to take up the position a champion of my class, with a view
to my standing on other questions'[66] – by which of course he meant
the Corn laws. After Ashley's bill had been modified in accordance
with Graham's wishes, it was passed without any divisions. According to Ashley, Cobden gave it 'positive support'[67]; and since it
went no further than banning the employment of children under
eight, and night work for women and children between the ages of
eight and 13 years, he cannot have found that very difficult.

In principle, Cobden could not accept the right of the state to
interfere in the way one man ran his business, or restrict the right of
another to dispose of his labour as he thought fit. He commented
adversely on the '*socialist* doctrines' behind the 1844 Factory Act.[68]
But he accepted that children, being too young to protect themselves, must be protected by law from economic exploitation.[69]
Protecting the child, however, often had the effect of restricting the
adult's right to work as long as he liked. Cobden could not resolve
this dilemma. Instead, he took refuge in pointing out that economic
necessity often made parents as guilty of exploiting their children as
employers, if not more so; and if society was in such a state that
parents were willing to work their children almost to death, then
society must be improved by, among other things, making the
necessities of life cheaper – in other words, by repealing the Corn
law.[70] For Cobden, most issues came round to the Corn law in the
end.

Cobden described the 1844 parliamentary session as 'unprofitable'.[71]
The free traders had not helped themselves by seriously falling out
with the Whigs; 'we are at war to the knife with the Whig politicians',
Cobden reported to Wilson in April.[72] One reason was the League's
too pertinacious lobbying of Whig MPs, including Thomas Macaulay. Another was its interference in recent by-elections, which had
benefited nobody but the Tories. The breach was widened when
about a dozen free traders, led by Cobden, supported Peel's proposal
to reduce the imperial preference enjoyed by colonial sugar. The
government was defeated on a hostile amendment moved by a Tory
protectionist. But with the crucial help of the free traders' votes,
Peel successfully moved a second amendment which in effect re-
versed the first. The Prime Minister had threatened to resign over
the issue, and Cobden was sharply criticised in some of the Whig
journals for sticking to his principles at the expense of party advan-

tage.* He was equally disgusted with the Whigs – 'It is really too bad to see the Whigs combining with the *ultra protectionists* against the Government for merely factious and party purposes.'[73]

Macaulay had fallen out with his League constituents in Edinburgh because they would badger him to support the total and immediate repeal of the Corn law, while he was convinced that a fixed duty (instead of a sliding scale) was the most that could be hoped for in the immediate future.[†] He was of the opinion that the League overestimated its influence. 'It is easy', he told Duncan McLaren,

> for the members of any Anti-Corn Law League to deceive themselves about their strength. They are generally inhabitants of great towns. Everybody with whom they converse is for Free Trade. If they attend a meeting on the subject of the Corn laws, they see every hand held up for total and immediate repeal. No supporter of the sliding scale, no supporter of a fixed duty, can obtain a hearing. It is not strange that even people so intelligent as my constituents should go home from such meetings with the conviction that the voice of the nation is the voice of the League, and that the good cause is on the point of triumphing. I am certain that you deceive yourselves.[74]

Cobden would have regretfully agreed. His correspondence was no longer sprinkled, as it had been in the early days of the movement, with jubilant prophecies of the League's imminent success. There was too much evidence to the contrary. The assiduous efforts of the League's lecturers during 1843 seem not to have made much permanent impression on the farmers, even when they had seemed successful at the time. Moreover, the campaign to educate the electorate, launched with high hopes the previous autumn, had been hampered by lack of funds and made disappointing progress. Cobden was forced to realise that the walls of the fortress of monopoly were not going to fall down at a few blasts of the League's trumpets. '*Time* alone can effect the business', he told his brother early in June. They had been wrong, he added, to think they could carry it by storm. At any rate – he anticipated optimistically – the League's change of gear would make his own life less hectic, and he

---

* On 24 June, Cobden wrote to Duncan McLaren: 'The "Tadpoles and Tapers" (read Coningsby) have been guiding nearly all the editorial pens of the "liberal" press for the last week against us.' *Coningsby* was published in May 1844, so Cobden had lost no time in reading it. (Cobden Papers, 71)

[†] On 26 June, Macaulay did reluctantly vote for Villiers's motion for total and immediate repeal. According to Bright, he spent the preceding hours of debate stretched out on a bench up in the gallery, either asleep or pretending to be. (Trevelyan, G. M. *John Bright*, p. 122)

would be able to give more time to his private affairs, 'which, Heaven knows, have been neglected enough'.[75]

His most urgent priority – at least in his own eyes – was not his business, but a permanent home to replace the house in Quay Street, which his brother-in-law, John Sale, had managed to let the previous August. 'What shall we do with ourselves?', he had then asked his wife.[76] The question was still without a permanent answer in June 1844, and was not finally settled until the following April, when the Cobdens, who by then had another baby daughter in addition to young Richard, moved into a large corner house in Park Crescent in the Manchester suburb of Rusholme.

Circumstances had not helped the League's campaign in the countryside. Many farmers were in financial difficulties after the bountiful harvest of 1843 had brought down prices, and although the League could hardly be blamed for the workings of nature, the farmers' general sense of grievance must have encouraged the beginning of an organised movement against the League during the winter of 1843–44.* It was started by an Essex tenant farmer, Robert Baker, who formed a local Agriculture Protection Society. Baker's initiative was immediately supported by aristocratic landlords, led by the Duke of Richmond; a central office was set up in London; and by March 1844 nearly 100 societies had been formed in various parts of the country. 'I am glad', wrote Lord Willoughby's bailiff in Lincolnshire, 'to see that the agriculturists throughout Lincolnshire are now aware of the danger they stand in from Mr Cobden and the "League".'[77] Cobden and his associates naturally did their best to belittle the 'Anti-League', claiming that it was really nothing but a ploy by the landlords to protect their monopoly by means of their tenants. This was unfair to the farmers, who were certainly active in some districts in promoting Anti-League societies, although modern historians have found it hard to agree on the respective roles of farmers and landlords in the societies as well as on the importance of the movement as a whole. In any case, whatever they might say in public, Cobden and Bright were thoroughly discouraged by their

---

* There was a spate of rick-burnings in the summer of 1844 by unemployed farm labourers who had fallen victim to their employers' economies. In one of his speeches, Cobden cited the case of a Suffolk man, James Lankester, who had read that wages rose and fell with the price of corn, and that the price of corn rose and fell according to whether it was scarce or plentiful. So he had set fire to Farmer Hobbs's stacks and was to be transported for life. He knew, said Cobden, there was a difference in law, but what difference in principle was there between creating an artifical scarcity by stopping imports and by setting fire to Farmer Hobbs's stack? (Prentice, *History of the Anti-Corn Law League,* 11, pp. 224–5.)

failure to make more of an impact on the farmers, and by April 1844 had privately agreed to abandon them as 'hopeless' and concentrate their efforts on the boroughs.[78]

The League's task in the boroughs was not only to win over the voters, but to make sure that the right to vote of its supporters could not be questioned. The electoral laws were complicated and full of loopholes.* Some voters did not realise they had a vote, others did not bother to register their claim to one. It was common practice for the local organisations of both Whigs and Tories to manipulate the electoral laws to increase their voting strength and to find flaws in their opponents' voting qualifications. The League was well placed to play the same game, because the distribution of its literature to electors made it necessary for every League agent to study the voting registers and maintain an up-to-date record of the electoral situation in his own district. He could also discover each voter's political loyalty which, before the introduction of the secret ballot, there was no point in hiding. Throughout 1843 the League had expanded its efforts to place free traders on the electoral registers and to expel protectionists. But by the spring of 1844 Cobden was not at all satisfied with the progress made. 'Depend on it', he assured the long-suffering and hard-working George Wilson, 'we must work more to a point and upon a system. A great deal of random firing has been kept up, and now the smoke blows off and discloses the two contending armies in nearly the same positions as regards their numbers at the poll as two years ago – *We have made less real progress than we imagined*. But there is a great am[oun]t of opinion going astray which we may gather into our fold with a little careful shepherding.'[79]

Renewed afforts were made to prevent opinion 'going astray'. Sometimes a delegation from the League would visit a borough and stir up the local free traders to apply themselves more energetically and methodically to the electoral registers. Sometimes the stirring up was done through the post. (Cobden impressed upon Wilson the importance of *writing* to supporters because people did not pay much attention to *printed circulars*.[80]) Sometimes agents, of varying quality, were employed to organise the scrutiny of the registers. Progress was made, but not enough to prevent the League from losing several

---

* The 1832 Reform Act for the first time laid down systematic arrangements for compiling official electoral registers and for keeping them up-to-date through special 'revising barristers' and annual registry courts. In the boroughs, the occupier, as owner or tenant, of a property with a rateable value of £10 was entitled to vote provided he fulfilled certain conditions. In the counties there were four main categories of voters, with freehold, copyhold, leasehold and occupational qualifications, but there were hundreds of different ways of describing these qualifications.

by-elections that summer, and not nearly enough to satisfy Cobden. So in the autumn of 1844 the League turned its attention to the county seats and launched a new campaign to build up its voting strength in those strongholds of the aristocracy.

It is not clear who first realised that League supporters could qualify for a county vote by acquiring a 40/- freehold. But whoever it was, Cobden at once realised the potential of the device and pushed it with the whole force of his authority and enthusiasm. At a great meeting in the Free Trade Hall on 24 October, he pointed out that freehold properties worth 40/- a year, which gave a man a vote in the counties, could be multiplied more or less indefinitely. 'I think', he added, 'our landlords made a great mistake when they retained the forty-shilling freehold qualification; and, mark my words, it is a rod in pickle for them.' Realising no doubt that a good many of his audience would have qualms about using that particular rod, Cobden presented the matter in the light most likely to appeal to them: 'It is the custom sometimes for many to put their savings into the savings' bank. I believe there are fourteen or fifteen millions or more so deposited. I would not say a word to lessen the confidence in that security, but I say there is no investment so secure as the freehold of the earth, and it is the only investment that gives a vote along with the property.' He even suggested that a parent might teach his grown-up son the virtues of thrift, not by opening an account for him in a savings bank, but by laying out £60 or so on making him a freeholder – thus giving him the status of an independent freeman and placing him, electorally speaking, on the same footing as the biggest landowner in the country.[81]

Although this method of making votes was not actually illegal, not everyone saw it in the same estimable light that Cobden did. And when the League, warming to the work, proceeded to buy houses, divide their ownership into shares (the owners of which would qualify for a vote by receiving at least 40s in rent from the actual tenant), many contemporaries felt it had crossed the shadowy line between what was permissible in electoral manipulation and what was not.* Cobden, however, had no qualms, and since residence was not a necessary qualification, he bought a part share in a house in Brighton so as to obtain a vote in his native Sussex. The legal work for this and similar purchases was carried out by solicitors employed by the League; and by 1845 an impressive administrative apparatus had been set up in two special offices, in London and Manchester, for checking the registers and buying freehold qualifications.[82]

* In the past the device had been widely used and widely condemned. It had been prohibited in the first and second Reform bills in March and June 1831, but not in the final Reform Act of 1832.

The scrutiny of the county registers was pursued with aggressive – and sometimes, it seems, rather slapdash – zeal; 23,000 objections were posted by the League's Manchester office (incidentally swamping the local post office) on 24 and 25 August, 1845, the last days on which they could be lodged for that year's registers.[83] Of course, it was a game that two could play, but the League claimed that the combined effect of opponents purged and friends added, either by taking up existing qualifications or buying 40s freeholds, was always to improve its numerical position on the register.

In 1846 a judgment by the Lord Chief Justice, in a test case brought by the Tories, removed the shadow of illegality that had hung over the practice of buying and dividing properties in order to create votes. Sir Nicolas Tindal ruled that: 'The object of increasing the number of freeholders at a county election is not an object, in itself, against law or morality, or sound policy.'[84] But by that time the battle was nearly over, and it was never necessary for Cobden to demonstrate in the general election, due in 1847, how effective the 'tremendous engine' of the 40s freehold could be in unseating protectionists.[85]

CHAPTER 8

Repeal (1845–46)

By 1845 Cobden had overcome the more or less open hostility with which he had had to contend during his first years in the House of Commons. The quiet reasonableness with which he usually spoke appealed to the House, which gradually realised that beneath the northern manufacturer was a very likeable man. He was by nature friendly and good-humoured, entirely without pomposity, and much more inclined to a friendly than an abrasive approach. 'Strange as it may sound', he wrote to a friend in May 1845, 'I am on the most cordial terms *now* with all parties in the House, and especially with those ultra monopolists who 3 years ago would have skinned me alive.' He added that Lord Ashley (who was too saintly to bear him malice for his attacks on Dorset landowners) had just assured him that he was the most popular man in the House.[1] Like most people, Cobden liked to be liked. In his case it had the added advantage of usually securing him an attentive audience. By contrast, his combative and intolerant friend, John Bright, whose manners (in Ashley's too fastidious opinion) made him almost unfitted for educated society,[2] cared nothing for the good opinion of his political opponents – or for that of his nominal political allies, the Whigs, either. His penalty was often an unreceptive, and sometimes a noisily hostile, audience.

Not long before Parliament reassembled for the 1845 session, Cobden told one of the League's huge meetings in Covent Garden that he had spent the past two months visiting nearly all the principal towns in Yorkshire and Lancashire, and had seen much prosperity where four years ago there had been great distress. But his meetings, he claimed, had been larger and more enthusiastic than during the worst of the economic recession because in the interval people had been able to see for themselves that when abundant harvests brought

PAPA COBDEN TAKING MASTER ROBERT A FREE TRADE WALK.

7 *Punch*, Vol. VIII, 1845.

down the price of bread, wages did not automatically follow.[3]

Peel, brooding over the country's finances, saw that another of the free traders' theories had also been proved correct: in the long run, lower tariffs made for more, not less, revenue. So in his budget speech on 14 February 1845 he took another big bite at the cherry of tariff reform; import duties on more than half of the remaining dutiable articles (mainly cotton and other industrial raw materials) were abolished; so were export duties on British goods; the import duty on sugar was reduced; and to compensate for the temporary loss of revenue, the hated income tax was extended for three years. It was not a budget the Whigs and free traders could seriously oppose, however much they might rail at the 'inquisitorial' nature of the income tax. And according to Greville, Peel's own supporters were too crestfallen to resist,[4] although during the budget debates several of the more extreme country gentlemen referred indignantly to the Prime Minister's deafening silence on the subject of agriculture and its problems.

Agriculture was indeed the only important sector of the economy not to share in the return of prosperity, and farmers' delegations from all over the country made their way to Whitehall to complain to the Prime Minister that they could no longer pay their rents, or only by digging into the remains, if any, of their working capital. Cobden and Bright, apparently discarding their view that the farmers were 'hopeless', felt encouraged to make another effort to win them over. Bright led the way, on a slightly peripheral front, with an attack on the Game Laws. Designed to preserve game for the benefit of sporting landowners, they caused the wholesale destruction of farmers' crops by marauding pheasants and rabbits. Bright, moved by honest indignation, had done his homework with devastating thoroughness, and he presented his case so well and – for once – so moderately, that he got a committee of inquiry without further ado*. 'Bright did his work admirably', wrote Cobden afterwards, 'and won golden opinions from all men. His speech took the squires quite aback.'[5] He himself made a short speech supporting everything that Bright had said. Sensing the discomfiture on the benches opposite, he commented mockingly that the country gentlemen seemed to know less about the farmers' feelings than did the members of the 'much-maligned' League.[6]

A fortnight later Cobden moved for a committee of inquiry into the agricultural distress and the effect of protection on the rural classes. He prepared himself with particular care, asking a well-known Hertfordshire farmer and free trader, Mr Lattimore, to come

---

* The select committee confirmed Bright's allegations, but it was not until 1880 that the Ground Game Act was passed to protect tenant farmers.

up to London to brief him. But he was still unusually nervous about
the speech he had to make. Two days beforehand he told Kate he was
'quite in a fidget' about it. 'You will think it very strange in an old
hack demagogue like me, if I confess that I am as nervous as a maid
before her wedding. The reason is I suppose that I know a good deal
is expected from me, and I am afraid I shall disappoint others as well
as myself.'[7] Two days later, when he got up to speak, he was still 'all
in a maze'. He then proceeded to make one of the best speeches of his
career. With facts, figures and apposite examples, he made a careful,
moderate analysis of the agricultural industry, demonstrating that
what it needed was not protection, but more capital with which to
modernise farming methods and make use of technological improvements to raise productivity. He spoke so knowledgeably that some
of his listeners thought he must be a practising farmer himself and
asked him afterwards where his estate was.

Unlike many of the new breed of businessmen, Cobden did not
ignore or dismiss the past; he was too interested in it for that. On this
occasion he tried to link the past with the present and the future, in
order to persuade the country gentlemen – in his characteristically
conciliatory way – that it was both their interest and their duty to
shake off the old ways and come to terms with the new.

> You have been Englishmen. You have not shown a want of
> courage or firmness when any call has been made upon you. This
> is a new era. It is the age of improvement, it is the age of social
> advancement, not the age for war or for feudal sports. You live in
> a mercantile age, when the whole wealth of the world is poured
> into your lap. You cannot have the advantage of [both] commer-
> cial rents and feudal privileges; but you may be what you always
> have been if you will identify yourselves with the spirit of the age.
> The English people look to the gentry and aristocracy of their
> country as their leaders. I, who am not one of you, have no hesi-
> tation in telling you, that there is a deep-rooted, an hereditary
> prejudice, if I may so call it, in your favour in this country. But
> you never got it, and you will not keep it, by obstructing the spirit
> of the age. If you are indifferent to enlightened means of finding
> employment to (sic) your own peasantry; if you are found ob-
> structing that advance which is calculated to knit nations more
> together in the bonds of peace by means of commercial inter-
> course ... why, then, you will be the gentry of England no
> longer, and others will be found to take your place ...[8]

When Cobden sat down, Peel, who had been listening intently,
crumpled up the piece of paper on which he had been making notes
and whispered to his neighbour, Sidney Herbert: 'You must answer
this, for I cannot.'[9]

But it did not need Peel's failure to rise to the challenge of Cobden's speech to alarm his supporters about the course he seemed bent on pursuing. For some time Peel had seemed indifferent to the paramount importance – as they saw it – of preserving the dominance of the landed interest in English society. He had also clearly announced his conversion to the principles of free trade in his speeches, and to its practice in two reforming budgets, the second of which was still passing through Parliament. How soon would it be before corn was exposed to the chill blasts of foreign competition?

In another debate on agriculture, initiated this time by a Tory backbencher, the landed interest made a concerted effort to ward off that evil day. In particular Disraeli, who had begun a deliberate bid to wrest the leadership of the Tory party from Peel, made a scathing attack on the leader who – he sneered – was now spurning the country gentlemen whom, when in opposition, he had courted and flattered: '. . . For my part, if we are to have free trade, I, who honour genius, prefer that such measures should be proposed by the hon. Member for Stockport, than by one, who through skilful Parliamentary manoeuvres, has tampered with the generous confidence of a great people and of a great party.' Disraeli ended his speech by declaring, amid cheers and laughter, that in his opinion a Conservative government was an organised hypocrisy.[10] The House of Commons neither liked nor trusted Disraeli, but it could not help enjoying his speeches. Next day, Sir James Graham, a born pessimist and fond of expressing his misgivings in melodramatic terms, reported to the Lord Lieutenant in Dublin on the bad mood of the government's supporters. 'The House is surcharged with Electric Fluid and an explosion after Easter is quite possible.'[11]

The explosion, when it came, was sparked off, not by free trade, but by religious prejudice. In Ireland, O'Connell's repeal movement was a spent force and Peel, anxious to conciliate Irish opinion, decided to introduce some educational reforms. The college at Maynooth, set up in 1795 to educate Catholic priests, was seriously under-financed, and one of Peel's measures proposed to increase the annual government grant to the college from about £9000 to £26,000, and to give a special building grant of £30,000. Although no new principle was involved, the bill rasped two raw nerves in English society. One was the nonconformists' fanatical horror of any state subsidy for religion – any religion. The other was the ancient phobia about 'popery', which had been given a new lease of life by, among other things, the widespread exasperation at the continued unrest in Catholic Ireland, as well as by the extreme alarm of evangelical Anglicans at the 'Romish' tendencies revealed in Oxford by the Tractarian controversy. When the terms of the Maynooth bill became known, the storm of protest was overwhelming. More than 10,000 hostile petitions flooded into the House of Commons; a huge anti-Maynooth conference assembled in London; and *The Times* repeatedly attacked Peel in articles described by Greville as 'as mischievous as malignity could make them'.[12] The prime minister thought the government might fall, but he had no intention of giving way.

Many of the most influential members of the Anti-Corn Law League were nonconformists who disapproved of state funding of education as passionately as they had disapproved of the education clause in the Factory bill two years earlier. Cobden was even less disposed to give way to them now than then. In his opinion the 'outburst of fanaticism' over Maynooth was, in 99 cases out of a 100, simply a revival of the old no-popery spirit. 'It is pretty evident, I think', he wrote to his agent in Stockport, 'that in matters of religious toleration the government is in advance of Parliament, and the latter is ahead of the people.'[13] His Stockport constituents were well in the rear and sent him an anti-Maynooth petition. Cobden duly handed it in, afterwards explaining to one of them why he could not agree with it. 'It is . . . difficult to deal with *Irish* questions on *English grounds*. The state of the country is such that I should be willing to do anything short of a violation of a great principle to conciliate its unhappy people. The question now before us is not one of principles. Everybody concurs in voting the smaller sum. I vote for the larger in order to conciliate the Irish nation.'[14] The Commons spent six evenings debating the second reading of the Maynooth bill. Cobden, refusing to take refuge in a 'silent vote', spoke on the last evening. He tried to introduce some cool common sense into the debate, pointing out that they were not discussing a religious issue, but simply an extended educational grant. For about 12 years Ireland (unlike England) had had a moderately successful national system of non-sectarian elementary education. Cobden asked the Commons why, if they were ready to provide elementary instruction for Irish farmers, shoemakers and tailors, they refused a comprehensive liberal education to those who were to be these people's spiritual leaders. But it was the tragic state of Ireland that influenced his vote most deeply.

> I know I am taunted by some of my friends with giving a bad vote on this occasion. I shall give a conscientious vote, and if in doing so I am to make personal sacrifices, and lose the good opinion of those with whom I have acted and have a deep respect for, I shall regret it, but next to the satisfaction of having acted conscientiously, will be that [satisfaction] I shall feel in voting for that which I believe will tend to heal the festering wounds of Irish society.[15]

The Maynooth bill passed its second reading very early on 19 April by the surprisingly large majority of 147. The delegates at the anti-Maynooth conference were stung into even more frantic lobbying of MPs. Cobden described their zeal as 'most formidable', and their leader as being 'in a fit state of mind to qualify for a straight waist-coat' (sic).[16] There were even hints of secession from the League. But Cobden, 'exceedingly disgusted' at the conduct of his nonconformist supporters, insisted on supporting the bill all the way – 'as a small peace offering to Ireland'.[17]

Cobden emerged unscathed from the Maynooth controversy. Peel, with even more at stake, did not. The third reading of the bill was carried by a comfortable majority, but the vote of the Tory party – traditionally the champions of the Established Church – was split down the middle: 148 for and 149 against. Some observers felt that the Tories would not have been so hostile to Maynooth if their leader had not already aroused their resentment and fears by his tariff reforms and his equivocal attitude towards the Corn laws. However that may be, Peel and Graham were well aware that the Maynooth bill had 'mortally offended' a large section of their party; they were ready to take the consequences.[18]

Maynooth was not the only issue on which Cobden was at odds with other members of the League. In the autumn of 1843 the League Council had publicly pledged itself to put up a League candidate at every by-election. Ever since, the dubious wisdom of this pledge had become increasingly apparent. In some cases, as we have seen, it had soured relations with the Whigs by splitting the anti-Tory vote, and in others it had exposed the League to the bad publicity of a crushing defeat. Moreover, it was difficult to find suitable candidates who could be trusted to do credit to the League. In the spring of 1845 Cobden was asked by the League Council in Manchester to find a League candidate for a by-election at Leominster. He made some inquiries, discovered that a League candidate would not have the slightest chance of winning, and refused to take any action. When he was criticised by some members of the Council, he sent, through George Wilson, a stinging reproof which included a defiant assurance that if the Council passed a vote of censure on his conduct, 'it will not deter me in future from pursuing the same rational course'. After this, no more was heard of 'the ridiculous pledge of 1843'.[19]

In other respects, however, Cobden had no reason to be dissatis-fied with the League's activities while he was tied to his parliamen-tary oar. Its most spectacular effort in 1845 was a grand Free-Trade Bazaar for which George Wilson's organising genius was largely

THE ANTI-CORN LAW LEAGUE BAZAAR.

THE conversion of Covent Garden Theatre into a Gothic Hall is a transformation so complete, as to be worthy the best days of Pantomime and the high reputation of our old friend GRIEVE. The massy beams of ⅜ canvas, emblazoned with the Anti-corn Law cognizance—the roof of stained calico admitting "a dim rushlightish light," the Chinese lanterns trying to look Gothic, all tend to aid the delusion without entirely dispelling it. The aspect of the place is not, however, more marvellous than the regularity of the proceedings, when it is remembered that a committee of *one thousand ladies* has had the management of the arrangements. Scarcely a town has been without a female secretary and a committee of local ladies, all of whom have had a voice in the matter ; so that the unanimity with which the plan has been carried out is indeed wonderful.

The contributions to the bazaar comprise every conceivable commodity. We were particularly struck with three or four free millstones, which would form an elegant addition to the *bijouterie* of a lady of fashion. Some highly-polished circular saws seemed to be objects of great attraction, and we can fancy a gentleman presenting to his lady-love one of them, labelled, " A trifle from the League Bazaar."

There is a post-office, too, where you may buy one of our old jokes and a smile—such a smile !—for sixpence. The pretty politicians who preside at the various counters fulfil their task with admirable tact, and we repeatedly found our hands diving into our pockets, in obedience to the mute solicitations of the bright eyes of the fair Leaguers.

Contributions to the Bazaar.

8 *Punch*, Vol. VIII, 1845.

responsible. It was held in May in Covent Garden Theatre and lasted for nearly three weeks. The pit and stage of the theatre were boarded over and transformed into a 'Norman Gothic Hall' with a gaily decorated arched roof, supported by ornamental pillars, and with a large imitation stained glass window at one end. In the body of the theatre there were rows of stalls, each exhibiting the products of a provincial town or a district of London. No opportunity to publicise the League's message was lost; cushions, waistcoats, handkerchiefs and so on were decorated with free-trade devices, while portraits of Cobden, Bright and Villiers adorned fire screens, pottery and even shears. The refreshment room contained a vast plum cake, about five feet in diameter, covered with white iceing on which a variety of League mottoes were tastefully inscribed. (It was cut up and distributed on the last day.)[20] Both as propaganda and as a money-spinner, the Bazaar was a runaway success and raised over £25,000. Indeed, the organisers' main problem was the pressure of the crowds, which by the end of the first week caused the lady stall-holders to send a strong protest to League headquarters. The problem was eased by raising the price of admission and keeping the Bazaar open until ten in the evening. Cobden, who put in an appearance every day, reported to Kate, when the Bazaar was in its third week, that the ladies were bearing up 'uncommonly well'.*[21]

By this time a large slice of Cobden's time was being taken up by a subject far removed from the Corn laws but intimately linked with the expansion of the British economy. The 'railway mania' of the mid-1840s was in full swing, and every private railway bill (or every group of sometimes conflicting proposals) had to be scrutinised by a committee of each House of Parliament. During the 1845 session there could be between 20 and 30 separate Commons railway committees sitting at the same time. The 'odious Committee' to which Cobden was appointed met from 12 noon to 4 p.m. on six days a week, and he could never get a day off because without him it would not have the necessary quorum of four. (The fifth member – 'very luckily for him', according to Cobden – was pitched from his horse on to his head on the committee's second day and excused from further attendance.)[22] Cobden found it exceedingly tiresome to sit day after day 'hearing witnesses, and listening to the tedious harangues of counsel about a lot of paltry lines among the little towns and villages in Norfolk and Suffolk'. And to make matters

---

* But about a week after the Bazaar ended, Cobden reported that 'Mrs Taylor ... had been suffering a reaction of languor consequent upon her great exertions at the Bazaar'. (WSRO, Add. Mss. 6016, 5 June, 1845)

worse, the committee had no powers to restrain the verbosity of the barristers, 'who are paid in proportion to the length of time they can waste'.[23]

Cobden might have been more philosophical about his time-consuming railway committee – he might even have enjoyed it – if he had not had so much else on his mind. He was becoming the victim of his own success as a public figure. The demands on his time and energy were always mounting; and the vexatious disagreements with Council colleagues in Manchester and nonconformist supporters all over the country added to his burden. 'I can't', he wrote to Kate on 19 June, 'go through another period such as the present session, to be harassed and annoyed as I have been in every possible way; it would kill me.'[24] What was most harassing of all was the imminent prospect of the failure of his business. He had been pleased by his success in getting a commission on railway gauges set up because it helped to give him 'the standing of a man of business' in the House of Common.*[25] But in his private capacity he was rapidly heading towards exposure as a bankrupt failure.

Cobden's business difficulties had apparently come to a head sometime during the previous winter. He had sought the advice of two Manchester friends, who had told him frankly that his business lacked an effective head, and if he continued to leave it in his brother's incompetent hands he would inevitably be ruined. Cobden could not bring himself to give up a public crusade which seemed close to success. But his letters to Frederick during the spring of 1845 show how deeply worried he was by the firm's inability to pay off its debts, let alone make a profit.

> The fidgets – he wrote on 7 April – have so got possession of me that I cannot master them. For the first time I feel fairly down and dead-beaten. It is of no use writing all one feels. Entreat J. S. [his brother-in-law] to work down the stock of odds and ends of cloth, and keep down everything as low as possible. And remind Charles [his younger brother] of the critical importance of finding something for the machinery to do in the interval between the seasons.

* Most of the railway companies laid down the standard narrow gauge line which George Stevenson had pioneered. But the rapidly expanding Great Western Railway used the broad gauge favoured by Brunel, which made for swifter and more comfortable travelling. When the two gauges met, everything had to be transferred from one set of carriages or trucks to another, causing inconvenience, delay and damage to goods. Cobden advocated going over to the narrow gauge, because there was so much more of it already and because it would be easier to adapt the broad to the narrow gauge than *vice-versa*. The commission's report was on the whole in favour of the narrow gauge, which was eventually adopted as the national gauge.

It is of no use your writing bad news to me. I can't help it while here.[26]

But the bad news continued relentlessly to come in, keeping Cobden on tenterhooks and increasingly frustrated because his enforced attendance at the railway committee prevented him from investigating the situation at first hand in Manchester. Eventually, after much agonising, he told his brother, on 24 June, that he had decided to retire from public life. 'I have made up my mind to this, and shall not have a moment's peace of mind until I have fairly got out of my present false position. In fact, I would not go through another four months like the past for any earthly consideration whatever.'[27]

But he still hesitated, paralysed by the conflict between public and private duty. Nearly three months later he at last told Bright of his decision. Bright received Cobden's letter while on holiday with his sisters in Scotland. He was deeply distressed by the plight of his friend and appalled at the consequences of his decision for the League. 'I am of opinion', he wrote, 'that your retirement would be tantamount to a dissolution of the League; its mainspring would be gone.' He added that he himself could not take Cobden's place; he realised that he had 'incapacities' which prevented him from being more than a second in their campaign, and he urged Cobden to delay making his decision public for as long as possible.[28] Bright had at first felt unable to disrupt his sisters' holiday by going straight to Cobden's side. But after a few days, he changed his mind, hastened south to Manchester and there, with the help of one or two friends, managed to raise enough money to tide Cobden over his immediate difficulties. They both felt that the victory which would release Cobden from his public commitments could not be long delayed. It was, in fact, closer than they realised.

The summer of 1845 was abnormally wet and cold. By mid-August it was clear to Peel and Graham, anxiously studying the barometer, that the run of good harvests was at an end. At the same time they heard that a blight had destroyed the potato crop in parts of Kent, Essex and Sussex. By the beginning of October the blight had spread to Ireland, and by the middle of the month the Dublin government confirmed that almost the entire Irish potato harvest had been ruined. It was bad enough for the poor in England to be deprived of potatoes, especially when a bad wheat harvest put up the price of bread. For the four million Irish peasants, who had to exist on potatoes and on nothing else at all, the potato blight was a catastrophe of horrendous proportions. It did not strike them immediately, while they were consuming whatever bits of their ruined potatoes were still edible; but after a few months they would certainly start to starve unless succoured by public or private charity.

On 1 November, Peel summoned his Cabinet and proposed various relief measures to alleviate the impending famine in Ireland. He was well aware of the implications for the Corn law of what he proposed: 'Can we' – he asked his colleagues – 'vote public money for the sustenance of any considerable portion of the people on account of actual or apprehended scarcity, and maintain in full operation the existing restrictions on the free import of grain? I am bound to say that my impression is that we cannot.'[29] For Peel, the prospect of repealing the Corn law was the logical culmination of his gradual conversion to the principles of free trade over the past three years. He had begun to dismantle the trade barriers holding back Britain's economic expansion and there had been none of the dire consequences the protectionists had prophesied. On the contrary, the economy was expanding and living standards were improving. There was really no valid reason why cereals should not be included in a tariff reform which already included a wide variety of farm products. The only question remaining, as Cobden told a League meeting at Covent Garden in June, was 'When?'[30]

The prospect of mass starvation in Ireland gave a compelling urgency to that question. Peel's private opinion was that the only real remedy for the Irish famine would be 'the total and absolute repeal for ever of all duties on all articles of subsistence'.[31] But he did not attempt to inflict such strong medicine on his Cabinet. He merely proposed, on 1 November, that the Corn law should be suspended and later replaced by a more liberal one. All but three of his colleagues (Sir James Graham, Lord Aberdeen and Sidney Herbert) found even this mild medicine too nasty to swallow. They would probably have agreed to a temporary suspension if Peel could have guaranteed that the 1842 law would be reimposed. But they realised as well as he did that once the ports had been opened to the free entry of grain, it would be politically impossible to close them again. They no longer claimed with any conviction that the Corn laws were of much benefit to agriculture, but they remained an irreplaceable symbol of the old order which the rising tide of industrialisation and democracy threatened to overwhelm. Moreover, for a Tory government to abolish them would be a shameful act of political inconsistency which would split and probably destroy the party. As for the crisis in Ireland, Peel's colleagues claimed that it might well turn out to be not as bad as he feared.

The Prime Minister gave his Cabinet more than a month to discover that he was not exaggerating. Meanwhile, he went ahead with preparations to meet the impending famine in Ireland, setting up a Relief Commission and arranging to buy £100,000 of Indian corn (maize) from the United States for an emergency store. On 15 November, the three-man Scientific Commission which Peel had asked to investigate the Irish potato blight produced an extremely gloomy report. Armed with this confirmation of his fears, Peel asked the Cabinet to agree to a new Corn law with a revised scale of duties which would be gradually reduced until after eight years they disappeared altogether. Next day, 3 December, 12 members of the Cabinet 'reluctantly' agreed, but Lord Stanley and the Duke of Buccleuch said they must resign. With his Cabinet openly split, Peel felt he had no hope of carrying his party with him in the House of Commons. On 5 December, he told the Cabinet he must resign. The Queen, by now a convinced repealer, had 'very much' hoped that none of his colleagues would prevent him 'from doing what is *right* to do'.[32] On the 6th, he went down to Osborne to tell her that they had.

Meanwhile, the public clamour that the ports should be opened had grown steadily louder and more excited. The League was of course at the head of the agitation. On 28 October, some 8000 people crowded into the Free Trade Hall to hear Cobden declare that the prime minister would be a criminal and a poltroon if he did not open the ports.[33] But Peel was wrestling with his colleagues' fears and prejudices, and the announcement which many people were confidently expecting was not forthcoming. The League geared itself up to a final effort. Factory workers, who had been so hostile to the League, began to organise meetings to demand, not the vote, but cheap food. *The Times* added its powerful voice to the agitation, and on 22 November Lord John Russell announced, in an open letter sent from Edinburgh to his constituents, the completion of his slow and tortuous conversion to total and immediate repeal.

Lord John's announcement was no help to Peel, whose wavering colleagues naturally shied away from appearing to succumb to Whig pressure. For the League, it was a great triumph to have the Leader of the Opposition, in effect, enrolling himself under its banner. But for Cobden there was many a slip, and in his opinion the apparent imminence of victory called for more, not less, effort. There might still have to be a general election before repeal was won, and he and Bright plunged into a whirlwind tour, from the Scottish borders down to Somerset, to put fresh vigour into the campaign to register 40s freehold voters. By 4 December they had reached Stroud, where Cobden reported to his wife: 'Our meetings are everywhere gloriously attended. There is a perfect unanimity among all classes; not a syllable about Chartism or any other *ism*, and not a word of dissent. Bright and I are almost off our legs, five days this week in crowded meetings.'[34]

That morning *The Times* announced that the government intended
to summon Parliament early in the New Year to repeal the Corn
law. The news was not true, but it caused tremendous excitement.
Bright felt 'almost ill' when he read the announcement and believed
it was true.[35] Cobden was more sceptical and immediately wrote to
Wilson; 'For Heaven's sake, let there be no throwing up of caps.'[36]
The following evening he and Bright arrived in Bristol after 'a very
delightful meeting' in Bath. Cobden told Kate he thought they
would have to go on with their nightly meetings until Parliament
met. 'But I hope we are getting to the death struggle.'[37]

The news of Peel's resignation reached Cobden shortly before he
was due to address a huge meeting of his constituents in Stockport.
He gave the news early in his speech. The entire audience sprang to
its feet and gave three times three cheers. For once Cobden's self-
control snapped and he responded with an impassioned and savage
attack on the fallen prime minister.[38] His elder brother and many
of his friends – George Combe and Harriet Martineau among
them – were shocked by the violence of his outburst and wrote to
reprove him. In his reply to Frederick, Cobden acknowledged that
he had 'perhaps' been 'too strong' upon Peel, but he had wanted to
guard the country against sympathising with him and calling for his
return. 'For in my opinion he would infallibly trick us. I am confirmed in this view by what I hear in London . . . although he gives
out that he'll never take office again I don't believe it. I believe he is
ready to come back again and trick all parties if he can. The truth is
not in him.'[39] On the same day that he penned this uncharacteristically
vindictive outburst, Cobden launched further insulting attacks on
Peel at a huge Covent Garden meeting, at one point declaring that
Peel was the only man in the House of Commons to whom he could
never speak a word in private without forfeiting his self-respect and
the respect of others.[40]

The fact was that Cobden had never forgotten or forgiven what he
saw as Peel's failure to withdraw the accusation he had made in
February 1843 that Cobden wanted to incite someone to murder
him. To Cobden it was a deliberate attempt at character assassination, and he seems to have brooded on it with renewed anger in the
frenetic atmosphere of the closing months of the anti-Corn law
campaign. (He had referred to it during a public dinner at
Birmingham in November, declaring scornfully that he himself
would not touch a hair of the prime minister's head.)[41]

But as the days passed, Cobden began to feel thoroughly ashamed
of his outburst at Stockport and anxious to put himself right in the
eyes of his friends. In a letter to George Combe on 29 December, he
claimed that it had been an 'unpremeditated ebullition'; he had been
taken aback by the jubilation of the men before him and had vividly

remembered their 'terrible suffering' in 1841 when Peel had taken office and done nothing to relieve them.[42] This is contrary to the implications of his first explanation to his brother, but it certainly tallies more convincingly with the report of his speech given in *The Times*. Several weeks later, however, he told Combe that however much he regretted his failure in magnaminity, he still felt that Peel's 'atrocious conduct' towards him should not be forgotten.[43]

'The Government', wrote Greville on 20 December, 'is really like a halfpenny whirling in the air, with J. Russell's head on one side, and Peel's on the other.'[44] That same day the halfpenny fell to the ground with Peel's head uppermost. Lord John had abandoned his rather half-hearted attempt to form a government 'for no better reason', as Peel contemptuously put it, 'than that one intemperate and head-strong man objected to another gentleman having one particular office.'[45] In other words, Earl Grey would not have Lord Palmerston at the Foreign Office. The day before, Russell had written to Cobden offering him the post of Vice-President of the Board of Trade. Cobden promptly declined, on the grounds that he could better help Lord John carry out 'our principle' from outside the government.[46] This was almost certainly true and, since Cobden had a poor opinion of Russell, he must have been glad that his personal preference did not clash with his duty.

Peel had no doubt where his duty lay. Since the Queen must have a government, and neither the Whig Opposition nor the Tory pro-tectionists could provide one, he must step into the breach. The only alternative, he told his Cabinet, was Grey and Cobden. His collea-gues agreed, and this time without their former reluctance. Stanley alone persisted with his resignation, and was replaced at the Colonial Office by Gladstone, a recent convert to repeal. Peel told the Queen and Prince Albert that he had intended to announce publicly before the next general election that the Corn law would have to go. But now events had overtaken that decision, and he would deal with the Corn law at once, as part of a programme of agricultural reform, before he was forced to do so by some national calamity. He added that the League had made 'immense progress and had enormous means at their disposal'.[47]

On the same day, at a triumphant meeting in Manchester Town Hall, the League launched an appeal for £250,000. Within an hour and a half, £60,000 had been promised by members of the audience. With victory in sight, they were more than ever determined to keep up the pressure. Cobden told the meeting that if 'Sir Robert Peel will go on in an intelligible and straight-forward course ... he shall have the support of the League and the country as fully and cordially as any other prime minister'.[48] When he could shake himself free from his personal grudge, Cobden had no doubt that Peel was at heart a more convinced free trader than Lord John. Moreover, it was obvious that only Peel had any chance of winning over enough Tory MPs to carry repeal. The protectionists organised meetings all over the country in an attempt to stop him.

When Parliament met on 22 January, 1846, Peel frankly admitted that he had changed his views about protection and, after explaining why, concluded that he could no longer defend the Corn laws. According to Cobden, this threw the Tories into 'a state of frantic excitement', but they and he had to wait another four days before the prime minister unveiled his detailed proposals. Cobden spent the intervening Sunday visiting George Grote, a few miles from Slough. They went for a 12-mile country walk which left him next day 'like an old posting-horse ... stiff and footsore', waiting with 'great anxiety' for Peel's plan.[49]

'Peel is at last delivered', Cobden told Kate two days later, 'but I hardly know whether to call it a boy or a girl. Something between the two, I believe.' Peel had stopped short of the League's goal of total and immediate repeal. Instead he proposed a progressive reduction of duties over the next three years until in 1849 they disappeared entirely. To compensate the agriculturists he announced various measures to reduce the county rates, and public loans to finance agricultural improvements. 'It was', thought Cobden, 'too good a measure to be denounced, and not quite good enough for unqualified approbation'.[50]

The League in Manchester was also uncertain how to react. At a crowded and excited meeting on 29 January those hostile to any compromise seemed to be gaining the upper hand. But Cobden realised that the League would ignominiously fail if it now tried to mount a national campaign against Peel's plan. He went up to Manchester and, with the backing of Bright, Villiers and Milner Gibson, persuaded the diehards on the Council that the best must not be allowed to become the enemy of the good.*[51]

For the sake of political consistency Cobden discouraged Villiers from abandoning his annual motion for total and immediate repeal. But he had already made up his mind that if it were rejected, Peel's bill must be supported 'through thick and thin'.[52] The official party line, published in *The League* on 7 February, reflected Cobden's thinking. 'The League will offer no factious or fanatical opposition to Sir Robert Peel's measure.' If, it added, the Leaguers in the Com-

---

* He still had a very faint hope of getting the best, and published a letter addressed to the farmers of England, explaining why it would be better to repeal the Corn law at once and completely. (Speeches, I, pp. 449–52)

mons failed to get a majority for their own principles, they would
support whatever 'proximately' realised them. So although *The
League* continued to publish (gradually diminishing) lists of subscribers to the League's latest and largest fighting fund, the lengthy
accounts of League meetings that used to fill its columns were gradually replaced by even longer accounts of parliamentary debates.

Cobden began to look forward joyfully to his emancipation from 'a
vortex of agitation, in which for nearly seven years, I have neglected
almost every private claim and domestic duty, almost to the forget-
fulness of my own identity'.[53] The long years of unremitting strain
were beginning to tell. He returned from Manchester to London on
5 February suffering from acute neuralgia and a tormenting ear
infection. 'The prostration that has accompanied this local attack',
he told Frederick, 'tells me I have little reserve strength. In fact I feel
"all to pieces".'[54] For most of the rest of the month he was either
confined to his lodgings or convalescing in a friend's cottage just
outside London.

Fortunately, Cobden was in his place in the Commons on 27
February when an opportunity suddenly arose for Peel to put the
record straight between them. The prime minister genuinely
believed that he had fully withdrawn his incitement-to-murder
accusation against Cobden. He had been greatly surprised to learn,
through various channels, that Cobden had made the incident the
excuse for his intemperate attack on him at Stockport, but felt it was
too late to do anything about it now. He reckoned without the
intrepid Miss Martineau, who took it upon herself to act as
peacemaker. On 22 February she sent an adroitly worded appeal to
the prime minister (whom she did not know personally) to put
matters right with Cobden who, she said, had suffered most bitterly
over the affair. She went on to express her firm belief that in spite of
Cobden's insulting speeches, Peel could be counted on to do the just
and generous thing. Peel sent a friendly reply, explaining that he
thought he had withdrawn his accusation years ago.[55] Miss
Martineau then sent Cobden 'the most artful letter I ever penned',
leaving him under the impression that Peel might be contemplating
some gesture towards him.[56] She also wrote again to Peel, assuring
him that Cobden was likely to go more than half way to meet an
adversary.

After all this careful preparation, it was Disraeli, of all the unlikely people, who inadvertently allowed Miss Martineau's efforts
to be crowned with success. In his attempt to defend a typically
intemperate attack by Ferrand on George Wilson, he referred to
Peel's attack on Cobden three years earlier. The prime minister

seized the opportunity to withdraw 'fully and unequivocally . . . an imputation on the hon. Member for Stockport which was thrown out in the heat of debate under an erroneous impression of his meaning'. Cobden jumped up to accept Peel's retractation and to regret the terms in which he had referred to him 'whilst the remembrance of what had passed in this House was rankling in my mind'.

Before he went to bed that night Cobden scrawled a note of thanks to Miss Martineau for helping to ease his mind of 'a load which had burdened it for long and miserable years'. Apparently he was not told of her correspondence with Peel, and so never learned the full extent of her peacemaking diplomacy.[57]

The debate interrupted by the reconciliation of Peel and Cobden was the twelfth and final instalment of the protectionists' preliminary assault on Peel's Corn Bill. When Cobden got up to make his contribution, he was received with cheers and listened to in complete silence. He told the House that although he had missed the previous debates he had read every word of them, and he scathingly assured the protectionists that their repeated abuse of the prime minister was turning him into the most popular man in the country. Public opinion, he said, had turned decisively against them, and in his quiet, reasonable, factual way he spelled out why he was convinced that they would not be returned with a majority if they forced the government to go to the country on the issue of the Corn laws. As for the mass of people without votes, he challenged the protectionists to call a genuinely open public meeting anywhere and get it to support the Corn laws. The people were no longer frightened of free trade, and they had come to regard protection 'as they do witchcraft, as a mere sound and a delusion'. He did not, he said, want any triumph for the Anti-Corn Law League. He only wanted the protectionists 'to put an end, from conviction, to an evil system', and his final remarks included some good-humoured advice to them to try to get a correct grasp of the principles of political economy.[58]

Charles Greville described Cobden's speech as 'extraordinary. . . one of the ablest I ever read, and it was (I am told) more striking still to hear, because so admirably delivered'.[59] Shortly after Cobden sat down, the House at last divided on Peel's motion for a committee on his commercial policy. The government's majority was only 97, and more than two thirds of its supporters were in the minority. In a letter to Peel, Prince Albert acknowledged that the government did not now look strong. But he added consolingly that it had a moral strength which must tell more every day. 'Mr Cobden's speech, which we read with much attention, and which was certainly a very able one, points to that very strongly.'[60]

When the Commons next met, Villiers moved for complete and immediate repeal. His motion won even fewer votes than usual. He

himself had been afraid of rocking the government's boat and some
of the Radicals castigated him for doing just that. 'You have no idea
how poor Villiers was badgered for bringing on his motion',
Cobden told George Wilson, 'even by such men as Jo Hume. The
Peel fever is upon them and they seem to have no faith in anybody
else.'[61] He himself was sure the debate on Villiers' motion would
have helped Peel: 'If we, the Leaguers, had all jumped into the same
boat with Peel, and eagerly accepted his measure, the malcontent
protectionists would have said: "see how the rascal has sold us, he
might have made better terms for us, and the League would as
readily have accepted them".'[62]

But nothing that Cobden could contrive had the slightest chance
of mollifying the diehard protectionists in Peel's party. Lord George
Bentinck, who had emerged as their leader, described Peel and his
colleagues as no better than common cheats who in 'the good old
days' would have been put in the pillory and had their ears cropped.[63]
Fury at Peel's 'betrayal' and fear of the consequences of repeal made
the protectionists implacably determined to fight the Corn bill every
inch of the way. And when the bill had got through its second
reading on 26 March, the government inadvertently helped their
delaying tactics. The starving Irish were reacting violently to their
plight, and the Cabinet decided that a bill to contain their unrest,
which had already gone through the Lords, must be given at least its
first reading in the Commons. Although not particularly repressive
by Irish standards, to the Irish members the measure was only the
latest in a long line of 'coercion' bills, and, with Bentinck's private
encouragement, they mounted such a successful campaign of obstruction that all other government business was held up, and the
Irish bill itself did not get its first reading until 1 May.

A fortnight later the final battle in the campaign to get the Corn
bill through the Commons was fought. It was a tragic struggle
between Peel and the greater part of his own party in which Cobden
could do nothing to help except keep quiet. Disraeli launched the
last of his venomous diatribes against his former leader, and when
Peel wound up the debate with a brave and moving speech, the
benches behind him erupted with screams and hoots and jeers. 'They
hunt him like a fox', wrote Greville, 'and they are eager to run him
down and kill him in the open.'[64] But Peel had not yet run his
course. With two thirds of his party voting against him, his Corn bill
still got its third reading by a majority of 98. There was a good deal
of cheering and waving of hats, and several members, including
Macaulay, shook Cobden's hand and congratulated him on the triumph of his cause. For him, unlike Peel, there was no bitterness to
mar the occasion.

It was a further six weeks before the Corn bill got through the

House of Lords, and Cobden never took its safe passage for granted. But the suspense was eased by a flowering of his social life. The approaching triumph of the cause of which he had become the symbol; the conversion to that cause of the leader of the Whig Opposition the previous November; Cobden's pleasant and unassuming personality – all these combined to make him *persona grata* in the aristocratic Whig political world. He found himself investing in a white cravat because his black stock was clearly quite unsuitable for taking titled ladies in to dinner. At one party he heard some very good singing, at another the dinner was first-rate, at a third (Lady John Russell's) he met 'a select company' whose names were all in the papers next day. He went to a breakfast party where the guests included Prince Louis Napoleon, Suleiman Pasha and Disraeli, and an evening 'squeeze', where it was hardly possible to get inside the drawing-room doors. He assured Kate that he would much rather find himself taking tea with her than dining with lords and ladies. But a few days later he wrote: 'I am afraid if I associate much with the aristocracy, they will spoil me. I am already half seduced by the fascinating ease of their parties.'[65]

Before he was wholly seduced, Cobden was able to remove himself from further temptation. On 25 June the Lords at last gave the Corn bill its third reading. Next morning Cobden scribbled a hasty note to his wife: 'My Dearest Kate, Hurrah! Hurrah! the Corn bill is law, and now my work is done. I shall come down tomorrow morning by the six o'clock train in order to be present at a Council meeting at three, and shall hope to be home in time for a late tea.'[66]

What Cobden did not have time to tell his wife was that a few hours after the Corn bill became law, the government had been defeated in the Commons on the third reading of the Irish bill by what the Duke of Wellington called a 'blackguard combination'[67] of Whigs, Radicals, Irish and more than 70 of Bentinck's supporters who, in ordinary circumstances, would have been enthusiastic supporters of an Irish coercion bill. Peel's resignation was a foregone conclusion. The following day the Queen sent for the Whig leader, Lord John Russell.

Those free traders like Cobden, who had consistently opposed Irish coercion bills, had been in a distressing dilemma. But Peel, who knew that abstentions by free traders and Radicals could not save him, had encouraged them to vote according to their beliefs. Cobden, who wound up the debate on its sixth and final night, said he did not want his vote to be misinterpreted, but it would be pointless for him to vote against his convictions when a majority were determined to throw the prime minister out. He ended with a

warm tribute to Peel, giving him 'my heartfelt thanks for the un-
wearied perseverance, the unswerving firmness, and the great ability
with which he has during the last six months conducted one of the
most magnificent reforms ever carried in any country through this
House of Commons.'[68]

As Peel listened he must have thought of the exchange of letters
that had recently taken place between him and the man who had been
so remarkably transformed from bitter opponent to warm defender.
Two days earlier Cobden had sent Peel an immensely long letter in
which he urged him not to resign (as it was rumoured he intended to
do), but to dissolve Parliament and appeal to the country.[69] 'Are you
aware of the strength of your position with the country? If so, why
bow to a chance medley of factions in the Legislature, with a nation
ready and willing to be called to your rescue?' He insisted that there
were no longer any substantial differences of opinion between the
Peelites and the Whig or Liberal party; the rank and file of both were
ready for a fusion. Peel would not be embarrassed by any questions
of organic (constitutional) reform which for the time being aroused
no interest in the country or Parliament. 'Practical reforms are the
order of the day, and you are by common consent the practical
reformer. *The Condition of England Question – there is your mission.*'

To this stirring appeal the prime minister returned a firm but
friendly refusal.[70] If, he wrote, a dissolution had been necessary to
secure the repeal of the Corn law, he would have instantly advised
one. But he did not feel a minister would be justified in advising a
dissolution when he was not at all sure he could obtain a majority
'based not on temporary personal sympathies...but on general
approval of his whole policy'. Moreover, if the expected defeat of the
Irish bill were followed by a general election, Ireland would
inevitably – and deplorably – become an issue. Finally, after the
uncertainty and excitement of the Corn law struggle, the country
and its economy needed '*repose*' more than anything. He himself
certainly did.

It is unlikely that Peel had any difficulty in rejecting Cobden's
suggestion, but he would have been less than human if he had not
been gratified by the flatteringly cordial terms in which it was put.
He was sorry, he told Cobden, to hear that he intended to leave
London immediately, because he had hoped to make his acquaintance privately and express to him 'a hope that every recollection of
past personal differences was obliterated for ever'.

So Cobden was not in his place in the House on 29 June when Peel,
even paler and cooler than usual, made his formal resignation speech.
It was a quiet businesslike performance until, at the end, some of his
suppressed emotion broke through. To the great surprise of his listeners, he paid a warm tribute to the man who had so often attacked

him in the past: 'The name which ought to be, and which will be, associated with the success of these measures [in particular, Corn law repeal] is the name of one who, acting, I believe, from pure and disinterested motives, has advocated their cause with untiring energy, and by appeals to reason, expressed by an eloquence, the more to be admired because it was unaffected and unadorned – the name . . . is the name of Richard Cobden. Without scruple . . . I attribute the success of these measures to him.'[71] A few days later, Prince Albert remarked to Peel that his eulogy of Cobden had created an immense sensation.[72] But Peel was not to be drawn upon his motives. Whatever they were, he had surprised, shocked and even angered many of those around him. It was not just that this personal tribute to another member was considered 'unparliamentary'. Or that it was hard on members of his own party not to receive even a modicum of praise when they had loyally stifled their doubts, and perhaps risked their seats, to support him. It was also the fact that in an acutely class-conscious society Peel had touched on a tender spot by praising the middle-class demagogue who had repeatedly reviled the aristocracy as knaves, plunderers and fools. Gladstone, characteristically, carefully analysed why he had been so upset by Peel's tribute to Cobden. He concluded that although everything that Peel had said was true, it was not the whole truth. 'For if his [Cobden's] power of discussion has been great and his end good, his tone has been most harsh and his imputation of bad and vile motives to honourable men incessant.'[73] This was true also, but Gladstone could not have known how often Cobden had regretted that his tongue and his emotions had run away with him.

If, as Gladstone loftily opined, Peel 'like some smaller men, is, I think, very sensible of the cheers of opponents', it was an endearingly human trait in a man whose reserve often made him seem frighteningly untouched by human emotion. But there was a much deeper bond between Peel and Cobden, which the prime minister had perhaps come to recognise and to which he pointed in the famous closing words of his resignation speech. He knew, he said, that he left a name censured and execrated by many; 'but it may be that I shall leave a name sometimes remembered with expressions of good will in the abodes of those whose lot it is to labour, and to earn their daily bread by the sweat of their brow, when they shall recruit their exhausted strength with abundant and untaxed food, the sweeter because it is no longer leavened by a sense of injustice.'[74] Cobden would never, as Greville did, call this claptrap. Like Peel, he could never forget the terrible winter of 1841–42. For both, the repeal of the Corn law was basically part of the 'Condition of England Question', although each emphasised a different aspect of the beneficial consequences they anticipated from repeal. Cobden believed that it would not only bring cheap bread, but it would also lead to a general economic expansion from which all would benefit. Peel had more modest economic expectations, but he hoped that the repeal of what was undeniably a blatant piece of class legislation would have a psychologically healing effect on a divided society.

Peel's critics might justifiably have complained that in his resignation speech he had been too modest. It was Peel himself, and no one else, who had had sufficient authority, prestige and iron determination both to win over his Cabinet and get repeal through both Houses of Parliament. Only Peel could have won over sufficient members of his party to secure a majority in the Commons – and the Lords – for a measure which their deepest instincts rejected. Cobden's contribution was two-fold. First, in the House of Commons his lucid, tireless expositions of the case for repeal seem to have had a major – perhaps even a decisive-effect on Peel's intellectual conversion. Second, although the League was the product of many men's dedicated hard work, Cobden provided its chief inspiration and guiding force; and it was his personality, more than anything else, which in the end gave it the stamp of respectability.

The contribution of the League to securing repeal was not as great as it was made out to be in the euphoria of the post-repeal years. When Peel brought in his Corn bill the League was left cheering rather half-heartedly on the sidelines. It had not even secured the 'total and immediate' repeal for which it had always campaigned; and Cobden's conviction that its registration campaign would secure a free-trade majority at the next election was never tested. But the League did succeed in turning the Corn laws into a major national issue which, it was realised, would have to be settled sooner rather than later. It created a climate of opinion in which it was impossible to contemplate any tinkering with the 1842 Corn Act, or any limited suspension to meet a temporary crisis.* The only choice was between sticking to the existing law or having no law at all. Peel was not the sort of man to bow to external pressure if he thought it wrong to do so. But when he had become convinced that repeal was the right course, the League lent strength to his arm to a powerful degree. It was not itself responsible for repealing the Corn laws – how could it be? – but it prepared the ground, it intimidated the laws' champions and it made it impossible to bring them back.

Peel claimed that the repeal of the Corn law was the most conservative act of his life.[75] He was probably right. The Corn laws had become the symbol of selfish class domination by the landed aristo-

---

* Because of the situation in Ireland and a general shortage of grain, Peel's 1846 Corn Act was suspended in January 1847 until March 1848. The act expired the following January.

THE GREAT ANTI-CORN-LAW LEAGUE MEETING, IN COVENT GARDEN THEATRE.

9 Anti-Corn law League Meeting in Covent Garden Theatre

cracy. Their abolition removed a dangerous obstacle to the country's peaceful social and political evolution. It also demonstrated once again that peaceful change could be achieved without revolution.

The practical effect of repeal was modest. When the domestic harvest was bad and continental harvests good, unimpeded supplies of foreign corn were now able to make prices in England lower than they would otherwise have been, and keep them steady. But when foreign as well as domestic corn was in short supply (as in 1846–47), prices inevitably rose. As for the Irish, the peculiar conditions of their existence (which were not understood in Whitehall) made repeal largely irrelevant to their plight. In 1846 their potato harvest again failed, this time suddenly and completely. Within five years, nearly a million had died of hunger and disease and about a further million had emigrated.[76]

To Cobden, the practical effects – or non-effects – of repeal seemed less important than its moral and social significance as the symbol of a new era, in which the establishment of the principles of Free Trade would make the whole world a better place. In his vale-dictory speech at the last meeting of the League Council on 2 July, 1846, he said that they might come to look back on the occasion as 'the germ of a movement which will ultimately comprehend the whole world in its embrace'.[77] For the rest of his life he tried to make a reality of that vision.

CHAPTER 9

European Celebrity (1846–48)

The day before the League Council held its last euphoric meeting Cobden confessed to a friend how much he needed a complete rest. 'I have been galvanized into an activity beyond my physical force and unless I now let my brain and nervous system lie fallow for a long season I shall be incapable of usefulness hereafter.'[1] In the months leading up to the final repeal of the Corn law, nervous strain and physical exhaustion had left him vulnerable to the insistent prickings of his conscience over his neglected private affairs. He had felt himself to be in a false situation – forced into a position of prominence which led the public to expect him to go on playing a leading part in public affairs while the state of his private affairs made that impossible. The arrangements made to bail out his firm the previous autumn had only been provisional. He had not the slightest desire to go back to the life of a Manchester businessman even for a limited period, but there seemed no alternative. By the beginning of April 1846 he had made up his mind to apply for the Chiltern Hundreds as soon as the repeal bill had received the royal assent.[2]

His situation was transformed by the League's decision to raise a public subscription for him. Even before he knew exactly how much would be collected – more than £75,000 – he seems to have felt confident that it would be enough to stabilise his firm's finances and restore his own. He hoped that by appointing a new manager, injecting some more capital and temporarily leaving his own name in the firm, he would in a year's time be able to leave his brother a flourishing instead of a sinking concern.

But he still could not accept a public gift without serious qualms. It was distasteful to him to be paid for public services, and he feared it would impair his 'moral influence'. He would have preferred either to refuse the gift altogether or use it to endow some public institu-

169

tion. But with his family responsibilities as well as a load of business debt, he simply could not afford to do so. What distressed him most was that the public's generosity should be concentrated on him when so many others – Bright, Colonel Thompson and, in particular, Villiers – were in his opinion equally worthy of public recognition. He never forgot that he had supplanted Villiers as leader of the free-trade cause in Parliament, and perhaps he sensed the mixed feelings with which Villiers had unselfishly continued to give him loyal and energetic support – '*I love and venerate him more than he is aware of*', he told Joseph Parkes in an agitated outpouring about the neglect of Villers.*[3]

Cobden did not, after all, resign his Stockport seat. Instead, his agent persuaded him to explain to his constituents that his doctors strongly advised him to go abroad for a year to restore his health. So after the League's last meeting he set out for his father-in-law's home at Machynlleth in mid-Wales, intending to settle his private affairs; then to cross the Channel with Kate and make a leisurely progress south to Italy and the mild winter climate of Egypt. But within little more than twenty-four hours of his departure from Manchester all his plans for a 'thorough relaxation' had gone by the board. They had been blown away by a letter from the famous geologist, Sir Roderick Murchison, who was a friend of the Russian Emperor, suggesting that Nicholas would listen sympathetically to the free-trade gospel if Cobden went to St. Petersburg to preach it to him.

As his speech in Manchester a few days earlier had showed, Cobden was already turning over in his mind the possibility of spreading the free-trade gospel throughout a largely protectionist world. He had already received hints that he would find a receptive audience in various European capitals. When St Petersburg was added to the list, the temptation to go on 'a private agitating tour through the Continent of Europe' became irresistible. Yet he succumbed at first with some foreboding. Finding himself at Llangollen in 'the loveliest valley out of paradise' on his way to Machynlleth, he was appalled to find himself suddenly 'blind to the loveliness of nature' and eager only to set out on his mission. He feared he might never be able to settle down again. But on the same day his mood shifted from apprehension to enthusiastic acceptance. 'Why' – he

---

* But according to Lord John Russell, Villiers refused any government post. And when the League belatedly offered him a 'testimonial', he at once refused a money gift, saying 'the reward of public services is public confidence' – which must have turned the knife in Cobden's wound. More than £5000 was subscribed for Bright; he spent it on a 1200-volume library. The League gave George Wilson £10,000, and other prominent members of the League council each received a silver tea and coffee set. Minor employees also received gifts, and in later years Cobden and Wilson tried to help those who had fallen on hard times.

asked another friend – 'should I rust in inactivity? If the public spirit of my countrymen affords me the means of travelling as their missionary, I will be the first ambassador from the people of this country to the nations of the continent. I am impelled to this step by an instinctive emotion such as never deceived me.'[4]

The message he wanted to preach was the profound conviction, which he had expounded in his first pamphlet eleven years earlier, that commerce was the 'grand panacea' that would heal all the world's discords. The triumph of free trade, he had explained at one of his huge meetings in the Free Trade Hall, implied the triumph of pacific principles throughout the world. It was simply a question of teaching people that 'they could better profit by the prosperity and freedom of other nations, through the peaceful paths of industry, than they could triumph through the force of war or military conquest'. Although he preached his message with the dedicated fervour of a visionary, he did not believe it was an impractical dream. And if it was 'founded in reason', it was '... a cause worth contending for; one that not merely the merchant and the manufacturer, but the philanthropist and the Christian might well lay hold of, and glory that he lived in an age when he might take a share in the conquest over selfishness and monopoly'.[5]

The few weeks before Cobden set off on his mission were clouded by a threat to his relationship with Bright. His friend's name had been put forward as candidate for one of the Manchester seats at the next general election. Bright was very anxious to abandon Durham for such a prestigious seat, but his extreme views and overbearing manners had not made him universally popular in Manchester liberal circles, and some of Cobden's friends asked him to stand instead. Bright sent Cobden a distinctly disingenuous letter in which his professed readiness to defer to his friend did not disguise from Cobden his 'obvious ambition' to sit for Manchester. He did not want to stand in Bright's way and, in any case, he much preferred to stay with Stockport where his constituents made few demands on him. But he shrank from offending the Manchester friends whose initiative had given him financial security, and he could not bring himself to make the public repudiation of their overtures which Bright sought from him before he went abroad. He may have been unduly sensitive, but he was clearly greatly distressed, and the day before he set out he appealed to George Wilson to rescue him from his dilemma.

> Would to God you could induce our friends about you to let me off! The truth is, it is a matter of feeling and deep gratitude to them which alone prevents my writing a positive negative. I am not in a position to refuse any thing which they persist in desiring and demand as a *reasonable* service, even if I knew that it would

endanger my life and fortune. Do what you can to induce *them* to have mercy on me.[6]

Eventually, in one of the many letters from Manchester that pursued him on his travels, they did have mercy on him – or so he felt – and on 17 September he wrote to the president of the local reform association definitely refusing to stand for Manchester.[7] Bright was duly nominated instead, but temporarily the episode left a slight shadow between the two men.

On the evening of 4 August, 1846 Cobden and his wife caught the seven o'clock train to Brighton and next morning crossed to Dieppe.* At eight o'clock that same evening they found themselves being very civilly received by the King and Queen of France at the Chateau d'Eu, a royal residence near the little Normandy port of Tréport. It was a foretaste of the astonishing reception given to Cobden all over Europe, from Paris to Naples, from Madrid to st Petersburg. He had no more time to worry about his delicate health and mental exhaustion. For 14 months it was a formidable programme of public banquets, receptions and meetings, innumerable private discussions, enthusiastic sightseeing, indefatigable information-gathering and constant travelling. So greatly had this English politician captured the Europeans' imagination that he even saw a silk handkerchief, printed with his name and portrait, in a shop window in Dresden. Europe was still heavily criss-crossed with tariff barriers, but free-trade ideas had become a familiar subject of discussion and controversy. Charles Dickens, visiting Lausanne that October, reported that one of the local papers 'treating of free trade has been very copious lately in its mention of LORD GOBDEN. Fact; and I think it a good name.'[8] Moreover, as the personification of a successful popular movement, Cobden was an object of intense interest to all the European liberals whose unrest was to erupt so spectacularly less than two years later.

As soon as he arrived in Paris, Cobden began daily lessons to improve his French; in less than a fortnight he managed – 'by dint of a good deal of preparation' – to deliver a speech in French at a public banquet 'without a fault'. He saw the leading men of all parties, but was especially sought after by opposition leaders, like Odilon Barrot, who were already organising a campaign of peaceful protest against Louis-Philippe's regime and were anxious for Cobden's advice on how best to manage it. 'Never was I in such a vortex', he assured his brother, 'as here among the politicians, philosophers and economists – I have not a moment to myself – a plate full of cards before me and not an hour to return visits.'[9]

---

* Their two small children were of course left behind – the little girl with Mrs Cobden's sister and young Richard at a nursery school at Southport.

At the end of August the Cobdens set off southwards through France to join some Manchester friends, Mr and Mrs Salis Schwabe, at Pau in the Pyrenees. On the way they visited Bordeaux, a prosperous commercial centre with strong trading links with Britain, where free-trade sentiments were already strong. Cobden's reception was so enthusiastic that after a few days he felt an urgent desire to escape before the mayor killed them with feasting.[10] Even at Pau, where he hoped for a real holiday, the local paper published a poetic panegyric on him, and the local notables bombarded him with their hospitable attentions.

By the beginning of October the Cobdens and their friends had begun a slow and uncomfortable journey through northern Spain during which Cobden, to his great irritation, had to submit to no less than three customs inspections. In Madrid, however, they were greeted by a musical serenade, deputations and declarations in favour of free trade in almost all the town's newspapers. How much more the authorities would tolerate was uncertain, so Cobden confined himself to private discussions and made the most of the picture galleries, which, he decided, were the best he had yet seen. (Murillo was his favourite painter.) He happened to be in Madrid at the time of the marriages of the young Queen and her sister – the Queen to her cousin Don Francisco, and the Infanta to the French Duke of Montpensier – which greatly perturbed the English government and press. Cobden was greatly disgusted by all the fuss, but did not reject the tickets that allowed him and his party to attend the ceremony. He also went to a gala bullfight held in the presence of the royal court to celebrate the double marriage. Kate and Mrs Schwabe had had enough after half an hour, but Cobden 'did violence to my nature' and stuck it out because he believed that nobody could really understand the character of the Spanish people without observing their national pastime.[11]

After leaving Madrid, the Cobdens spent nearly two months touring southern Spain, with the usual round of banquets, private discussions and sights. At Seville Cobden was elected an honorary member of the local Economical Society – 'an old society which has done but little good'. At Cadiz his sightseeing was hindered by the crowd of callers. In Malaga a free-trade banquet was well attended, but Cobden doubted whether one in half a dozen of the guests understood anything about the principles of free trade. He invariably took a sober and disenchanted view of the enthusiasm he aroused. He thought the Spaniards were more sympathetic towards free trade than the French, who talked too much of war and national independence, but at Cadiz he confessed to his brother that although he hoped to do some good by indoctrinating individuals, he could not see any 'tangible' result from his labours.[12]

Early in the new year of 1847 Cobden arrived in northern Italy,

still with Kate, but without the Schwabes who had left them for
home at Narbonne. Much of Italy was in a state of simmering
agitation, not yet for unity, but against foreign or oppressive rule, or
both. Fortunately, the authorities, whether Austrian, Piedmontese,
papal or Neapolitan, considered that free trade belonged to the
harmless science of political economy and not to the dangerous
domain of politics.[13] (In fact in Naples the minister of police sent
Cobden a copy of a pamphlet in favour of free trade which he himself
had written.)[14] So although public banquets, with toasts and
speeches, were previously unheard of, no official objection was
raised to those held in Cobden's honour. After the first, in Genoa,
the governor, meeting him at a public reception, complimented him
on his tact and confessed that he had felt a little anxious beforehand.[15] To the Italian liberals who organised them, any public dinner
was a step forward and, they hoped, a useful precedent. Cobden was
well aware of the mixed motives behind these affairs and of the
potential danger to his hosts; but as he was careful what he said
and was as well received by the authorities as by the opposition, he
felt that no harm would come of them.[16]

In Rome, Cobden had a private audience with Pope Pius IX, who
had been elected the previous June and had inaugurated his ponti-
ficate with a series of conciliatory gestures which had given him a
somewhat misleading reputation as a liberal. But the Pope was a
genuine advocate of free trade and he was already trying to promote
a customs union between the Italian states. He gave his visitor a
flatteringly warm reception and, at the end of their conversation,
Cobden was encouraged to appeal to him to put a stop to the Spanish
practice of celebrating saints' days with special bullfights. His appeal
was well received, and Cobden, who had no use at all for the
religious intolerance of so many of his fellow countrymen, left the
Pope's study convinced that he was 'one of the best men that ever
lived'.[17] He reacted more critically to King Ferdinand of the Two
Sicilies, whose treatment of political prisoners was to evoke a
hurricane of public indignation a few years later from another
English visitor, William Gladstone. Like the Pope, Ferdinand was
also genuinely interested in breaking down Italian customs barriers.
But his discourse on free trade did not greatly impress Cobden who
dismissed him as of 'restricted capacity'.[18]

Cobden took his sightseeing seriously, sometimes even deploring
the flood of visitors who prevented him from indulging in it as much
as he would have wanted. He knew what he liked and why.

I felt impressed with more solemnity in entering York Minster for
the first time than in St Peter's. The glare and glitter of so much
gold and such varieties of marble distract the eye, and prevent it

taking in the whole form of the building in one *coup-d'oeil*, as we do in the simple stone of our unadorned Gothic cathedrals. I was disappointed too in the statues, many of which are poor things.[19]

After a visit to the Sistine Chapel to see Michaelangelo's frescoes, he decided it was 'a deplorable misapplication of the time and talent of a man of genius to devote years to the painting of the ceiling of a chapel, at which one can only look by an effort that costs too much inconvenience to the neck to leave the mind at ease to enjoy the pleasure of the painting'.[20] But the galleries of the Vatican, where he could indulge his enthusiasm and perceptive interest in sculpture, more than fulfilled his expectations. 'Not only is the human figure of both sexes and all ages in every possible graceful attitude transferred to marble, which all but breathes and moves, but there are perfect models of animals too, and all arranged with consummate taste and skill in rooms that are worthy of enshrining such treasures.[21]'

But of all that Cobden saw in southern Italy – and he ranged as far south as Paestum – what caught his imagination and admiration most of all was Pompeii, especially all the simple, everyday artefacts of domestic life found there – from pastry moulds to toilet articles, from lamps and jugs to surgical instruments and theatre tickets.* They gave him, he felt, a far more vivid conception of the domestic life and social conditions of the ancients than any number of volumes of history. And, with a temporary loss of his usual faith in the progress of contemporary civilisation, he was moved to reflect, 'if ancient Italy, with its 30 millions of people living as comfortably and luxuriously as did the inhabitants of Pompeii, was overwhelmed with barbarism and darkness, what is to guarantee *us*? Will the tourist from New Holland or Michigan be some day amusing himself with digging up antique steam engines at Manchester?'[22]

To Cobden his travels sometimes seemed like a progress from one 'vortex' to the next, with each one worse than the last, and by the end of March 1847 he was beginning to wish he had settled in one place for the winter.† In the Naples 'vortex' he dined out nearly every day, sometimes attended three receptions in one evening, and

---

* He could have too much of the actual excavations. The authorities insisted on specially excavating a house for his benefit. Nothing of interest was unearthed and he begrudged the time he had to waste standing about watching the navvies. (MCL Cobden Papers, to J. Potter, 28 March, 1847)

† He also suffered from never feeling warm. He wrote to the author of a book on climate suggesting he should bring out a new edition 'with a dire warning to all invalids against leaving English firesides and carpets in future, for houses in the south of Europe with brick floors, where each room has three windows and four doors, none of which close, and with fires that would excite a revolt in an English Union workhouse.' (MCL Cobden Papers, to J. Potter, 28 March, 1847)

when he left had to send out 100 cards *pour prendre congé*. But when
he reached Florence, he found himself in his greatest 'vortex' yet,
being 'feted and dined and honored in the most undeserved
profusion'.[23] The Florentines felt they had a special bond with
Cobden because liberal commercial policies had been introduced into
Tuscany more than half a century earlier. For once Cobden could
replace his free-trade sermons with eulogies on the converted,
conveniently – or tactfully – overlooking that it was an enlightened
Austrian grand-duke, Leopold I, who had imposed the conversion.
Throughout Tuscany, the people were seething with revolt against
Leopold's descendant and, as elsewhere in Italy, Cobden's visit
provided an excuse to relieve their feelings. A 'poetical address' made
to him during a dinner at a villa near Florence contained some
patriotic allusions to Italy which – Cobden observed – 'drew tears
from the eyes of the ladies and made the men clench their teeth and
look sternly at each other'.[24] At a public banquet in Florence a few
days later – the first ever held there – the chairman over-indulged in
champagne and 'in the ardour of his feelings' hugged Cobden and
kissed him on both cheeks. It was not hard to guess what, apart from
champagne, fuelled his ardour.[25]

Turin was less emotional, more matter-of-fact. The King, Charles
Albert, talked to Cobden of practical things like railways and
machinery, while the minister of finance – 'a sensible man' – had a
long discussion with him about free trade. He attended a lecture at
the university by the professor of political economy; the audience
applauded when the lecturer referred in flattering terms to the
English visitor, and afterwards Cobden was cheered by a crowd of
students waiting outside.[26] In Milan there were more lectures, a visit
to Leonardo's Last Supper – 'fast perishing from damp'[27] – and a
public banquet which nearly got out of hand, thanks to the effect of
wine on the pent-up patriotic feelings of aspiring orators; but 'by
dint of management and entreaty the excited spirits were
calmed . . .'. Afterwards Cobden received an anonymous letter
begging him not to propose the health of the Austrian Emperor; it
was hardly a likely gesture for him to make.[28]

From Milan Cobden went for a brief rest to Lake Como. He
'lounged away the morning over Madame D'Arblay's Memoirs and
Lady C. Bury's George IV';[29] went up the lake in a steamboat; and
listened to some improper gossip about the people living along the
lake-side. He noted discreetly in his diary:

> The society on the shores of Lake Como has not always been the
> most select in the world. There have been dancers and actresses
> famous all over Europe in more ways than one, and there have
> been Englishmen of rather equivocal character, but at present this

lovely spot is attracting the notice of the respectable and wealthy inhabitants of Milan, to which it will become a sort of suburb when the railway now in progress is finished.[30]

Cobden ended his Italian tour in Venice. He was told that the Austrian authorities had not allowed his arrival to be published in the local press. But a few days later they provided an excellent regimental band to play during a public banquet given in his honour on the Giudecca. Seventy guests sat down to a 'sumptuous repast' under a canopy of vines. The Italian hosts discreetly banned all speechifying apart from a toast to the guest of honour and his brief reply in French. Afterwards the guests – and the Austrian band – embarked in gondolas and travelled in procession down the Grand Canal to the Rialto bridge, watched by a curious crowd from their balconies. As they returned the moon rose, adding a fresh charm to a scene 'which was sufficiently romantic to excite poetical emotions even in the mind of a political economist'.[31]

Not surprisingly, when the Cobdens arrived in Vienna a week or so later and were entertained to dinner by the Metternichs, Kate felt 'rather uncomfortable' to find herself sitting next to the man whom 'our good kind Italian friends' believed to be the cause of so many of their country's misfortunes.[32] Metternich himself, when talking privately to Cobden, seemed well aware of his own unpopularity within the Habsburg Empire and of the disapproval he aroused outside it. He appeared to be very much on the defensive, admitting that he feared the outbreak of violent disorders in Italy.[33] But he would probably have been surprised to be told that in less than a year the Viennese would have risen and forced him to flee into exile. Cobden, who formed a poor opinion of the Viennese, might have been equally surprised; 'there is perhaps no capital in Europe', he wrote, 'where there is so little taste for intellectual pursuits, and so great a devotion to eating, drinking, smoking, intriguing and other animal propensities.'[34] Perhaps the Viennese showed insufficient enthusiasm for the free-trade gospel.*

The Cobdens left Vienna in the middle of July and continued their journey by way of Dresden and Prague to Berlin, where Cobden learned about the progress and problems of the German Zollverein, but thought the contents of the museum very inferior to what he had seen in the galleries of Italy, Vienna and Dresden. He was

* But in October 1848 Mrs Cobden told a friend that the startling events in Vienna 'did not at all surprise us, but they came rather sooner than was expected. I recollect, when at that city, Mr Cobden foretold that these things would come to pass someday, in consequence of the heterogenous nature of the empire'. (Schwabe, Mrs Salis, *Reminiscences of Richard Cobden* p. 79.)

entertained to dinner by the King of Prussia at Sans Souci, and on the same day attended a three-hour public banquet at which the speeches were 'rather long' and the guests seemed 'phlegmatic' by comparison with Italians.[35] How he struck the guests was described afterwards by the *Allgemeine Preussische Zeitung*:

> The mighty orator is of a slender, weakly, slightly nervous constitution; his features are delicate, his physiognomy bears the stamp of thoughtfulness and calmness, with a shade of resolution; there is nothing domineering and his physiognomy is agreeable rather than impressive ... The secret of his physical strength lies in his unusual temperance and in his happy ability to sleep whenever he wants to. The secret of his moral strength, however, is to be found not only in the superiority of his mind and in the unbending firmness of his character, but also in the modesty and in the simplicity of his manners.[36]

By this time Kate had had more than enough of foreign travel. She had in fact begun to complain months earlier, when they were in Rome, about missing the children, and Cobden had had to promise never to take her abroad again without them – which meant, he felt, never again taking a long continental tour.[37] After coming so far, he could not bring himself to abandon what might well be his only opportunity to visit Russia. Kate, for her part, felt that now that her husband was in excellent health, she was free to rejoin her children. So on 7 August they said goodbye on Hamburg railway station, and Cobden turned his face eastward to begin the first stage of his long journey to St Petersburg.

He went by way of Danzig and Königsberg and, after he had passed the Russian frontier, travelled for three days and nights continuously in the mail coach before arriving in the Russian capital. He had no complaints; the roads were good, the inns very superior to those in Spain, and the tea incomparable.[38] In St Petersburg he thought the river Neva was one of the finest sights in Europe, but the houses and palaces seemed lost and insignificant in the vast squares and wide streets. 'The appearance of the city altogether is that of a parvenu who has just entered fashionable life and has copied all the newest modes, but there is too much gloss and glitter generally about such imitations.'[39] Moscow took him by surprise; so many of the people were Asiatic in dress and appearance and there was so much 'bowing and crossing' at every church door and opposite every religious shrine. He was everywhere 'struck with astonishment at the novel and beautiful features of this picturesque city of the Czars'.[40]

Two days more of continuous travelling eastwards brought him to the famous commercial centre of Nizhni-Novgorod (now Gorkiy). It was a monotonous journey; 'the country so flat and the view so

constantly bounded with straight lines of fir forests, that I was
frequently under the illusion that the ocean was visible in the distant
horizon. At Nizhni he visited several of the merchants who had just
arrived with one of the great caravans from Bokhara, and picked the
brains of the chief government trade official in the town. The latter
fortunately happened to be an intelligent German with a large store
of facts and figures for Cobden to copy into his diary. On his return
journey he visited one of the cotton spinning mills which had taken
advantage of Peel's repeal of the ban on the export of English
machinery five years earlier. Afterwards he deplored the contrast of
the 'masterpieces of machinery' he had just been inspecting and the
peasants' primitive ploughs, scythes and reaping hooks which
might, he felt, have been used by the ancient Scythians.[41] Everywhere he went he was confirmed in his opinion that the rest of
Europe had nothing to fear from a country that, although so vast,
was backward, thinly populated and hampered by great climatic and
geographical disadvantages.

During his round trip of 17 days from St Petersburg to Moscow
and Nizhni-Novgorod, Cobden spent as many as 10 nights jolting
along in a carriage. He was none the worse except for a slight cold
and some inflammation of the eyes, but allowed himself a little
relaxation when he got back to the capital. One day he went to the
races at Tsarsköe Selo, travelling there on Russia's first, and as yet
only, railway, which had been opened less than 10 years earlier. It
turned out to be a fashionable but – to Cobden – dull occasion. More
enjoyable was an excursion by steamboat to Peterhoff followed by a
visit to Prince Potemkin's new country mansion. He found himself
in 'a pleasant and intellectual society' where there was plenty of talk
about Russian politics and society, and where the ladies knew all
about the Anti-Corn Law League. He stayed the night and left the
following afternoon with a basket of preserves and a pair of slippers
for Kate.[42] It must have seemed like a scene straight out of
Turgenev or Chekhov.

Cobden did not after all get an opportunity to persuade the Tsar to
demolish the high tariff walls surrounding Russia. But the minister
of finance, although alleged to be ignorant and incompetent, listened
patiently and intelligently to half an hour's lecture on free trade. It
was also the subject of a lively discussion after Cobden had dined
with the foreign minister, Count Nesselrode. 'A Free Trade debate
in Nesselrode's drawingroom must', he felt, 'at least have been a
novelty.'[43] Outside the foreign minister's drawing-room it was
becoming less of a novelty, and the 'splendid banquet' given in
Cobden's honour before he left St Petersburg was attended by some
200 guests, including leading government officials as well as
merchants from many countries.[44]

By this time Cobden had at last had enough. He was feeling too
unsettled and homesick to visit Sweden, as he had planned, and
decided to come straight home instead. 'I am like a watch run down',
he told Kate, 'and which must be wound up again before it can be of
any use.'[45] He sailed from Cronstadt on 26 September, and after a
comparatively quiet visit to Lubeck – a public dinner with only some
70 guests and a visit to a beer cellar full of distinguished German
literati – he arrived in Hamburg to undergo the last and perhaps most
spectacular banquet given in his honour. About 700 guests sat down
in a riding school, with a sort of tribune like the bow of a ship at one
end from which the speakers addressed the company. 'The speeches
were long', reported Cobden, 'and the people very patient – we
began as usual speaking with the fish and had a toast between each
course ...' After the public banquet there were several private
dinner parties which he felt unable to refuse. 'I shall', he told Kate
gloomily, 'be knocked up with the heavy feeding.'[46]

He sailed at last on Saturday, 9 October, arrived in London the
following Monday, slept that night at the Victoria Hotel, Euston
Square, caught the early morning train to Manchester and reached
home at three o'clock that afternoon.

On the day that Cobden began the final stage of his tour and turned
towards Russia, *The Times* fulsomely described him as 'the
undiplomatized but not unacknowledged internuncio of a new
economic creed, which his country was the first to profess. He has
been received with the respect due to an ambassador, and the
reverence which belongs to a discoverer ...'.[47] If he ever read it, this
pretentious tribute (and there was a lot more of it) might not have
pleased Cobden. He was never inclined to over-estimate either his
own role or the effect of what he said. He was shrewd enough to
perceive that the popularity he enjoyed often arose principally out of
frustrated political and nationalist aspirations. Moreover, he realised
that it was authoritarian governments more than popular opinion
that had to be converted; and as the representative of the country
whose overwhelming lead in industrial development gave it an
obvious interest in sweeping away tariff barriers, he knew he was
bound to meet a certain amount of scepticism. If he had succeeded in
turning free trade into a live, publicly discussed issue and perhaps
made some individual conversions, his exertions would, he felt, have
been justified.

What had Cobden himself learnt from his long discussions with
the rulers and leading statesmen of Europe? It is fair to say, not
much. Some 12 years earlier he had published a couple of pamphlets
in which he had set out his views on the post-1815 European system
and Britain's involvement in it. But instead of now testing these

armchair conclusions against his firsthand impressions, he retained only those impressions which could be reconciled with his conclusions, apparently conveniently forgetting or, more probably, simply not noticing, those that could not. He had always had, as he told Bright from Madrid in October 1846, 'an instinctive monomania against this system of foreign interference, protocolling, diplomatising, etc.'[48] And on his return he saw no reason to modify his root and branch condemnation of the traditional methods of regulating relations between states. On the contrary, he was confirmed in his view that it was all humbug and unnecessary mystification. Metternich, he declared, was the last of the old order of statesmen 'because too much light has been shed upon the laboratory of governments to allow them to impose upon mankind with the old formulas'.[49]

In spite of all his reading and all he had been told, Cobden seems to have acquired only a limited perception of the complicated maze that European statesmen had to find their way through – the territorial ambitions, national aspirations, political frustrations, economic rivalries, the fears and jealousies rooted in centuries-old and mostly hostile relationships. There was a great deal to deplore in the motives and methods of Europe's rulers. But Cobden refused to acknowledge that they were dealing with real problems (even if they sometimes helped to make them worse) and not indulging in a game of make-believe. He always persisted in the dangerously simplistic view that nations were just collections of individuals with similar interests and relationships. On Russia – and it was a very important exception – he was more perceptive than most of his countrymen. But he failed (unlike Metternich) to take very seriously the simmering unrest in Italy; it was 'an undefinable passion', lacking a practical basis or any foundation in the country's past history.[50] And after the crisis over the Spanish marriages had been explained to him by the British minister in Madrid, he noted dismissively in his diary that 'the marriage of a boy and girl' was after all 'but a paltry matter with which to embroil England and France'.[51] The issue may have been blown up unnecessarily, but there was more to it than Cobden was prepared to admit.

'In all my travels', he wrote from St Petersburg, 'three reflections constantly recur to me – *How much unnecessary solicitude and alarm England devotes to the affairs of foreign countries; with how little knowledge we enter upon the task of regulating the concerns of other people; and how much better we might employ our energies in improving matters at home.*'[52] Many people, not least his own colleagues, thought that Palmerston often pushed his blustering interventionist foreign policy too far. Not enough people felt, as Cobden did, that domestic problems merited more attention than they got. But when he deplored other people's 'lack of knowledge' of foreign issues, it did not occur to him that he himself, despite all his facts and figures, might not have a full *understanding* of them.

Cobden's return to England, like his departure 15 months earlier, was clouded by worries over his parliamentary seat. During the summer of 1847, while he was still abroad, a general election was held in England. Cobden had assumed that if this happened he would be returned in his absence for Stockport. So he was, but when he reached St Petersburg he found a letter announcing that he had also been elected for one of the two county seats in the West Riding of Yorkshire. He had been nominated after a last-minute intervention by a delegation of Manchester free traders, who had persuaded the Leeds Liberals to sponsor Cobden's candidature as a demonstration of the West Riding's endorsement of free-trade principles. Support for Cobden grew throughout the constituency, the Tory candidate withdrew and eventually Cobden and Lord Morpeth (a Whig free trader and a lesser member of the Cabinet) were returned unopposed.

The West Riding was the largest, and one of the most prestigious, constituencies in the kingdom, and to be returned for it without any solicitation and while he was abroad was, as Cobden well knew, a very great compliment. He was, however, 'very much embarrassed and annoyed' by the news.[53] He felt as he had done over the Manchester seat and, if he had been in England, would not have let his name go forward for the West Riding. He knew he would hate to have much of his time taken up with the rather petty and humdrum duties of a good constituency MP. (A foretaste of what he might expect followed him to St Petersburg in the shape of pressing invitations from the Bradford Mechanics' Institute and the secretary of the local Athenaeum.) As he confided to his brother, 'the public and private business in which it [the West Riding] will involve me will militate against my plans of usefulness on certain large questions to which I should like to give my attention'.[54] If he accepted it, he would have to make some awkward explanations to his Stockport constituents and, moreover, his lack of any local footing in Yorkshire might make it difficult for him to hold the seat after the free-trade euphoria was over.[55] (There was indeed great indignation in the West Riding, among Whig as well as Tory gentry, at the election to one of their county seats of someone who was not only a 'foreigner' from Lancashire, but a manufacturer as well.*) Cobden

---

* The great Yorkshire magnate, Lord Fitzwilliam, who was a free trader and admired Cobden personally, was so indignant at his nomination that he offered his support to Denison, the Tory candidate, who, however, had just committed himself to withdraw.

postponed a decision until his return to England, but once back in Manchester let himself be persuaded by his friends that he could not turn down the West Riding seat. He never regarded it as more than 'temporary lodgings', and 12 years later was still having qualms of conscience about his Stockport constituents.[56]

Cobden arrived back in England at the climax of an alarming financial and economic crisis. It had been brought about by a renewed bout of speculative 'railway mania'; a partial failure of the American cotton crop which seriously affected the country's most important industry; and – most disastrous in its consequences – a collapse of the grain market. The 1846 harvest had failed not only in Britain but also in most of Western Europe. Large supplies were ordered from Russia and America but, by the time they began to arrive in the summer of 1847, it was clear that Britain's harvest that year would be a bumper one. Corn prices collapsed, corn brokers began to go brankrupt and there was a general loss of confidence. The heavy drain of gold abroad to finance investment in foreign railways and speculative purchases of grain prevented the Bank of England from providing the credits that might have stemmed the panic. By October ten or more banks had closed their doors and over 100 firms had failed. Towards the end of the month the government took action to stop the rot.* It was successful, but much damage had been done, trade failed to pick up and the Lancashire textile industry remained depressed. Worst of all, there were the repercussions on the far more disastrous situation in Ireland. The government claimed that the loss of revenue due to the economic recession ruled out any more financial aid to the Irish. The potato was not blighted in 1847, but, after two terrible famine years, the Irish were in no state to fend for themselves.†

When Cobden travelled to Stockport early in December to make his appologies and farewells to his former constituents, he devoted much of his public speech to explaining that the country's current difficulties could not – as the protectionists alleged – be blamed on the repeal of the Corn law. If the country was to prosper, he claimed, what it needed was not a return to protection, but cheaper government, especially cheaper defence, so that the heavy burden of taxation could be lifted. The impetus thereby given to trade and industry would have a beneficial effect on the condition of the great

---

* Under the Bank Charter Act of 1844 the Bank of England was strictly limited in the amount of credit it could issue. On 25 October, 1847, the papers published a letter from the government authorising the Bank to exceed these legal limits if necessary. This was enough to restore confidence.
† In 1847 the potato yield was excellent, but a very much smaller acreage had been sown because so many seed potatoes had been eaten.

mass of the people, whether they worked in factories or on the land. Financial retrenchment and reform – that was his new rallying cry. He did not expect that it would be a popular one.

> In the present chaotic state of public opinion – he wrote to George Combe – upon great social and political questions, I fear I cannot do much more than cry aloud like one in the wilderness, and resign myself to my fate of being again in a minority. I do not think we are sufficiently alive to our financial and economic difficulties. We are over-taxed and over-indebted. When individuals are in pecuniary embarrassments, they retrench their expenditure. But nobody seems to dream that the same rule applies to communities ... I have returned home with the conviction that England with its debt and taxation, its Ireland and its Colonies, has the most dangerous *future* of any state in Europe ... The public mind is too arrogant and the man who should venture to humble it by a fair statement of our public affairs, would be liable to be denounced as a croaker and a traitor.[57]

Even making allowances – as Cobden went on to do – for the effect of the gloomy November weather, this was a strangely pessimistic letter to be written by a politician who had just returned from a triumphant tour round Europe and whose position at home was such that the Prime Minister felt obliged to try to find him a seat in the Cabinet.

What to do about Cobden had exercised Lord John Russell when he was forming his Cabinet in the summer of 1846. Many people felt that a man who had to be rescued from his private financial difficulties by a public subscription was not well qualified to help run the country. How much this weighed with Lord John is not clear. He told Prince Albert that it was difficult not to offer a Cabinet post to Cobden after Peel's tribute to him, but it would affront many people and might cause dissension in the Cabinet.[58] The news that Cobden intended to go abroad for at least a year provided a reasonable excuse to shelve the matter, but Russell wrote to Cobden expressing an unenthusiastic hope that he would join the government on his return.[59] Cobden thought that in the circumstances an offer would have been a 'silly compliment'.[60]

The general election the following year did little to strengthen the government and nothing to clarify the confusion into which party politics had fallen after the break-up of the Tory party. The emerging Liberal party comprised the old-style Whig party, moderate reformers who preferred to think of themselves as liberal rather than radical, genuine Radicals (like Cobden) who also called themselves Liberal but were idiosyncratic and independent, and a majority of the

Irish members. It gave Lord John only an unreliable majority and the Peelites, whom he had hoped to attach to his government, preferred to remain aloof. Cobden could not, any more than anyone else, speak for the heterogeneous collection of Radicals but, with his newly-acquired prestige and influence, he would clearly be a useful addition to the government. So three days after Cobden landed in England, the Prime Minister wrote to the Queen, proposing to make him President of the Poor Law Commission with a seat in the Cabinet. 'His ability, his popularity with the working classes and his knowledge of sound principles of political economy are undoubted.' And remembering the Queen's great admiration for the former prime minister, he shrewdly reminded her of his tribute to Cobden which 'has raised him both on the Continent and in this country, so that his presence in the Cabinet would give satisfaction to many.' But without even sleeping on the suggestion the Queen turned it down flat. Cobden, she told Lord John, was 'well qualified in many respects' for the Poor Law Commission, and it would be 'advantageous' to secure his services, 'but the elevation to the Cabinet directly from Covent Garden* strikes her as a very sudden step, calculated to cause much dissatisfaction in many quarters, and setting a dangerous example to agitators in general (for his main reputation Mr Cobden gained as a successful agitator).' She felt that Cobden ought first to serve in a lesser government post before being promoted to the Cabinet.[61] In other words, he should work his passage back to respectability. Lord John did not press the matter at Windsor. Nor did he offer Cobden anything else.

If Cobden had been offered a post in the government, either inside or outside the Cabinet, it seems unlikely that he would have accepted it or, if he had, that he would have stayed in it for long. The Whigs were the effective source of power in the emerging Liberal party. But they were essentially aristocratic and landowning. When they were in opposition, Cobden's relations with them had generally been cool, and usually uneasy or severely strained. When they were in office, with the Radicals as their nominal allies, he saw no reason to think better of them or of their leader, for whom he scarcely ever had a good word to say. He could never believe in the sincerity of the Whigs as reformers. 'The fact is they [the Whigs] are the allies of the aristocracy rather than of the people, and they fight their opponents with gloves, not meaning to hurt them.'[62] With free trade – he assumed – a dead issue, Cobden could see little to choose between 'the two aristocratic factions'.[63] He never seems to have considered the possibility that he (and the other Radicals) might have more to gain by working with and through the Whigs than by

---

* A reference to the League's rallies in the Covent Garden theatre.

continually sniping at them, and thereby making a weak government still weaker.

Although outwardly he seemed to have become an experienced and adroit House of Commons man, he still really felt himself to be in an alien and uncongenial world. This was partly a purely physical reaction natural in someone with his asthmatic tendencies. He once tried to explain how he felt to George Combe. 'There is something too in the atmosphere (physically speaking) of the House, which always produces a sense of oppression, a kind of vacuum in my head, and a driness (sic) in my throat, which interferes much with the working of my brain, and the delivery of my observations. Perhaps it is dust from the floor through which Doctor Reed pumps up the air from below, or else the want of moisture in the air.' But it was also due to a sense of complete estrangement from those whom he was trying to convert to his point of view. 'You can have no idea', he went on,

> what an effort it requires to work myself up to an effort in the right direction in the House. It seems as if I leave my better nature outside the doors. I sometimes compare it to thrusting a man back into a generation two centuries ago. Principles which in my mind have been indisputable truths ever since I began to reason are *there* regarded by the majority as unheard-of novelties and daring innovations. Sending a man of my nervous and anxious tempera-ment into such a battlefield is almost as certain slaughter as if I were under Lord Gough's command in face of the Sikh batteries.[64]

Whether or not Cobden was sometimes guilty of intellectual arrogance, it is quite certain that he was not, and never pretended to be, a party politician. 'Party trammels', he wrote in March 1846 when considering his future after repeal, 'unless in favour of some well-defined and useful principle, would be irksome to me, and I should be restive and intractable to those who might expect me to run in their harness.'[65] In the Parliament elected in 1847 party loyalties and alignments were unusually tenuous and confused. Yet on one occasion Cobden reproved his fellow members for voting on party rather than conscientious grounds. 'I have made up my mind to give my vote independently of all parties; and I believe the country will never have a chance of getting good measures until we totally fling aside the whole distinction of parties, and decide on measures according to their merits.'[66] Perhaps he would not have denounced the system if he had not despaired of ever fitting into it. If Peel had responded to Cobden's appeal in June 1846 to dissolve Parliament, and had then been returned with a large majority and a mandate for reform, Cobden would presumably not have refused to join his Cabinet. He was not without ambition, but this lifelong feeling of alienation from the British political system had given him a deep temperamental reluctance to accept the commitment to party and colleagues implied in taking office. He once told Bright that if he lived in the United States there would have been no limit to his ambition, but at the beginning of his career 'my judgement told me ... that if I aimed at office in this country, it must lead either to disappointment or an abandonment of objects which I cherish far before official rank, and therefore I preferred pioneering for my convictions to promotion at the expense of them.'[67]

The prospect of the stony path in public life which he had marked out for himself did not, however, tempt Cobden to return to a private career in commerce. During his absence abroad, his optimistic hopes for the future of the family firm had been destroyed by the storm that had overtaken the Lancashire textile industry with gathering force throughout 1847. In March, he wrote to his brother from Naples with unaccustomed asperity, urging him 'for Gods's sake' to try to think of ways to make the business pay – and if it could not be done there was no point in going on.[68] Frederick, as so often in the past, could not cope, and soon after Richard returned to Manchester, their business was wound up. He was not exaggerating when he described the pecuniary sacrifice this involved for him as 'enormous'[69]: altogether, more than half – £40,000 – of the public subscription raised for him had to be spent on paying off the firm's debts. But he knew by now that he could never successfully combine politics with private business. 'In fact', he confessed to a friend, 'I have never done any good in trade from the time I became a public man.'[70]

Another link with the North was broken when the Cobdens decided to move to London. Cobden no longer had any business ties to keep him in Manchester, he found the long absences from his family while Parliament was sitting intolerable, and he could not afford to keep up two establishments. Moreover, he was convinced that the damp cold climate and clay soil of south Lancashire did not agree with his constitution nearly as well as the milder, dryer climate of southern England.[71] He was not turning into a valetudinarian, but the asthmatic and bronchial complaints to which he had always been prone – and which evidently got worse rather than better as he grew older – made him more careful about his health than a normally healthy man in his mid-forties would have been. Moreover, the mental and emotional strain of public life took a great deal out of him. Behind his calm exterior he took this immensely seriously, worked at it tremendously hard and was deeply frustrated when the rest of the world failed to followed his lead.

As soon as Cobden reached London for the opening of Parliament in January 1848 he began to look for a suitable house for himself and the family. He soon found one in Westbourne Terrace, 'near the

great Western Railway, Paddington, the highest part, as well as the
driest, of the metropolis'.[72] The house had the added advantage of
congenial neighbours. On one side of Number 103 lived Cobden's
old Manchester friend and colleague in the anti–Corn law struggle,
J. B. Smith; on the other side was Sir Joshua Walmsley who, having
made his fortune as a Liverpool corn merchant, devoted the rest of
his life to active campaigning for parliamentary reform and other
radical causes. (That part of Westbourne Terrace came to be
nicknamed 'Radical Row'.) Kate paid a brief visit from Manchester
to approve the house, Richard established himself next door at the
Walmsleys' and for the next few months divided his time between
criticising the government in the House of Commons and overseeing
the preparation of his new family home. His letters to Kate were full
of questions, assurances and suggestions. Which were the rooms
where she would like to have bars on the windows to prevent the
children from falling out? The lower part of the house was as dry as
she could wish. The back premises of the Walmsleys' house had been
whitewashed, which gave a more cheerful aspect to the back room
behind the dining room. What about the colours and patterns of the
wallpapers? Would it not be better to have a plain rather than a
patterned carpet, provided there were pictures on the wall?[73] And so
on. By early June the move from Manchester had been accomplished
and Cobden was cheerfully reporting to Frederick that they would
very soon have the house in order.[74] Henceforward, the centre of
gravity of his life was permanently established in the south, although
he continued to pay regular visits to his friends and old League
colleagues in and around Manchester.

In the new year of 1848 the country was in the midst of one of its
periodic panics over the supposed aggressive intentions of the
French. It was not a propitious atmosphere in which to launch a
campaign against defence spending. 'I thought', Cobden wrote sadly
to an old Manchester friend, 'Free Trade was the beginning of a new
era, but it is evident we repealed the Corn Laws by accident, without
knowing what we were about. The *spirit* of Free Trade is not yet in
us.'[75] But it did not occur to him to wait for a more sympathetic
climate of public opinion. Instead, he exhorted his friends to bestir
themselves to change that climate – '. . . and until then,' he told
Joseph Sturge, 'We can afford to be in the minority in so holy a
cause'.[76] He wrote to George Wilson, who had done so much for the
success of the Anti–Corn Law League, emphasising the importance
of stirring up the country on the armaments issue. 'I consider', he
added (perhaps a little to Wilson's surprise), 'this struggle against
armaments to be the real Free Trade battle.'[77]

At a big public meeting in Manchester on 27 January, Cobden devoted most of his speech to deriding the fears of a French invasion and criticising the government's defence policy. (Bright reported approvingly that 'Cobden was rather strong'.[78]) Afterwards, one of his staunch supporters in the anti-Corn law struggle remarked to him: 'this peace question is the *second* chapter of Free Trade and the *best* chapter'. No comment could have chimed in better with Cobden's feelings. 'Certainly', he told Sturge, 'the speakers and the audience seemed to rise and expand with the grandeur and loftiness of the subject.'[79] In fact, it was not a campaign he had embarked upon, but a crusade.

Cobden was no longer a pacifist in the uncompromising, 'non-resisting', sense that his Quaker friend Joseph Sturge was.* He greatly admired and single-minded dedication of men like Sturge, and during the period leading up to the Crimean war he worked closely, but never uncritically, with the peace movement in Britain, although he sometimes regretted that his association with the Quakers damaged his reputation as a practical politician.[80]† He did not deny that the country should have adequate defence forces and should use them if attacked. But he did not believe there was any danger of attack (apparently discounting the bellicose atmosphere he had found in France in 1846)††, and he complained, as he had done in his pamphlets some years earlier, that the armed forces were both unnecessarily large and used for unjustifiable purposes. Why should ships of the Royal Navy be kept for month after month in the Tagus simply to protect the Queen of Portugal from her own subjects? What was the point of leaving ships idle for months at a time at Malta – the Navy's 'great skulking-hole'? The crusading fervour with which Cobden went on persistently probing these practical questions sprang from his profound conviction that permanent peace could only be secured by reducing arms to a minimum, and Britain, the greatest naval power, had a duty to show the way. Many people, especially if they had had any actual experience of government, felt that Britain had already done as much. In the years after the defeat of

---

* When George Combe first met Cobden in 1837, the only point on which they disagreed was Cobden's extreme pacifism which Combe thought was 'nonsense'. Ten years later Cobden seems to have thought so too, (Gibbon, 11,11)

† The peace movement in Britain, which began in 1816, was at its most active, with meetings, lectures and pamphlets, in the 1840s and early 1850s. Its chief organisations were the Peace Society and its offshoot, the Peace Congress Committee, set up in 1848, together with numerous local societies. The English campaigners kept in close touch with similar American societies. A reputation for religious fanaticism did not help the movement's propaganda.

†† 'At present France is under arms – her children are taught to look only to the battlefield for the scene of future glory ...' B.L. Add. Mss. 43, 674, A, Diary, 6 August 1846.

Napoleon, persistent pressure by Treasury, Parliament and taxpayer had drastically whittled down the expenditure on the armed services. In 1835 it reached its lowest point, £11.7 million (compared with £71 million in 1814); by 1845 it had climbed back to £16 million. The Duke of Wellington's constant lamentations about the country's defenceless state might be largely put down to his advanced years. But many level-headed people, who had not the slightest wish for an arms race with France and were not susceptible to the hysteria of the press, genuinely feared that with the advent of steam the Channel was no longer the sure barrier against invasion it had always been assumed to be. For several years relations with France had been precarious. The French were said to be busily building armed steamers at Cherbourg, and it was not difficult to construct an alarming scenario of what they might achieve against the South coast with the aid of a 'steambridge'.

Early in January 1848, the Chancellor of the Exchequer, Sir Charles Wood, wrote to the Prime Minister deploring the habit people had fallen into of talking about a French landing on the Sussex coast almost as if it were a matter of course. He pointed out that steam vessels were an asset for defenders as well as attackers, but agreed that the country's defences ought to be improved.[81] Most of the Cabinet felt the same, Palmerston even threatening to resign if something was not done.[82] The government was already in serious financial trouble; its receipts had been depleted by the economic recession and its expenditure pushed higher than estimated by, among other things, the cost of Irish relief. Russell told the Commons that half a million could be added to the defence estimates if income tax, due to expire in 1849, was extended for another five years and the rate raised from 7d to a shilling. This plan, however, raised such a storm of indignation throughout the country that it had to be dropped. The proposed increase in the defence estimates was cut by half and income tax was extended for three years only. Cobden pressed on with a proposal for an actual reduction in the defence estimates, but only 38 members would support him. 'The blue jackets and red coats', he wrote next day, 'are down on me with a savageness that reminds me of the early days of the Corn debates.'[83] It was a disheartening outcome to his repeated attacks on the naval estimates, a poor recompense for being 'bullied in the House and sneered at out of doors'.[84]

While the House of Commons was arguing over the budget, the French in Paris were getting rid of Louis Philippe. The news was received with general amazement in London, not least by Cobden, who confessed as much in the Commons, but he hastened to add that there was now no reason to fear an attack by France – you need not fear an enemy ship whose crew was in open mutiny.[85] (The

Chancellor of the Exchequer used the same argument to justify his retreat on the income tax.) A month later, the kings of Prussia and Sardinia had granted constitutions, Metternich had fled from Vienna, and the revolutionary winds were blowing hard through Italy and central Europe. 'What astonishing news we have from the Continent!', wrote Cobden on 21 March. 'Almost every post brings us accounts of a revolution or the formation of a republic.'[86]

In the manufacturing districts of England and Scotland, where the severe economic recession had brought unemployment and distress, the news of the continental upheavals sparked off an alarming revival of Chartism. There were serious outbreaks of mob violence in Glasgow and other northern towns. In London the Chartists held several large public meetings and, after much fierce private argument, collected a third mammoth national petition and announced their intention of carrying it, on 10 April, in a procession led by Feargus O'Connor, from Kennington Common to Westminster. There was great alarm in London – much swearing-in of special constables (including Gladstone), barricading of windows and doors, discreet stationing of troops at strategic points and so on. But when the day came, the huge demonstration collapsed into a pathetic fiasco, destroyed by the government's resolution and O'Connor's lack of it.

With the benefit of hindsight, Cobden thought that the government and the newspapers had made far too much fuss about the Chartists' activities.[87] He was, all the same, greatly moved by the events on the continent and their repercussions in England. When he returned from his European tour, he was determined to concentrate on financial retrenchment and disarmament. He refused to get involved in any movement for 'organic' (political) reform, although, by his own account, he was strongly urged to lead a political reform party in the Commons.[88] But the upheavals at home and abroad in the spring of 1848 gave him second thoughts. Three days after the Kennington Common fiasco, he helped to launch Joseph Hume's 'Little Charter'* at a meeting attended by 50 MPs, including Cobden's new neighbour, Sir Joshua Walmsley. Shortly afterwards he attended a meeting of prominent Leaguers in Manchester, including George Wilson, at which it was decided to send a circular to everyone who had contributed at least £5 to the League's funds, asking them to support a campaign in favour of Hume's 'Little Charter'. The response was encouraging; local meetings were held, local associations formed and petitions organised. Cobden was impressed. He felt that a strong current was setting in for another

---

* It had four points: household suffrage; vote by ballot; triennial parliaments; a redistribution of seats.

reform bill, but he found it hard to decide what the new bill should
contain. All his most enthusiastically radical instincts were aroused;
'. . . many very good men are for universal suffrage', he told Wilson,
'and I confess I wish we could be with *them*, for they are the most
earnest of the movement party.'*[89] A few days later he told the
House of Commons that 'the people . . . expect to hear that the
government are prepared to put our representative system more in
harmony with the spirit of the age. The people of this country are
not prepared to see all the world in motion while they are standing
still . . .' He went on to suggest that if Parliament wished to preserve
the monarchy against republican innovations, it should cut away
some of its 'barbarous splendour' which was out of date, cost the
country so much and was maintained 'solely for the aggrandisement
of the aristocracy'.[90] These remarks were not well received either by
the Commons or the newspapers; ' . . . whenever I speak', complained Cobden, 'I am sure to upset the fat in the fire'.[91]

On 6 July Joseph Hume introduced a motion in favour of
parliamentary reform. Cobden of course supported it, but he was
careful to destroy any impression he might have created that he was a
dangerous iconoclast. He assured the House that he was not in
favour of universal suffrage, that he did not want to overturn the
country's institutions, and that those who supported the extension of
the suffrage were 'the real conservators of peace'.[92] What he was
really getting at, in a rather circuitous way, was that Parliament as at
present constituted was incapable of responding to the people's
needs, and it could not expect to survive indefinitely unless it
equipped itself to carry out its duties efficiently. Not surprisingly,
Hume's motion, although mild and carefully-worded, was resound-
ingly defeated by 358 votes to 84.

This rebuff seems to have knocked the stuffing out of the
movement for political reform which had sprung up with such
enthusiasm a few months earlier. Cobden's hopes – well-founded at
the time – that the Chartist fiasco on 10 April would incline the
moderate Chartist leaders towards co-operation with the middle
classes, also came to nothing. But the extremists, whose distrust of
middle-class radicals was insuperable, had nothing better to offer. In
the middle of August pre-emptive action by the authorities thwarted
a carefully laid plan for a nation-wide Chartist rising. It was the end
of the Chartist revival, destroyed not only by the government's
vigilance, but also by the growing indifference of the working class.

---

* Lord Ashley wrote in his diary on 13 April: 'A Sanitary Bill would, in five years,
confer more blessing and obliterate more Chartism than universal suffrage in half
a century; but the world, when ill at ease, flies always to politics, and omits the
statistics of the chimney-corner, where all a man's comfort or discomfort lies.'
(Hodder, *Shaftesbury*, Vol II, 243.)

Towards the middle of September 1848, Cobden retreated with his family (which had recently been enlarged by the arrival of a second daughter) to a furnished house on Hayling Island. They stayed there for six weeks, living the 'life of a family Robinson Crusoe', five miles from the nearest butcher's shop or doctor, and – what was much more important – many miles from any politicians.[93] But it was not in Cobden's nature to relax completely or to stop brooding over the world's problems. One was Ireland, where a pathetic attempt at revolt had just been foiled and where the potato harvest had failed once again. George Combe had just visited Ireland and been appalled by what he saw. Assuring Cobden that no 'patching measures' would do, he urged him to go and see for himself and then report fully to Parliament. As 'a moral and independent Englishman', Combe believed Cobden could do much to open the eyes of England to Ireland's needs.[94]

It was the sort of challenge that Cobden might have been expected to take up with enthusiasm. But he did not. In his first pamphlet he had castigated the British people's callous neglect of Ireland. During his recent continental tour he had everywhere been ashamed to find intelligent foreigners more impressed by Ireland's troubles than were politicians at home. He himself regarded it as Britain's most serious domestic problem. Yet, apart from opposing coercion bills, he never took part in Irish debates in the House of Commons and he never, either now or at any other time, seems to have contemplated using his talents and prestige to campaign for Irish reforms. He confessed to George Combe. 'I do not like to talk or think about Ireland or Irishmen. The politics of Ireland like its bogs *may* be reclaimable, but they have been a pestilential swamp from the beginning of time and I almost despair of their harboring anything better than beggars and traitors till the end of the world.'[95] But he did think about Ireland, even if he did not say much. In the years since he wrote his first pamphlet he had come to think that the worst evil there was not the Protestant Church Establishment, but the concentration of so much of the land in the hands of absentee landlords. He wanted to divide the great estates into small properties. 'In other words', he told Combe, 'I would give Ireland to the Irish.'[96] But he did not know how.* Something about the Irish temperament and outlook – their inability to agree to help themselves – filled him with despair. He felt, perhaps, the involuntary guilty exasperation that helpless victims sometimes arouse.

* In January 1847, Cobden unburdened himself about 'that scandal of Europe and the civilized world, the state of Ireland', in a letter to Bright, written from Genoa. 'You cannot elevate or alter materially the condition of the mass of her [Ireland's] population but by a redistribution of a large portion of the soil. How this is to be effected legally, honestly and peacefully is the real problem you have to solve.' (A.M.43, 649. 18 Jan., 1847).

In any case, Cobden was convinced that his primary duty was to press on with his campaign to cut down government expenditure, especially on defence. To his disgust, the defence estimates had eventually amounted to £18 million – 'and this vast sum is as much lost for reproductive purposes as if it had been thrown into the sea. What wonder, with all this waste, that we should have distress, Chartism, pauperism and an insolvent Exchequer'.[97] There was also the wider issue of general disarmament to preserve peace. Joseph Sturge was about to attend in Brussels the first of a series of peace congresses, and Cobden sent him a long briefing on the size and cost of the armaments of the European powers. It was, he wrote, 'a scandal to the boasted civilization of the age' that the powers should demonstrate their total want of confidence in each other by maintaining these huge armaments in time of peace. 'You will probably be treated with ridicule on the continent, as I have been in England, for advocating such a utopian scheme as a general disarmament ... But we know that in contending for a principle based upon truth, and sanctioned by the law of God, we have only to persevere to convert our minority into a majority.'[98]

By the autumn Cobden had lost his enthusiasm for political reform as an immediate practical objective. He was disgusted by the 'misconduct' of the Chartist extremists, and he doubted whether there was much popular interest in an extension of the franchise, and even if there was, he did not believe the present House of Commons would concede it. The only certain – although admittedly slow – way forward was 'by making ourselves strong in the polling booths' – in other words, by continuing the work which the League had begun of creating new voters through the 40/– freehold qualification.[99] And while this admittedly slow process was being carried forward, the country must be educated about the importance of cheaper government, less taxes, fewer armaments, colonial incubuses and so on. There was, Cobden felt, 'a fearful mass of prejudice and ignorance to dispel upon these subjects ....'.*[100]

Other people too were becoming actively concerned in promoting retrenchment and financial reform. Early in December Cobden paid a visit to Liverpool in order to meet the leading members (who included Gladstone's brother Robertson) of the Liverpool Financial Reform Association. He was impressed by their earnestness, but felt – characteristically – they lacked direction and drive; and in order to

---

* The *Labour League*, for example, asked what was to become of all the soldiers and sailors Cobden wanted dismissed, and how much of the money he proposed to save would fall to the share of the working man.

concentrate their minds, he sent them his own budget plan. He proposed to save £10 million, most of it (£8.5 million) by slashing defence expenditure; to raise £1.5 million by a new probate and legacy duty on land; and to use the £11.5 million thus saved or raised to reduce or abolish duties on a wide range of articles, including tea, soap, butter and cheese.[101] The Liverpool association felt that Cobden did not go far enough,* but it published his proposals, and they aroused a good deal of interest. The *Morning Chronicle* rather unkindly commented that Cobden had rescued the Liverpudlian reformers from 'groping about, like men blind and benighted, in the mazes of economic statistics'.[102] That was exactly what he had wanted to do.

Other financial reform associations sprang up, and Cobden wanted to continue the good work. But John Bright, supported by George Wilson, argued that the reform of Parliament was the great goal to aim for; then all other reforms would follow. But Cobden was not convinced, and as always, believed in concentrating on one thing at a time. Anxious to harmonise their views the two men exchanged an increasingly cool series of letters. Cobden assured Bright that he still supported Hume's Little Charter in principle, but was sure that to try to run a 'mongrel agitation' for both political and financial reform at the present time would win no support.[103]

Yet in the end a 'mongrel agitation' was what they had. Early in January 1849 a public meeting was held in Manchester to launch a new financial and political reform association. Cobden spoke about the first and Bright about the second. The audience seemed enthusiastic, but Bright's 'Commons' League' (as he wanted to name it), although for a time active with meetings and lectures, never really got off the ground. Perhaps it was too obvious that its chief sponsors did not speak with one voice. In London, a similar enterprise launched by Walmsley and Francis Place, was more successful. It began by following Cobden's advice and concentrating on financial reform, but after a few months decided to work for parliamentary reform as well. By the end of 1849 it was acting as the focus for about 35 local associations, some working for financial and some for political reform, and Walmsley felt justified in substituting 'national' for 'metropolitan' in the name of his society.[104]

Cobden gave Walmsley encouragement and a subscription. He was 'grateful to anybody that does anything but stagnate', and pleased by the way in which Walmsley had managed to bring middle–class people and moderate Chartists together without them falling out. But he did not disguise his view that the reform

---

* The Liverpool reformers wanted to substitute direct for indirect taxation. Cobden agreed in principle, but thought the practical difficulties too great.

associations were really only talking-shops, and that nothing would actually be achieved to extend the franchise without 'an organised system of working' – by which he meant creating new votes through the 40/– freehold and the registration courts.[105]

A beginning had already been made by a Birmingham artisan, James Taylor, who after taking the pledge in 1841, put aside part of his wages until five years later he had saved enough to build his own home, which he called 'Temperance Cottage'. In 1847 Taylor started a society in Birmingham for promoting the purchase of 40/– freeholds. Like Cobden, his interest was political as well as social. Within a year there were half-a-dozen freehold land societies in the Midlands.* Cobden was delighted and gave Taylor his public encouragement. In the autumn of 1849 he suggested that Taylor should organise a delegate conference of land societies in Birmingham. Anxious that the movement should not stray from what he believed to be the right lines, he attended the conference himself. 'Societies are springing up in all directions', he wrote on 15 October, 'and many of them are upon unsound principles. It is desirable that there should be a comparing of notes.'[106]

Meanwhile some leading members of what was still called the Metropolitan Financial and Political Reform Association, including Walmsley, Cobden and Joseph Hume, were planning to launch a freehold land society in London. (One of those present remembered Cobden at the first committee meeting – 'keen, calm and prescient'.[107]) The National Freehold Land Society held its inaugural meeting in the London Tavern on 26 November. Cobden was the chief speaker, and *The Times* devoted three columns to his speech the following day. He said that the society had two objects and the first was to be a deposit for savings.

> One man buys Spanish bonds, and another Russian and Austrian bonds. Others, again, buy railway shares, which are running all over the country, and some of them running away. But give me a freehold investment in the earth, which never does run away, and it does not matter whether it is in my own parish or not, so that I have good title-deeds and receive my rent by the penny post.[108]

The society's other object, said Cobden, was to provide a way of obtaining the vote. He conceded that this could not be expected to

---

* To acquire a legal existence, the freehold land societies had to be registered as building societies. As this precluded them from owning land, they had to act through trustees who bought suitable estates and divided them into plots worth at least 40/– a year. In 1856 the Company Act made it possible to form a British Land Company to take over the responsibilities of the trustees.

lead to any great change in less than seven years. But he spelled out what he hoped it would eventually bring about. '... I want, by constitutional and legal means, to place, as far as I can, political power in this country in the hands of the middle and industrious classes; in other words, the people. When I speak of the middle and industrious classes, I regard them, as I ever did, as inseparable in interest ... I defy any person to draw the line where one ends and the other begins.'[109] The idea caught on among artisans who liked the idea of investing their savings in land and obtaining a vote into the bargain. The National went from strength to strength and remained the most important of the land societies. By 1853 there were 130 of them altogether with a total membership of 85,000, and a Scottish journal commented that in London there was 'quite a mania for freehold land societies' and something similar in most places elsewhere.[110]

Socially, the land societies were a success, both in their own right and as a stimulus to the rapidly developing building society movement. Politically, they were a failure. They seem to have had little or no effect on voting behaviour in the counties in either the 1852 or 1857 elections. Some of the members who acquired voting rights chose to vote Tory, some chose not to vote at all, and a steadily increasing number joined societies as a safe haven for their savings, with no intention of acquiring a freehold. Cobden did not, as he had rashly and publicly promised, give up part of every working day for seven years to the movement, but he continued to take a friendly interest in the National Society, and was its president when he died.

From the beginning, Bright assured Cobden that the freehold land movement was, politically, a waste of time. Much better, he urged, to campaign for an extension of the franchise in a straightforward way. Inevitably, Cobden's reluctance to do this made Bright suspect that he regarded the freehold campaign as a substitute. Cobden assured him he did not; it was only a stepping-stone to a wider reform. At present, the aristocratic minority were so strongly entrenched in power that the property-owning middle class could not hope to oust them except by 'raising up a portion of the working-class to become members of a propertied order'.

And what of all the rest? In an unguarded sentence in the same letter, Cobden hinted at what he thought of them. If, he wrote, enough new freeholds were created to double the county electorate, some shrewd Tory aristocrats 'would be found advocating universal suffrage, to take their chance in an appeal to the ignorance and vice of the country against the opinion of the teetotallers, nonconformist and rational Radicals, who would constitute nine-tenths of our phalanx of forty shilling freeholders.'[111] In Cobden's mind there was always a tension between theory and practice, between the principle that every man should have a vote, and the reality that many were not fit to use it. Subconsciously, perhaps, the 40/– freehold campaign was a way of reducing the tension.

CHAPTER 10

Campaigning for Peace (1849–52)

By the middle of January 1849, according to Charles Greville, the campaign to cut government spending which Cobden had launched in Liverpool and Manchester was making 'a grand stir', and the government was 'moving heaven and earth' to find ways of saving money.[1] Conscious of past, and present, failures to balance the budget, the Whig Cabinet was indeed anxious to respond to the popular demand for economy. But it had very little room for manoeuvre, especially with the starving Irish insistently knocking on the Treasury's door. Cobden, however, had no doubt at all where massive cuts could and should be made.

> You know – he wrote to George Combe early in January – that of old I have felt a strong sentiment upon the subject of warlike armaments and war. It is this moral sentiment, more than the £.s.d. view of the matter, which impels me to undertake the advocacy of a reduction of our forces. It was a kindred sentiment (more than the material view of the question) which actuated me on the Corn Law and Free Trade question. It would enable me to die happy if I could feel the satisfaction of having in some degree contributed to the partial disarmament of the world.[2]

For more mundane reasons, the Cabinet decided to make some fairly modest cuts in the army and navy estimates. Cobden's plan, which he unveiled to the Commons on 26 February, was far more drastic. He proposed that government spending, civil as well as military, should be reduced to its 1835 level by making cuts amounting to some £10 million, most of which were to come from the defence estimates. He argued that the armed services had been chiefly responsible for the increase in spending since 1835, and that it had been increased in response to successive foreign crises but never reduced when each crisis blew over. So long as the country minded its own business, avoiding 'rash and needless disputes with other countries', there was no danger of war breaking out, and productive industry would benefit greatly from reduced taxation.[3]

In spite of all the interest in retrenchment, only 78 members supported Cobden's motion. He had carefully stated that the cuts were to be made 'with all practicable speed' because – he claimed privately – he was 'too practical a man of business' to think they could be made all at once. But he seems to have genuinely hoped that people would be more likely to sit up and take notice if he made a sufficiently startling proposal instead of 'nibbling at details'.[4] It does not seem to have occurred to him that those who had been made to sit up might then fall back in alarm at the magnitude of his proposals.

Later in the session Cobden tackled an aspect of the 'warlike armaments and war' issue which had already been raised a few months earlier in both the French Chamber and the American Congress. He asked the Commons to approve a plan for bilateral arbitration treaties. The ground had been well prepared by the Peace Congress Committee, which had sent out lecturers to tour the country, organised many hundreds of petitions to Parliament and held a well-attended rally in Exeter Hall just before Cobden introduced his motion on 12 June. Well aware of the danger of being dismissed as a hopeless Utopian, he explained his proposal in the most practical and moderate way. It was not in any case a novel idea. International disputes were regularly, if infrequently, successfully settled by arbitration. Cobden wanted to make it an obligatory, not an occasional procedure. Britain and, say, France, would commit themselves to refer any dispute to arbitration before resorting to war. He did not even insist, apparently, that the award should be compulsory. And he emphatically disclaimed any wish to establish a permanent court or congress for the settlement of disputes, as his Quaker friends were anxious to do. With his profound distrust of government intervention, he could only fear the worst – corruption, intrigue and armed interference – from any plurality of governments authorised to act collectively.[5]

Palmerston, who had in fact considered trying to negotiate an arbitration treaty with the United States, discussed Cobden's motion sympathetically and courteously and without directly negativing it. Only 79 members voted for it, but Cobden was not dissatisfied. The issue had been well aired, both inside and outside Parliament, and it had provided useful advance publicity for the Peace Congress due to be held in Paris in August.*

---

* Cobden tried to put down another arbitration motion during the 1850 session, but was unlucky in the ballot. He gradually became disillusioned with the importance

With 670 delegates from across the Channel, the congress was overwhelmingly a British occasion. The French, contrary to their promises beforehand, produced only 100 delegates, and there were 70, mostly Americans, from the rest of the world. Victor Hugo, whom Cobden thought seemed to have 'more tact than the rest', was chosen chairman and made a 'very effective' opening speech. But in Cobden's opinion, the other French speakers were not good, some of them, whom he had been told were socialists, being 'evidently half-crazy'.[6] Cobden spent much time and trouble on preparing his own speech with the help of his friend and admirer, the French economist Frederic Bastiat. He delivered it in French, and then repeated most of it in English for the benefit of the Americans. According to his own report, there was really very little in it, but it produced 'a famous effect' on the audience.[7]

The sceptical French press had a good deal of fun at the expense of the congress, but the French public were sufficiently interested – or curious – to pack a conference room holding 2000 for three hot August days to listen to speeches that endlessly repeated the same themes. The French authorities also went out of their way to be civil and hospitable, even organising a day excursion (by special train) to Versailles, where the delegates were taken all over the palace, given luncheon in the famous tennis court and entertained with a special display of the fountains.* Cobden reported that the crowd of French people in the grounds were very good-humoured and polite, but 'seemed to be unable to suppress their smiles at the Quakeresses' bonnets'. Later that day the whole party was taken on to St Cloud, where again the fountains, this time illuminated, were turned on specially for their benefit.[8]

Privately, Cobden had less reason to be satisfied with the French government. When he suggested (unofficially, of course) to the minister of finance, M. Passy, that the two governments should agree on a mutual reduction of their naval forces, he was put off with allusions to the vanity of the French people which would not be satisfied without a large display of force. When he tried again, at a dinner party given by M. Passy, he 'found very little common sense upon the subject'.[9]

But these private setbacks did not diminish Cobden's enthusiasm

---

of arbitration treaties as a means of preventing war. At the end of the Crimean war he played only a very minor part in Henry Richard's efforts to get the issue raised at the Paris peace congress. Lord Clarendon was sympathetic, but he could only get the conference to agree to a guarded statement (Protocol 23) in favour of international arbitration. (W. O. Henderson, *Crimean War Diplomacy*, p. 146–50.)

* After the meal Cobden presided over the presentation of a copy of the New Testament in French to each of the American delegates as a tribute to their zsal in coming so far to attend the congress.

for the congress itself. It had at any rate made people talk about peace, 'even in France'. When he called on the French foreign minister, M de Tocqueville, and found most of the congress delegates crowding the minister's reception rooms, he told him he had never before had so large an amount of moral worth under his roof at one time. The minister, noted Cobden complacently, 'did not seem disposed to dispute the fact'.[10] Cobden's deep distrust of governments – and hence of any organisation controlled by governments – was balanced by his profound faith in what could be achieved by individual men of goodwill working together. After his return to England, he wrote a euphoric account of the congress to Henry Ashworth.

> ... the *novelty* of the scene was inexpressibly striking. In spite of all sneerers, depend on it that these international visits, where people become their own ambassadors, will do a great deal of good. More than 600 Englishmen have now returned to their homes, scattered over the face of the kingdom, who are busily narrating to their neighbours all the kindnesses received from the French government and people. What mountains of prejudices will thereby be removed![11]

There were four more peace congresses before the outbreak of the Crimean war. Cobden attended them all, and once there, did his best to make them a success. But he left it to others to set them up and he soon lost his unrealistic expectations of what they could achieve. At the next congress, in Frankfurt the following year, his influence was exerted powerfully and effectively on the side of realism. During a heated debate on disarmament he helped to secure substantial amendments to the undiluted pacifism of the original resolution; after condemning the burdens and evils of armaments, governments were urged to prepare 'a system of international disarmament without prejudice to such measures as may be considered necessary for the maintenance of the security of their citizens'.[12]

When Cobden was speaking about non–intervention, disarmament and arbitration, he often referred to 'the spirit of the age'.[13] He meant that the factors which formerly used to govern relations between states, such as religious intolerance, dynastic ambitions and trade monopolies, all of which made for war, had been replaced by other factors making for peace, such as free trade – 'the mutual exchange of benefits' – and improved communciations through steam and the electric telegraph. But in the middle of the 19th century the 'spirit of the age' was in fact largely formed by a fierce nationalism which took it for granted that freedom and independence – whether for Italians, Hungarians or Poles – would have to be fought for, and by governments which still regarded war, or the threat of war, as an acceptable – and popular – way of maintaining national prestige or furthering national ambitions.

Most of the nationalist uprisings which flared up all over Europe during 1848 were quickly suppressed. But the Hungarians, led by Kossuth and helped by a large contingent of Polish exiles, put up such a brave fight that the Austrians were forced to appeal to Russia for help. In the early summer of 1849 Russian and Austrian armies invaded Hungary in overwhelming strength. By the middle of August the struggle was over. Kossuth and the Polish General Bem fled to Turkey and the Hungarians were left to the mercy of the brutal Austrian, General Haynau.

The Hungarian struggle seized the imagination of a large part of the British public, as the Polish one had done nearly twenty years earlier. With sympathy for the Hungarians was mingled alarm at the extent of the counter-revolutionary reaction throughout Europe, and fears of what the Russian intervention in Hungary might portend. At huge mass meetings throughout July, in Glasgow, London (where Cobden spoke) and many other major cities, middle-class radicals and militant Chartists appeared on the same platforms to denounce the invasion of Hungary. This united front did not last long because the Chartists insisted on demanding military intervention by Britain. It was an entirely unrealistic demand, but it was enthusiastically supported by working-class audiences. Cobden had a great deal of sympathy for the Hungarian refugees who began to appear in London. He entertained them in his house in Westbourne Terrace and served energetically on a small committee set up to raise money for them. But intervention by the British government was as anathema to him in the case of Hungary as in any other. He pinned his faith unwaveringly on 'moral power', and Britain could not condemn the Russian intervention with any moral force if its own record was not clean. Why intervene on behalf of the Hungarians, but not of the Romans or Venetians?* Above all, he worried about the effect of an interventionist policy on his major preoccupation – one might almost say obsession – the defence budget. If, he wrote to the editor of one radical paper, 'the liberal press takes that [pro-intervention] line, adieu to all prospects of reducing our warlike establishments. The Horseguards and Admiralty will rejoice to see us take that line'.[14]

Although Palmerston also had much sympathy for the Hungarian patriots, he had no intention of getting mixed up in the Hungarian tragedy, apart from protesting to the Austrians about the savageness

---

* The Roman Republic, which Mazzini and Garibaldi had set up after the Pope's flight in December 1848, was overthrown by French troops in July 1849. The Venetian republic, set up by Manin, was overthrown by Austrian troops in August 1849.

of their repression. But he was willy-willy involved when the Russian and Austrian governments tried to bully the Sultan into handing over the Hungarian refugees, including Kossuth, who had fled to Turkey. Stratford Canning, the British ambassador at the Porte, stiffened the Turks' resolve to resist with an implied assurance of British aid in case of war. The British government approved Canning's unauthorised assurances. So did the British public in what Palmerston described an an unprecedently 'strong and un-animous[a] burst of generous feeling'.[15] The Austrian and Russian governments climbed down, withdrew their demands for extradition, and the crisis blew over. Whether they were more impressed by the ebullition of British (and French) public opinion, or by the arrival of the Royal Navy off the Dardanelles is hard to say. Cobden, however, had not the slightest doubt that it was the strength of public opinion that 'scared the despots instantly from their prey'. If, he felt, there had been a similar unanimous display of public and governmental hostility to the invasion of Hungary, not a single Russian or Austrian soldier would have crossed its frontier.[16] But the government had said nothing and the press had been divided.

In the autumn of 1849 the Austrian government decided to raise a loan on the London market, and a few months later the Russians did the same. Cobden assumed that the loans were needed to pay for the suppression of the Hungarian revolt and he spoke out strongly against them on both practical and moral grounds. He warned the small investor not to be deluded into throwing away his savings on unsound securities. The Austrian government was already heavily in debt and more likely to go bankrupt than repay the loan, while the Russian government's finances, which he had had the opportunity to study two years earlier, were 'nothing more or less than a gigantic imposture'.[17] He argued passionately that it was morally wrong to lend money to be spent on arms and armies – 'I say that no man has a right to lend money if he knows it is to be applied to the cutting of throats.'[18]

Cobden's claim that there was anything either moral or immoral about the way a man disposed of his capital was highly resented in the prosperous business and commercial circles which he was supposed to represent. It was pointed out that, in seeking to restrict people's financial freedom, he was betraying his own free-trade principles. The Times claimed that he had the political economists against him. Cobden, however, was unimpressed. He was sure he had the master on his side – 'I can quote Adam Smith whose authority is without appeal now in intellectual circles, it gives one the basis of science upon which to raise appeals to the moral feelings ...'[19] But whatever intellectual circles might think, he had a good deal of popular support. When he left the London Tavern, after speaking at a huge meeting called to protest against the Austrian loan, he was escorted down the street by a cheerful crowd from whom he eventually had to take refuge in a bank whose staff let him escape out of their back door.[20]

By the beginning of 1850 the country had recovered from several years of severe economic depression and embarked on a period of unprecedented expansion and prosperity. Only the farmers had no cause to rejoice. Since 1847 the price of corn, with a few slight recoveries, had gone steadily down; in mid–December 1849, it was only 38/9d a quarter. The farmers naturally blamed free trade and demanded a new government and a new Corn law. They were enthusiastically encouraged by the Tory protectionists, smarting from their failure by a narrow margin to stop the repeal of the last great bastion of protection, the Navigation Laws, during the 1849 session. Throughout the country there were rowdy county meetings, some of which ended in violence. At a protectionist meeting in Dorchester the farmers were attacked with stones and had to beat off their assailants with their hunting-whips, while after a meeting in Stafford, a crowd of more than a thousand chased the farmers back to the station and stoned their departing trains.

The excitement was increased by rumours that the government intended to reimpose a fixed duty on corn, and by the government's failure to scotch the rumour. In fact, Lord John, his resolve stiffened by the private advice of Peel, did not intend to do any such thing. It would be political suicide. As the Peelite Sidney Herbert coolly remarked: 'In the face of the thriving and daily improving state of all classes, except the one which has to go through the process, never very pleasant, of giving up a pecuniary advantage which they enjoyed at the expense of the rest, it is hopeless to attempt the reimposition of the Corn Laws.'[21]

To Cobden, the protectionists' agitation was an opportunity to 'unmask landlordism, both here and in Ireland, without mercy', and to drive a wedge between the farmers and the landlords.[22] He denounced the landlords' campaign (assiduously promoted inside Parliament by Disraeli) to have the local taxes for which they were responsible transferred to the national budget, where they would have to be met 'out of the taxes wrung from the agricultural labourer upon his ounce of tea, and the half-starved needlewoman in London upon her half-pound of sugar'.[23] He told the farmers that there was bound to be a transition period and , instead of agitating for new legislation to raise the price of corn, they should be making their landlords reduce their rents in line with the lower price of corn. The rent issue, he was sure, was the 'sore-place',[24] and he

probed it relentlessly in a series of speeches during the winter of
1849–50, although he complained more than once to Kate about the
difficulty of finding something new to say.[25] At a big meeting at
Leeds just before Christmas he launched into a fierce attack on the
'whole aristocratic system' of landlordism, and warned that it would
be 'torn to pieces' if there were another struggle over the Corn
laws.[26] Afterwards, he wondered if he might not have appeared
'rather rough' with the landlords, but noted with satisfaction that *The
Times* 'pokes me about like a dog over a hedgehog not knowing how
to bite'.[27] Early in the new year he spoke at Aylesbury, in the heart
of Disraeli country, and got, as might have been expected, a rather
mixed reception. But a fortnight later, back in the friendly North,
there were 'great doings' at Sheffield, with a public meeting, a public
breakfast and a ringing of church bells.[28]

When Parl iament met at the end of January 1850, the protectionists were said to be very savage and to 'live in a state of perpetual
growl'.[29] But Disraeli, their leader in the Commons, who had refused Cobden's invitation to appear on the platform with him at
Aylesbury, had privately decided that protection was a dead duck.[30]
Since, however, he could not openly admit as much, he spoke
evasively and badly in the debate on the Address and, in Greville's
opinion, Cobden had much the better of him.[31] A protectionist
amendment on agricultural distress was defeated by 192 votes to
311. But a few weeks later, a carefully moderate motion by Disraeli
to reduce the burden of taxation on agriculture got 252 votes. By
contrast, a motion of Cobden's for a cut of nearly £6 million in
defence expenditure, attracted only 89 votes. The Tories may have
been deluding themselves about a return to protection, but they had
more support in the Commons than was given to their principal
opponent when he brought forward his favourite project.

For the Cabinet, the most important legislative business at the
beginning of the 1850 session was the bill preparing the way for the
introduction of responsible government in the Australian colonies.
What to do about the empire – more than forty separate colonies –
was much debated by mid-century Victorians, and the interpretation
of their debate has been much argued over by modern historians.
The vast majority of those who thought about the problem were
undoubtedly strongly opposed to adding to the empire; but only a
small minority were anxious to slough it off altogether. The
argument was over what best to do with the existing colonies, in
particular the 'colonies of settlement', Canada, Australia, New
Zealand and Cape Colony. To some they were a noble opportunity
to spread civilisation; to some they were a safety-valve for Britain's

increasingly overcrowded cities; and to others they were simply a duty that had to be discharged as creditably as possible. But there was in fact a good deal of agreement between the government (Whig or Tory) and the mostly Radical colonial reformers like Sir William Molesworth and Joseph Hume. Both were anxious to reduce the burden of the colonies on the British taxpayer; both wanted to transplant British self-governing institutions to the colonies. It was round the pace of colonial reform and the extent and nature of the remaining links between colony and mother country that the debate largely revolved. The reformers laid most stress on releasing the colonists from the Colonial Office's leading strings, while the Colonial Secretary, Earl Grey, although not opposed to change, was anxious about the unity of the empire.[32]

Empire unity was the least of Cobden's worries. He was one of the small minority to whom the colonies were nothing more than a source of lucrative patronage for the aristocracy and an unnecessary financial burden on everyone else. The only exceptions were defence bases like Gibraltar, which he conceded were necessary but insisted could be maintained at far less cost. As he had stated in his first pamphlet, once released from commercial constraints (as, since 1846, he claimed they were*), the colonies should be allowed to go their own way. He justified this unpopular view in a speech at Bradford on 20 December, 1849.

> ... If people tell me that I want to dismember the Empire and abandon the colonies, I say I want Englishmen who are free to possess them ... I admit that the political connexion between the colonies and the Mother Country must become less and less strong, and ultimately I can see that it will be but a mere thread of connexion, politically speaking. But, on the other hand, by giving the colonies the right of self-government, with a right goodwill shaking hands with them, you will retain the connexion commercially and morally more strongly than you could by any political bond; the one is by the sword, the other is by the strong hand of affection for the Mother Country.[33]

Cobden believed that this speech was 'calculated to diffuse sound information' about the subject of the colonies.[34] But neither here nor anywhere else did he address himself to the many practical problems with which the Colonial Office and the minister responsible (at this time Earl Grey) had to grapple. He did not accept that the British government had any responsibility either for settlers,

---

* After the repeal of the Corn law, the colonies were gradually released from the restrictions on their commercial freedom. But by the early 1850s they did not, as Cobden used to imply, yet enjoy complete commercial autonomy.

merchants, missionaries, or the native races who all too often
suffered at the hands of the newcomers; nor did he recognise that the
pace of change had to be adjusted to the different situation in each
colony; nor would he make allowances for the reluctance of some
colonies to shoulder more of the cost of their defence. Unlike such
reformers as Molesworth or Gladstone, he was not interested in the
future of the empire, only in reducing as quickly and drastically as
possible what to him was an intolerable drain on the mother
country's productive resources.*

Year after year he tried to block the drain by attacking individual
supply votes. What possible value could the Falkland Islands, with a
population of 200 at the very most, be to England? The climate was
impossible and he understood no ships stopped there.[35] Why was it
necessary to have a separate ordnance establishment on every small
West Indian island now that steam had so greatly cut down the
travelling time between them?[36] What return were the people of
Britain ever likely to get from laying out £20,000 on salaries for the
army, the church, the judiciary, and on roads, public works and so
on, in New Zealand? To Cobden it was an 'illustration of the folly
this country was perpetrating in all parts of the globe'. Missionary
work, he declared, should be voluntary, not subsidised by the House
of Commons. 'It was not the province of that House to promote
Christianity either by force of our arms or by the appointment of
bishops to New Zealand'.[37] But at least in New Zealand, with its
temperate climate, white men could establish permanent, self-
governing settlements. It was far greater folly, in Cobden's view, to
try to colonise tropical territories, like the West coast of Africa,
where the climate was lethal, the natives usually hostile, and the
government's involvement likely to be permanent. He denied that it
was necessary to develop cotton-growing in West Africa – sufficient
supplies could be obtained elsewhere – and as for extending
civilisation and Christianity, he told the Commons that 'they had a
great deal to do at home within a stone's throw of where they were
before they embarked on a scheme of redeeming from barbarism the
whole coast of Africa'.[38]

The gap between Cobden's attitude and that of the majority was
highlighted in April 1851 when Molesworth introduced a motion to
reduce civil and military spending on the colonies and give them self-
government as quickly as possible. Asserting that it was one of the
most important motions of the session, Cobden strongly supported

---

* The British government accepted an obligation to defend the colonies against
  external attack, but Earl Grey laid it down in 1846 that if they wanted a larger
  defence force than the British garrison allotted to them, they must raise and pay
  for it themselves.

it in the interests of the taxpayer. 'It was', he declared, 'childish, cowardly, humiliating and disgraceful to be continually crying out about the heavy weight of taxation, and to refuse to take the only possible way of reducing the burden.' Free trade had completely changed our relations with the colonies, 'and if it was folly before to garrison the colonies, it was now downright insanity'. When Cobden sat down, Lord John got up and said he agreed about the importance of the motion – because it concerned the maintenance or the dissolution of the Empire.[39] This was not quite fair on Molesworth, but it reflected the effect of Cobden's attitude on the prime minister of a goverment that had every intention of continuing to carry out its imperial duties in a responsible way.

Although Cobden believed so fervently in the beneficial effects of the spread of commerce, he was extremely reluctant to recognise that in remote and unfriendly places like the coasts of China or West Africa British merchants needed – sometimes, it is true, through their own fault – the support of consuls or the protection of the Royal Navy. His objection sprang partly from a desire for economy, but also from a basic reluctance to accept that commerce might ever depend in any way on armed force. He was implacably opposed to 'forcing the markets open at the point of the bayonet'.[40]

When Cobden complained that the need for naval protection was exaggerated, and that many ships allotted to protection duties found nothing to do, Palmerston rather scornfully replied that one might as well ask what was the use 'of all those men in blue coats . . . lounging about the streets with their hands in their button holes, who seem to have no earthly occupation but to stare decent people out of countenance . . . [41] In fact, merchants, whether in China or Chile or anywhere else, were always clamouring for more protection and complaining that they had not seen a British cruiser for months and months.* In the China Seas the Royal Navy felt particularly overstretched. But Cobden criticised the size of the military and civil establishments of 'that pestiferous rock',[42] Hongkong, overlooking the formidable difficulty of maintaining law and order in a place that was swarming with Chinese robbers, pirates and smugglers. He claimed indeed that piracy in this area was no more. That may have been true of the big ocean-going ships, but certainly not of the small junks that hugged the coast. In fact the local press at Hongkong complained that the Royal Navy did not try hard enough to hunt

---

* One West African trader maintained that even infrequent visits by single warships impressed the local chiefs enough for them to maintain order and refrain from aggression themselves; he suspected that his factories might have been driven into the sea without these visits. (Bartlett. *Great Britain & Seapower*, 263)

them down, although it had destroyed or captured nearly 150 pirate vessels between 1840 and 1849.[43]

Piracy was also endemic along the coast of Borneo, and it was a major ingredient in the controvery surrounding the activities of Rajah Brooke into which Cobden threw himself with passionate indignation. Brooke was admired in England for his audacity and enterprise* and when he returned home in 1847 he was knighted and enjoyed considerable popular acclaim. But the government's attitude towards him was always cautious. It refused his repeated requests to annex Sarawak, and only very reluctantly, and after strong pressure from commercial interests, agreed to take over Labuan, an island off the coast of Borneo, as a naval base. (The Sultan of Brunei ceded the island in December 1846.) In 1848, however, Brooke was given an official status by making him commissioner and consul-general to Borneo and governor of Labuan.

On several occasions Brooke had already enlisted the help of naval captains stationed in the area to crush the Saribas and Sekrang Dyaks who raided all along the coast, burning villages and massacring their inhabitants. But the pirates still flourished, and in the summer of 1849 Brooke, with the help of the Royal Navy, organised yet another expedition against them. At the battle of Beting Marau the pirates were completely crushed, several hundreds of them being killed by the guns and flailing paddle wheels of the British war-ships.[44] For a time peace was restored and trade revived along the coast of Borneo. But when accounts of the battle reached England, reactions were mixed. There was revulsion at the apparently callous way in which so many natives had been mown down, especially among Radicals who in any case thoroughly disapproved of what seemed to them Brooke's one-man exercise in colonial expansion. Cobden was beside himself with indignation about 'that horrid and cowardly butchery on the coast of Borneo'. 'It shocks me to think what fiendish atrocities may be committed by English arms without rousing any conscientious resistance at home, provided they be only far enough off, and the victims too feeble to trouble us with their remonstrances or groans.'[45] Throughout the winter of 1849–50, Cobden (together with Joseph Hume, who was even more indignant) did his best to bring the 'fiendish atrocities' home to the British public, writing letters and articles for the newspapers and urging the Peace Society and the Aborigines' Protection Society to organise public meetings, petitions and pamphlets.† Feelings were still further

---

* The Sultan of Brunei, who was the nominal suzerain of Borneo, made James Brooke Rajah of Sarawak in 1842 after Brooke had played an important part in suppressing a revolt there against the Sultan's rule.
† Hume and Cobden were horrified to discover that a new edition of Brooke's journals contained passages about bloodshed and executions which had been omitted from the first edition.

outraged by the practice of paying 'head money' to naval officers and ratings for pirates killed or captured; the total bill for 1849 came to £100,000. Cobden told the Commons that he 'objected, on principle, to paying £20 a head for killing people who had never done anything to us'.[46*] He did not deny that piracy existed along the Borneo coast, but he demanded proof that the natives killed at Beting Marau in 'what seemed to have been a complete *battue*, as of so many sheep or deer', really were pirates and really had attacked English ships.[47] But neither he nor Hume got much support for their contention that the Dyaks' warlike activities were much more likely to be tribal feuding than piracy.[48] Only 29 members supported Hume's motion for a royal commission of inquiry.

Brooke may have had over-ambitious ideas about what could be achieved among the tribal rivalries of Borneo. But he was liberal and humane in his outlook. He was genuinely anxious to protect the natives from both piracy and European exploitation, and he earned the lasting gratitude of many of them for providing a measure of peace and stability.[49] But among his own countrymen, in spite of his popularity with the general public, his flamboyant career and his efforts to protect the natives from white speculators easily aroused dislike, distrust and resentment. In particular, he made a lasting and most vindictive enemy of his agent, Henry Wise, by refusing to back his plans for the commercial exploitation of Sarawak.[50] On his return to England, Wise did his best to blacken Brooke's character and reputation, and well-meaning humanitarians, most of whom were woefully ignorant of the real situation in Borneo, did not doubt what he told them.

In the case of Sir James Brooke, Cobden and Hume seem to have mislaid their critical faculties, although Joseph Parkes, for one, warned Cobden that there were some 'queer customers' among those whom he and Hume were consulting over Sarawak.[51] When, in July 1851, Hume again asked for a royal commission on Borneo, one of the key documents he produced in support of his case against Brooke was convincingly exposed as a complete forgery. The following March he repeated his accusations, again citing his discredited witness, and when confronted with damning proofs of the man's criminal career, he simply refused to accept them.[52] Cobden, for his part, never seems to have doubted Henry Wise's reliability in spite of his quarrel with Brooke.

But there were more level-headed people who also worried about Brooke's ambitions, even if they did not, like Cobden, claim that he waged war in Borneo, not to put down piracy, but to enlarge the territories under his control.[53] In March 1853, Lord Aberdeen's

---

* The Head Money Act was repealed during the 1850 session, and replaced by grants made at the discretion of the Admiralty.

coalition government appointed a royal commission to inquire into the situation in Borneo. The commission sat at Singapore and listened to a string of witnesses who all declared that piracy, in its most violent and atrocious forms, was undoubtedly rife along the Borneo coast and undoubtedly had to be suppressed. Brooke was vindicated, but Cobden would not change his mind. A few years later he was still arranging for the publication of material hostile to Brooke that had been provided by Wise – and even suggesting that it would be better to publish it anonymously, since everyone knew that Wise and Brooke had had a deadly personal quarrel.[54]

In June 1850 Cobden took the first significant step down off the pedestal on which the British public had placed him and Bright in 1846. His action was provoked by what Greville had described in February as 'the worst scrape into which Palmerston has ever got himself and his colleagues'.[55] It arose from Palmerston's decision to use the Royal Navy to enforce payment of several small claims against the Greek government by British subjects, of whom the most notorious was a Gibraltar Jew, Don Pacifico, whose property had been lost and damaged by an Athenian mob nearly three years earlier. On 15 January, 1850 a British fleet anchored off the Piraeus, and Admiral Parker submitted a list of payments to be made within 24 hours. When the payments were not forthcoming, he first seized a Greek naval vessel and then blockaded the harbour.

Lord John's reaction, when he first heard what was afoot, was to tell Palmerston that Don Pacifico's debt was 'hardly worth the interposition of the British Lion'.[56] But Palmerston argued that if British warships were not used to redress the wrongs of British subjects, the government might as well accept Cobden's motions for reducing this useless force and save the unnecessary expense.[57] But eventually, after the intervention of the French and Russian governments, he was forced to accept a compromise; Don Pacifico was compensated, but his demands were reduced to suitably modest amounts.

Two days earlier, on 17 June, a motion of censure on the government's policy towards Greece was carried in the House of Lords by 169 votes to 132. Lord John decided to fight. He stoutly defended his foreign secretary in the Commons, and a few days later Roebuck was put up to move a vote of confidence in Palmerston's foreign policy. On the second night of the debate, in the most famous speech of his career, Palmerston expounded and defended the whole of his foreign policy, making a highly flattering comparison of his country's peaceful, orderly progress – 'worthy of the admiration of mankind' – with the political earthquakes which had rocked all of

10 Cobden in middle age.

Europe. Finally, he likened the British subject, protected everywhere by the strong arm of England, to the ancient Roman who
'held himself free from indignity when he could say *Civis Romanus
sum*'.[58] It was a blatantly emotional appeal to the complacent
bellicose national pride characteristic of the mid-century Victorians.

Palmerston, moreover, although stubbornly hostile to further political reform at home, had acquired an undeserved reputation as a champion of oppressed nationalities abroad, even among Radicals. In the current climate of opinion he was virtually impregnable. Roebuck's motion was passed by a majority of 46.

Cobden made his contribution on the fourth and last night of the debate. His language, according to an eyewitness, was 'plain, earnest and sensible'.[59] It was absurd, he said, to send 15 warships to collect a debt of £6000, and after condemning Palmerston's handling of the dispute with Greece, he turned to the wider field of Britain's relations with Europe and made yet another plea for a non-interventionist foreign policy. 'I believe the progress of freedom depends more upon the maintenance of peace, the spread of commerce, and the diffusion of education, than upon the labours of cabinets and foreign offices . . . If I have one conviction stronger than another, it is in favour of the principle of non-intervention in the domestic concerns of other nations . . .'[60] He spoke for over an hour, cheered by the Conservatives and hooted and yelled at by his own side. Apart from Bright and Molesworth, only a handful of Radicals joined Cobden in opposing the motion.

Cobden cannot have been surprised to be 'famously abused' for his vote on Roebuck's motion.[61] A great many of his Yorkshire constituents happened to be in London for the wool sales and they had bombarded him with requisitions and round robins urging him, as he valued his popularity, to support the government.[62] But he was simply sorry and indignant that those who had cheered his advocacy of arbitration and non-intervention at public meetings in Yorkshire and Lancashire should now condemn him for not sacrificing principle to party. 'If they want a man who will put on and off his principles at the bidding of treasury whippers-in, they must look out for another and more pliant representative.'[63] He had, however, the consolation of finding himself on the same side as many of the most distinguished and able members of the House of Commons, including Peel, Gladstone and Graham. Peel's impressive contribution to the Don Pacifico debate was his last public speech. A few days later he was thrown from his horse while riding in the Park and died several days later. It was a severe blow to Cobden, who had become as friendly towards his former opponent as he had once been hostile. 'I have not been able to think of anything since', he told Kate after hearing of Peel's death.[64] He had convinced himself that Peel was developing strong sympathies for the issues he himself cherished – disarmament, international mediation, financial retrenchment and so on.[65] Rightly or wrongly, he felt he had lost a powerful ally in the making, and he could ill afford the loss.

In the autumn of 1850, Cobden retreated to the depths of the Sussex countryside and there spent the quietest six weeks he had known for 20 years. 'There seems', he wrote to Bright, 'to be no immediate market for political action of any kind, and why should we be ... always trying to cram ourselves down the throats of unwilling customers?'[66] It was an uncharacteristic frame of mind and it did not persist. Before long he was making his way north to campaign for a cause of which he had never entirely lost sight. After the repeal of the Corn laws in 1846, he told a friend that the only issue for which he would feel disposed to put on his armour for another 'seven years' war' was education.[67] During the previous seven years no progress had been made towards achieving a consistent, countrywide system of elementary education.* It was obvious that the two voluntary religious societies could not adequately supply the need. But greater state participation was blocked by religious extremists, especially among the nonconformists who feared that it would lead to more Church control of education. In the mid-1840s a 'voluntarist' movement developed among the nonconformists which condemned any intervention by the secular state in education as morally wrong; it was led by Edward Baines, the editor of the *Leeds Mercury*, who was adept at collecting statistical information to prove – to *his* satisfaction – that all the country's educational needs could be satisfied by voluntary effort alone. In 1847, while Cobden was still abroad, Baines organised a massive propaganda campaign, including a petition with 500,000 signatures taken to London by 500 delegates, to stop the government's scheme for teacher-training. The campaign was unsuccessful, but in the general election Baines did not hesitate to force voluntaryism on the West Riding electorate at the cost of the unity of the Liberal party.[68]†

To Cobden the voluntaryists were a political disaster – because they split the Liberals, especially in the West Riding – and a maddening setback to the cause of education. 'I am convinced', he wrote from Venice in June 1847, 'that government interference is as necessary for *education* as its non-interference is essential for *trade*. Any voluntary scheme is a chimaera.'[69] About the same time a small committee in Manchester, all but one of whose members had belonged to the Anti-Corn Law League, drew up a scheme of education for Lancashire based on the free, non-sectarian, rate-

---

* The annual government grant to schools had been increased, and a Committee of the Privy Council on Education set up in 1839 to dispense it. The committee's secretary, the dedicated James Kay-Shuttleworth, had managed to establish a school inspectorate and was about to launch a scheme for teacher-training.
† Twenty years later Baines publicly announced that he had been mistaken in opposing state aid for education.

supported Massachusetts system which Cobden had admired during his visit to the United States ten years earlier. When he got home that autumn, Cobden sent his blessing to the Lancashire Public Schools Association which had by then been formed, but did not become actively involved. He preferred to keep quiet about education for the time being so as to give the voluntaryists a chance to cool down after their recent heated agitation against teacher-training – a chance they did not take. Other issues quickly monopolised his attention – he could, he once confessed, only do one thing at a time[70] – and it was three years before he felt able to give his active support to the Lancashire reformers who by now had won enough backing to describe their association as 'National' instead of 'Lancashire'.

Cobden realised that the educational reformers had little to hope for from Parliament. During the previous session he had listened to a Commons debate on W. J. Fox's plan for secular education which he afterwards described as 'an outpouring of bigotry . . . such as would have done credit to Spain in the palmy days of its autos-da-fé'[71] Nor did the subject arouse any great interest in the country as a whole. So Cobden went up to Manchester for the NPSA's conference in October 1850 in order to help create a public demand that would eventually force Parliament to take action. He wanted to make education 'a hustings question'. He argued that to rely on voluntary effort was utterly inadequate, and he laid special emphasis on the rural poor. Too many villages had no resident gentry or clergy to finance and organise schools; too many of the existing schools were woefully inadequate; and too many of the village poor were too ignorant to have any spontaneous desire for education. The answer, said Cobden, was a compulsory education rate. 'I say, tax the property of the country to give us common schools, and you will save the money and fivefold that expense which you incur for gaols and for barracks and the rest of the paraphernalia by which you must rule in ignorance the people you deny the intelligence to rule themselves.'[72] Later, at a public meeting, he put his argument on a higher plane. It was not, he told his affluent, middle-class audience, a matter of self-interest, but of *duty*. And he rounded on those who claimed that the poor were always drunk and not worth bothering about.

> Would not *you* be drunken? – I speak to those of a more elevated class, and those in easy circumstances – would not *you* be drunken now, as your forefathers were not one century ago, if you had not some stimulus applied to your intellectual powers, some other resources besides the dram to produce that excitement which, mental or physical, is necessary to the health and existence of man.[73]

It was not only social prejudice that had to be fought. After hoping for many years to involve the various religious denominations in a national system of education, Cobden had come to realise that their mutual suspicion and intolerance made this impossible. But the alternative of a secular system was widely assumed to be atheistic and aroused enormous prejudice. Not all the members of the NPSA recognised this as clearly as Cobden did. At the Manchester conference it was wtih considerable difficulty, and after three interventions, that he disposed of a move to call the association 'secular' instead of 'public'; he pointed out that secular meant non-religious, whereas they were simply non-sectarian.[74] He also upset the extreme secularists by insisting that the reading of the Bible should not be excluded from a school's curriculum if the parents wanted it, although the interpretation of what the children heard would be left to pastors and parents outside the school. He strongly believed that it would be both absurd and intolerant to try to exclude the Bible from schools by law. He had his way, and prevented the NPSA from disqualifying itself as an influential moulder of public opinion. Opponents of the Manchester reformers, however, continued to use the epithet 'secular' as a weapon against them. The following year Cobden told the Commons, with some exasperation, that the provision for religious training already existed

> ... and therefore I wish to provide for secular education. I want people to be able to read and write – to be able to write their names when they sign a contract, or register the birth of their children; I want people to be trained in habits of thought and forethought; and I do not know any other term than 'secular' for this kind of education ... I say, once for all, that I am not opposed to the Bible or any other religious book being read in the schools.[75]

Some years later it occured to him that the supporters of a secular system of education should really be called 'separatists', because they advocated 'the *separation* of the religious from the secular instruction so that both may be had to the best advantage by all'.[76]

After the Manchester conference in 1850 Cobden held a series of private discussions with nonconformists and Anglicans in Birmingham, Huddersfield, Leeds and elsewhere. Many years earlier George Combe, the phrenologist, had told him, after examining his head, that if he had lived in the middle ages he would have made a capital monk.[77] Cobden was much gratified by this diagnosis from which he deduced that he had a special knack for getting on with religious people. Public discussions, he felt, were liable to arouse antagonism, but in private, with the aid of tea, tact and patience, much might be achieved.[78] He claimed to have had no difficulty in beating the opponents of secular education in argument, but it did not follow, he admitted, that they were converted to his ideas.[79]

Religious prejudice of another sort swept through the country during the winter of 1850–51. Towards the end of September, the Pope announced that he was dividing the country into 12 bishoprics with territorial titles. He appointed Dr Wiseman Archbishop of Westminster, and made him a cardinal. Wiseman produced a pastoral letter which implied that the people of England were about to return to the Church of Rome. This was obviously nonsense, but it was enough to spark off a tremendous wave of anti-Catholicism. Speeches, addresses, letters, articles, were poured forth from one end of the country to the other. Lord John Russell added fuel to the flames by sending the bishop of Durham an open letter in which he denounced the Pope's 'aggression' as 'insolent and insidious' and described Roman Catholic ceremonial as 'mummeries of superstition'. Early in the new session of Parliament he introduced a bill to prohibit the assumption of territorial titles by Roman Catholic bishops in Britain. The Irish members were furious and the Peelites were disgusted. So were all those Radicals who had not succumbed to the 'no-popery' storm.

Cobden did not succumb to the storm. He publicly and passionately deplored the revival of religious intolerance and the threat it implied to religious liberty and equality. He mocked the idea that the Queen's prerogatives and privileges would be invaded by the Pope unless the government intervened. He was particularly upset by the inflammatory effect of Lord John's Ecclesiastical Titles Bill on the Irish Catholics. When it was clear that the bill would become law, he told Sturge that he had never before felt so disgusted with political life and, had he not been so prominent, would have retired from it altogether. Only the Americans, he added, really understood about religious liberty.[80]*

The furore over the papal 'aggression' was not the only cause of Cobden's disgust with political life. The main reason, which the Catholic affair had strongly reinforced, was his alienation from the Whigs to whom he was supposed to be allied. The link had never

* The Ecclesiastical Titles Act remained a deadletter and was repealed by Gladstone in 1871.

Cobden was not immune to the instinctive disapproval of Roman Catholicism felt by so many Protestants. In April 1851 he went to a service in Chichester cathedral and thought it 'more like Romanism than ever. In fact, give the singing boys censers, and let them learn a few genuflexions, and the entire staff of a mass-house is ready to the hand of Cardinal Wiseman'. (to F. Cobden, [April 22], 1851, B. L. Add Mss. 50751).

fettered his independence and was becoming increasingly frayed, although in March he accepted an invitation to a meeting of 'the great liberal party' at Downing Street. (According to Cobden's rather malicious report, 'Johnny', who was small of stature, addressed the company standing on a chair before a looking-class.)[81] But he made no effort, either in public or private, to hide his opinion that there was little to choose between Whigs and Tories. Not surprisingly, some unfriendly newspapers dubbed him a disappointed demagogue. Cobden denied the charge at a big meeting of Liberal supporters at Manchester in January 1851. 'This disappointed demagogue wants no public employment; if I did, I might have had it before now ... I want nothing that any Government or any party can give me; and if I am in the House of Commons at all, it is to give my feeble aid to the advancement of certain questions on which I have strong convictions.' If he was told he must keep quiet for fear of destroying a government with which he could have no sympathy, then 'the sooner I return to printing calicoes, or something more profitable than sitting up in the House of Commons night after night ... the better both for me and my friends.'[82]

Cobden would never have found a parliamentary majority for his most cherished projects – cuts in government spending, especially on armaments. But many were frustrated by the near immobility imposed by parliamentary arithmetic and the self-isolation of the Peelites, who shunned the Conservatives because they still flirted with protection and Lord John Russell because of his personality, his quirkiness and, now, his outburst of religious bigotry. Lord John, for his part, had come to the conclusion that only another dose of parliamentary reform could deliver him and the country from a deadlocked and unworkable House of Commons. His Cabinet did not agree, and he was slow to act on his conviction. But on 20 February, 1851, after opposing a Radical motion for an extension of the franchise, he suddenly volunteered to introduce a reform bill himself in the next session.* His colleagues were annoyed, the Radicals delighted. A wider franchise suddenly seemed transformed from an impossible dream to a practical possibility. Walmsley's National Association, which had been weakened by lack of money and internal disputes, took on a new lease of life. Cobden, infected by the general optimism, told a meeting of the association in May that he no longer cared if they left financial reform out of their programme. 'Give me Parliamentary Reform and I will take my chance of getting all the rest'.[83]

---

* The motion, introduced by Mr Locke King, was in fact carried against the government by 100 to 52. Russell, exasperated by the unreliability of his majority, decided to resign. But the Tory leader, Lord Stanley, was unable to form a government, and Russell had to take up the reins again.

But the summer of 1851 was the summer of the Great Exhibition during which the country was more inclined to congratulate itself on its material achievements than agitate for political rights. Cobden was one of the commissioners chosen to organise the exhibition. He does not seem to have played a very active role – organisation not being his strong point – but he contributed unlimited enthusiasm which during the preliminary months of anxious preparation was sometimes in short supply. He persuaded sceptical Lancashire manufacturers that they should contribute their products to the exhibition, and insisted that the Peace Society's protest against exhibiting any 'warlike instruments' should include plenty of expressions of approval for the Prince Consort's 'truly magnificent project'.[84] For the exhibition, housed in its dazzling glass palace, was not just an impressive demonstration of national achievement. With half the exhibition space given over to foreign firms, it was also – or appeared to be – a heartening embodiment of Cobden's cherished belief that commerce was the true panacea that would bring international peace and understanding. To emphasise this aspect of the exhibition, a three-day peace congress was organised. Unfortunately, the 1200 delegates were overwhelmingly British, but at least the proceedings were well-reported in all the London papers.

Ten days after the opening ceremony which Cobden, true to his radical principles, refused to attend in court dress,* he wrote to a friend in the country: 'The exhibition is truly a spectacle that will make your heart expand. It marks an era of visible progress and warrants our aspirations for "the good time coming" . . . Description is powerless, and the imagination fails to picture the beauty and variety of the glass palace. Come and see it.'[85]

Altogether, more than six million visitors did go and see it. They included – or so it seemed to Cobden – his 36,000 constituents, all badgering him for some favour or other. It was 'enough to drive the most disciplined temper to madness'.[86] But for the exhibition itself he never lost his enthusiasm or his optimism about the benefits it would bestow on the cause of peace. 'It is a glorious work', he wrote a few days before the exhibition closed, 'successful even to the end, and will bear fruit in spite of Horse Guards, Admiralty and the Foreign Office.'[87]

Shortly after closing time on the last day of the exhibition, Cobden wrote to his brother from one of the committee rooms. 'We have had God Save the Queen and three times three, and now all the bells

---

* In spite of the mutual respect and liking which apparently developed between him and the Prince, Cobden refused a knighthood for his services to the exhibition. He was the only commissioner to do so. (Bennett, *King Without a Crown*. (1977) p. 211)

in the place are ringing the people out as fast as they can, but they don't seem to like to go. In fact it is the dying out of a great and pregnant event and nobody seems to be free from grave regrets'.[88] To contemporaries, especially foreigners with memories of the upheavals of 1848 still fresh in their minds, one of the most remarkable things about the Great Exhibition was the absence of disturbances of any sort. Mme Lieven, who had lived in England for many years as the wife of the Russian ambassador, reflected the views of many when she described the exhibition as a bold and rash experiment and feared a horrible explosion. But no bombs were thrown, no demonstrations were attempted, and the security was minimal. According to Cobden, the only serious damage was caused by a crowd surging forward to see the Duke of Wellington and breaking a statue and some other objects in their stampede. The incident was still fresh in his mind a year later, because few things grated on him more than the misplaced – as he felt – popular adulation of the country's greatest military hero.[89]

His attitude was quite different to the popular enthusiasm which greeted the arrival of the Hungarian leader, Lajos Kossuth, at Southampton on 23 October, 1851. The Turks had at last decided to defy Russian and Austrian threats and release the Hungarian refugees in their custody. Most of them accepted an offer of asylum in the United States, but Kossuth decided to visit England first. After the Mayor and Corporation of Southampton had given a banquet in his honour, the Radicals took him under their wing and arranged a triumphant tour through the country. Cobden was closely involved, sharing a platform with Kossuth at Winchester, advising him on what he should say in public and having a good deal of private talk with him. He shrewdly perceived that the secret of Kossuth's influence was his eloquence. 'Kossuth has really shown super-human ability. I question if another man in the world could have done what he has done – delivered five speeches without one mistake in a foreign language in less than ten days of his arrival from Turkey!'[90] On the whole, he was pleased with the moderation and good sense of what Kossuth said, publicly and privately, even though some of his admirers talked 'a little gunpowder'. The fact that the Hungarians were by now securely fastened down with Austrian fetters did not stop some of their British sympathisers from talking in a very bellicose way. Bright, due to speak at a big Kossuth meeting in the Free Trade Hall, was in a 'desperate puzzle' what to say after getting into a warm discussion in the League rooms with those who favoured 'a "tussle" with Russia *some time*, to put an end to Cossack domination, etc.'.[91] But neither Bright nor Cobden put popularity before principle. They could not condemn Russia's intervention in Hungary and at the same time urge a similar intervention by any other power. So Cobden assured Kossuth repeatedly that his only hope lay in the adoption of the principle of non-interference by the public opinion of the whole civilised world. It was a bleak and unsatisfactory message, and Cobden may have realised it was. It was difficult for him to resolve the conflict between his sympathy for the Hungarians, his sense of realism and his commitment to peace. Publicly, he urged that moral pressure by itself would be effective if those exerting it had a clean record – which, in his sympathy for the Hungarians, his sense of realism and his commitment to peace. Publicly, he urged that moral pressure by itself physical sanction.*

He found it easier to make up his mind about the oppressed Neapolitan liberals. In July 1851 Gladstone published a searing attack on the inhuman treatment meted out to the imprisoned opponents of King Ferdinand II, which he had witnessed while visiting Naples the previous winter. The pamphlet caused a tremendous sensation. There was a chorus of praise from the press, while Palmerston publicly congratulated Gladstone and sharply rejected the complaints of the Neapolitan minister. Cobden also was full of praise. In his opinion, Gladstone's exposure of the infamous government of Naples would do far more for the cause of humanity than anything that might be achieved through diplomatic channels. (He did not know that Gladstone's precipitate action had ruined the private representations that Lord Aberdeen was making to Ferdinand's patrons in Vienna.) But humanity was one thing, political rights another. When Cobden visited Naples in 1846 he had realised how small a minority the liberal politicians he met represented, and he had tried to persuade them to wait at least a generation before trying to bring in a constitutional government. Five years later he still felt that outside pressure could not hasten the process, and it was a cruel delusion to pretend it could.

> We cannot force the mass of the Neapolitan people to prefer our notions to their own. They have a right to revel in rags, and hug their fetters, and worship their priests' garments if they like . . . The small minority are dissatisfied, the rest neither know or care anything about the Government.[92]

---

* On 6 November, 1851, he wrote to Bright: 'Now I am satisfied that if public opinion in England can be shown to be unmistakably against [the] Russian invasion of Hungary, the Russian Government would no more think of risking a collision with the two most important maritime states [the other was the United States, mentioned earlier in the letter], than Tuscany or Sardinia would; for she is, if possible, more at the mercy of those powers. Therefore, to avoid the possibility of war, let us give the fullest development and expression to sound public opinion.' (Morley, *Richard Cobden*, 567)

Cobden did not long retain the optimism about political reform at home which had momentarily surged up in him after Lord John Russell's unexpected public commitment to reform. By the autumn of 1851 Bright was urging him '*to try to shake off your unbelief in political progress*'.[93] Cobden denied that he had lost his faith in political progress. He simply felt that there was no point in agitating for reforms when there was no popular demand for them.[94] He wrote from the seclusion of the Sussex countryside, and Bright, who had been touring the northern towns and campaigning for reform, felt he knew better than his friend about the state of popular feeling. He and George Wilson were determined to hold a conference in Manchester with the aim of influencing the contents of the reform bill promised by Lord John in the new session of Parliament. Cobden was unenthusiastic. He had been going through bundles of old letters from the League days, and thus his recollections of the men with whom he had then worked so successfully were vivid in his mind. He felt sure they would not, especially in their present prosperous state, throw themselves into an agitation for parliamentary reform.[95] Moreover, to launch the new movement from Manchester, the home of the successful League, would raise expectations which they could not fulfil. Above all – and here perhaps lay the root of his reluctance – people would expect *him* to do more than his fair share. '*Now*', he assured Bright, '*I have not another agitation left in me*.'[96] He did not suggest that nothing should be done, and he was willing to do something himself. But his physical stamina was no longer what it had been and he shrank from getting sucked into a campaign as intense and demanding as the League's had been. Towards the middle of September he told Sir Joshua Walmsley that in 'self-defence' he had refused to attend the proposed reform meeting in Manchester; his only chance of escaping the 'platform treadmill' was to refuse all invitations for a time.[97]

Cobden's so-much and no-more attitude must have been extremely frustrating for Bright. For both personal and public reasons he set the greatest store by his friend's support and co-operation. 'With you', he told him, 'I shall work with hope, indeed with a certain faith; without you, I should have no spirit in any political action.'[98] In the end, Bright won, and Cobden went to the conference. It was held in Manchester early in December, and attracted a wide range of support, from former Chartists to – as Cobden noted with satisfaction – 'many good and influential people from Lancashire and Yorkshire'.[99] With a heartening display of unity, the conference adopted the four points of Hume's 'Little Charter' which had been repeatedly rejected by the House of Commons.

In a number of other towns the radicals followed Manchester's example, shelving their differences and rallying their disparate forces behind an agreed programme. But in the rush of other events, it all came to nothing. Early in December Louis Napoleon seized power in Paris. Cobden scornfully dubbed him 'a mere hair-brained (sic) adventurer'[100] but, to the British public, stirred up by a violent anti-French campaign in the press, he was Bonaparte's nephew, and they wondered where his ambition would stop. Palmerston, acting entirely on his own initiative, sent his congratulations and approval to Louis Napoleon. The Cabinet, supported by the Queen, had wished to take a more neutral stance, and Lord John, also acting on his own initiative, seized the opportunity to dismiss an intolerably insubordinate colleague. No one – unless it was the Queen – was better pleased than Cobden, who described Palmerston's successor, Lord Granville, as 'a far sounder and more liberal man'.[101]

He was less pleased with the anti-French fever which continued to monopolise public attention. 'Last year', he complained to Bright on 29 January, 1852

> the invasion of the Pope. This year the French invasion – next year I suppose some modern Titus Oates will have some other plot – and all to divert attention from the real things. And all with success too ... Really I am half inclined to turn farmer and study the instincts of quadrupeds, and habits of plants, which are logical and rational compared with the folly of British bipeds ... really I meet with so many people here in London who have gone wild about the 'defences' from whom I expected better things that one never knows who are to be the next to take leave of their senses. *[102]

When Lord John proposed to improve the country's defences by forming a local militia, Cobden, who had been privately urging him to drop the subject,[103] argued passionately that the country's defences were perfectly adequate and anyway there was no danger of a French invasion. Palmerston took an exactly opposite line and moved that the militia should be national, not local. On 20 February his amendment was carried by 13 votes, and Lord John resigned. A few days later Palmerston wrote to his brother: 'I have had my tit-for-tat with John Russell, and I turned him out on Friday last.'[104]

The Queen sent for the Conservative leader, Lord Derby. He

---

* One of those he may have been thinking of was the historian and former Philosophic Radical George Grote, who wrote to Cobden on 26 December, 1851, warning him that Louis Napoleon would all too probably be warlike in order to preserve his throne. 'We know what a fund of dormant warlike impulse there always is in France, ready to be awakened, especially to avenge Waterloo which no Frenchman ever forgets. This Louis Napoleon affects to tread in his uncle's footsteps.' (B. L. Add Mss 43,668 6 December 1851.)

managed to cobble together a Cabinet that was richly endowed with aristocratic names but very short on experience. It also lacked a majority in the House of Commons. Disraeli, who had never held office before, found himself – with mixed feelings of delight and apprehension – both Leader of the House and Chancellor of the Exchequer. Cobden rejoiced over the elevation of the parvenu Disraeli which he considered a slap in the face for the aristocratic ruling caste. 'For my part', he told his brother, 'I should have no objection to see the new government supersede the Whigs for a while if it can only get rid of the tin kettle of protection.'[105]

This would not have been difficult if the new government had stated unequivocally that it accepted the verdict of 1846. Disraeli had long lost his illusions about a return to protection, but Derby still refused to abandon all his until the opinion of the country had been tested in a general election. Agreement to hold an election that summer was part of the price exacted by the Peelites for helping to sustain the government in office until the election.[106] In the meantime the Conservative leaders sent out confusing and ambiguous signals about their attitude towards protection. In his first statement as prime minister in the Lords, Derby appeared distinctly to favour a duty on imported corn and before he had even finished speaking, Cobden was sounding the alarm in a letter to George Wilson.[107]

When the League was wound up in July 1846, it was agreed that it should be immediately revived if there was any danger of a return to protection. Two days after Derby's statement, the League Council reassembled at its old headquarters in Manchester and before an enthusiastic audience inaugurated a new campaign to ensure that only free-trade candidates were returned at the forthcoming election. A campaign fund was started and the whole propaganda apparatus – lectures, meetings, petitions, leaflets, and so on – was again set in motion.* Two days later, Cobden addressed a meeting in Leeds. Although arranged at only twenty-four hours notice, the hall, which held up to 5000 people, was crammed long before the meeting was due to start. Afterwards, a cheering crowd followed Cobden back to his hotel. 'It is as I thought,' he wrote to Charles Villiers; 'the working people with their wives and families would *alone* prevent another Corn law being imposed. It is very different to what it was when I went to carry on a *middle class* agitation for the repeal.'[108]

---

* Cobden suggested to Wilson 'some telling placards' with woodcuts of the large 5d free-trade loaf and the small 9d protection loaf. But he was very disgusted with the placard Wilson later sent him because the free-trade loaf was disproportionately huge. '*It is not a caricature but the fact* you want to put forth.' (CP60 20 March, 1852.)

It was very different in other respects too, and not least in that it was really a sham fight against an enemy who had virtually given up the struggle. Before the end of March, Cobden – who, for a man of peace, was remarkably fond of military metaphors – was telling Wilson that 'we shall be in danger of wasting our strength in firing ball cartridges at a dead lion'.[109] What mattered to him was to get the election held as quickly as possible so that the free-trade issue could be laid to rest for ever (as he hoped) and the ground cleared for the other issues which now occupied the forefront of his mind. (Throughout the spring and early summer he was trying, through Joseph Sturge, to get up an agitation against the government's revised Militia Bill.[110])

The elections were held in July. Cobden had never felt at home in his West Riding constituency and had more than once declared privately that he would not stand for it again. The local Whig aristocracy were equally reluctant to have him again. But the election in 1852 was fought on the one issue about which Cobden and the whole West Riding Whig/Liberal party were united in their determination to demonstrate that they had had no second thoughts. Cobden agreed to stand, the party closed ranks behind him and he was returned unopposed. Elsewhere, it was a confused and confusing election. The protectionist candidates were hampered by their leaders' failure to give them a clear lead and, in the circumstances, they did well to gain more seats than they lost. But they still did not command a majority in the House of Commons and even Lord Derby abandoned all hope of restoring protection.

When Disraeli unveiled his budget proposals early in December, they were found to contain, reported Cobden, 'not a word or a figure . . . that a free trader could object to – the controversy is now fairly at an end'.[111] But with free trade safe, party politics took over. Through inexperience and lack of foresight Disraeli had made himself very vulnerable. The financial experts, including three ex-chancellors of the exchequer, arrayed on the Opposition front bench, did not spare him. After a debate lasting four nights had ended with a crushingly comprehensive indictment by Gladstone, the government was defeated by nineteen votes. Next day Derby resigned. The free-trade controversy had been finally laid to rest, but the political instability which was the legacy of repeal still remained.

CHAPTER 11

The Crimea and Democratic Responsibility (1852–56)

Dunford, Cobden's birthplace near Midhurst, was an out-of-the-way little hamlet, with fewer than three hundred inhabitants, sheltering under the South Downs. Its situation was beautiful, but in many respects it exemplified all that Cobden most disapproved of in rural life. The people were poor and ignorant, with little or no chance of bettering themselves. There was no resident landowner or clergyman. There was no school, apart from two dame schools run by illiterate old women who looked after small children while their parents were working in the fields. There was no post office or postal service, only an old man of about seventy, who went in to Midhurst each day and brought back letters (if there were any) and anything else that might be wanted, from legs of mutton to wheelbarrows.[1]

But Cobden had always cherished the hope of repossessing his old family home and when in 1847 he was offered a chance to buy the property, he eagerly took it up. The small estate of about 140 acres, including a considerable amount of woodland, cost him £3500, excluding the value of the timber.* There were two tenants, and the farmhouse, by now in a very tumbledown state, was occupied by three families of farm labourers.

Cobden first visited his new estate in October 1848, while he was holidaying on Hayling Island. He picked a leaf for Kate from the rose

---

* In January 1850, when there was a revival of protectionist agitation, Cobden told a rather hostile audience of farmers at Aylesbury that he himself owned a small estate in Sussex. Someone called out: 'You got it from the League funds.' Cobden agreed that he owed it to the bounty of his countrymen, adding that it had belonged to his ancestors, and 'I say that no warrior duke who owns a vast domain by the vote of the Imperial Parliament, holds his property by a more honourable title than I possess mine'. This was received with cheers. (Morley, *Richard Cobden*, p. 466–7.)

tree growing against the side of the house, and had a cursory look round the neighbourhood. Like everyone returning to a place they have not seen since early childhood, he was surprised to see how small everything looked.[2] At first his only interest in his acquisition was to behave like a model landlord. He carried out some much needed drainage at his own expense, gave his tenants unlimited authority to kill the hares and rabbits which were ravaging their crops and vegetables, and reduced their rent in line with the fall in the price of wheat.[3]

But sometime during the summer of 1849 Kate visited Dunford, fell in love with it and suggested that the farm house might be turned into a summer holiday home for the family. (A second daughter had been born the previous year.) Frederick, who by now had made a permanent home with his brother, approved of the idea. Richard, who had 'a great horror' of becoming saddled with two establishments, was cautious. But he was greatly worried about the 'disgraceful' overcrowding in which the families in the farm house were 'pigging together'. He feared an outbreak of fever or cholera for which he would feel himself responsible. And so, since something had to be done about the house anyway, it was an easy step to decide to make it habitable as a summer retreat where for a month or two the family could live a healthy outdoor life. But Cobden was very firm with Frederick that nothing more ambitious was to be attempted.[4]

Two of the families living in the house were found cottages in the neighbourhood which were repaired and made comfortable at Cobden's expense. The third family – an elderly labourer, his wife and daughter – would, Cobden decided, remain in part of the house and act as caretakers. Apparently anticipating criticism of this arrangement, he told Frederick: 'There may be objection to the helpless and wretched character of people of class – but if their character be good and they are encouraged and paid sufficient to keep themselves decently, they will not remain dirty or ragged from choice. We should be no better than they, if we led their precarious life.'[5] A year later, part of the house had been sufficiently repaired and renovated for the Cobdens to spend about six weeks there in September and October. The old farmyard, with its insalubrious outbuildings, had been cleared away, the drainage and sewage arrangements overhauled, and work on the garden and grounds was in full swing. By this time Cobden had become a keen gardener, and his letters to Frederick, who seems to have slipped into the role of overseer at Dunford in his brother's absence, were full of instructions about trees, plants and bushes. 'Remember', he wrote in November 1850, 'that any attempt to introduce ornamental shrubs or artificial arrangements into the grounds round Dunford would be in regular cockney taste and I should certainly root them up. Let us have consistency throughout, and therefore I am for wild evergreens, rather than rhododendrums or even laurels.'[6]

Dunford grew on Cobden every time he went there. In March 1851 he slipped down by himself for a few days after a bout of influenza, and reported enthusiastically to Kate that nothing could be better 'for a quiet temporary retreat'.[7] During the Easter recess he again visited Dunford alone. 'There is no want of life in the woods now', he told Frederick. 'I have not been to Midhurst or elsewhere, and have been so much interested in looking and walking about that I find myself in no want of company.'[8] His chief ploy in the garden during their visit was the planting, with the help of an elderly gardener, of nearly a hundred roses which he had very extravagantly ordered on his way through Chichester. 'I intend' – he told Kate – 'to have a bed of them on the rising ground just at the end of the house, not coming forward too far to interfere with the view of the Downs. I shall also have a bed in front of the house. We shall shine in roses ... I long for the time when we can be here with the children in the autumn. You will enjoy it beyond measure.'[9]

At the beginning of August, Cobden decided that young Richard needed some Sussex air after an attack of mumps, and the two of them went down to Dunford. 'We have been here just 24 hours', he reported to Kate, 'and your hopeful son has made the most of his time. He has been every where and seen every thing, from the roof to the cellar ... He has been three times round the wood with Quinell, for whom he has of course taken a violent attachment, and there is work enough cut out in fishing, trapping, bird-nesting and kite flying to give full employment for the week.[10] Cobden himself was feeling 'quite *done up*' after the labours of the parliamentary session and the turmoil of the Great Exhibition[11] and was thankful for a good excuse to escape from London. Kate, who had produced a third daughter (Emma Jane) in April, had had more than her fill of dispensing hospitality to exhibition visitors, but found it difficult to get rid to them. Cobden suggested a little ruthlessness. 'I should not scruple to begin clearing the drawing-room and leaving your visitors to content themselves with the little library'.[12]

Once the family was established at Dunford that autumn, only the closing of the Great Exhibition prised Cobden out of his rural retreat until past the middle of November. 'I thought', he told Frederick on the 17th, 'Kate would have been sick of this place when the cold weather came; but she grows fonder than ever of it and votes with both hands for never going back to Westbourne Terrace.'[13] That year the family spent the Christmas holiday at Dunford. To the children the place was no longer only a summer retreat; as Cobden was taking young Dick back to his boarding school in the train, the boy drew an old decayed leaf out of his pocket and solemnly told his father that it was a memorial of Dunford.[14]

A year later, Kate was finding it almost too difficult to wrench herself away from the country. Alone in London, Cobden wrote to a friend on 27 October, 1852, 'My wife seems half resolved never to bring the children back to London. They are so much happier and healthier where they are. Indeed she is advocating the building a good house for us all, and the giving up a town life altogether. Either it does not suit her or she it, for she is certainly not fascinated with West End existence'.[15] A month later he prevailed upon her to visit London for a few days. He was, he complained to his sister Priscilla, sick of being alone in a great empty house and 'having nobody to make a cup of tea for me'.[16] But as he himself was becoming increasingly attached to country life, he was not well placed to persuade Kate to consider London, rather than Dunford, as her permanent home.

He probably did not try very hard. By the new year of 1853 the die had been cast and the decision taken to pull down most of the old house and build a commodious family home on the old foundations. The accounts for the building work still exist. How they were settled is not clear, but expense does not seem to have worried Cobden; only the delays and temporary setbacks inevitable in any sizeable building operations. On 20 February he wrote to Kate,

> I am terribly put out about the front windows, both bed rooms and below. The pattern is in very common taste. Instead of the sash having one handsome pane, as I fully intended and hoped, it is divided thus [a sketch]. Now I have a great aversion to these side slips of glass. To my taste they are mean and common and I have written an abusive letter to Wehnert [the architect], who writes back he is quite resolved I shall not have anything always annoying my sight, and that he has a way of remedying it at little cost. I should wish you to see them before he comes ... I have found it very necessary to be here to have a voice about the contrivance for getting water to the wheel, which is more difficult than expected. The culvert is quite finished and a beautiful improvement it is. We are making good progress.

But he urged her to come for a few days so that they could reach a 'minute understanding' about the doors and fittings, because after seeing Wehnert's taste in windows they could not leave it to him.[17]

Later, from London, Cobden sent a string of exhortatory letters to his brother. 'Be sure you torment Grish [the builder] incessantly about the slates and all other materials. Unless you look ahead – depend on it you will be hung up for stuff of all kinds.' 'Tell Wehnert to bind Grish down for times as tight as possible. I am afraid the job will never be finished.' How are they to dispose of the old materials not needed in the new house? Would he get an estimate of the cost of the pump to the large cistern in the little tower? There were also plans for developing the grounds, and Frederick was adjured to plant hollies and yews rather than 'Cocknessy' laurels, to get the big tree out of the brook opposite the cottages, raise the border along the bottom of a field, and so on. At the end of April, Cobden took pity on his brother and suggested he joined them in London for a change. 'It must be very dull and dismal for you to be so much alone, especially in the midst of the ruins of the poor old house.'[18]

Towards the end of August, it was clear that the new house would not be habitable before Christmas. Kate, who had just produced a fourth daughter (Julia Sarah Anne), decided to evacuate Westbourne Terrace completely and establish a temporary home at Bognor, where Cobden could enjoy being with his family and still be reasonably near the operations at Dunford. Kate would drive him in her carriage as far as the Duke of Richmond's park and he would then trudge over Goodwood Down and the unenclosed country beyond until he reached his own domain.[19]

But even when he was not on the spot, a part – if not always the whole – of Cobden's mind was usually mulling over the progress and problems of his building operations. He was particularly concerned with drainage and sanitary matters. 'It may be a mere fancy, but I have a strong objection on sanitary grounds to open drains of any kind near a house and should feel much more comfort (sic) and a sense of healthfulness if the ditch in question were closed throughout its whole length.' His instructions to Frederick were precise and particular. The famous drain, or culvert, must be contracted by one inch at its upper end. A recess must be made in the hall just before the kitchen door to hold their flat hat and umbrella stand. In the orchard, loam must be mixed with the sandy soil – there must be some good strong loam available from the lowering of the road at the top of the hanger. The old tree trunks should be moved into an outhouse where they could be chopped into firewood when it was too wet to work outside: a great many fires would be needed to dry out the house.[20]

By the end of November, the date of the move had been fixed for 22 December. They must therefore, Cobden told his brother, press on with the essential work, especially the cesspit because of the water closets, and the tank because of the water supply for the house.[21] The move was postponed for a week, but even then – Cobden reported dolefully to a friend – 'the workpeople have still full possession and from the cellar to the attic nothing seems finished'. He dreaded the discomfort his wife would have to endure for the next two months[22] – and with reason, for in addition to the discomfort indoors, the winter weather made it impossible for them to go outdoors without stepping into a 'sea of sludge'.[23]

But in the long run they did not regret their migration to the country. And Cobden, in spite of his anxiety to remove all 'Cocknessy' traces from his grounds, seems to have been well satisfied with his villa, which in fact would not have seemed out of place if set down in an immaculate garden in the middle of Wimbledon. He had to reconcile himself once more to a solitary existence in London, but he made sure that the lodgings he chose – at 38 Grosvenor Street – were commodious and comfortable enough for Kate to stay with him.[24]

It might have been expected that once the issue of protection had been finally disposed of, the Peelites would have returned to their original home in the Conservative party. Gladstone indeed nearly did so. But most of the leading Peelites – Lord Abderdeen, Sir James Graham, the Duke of Newcastle (formerly Lord Lincoln) and Sidney Herbert – considered that they had more in common with the Whig/Liberal party, although they felt an instinctive aversion to the name 'Whig'. But in response to a suggestion that it might be dropped, Lord John Russell tartly replied that the name Whig 'has the convenience of expressing in one syllable what Conservative Liberal expresses in seven, and Whiggism in two syllables what Conservative Progress means in another seven (sic)'.[25]

It was more than a semantic disputation, but after the fall of Lord Derby's government in December 1852, it did not prevent Lord Aberdeen from forming a coalition Cabinet containing six Peelites, six Whigs and one Radical. The Whigs were disgusted that the Peelites, whose support in the Commons had shrunk to about forty, should have as many Cabinet seats as they. But Aberdeen was determined not to preside over a Whig Cabinet with a few Peelites thrown in, and on grounds of experience and talent there could be no complaint about the Peelite contingent. The solitary – one might almost say statutory – Radical in the Cabinet was Sir William Molesworth, who enjoyed an impeccably aristocratic background. So did Charles Villiers, who was given a post outside the Cabinet which Cobden indignantly told him was only tolerable as a stepping-stone.[26]

According to Bright, he and Cobden had made up their minds on the day of Derby's resignation not to have anything to do with the coalition which Aberdeen was about to put together.[27] They felt respect for the Peelites and a kind of fellow-feeling arising out of the battle for free trade. Cobden confessed to having 'always felt a sort of sneaking fondness for Lord Aberdeen',[28] and Bright described him as 'a quiet, sensible man, not likely to go wrong, judicious and liberal, and sincere'.[29] But they both still preferred to keep their independence, and support the government from outside when they thought fit.

In any case, they were never made an offer. And although Sir James Graham politely assured Bright, when he met him by chance, that he was entitled to a share in the government, it seems most improbable that he or Cobden were ever seriously considered.[30] They had said and done nothing to suggest that they would make comfortable colleagues in a government based on Abderdeen's concept of 'conservative progress'; in fact, rather the contrary.[31] Their views on national defence were particularly unacceptable. Cobden heard a rumour that it was because of these he had been excluded.[32] It may well have been true. Everybody wanted to cut government spending and taxation as much as possible. But Cobden's endlessly reiterated demand to reduce the cost of the armed services to a level which most sober men genuinely believed to be thoroughly imprudent and irresponsible, put him out of court as an acceptable Cabinet colleague. As Lord John wrote, when reflecting on the unlikelihood that Cobden and Bright (and Hume) could ever form or lead a party of their own, 'those who agree in many of their opinions will give their practical support to men less extreme and more judicious'.[33]

Throughout much of 1852 the hysterical alarm about Louis Napoleon's intentions simmered on, fed by the press and travellers' tales from Paris. Henry Richard, secretary of the Peace Society and editor of its paper, tried to dispel the alarm in the columns of the *Herald of Peace*. Cobden did his best to help him, sending facts, statistics, reasoning and any useful ideas that came into his head. Remembering that the League had offered prizes for essays on the Corn laws, he made the suggestion in one letter of offering a prize for an essay on European armaments – 'I send you the idea just raw as it enters my head.'[34] Early in December Louis Napoleon declared himself Emperor Napoleon III, and the anti-French alarm in England flared up afresh. In the new year of 1853 Cobden decided to make a contribution towards correcting the false version – as he saw it – of recent history which be believed to be a primary cause of the anti-French feeling in England. As most of his library was still in London – Dunford had not yet been rebuilt – a stream of requests went out to Henry Richard and other friends for dates, statistics, extracts from pamphlets and so on. A French friend, for instance, sent him statistics of French imports of raw materials, including coal for the navy, which demonstrated, to Cobden's delighted satisfaction, that the current rumour that the French were building a huge steam navy was quite without foundation. 'I confess it sorely tries my temper to write with moderation on this point.'[35]

The pamphlet, called *1793 and 1853*, was written in the form of three letters to an imaginary clergyman who had sent Cobden a copy of his sermon on the death of the Duke of Wellington. The pamphlet's aim was to dispel the fear of France, which threatened peace by producing constant demands for more armaments, thereby, in Cobden's view, making war more, not less, likely. He argued that, contrary to popular belief, the war with revolutionary France did not originate in any act of aggression by the French, but in the determination of the European despots, followed by the oligarchic British government, to destroy the revolutionary regime which was proclaiming dangerous and subversive ideas of liberty, equality and the rights of man. He declared categorically that 'England was the aggressor in the last French war',[36] and to prove his case he analysed the diplomatic correspondence that preceded the outbreak of hostilities in 1793. But he virtually ignored the basic cause of the ordinary Englishman's fear of the French, which was France's conquest of Europe under Napoleon's leadership.

Privately, he argued that after Nelson had destroyed Napoleon's sea power at Trafalgar it was quite unnecessary for Britain to intervene against him on the continent, and since most of Europe was still autocratically governed, it could not be claimed that Wellington had saved the liberties of Europe.[37] But these were hardly the arguments to put forward publicly a few months after Wellington's death. Instead, believing that everything in France 'is viewed by us through a distorted and prejudiced medium',[38] he set out to present a more accurate picture of French beliefs and attitudes. He pointed out that, in the context of the past 800 years, the French had more reason to expect an invasion by the British than vice versa. He went on to explain that the French set most store by the social equality which they had achieved through the Revolution, whereas the British (quite rightly, in his opinion) prized their personal liberties most highly. He then expounded all the arguments – economic, financial, commercial, military, social and political – why the French were extremely unlikely to attack the British in 1853.

Cobden believed that the most effective practical step towards reducing the danger of war between England and France was to stop their rivalry in the preparations for war. He was convinced that only the strong pressure of public opinion would move a British government to reduce its defence spending, and he called on the 'peace party', working 'in the manner of the League' to carry out a transformation of public opinion to this end.[39] He insisted that the abundant energy which had made the national character so aggressive and combative could be channelled into more worthwhile pursuits. 'Are not our people uneducated? juvenile delinquents uncared for? does not drunkenness still reel through our streets? Have we not to battle with vice, crime, and their parent, ignorance, in every form? And may not even charity display as great energy and courage in saving life, as was ever put forth in its destruction?' And in case anyone thought he was indulging in starry-eyed idealism, he gave a vivid and moving account of how some English Quakers had gone to help the Irish famine victims and found themselves in 'the charnel-house of a nation'.

Never since the 11th century, did pestilence, the gaunt hand-maiden of famine, glean so rich a harvest. In the midst of a scene, which no field of battle ever equalled in danger, in the number of its slain, or the suffering of the surviving, these brave men moved as calm and undismayed as though they had been in their own homes ... No music strung the nerves; no smoke obscured the imminent danger; no thunder of artillery deadened the senses. It was cool self-possession and resolute will ... And who were these brave men? To what 'gallant' *corps* did they belong? Were they of the horse, foot, or artillery force? They were Quakers, from Clapham or Kingston! ...[40]

Bright read his friend's pamphlet with 'intense pleasure' and considered it would have a powerful and very useful effect on public opinion.[41] At any rate, it sold well and was widely read. Most of the London press, absorbed in its anti-French scare stories, attacked it vehemently. *The Times* reprinted the whole pamphlet in three successive numbers, accompanying each instalment with a leading article.[42] It had decided, it wrote, to 'let Mr Cobden have his say fairly out, and introduce him to the public in his entirely new character of an historical lecturer'. In that capacity he was an easy target and the paper picked him off with patronising irony. It completely endorsed Cobden's plea for better relations with France, but could not believe that his version of history would influence present opinion in English. Few, however, would regret having read Mr Cobden's letters, 'for his composition, if he will accept the compliment, is better than his history, and his language than his logic. But he set out with a predetermined opinion, and fancied that he was confirming it conclusively by picking up one side of an old argument and omitting the other'.

It is difficult to disagree with *The Times*'s judgment. Cobden had an excellent case with regard to the anti-French phobia of 1853, but his dubious excursion into history made all it too easy to ignore or belittle it. Since Mr Cobden believed in a future of perpetual peace, concluded *The Times*, he was perfectly consistent in decrying all defensive preparations. As, however, most Englishmen did not share his confidence, what more natural 'than that they should seek to put their own shores beyond reach of danger without reference to the diplomatic correspondence of M. Chauvelin in 1792?' But Cobden, puzzled and pleased that *The Times* had given him so much space, was completely impervious to the paper's criticism. He was merely delighted with the free publicity; '... it is an abundant recompense for the little night-work, and the occasional cold feet it [the pamphlet] cost me, to see it sent to all the corners of the earth upon the *Times*'s broad sheet'.[43]

Cobden managed to finish his pamphlet in time for publication before the opening of the fourth Peace Congress at Manchester on 28 January. The meeting was, he told Kate, 'a regular cram'.[44] In his speech he reiterated the arguments of his pamphlet, declaring that the last war originated with the British, and that their ignorance about the French people was at the bottom of the invasion scare. In spite of his outspokenness, Cobden was acutely aware that he must appear moderate and reasonable if he was to get his message across. He was speaking from the platform of the British Peace Society which was resolutely opposed to war of any kind, and he emphasised that he himself did not believe in total non-resistance. 'I will put an end to war if I can, but will submit to no injustice if I can prevent it.'[45] Similarly, when, in the House of Commons a few weeks later, he begged the government to take the initiative in seeking a mutual reduction of armaments with the French, he added that if there was no response he would be ready if necessary to vote £100,000,000 in order to defend the country from invasion.[46]

During his visit to Manchester early in 1853, Cobden threw himself unsparingly into the meetings and deliberations of the peace movement; he had been, he rather quaintly told Kate, on 'the incessant trot'.[47] Afterwards he and Joseph Sturge led a large deputation to 10 Downing Street to present an address to a sympathetic Lord Aberdeen. It all seemed worthwhile. But to agitate for parliamentary reform, as Bright still wanted to do, did not. Cobden had convinced himself that in the circumstances of 1853 (as in those of 1837) the only political reform worth contending for was the secret ballot. 'You cut out,' he told Sir Joshua Walmsley, 'the very heart of the aristocratic system in applying the principle of secret voting.'[48] It certainly seemed indisputably necessary. Bribery and intimidation were recognised facts of electoral life, but during the 1852 general election they had been practised so excessively that the new Parliament was nicknamed 'the Bribery Parliament'. Cobden declared his blood almost boiled with indignation at the 'puerile pretences' with which the ballot was resisted,[49] and during the autumn of 1852 he encouraged the formation of societies in London and elsewhere to agitate for it.[50] They did not come to much, but Cobden's encouragement of them was deplored by those like Bright, Walmsley and Hume who wanted to reinvigorate the wider agitation for parliamentary reform.

Early in 1853 Bright and his friends began to organise another reform meeting to be held in Manchester about the same time as the peace congress. As he had done a year earlier, Cobden argued strongly against it. '. . . I am sick of this everlasting attempt *out of doors* to give the semblance of an agitation which don't exist . . . Our meeting and talking in Manchester positively misleads people.' The public would not be very radically disposed, he assured Bright, so long as the present prosperity lasted. ' "There is a time for all things", and this is the moment in my opinion to hold our tongues.'[51] A fortnight later he told Bright that he definitely would not attend his meeting. He added that, as he had other engagements in Yorkshire at the time, it would not look like a split.[52] Bright was greatly annoyed at Cobden's defection, not least because he feared that his friend was losing the will to take the lead in the political struggle.[53]

Cobden was certainly unwilling to lead what seemed to him a hopeless struggle. But was it? He believed that nothing by way of political reform could be expected from the country's aristocratic rulers unless they were irresistibly pushed from 'out of doors' – that is by public opinion, which, as everybody agreed, prosperity had made apathetic on the subject. But Lord John Russell was pledged to reform. He had introduced a reform bill just before his government fell in February 1852, and, when he was returned to office ten months later, he indicated that he intended to introduce another, if not immediately, then in the following session. Lord Aberdeen supported him and so did most of the coalition Cabinet with varying degrees of reluctance. They realised that, at the very least, the most corrupt boroughs would have to be disfranchised. Russell and many other Whigs were, it is true, opposed to the ballot, and according to Cobden, without the ballot, neither the extension of the franchise nor the redistribution of seats nor any other reform was worth anything.[54] But by making the ballot a *sine qua non* while believing, as he professed to do, that it would be 'opposed by the aristocracy and the "families" to the political death',[55] Cobden was in effect opting for stalemate.

The reform bill which Russell introduced in February 1854 was a modest but useful step towards a wider franchise and a fairer distribution of seats. Bright thought the franchise clauses were a useful half-way measure, and a meeting of Radical MPs, summoned by Hume, decided to vote for the second reading and then try to introduce the ballot and other improvements in committee. But Cobden dismissed it as a 'foolish' bill and told Bright he did not care what happened to it.[56] As it turned out, he was never to know how

the bill would have fared at the hands of Parliament. In April it was
dropped because of the imminence of war with Russia. 'The country'
wrote Sir Charles Wood '. . . is now bent on war, and will not
trouble itself about Reform.'[57]

It is not clear why Cobden was so opposed to accepting what was
on offer simply because it did not include everything. His attitude
towards the budget that Gladstone, the new Chancellor of the
Exchequer, introduced on 18 April 1853 was very different. It was
one of Gladstone's finest parliamentary performances, and even after
ten days' reflection Cobden still described it to the Commons as his
'very remarkable – I may say very marvellous – speech'.[58] The
centrepiece of the budget was the intensely unpopular income tax
which had just expired after having been renewed three times since
Peel reintroduced it in 1842. Gladstone proposed to continue it at the
old rate (7d) for two years and then to reduce it progressively until it
was abolished altogether in 1860. To increase the tax's yield he proposed to lower the exemption from £150 to £100 a year. In principle,
Cobden had always preferred the income tax to indirect taxes on
articles of consumption, including necessities like tea and soap,
which weighed most heavily on those least able to pay them. But he
had always strongly criticised the existing system of income tax as
unfair and unequal because it made no distinction between 'precarious' (earned) and 'permanent' (unearned) income.

Gladstone still refused to make any distinction between types of
income, so that on this count, as well as on the eventual abolition of
the tax, Cobden found the Chancellor's income tax proposals unsatisfactory. But Gladstone enlarged the existing legacy duty, which
applied only to personal property, into a general succession duty – a
reform for which the Radicals had long pressed but which was extremely unpopular with the upper classes. He also proposed another
hefty instalment of tariff reform, reducing, or removing altogether,
the duty on more than 250 articles. Finally, as guardian of the public
purse, Gladstone exhibited a ruthless determination to enforce the
strictest economy in all government spending. Altogether, Cobden
found Gladstone a Chancellor after his own heart. He felt he could
not deny him his support, although – as he confided to his brother –
it was rather awkward to do so when there was to be no change in
the system of income tax. He was not used to swallowing his words,
'and I expect Dizzy will rub my nose in Hansard. However, I shall
go for the budget as a whole.'[59]

But there was one item in Gladstone's budget which Cobden did
vehemently attack: the reduction of the tax on newspaper advertisements from 1/6 to sixpence. He wanted it repealed altogether, and so
it eventually was, by dint of persistence and some adroit parliamentary manoeuvring by a group of Radicals led by Milner Gibson,

Cobden and Bright. One of the three 'taxes on knowledge' – the other two were the newspaper stamp and the paper duty – which obstructed the development of a cheap press had been removed, and this was all the more welcome to Cobden because of the continuing deadlock over elementary education.

Since the winter of 1850–51 when Cobden made his passionate appeals, public and private, for a national system of education, there had been a good deal of activity on the education question but no progress. A predominantly Anglican group, the Manchester and Salford Committee on Education, had produced a scheme for providing free education by financing all the existing denominational schools in the Manchester area from a local rate. Unlike the NPSA, the Manchester Committee managed to embody its plan in a bill which was presented to the House of Commons in 1852 and then disappeared into a select committee. The provision of more education was so important to Cobden that he would have backed the Manchester Committee's plan or any other that had a chance of being accepted. But his bitter disgust at the religious intolerance which blocked progress made him deeply pessimistic about whether anything could be achieved. It perhaps also helps to explain why he failed to use his prestige and persuasive talents to better effect on the NPSA. 'If', he appealed to Samuel Smiles, 'we were half as anxious for the education of the people as we pretend to be, don't you think we should manage to get over the sectarian impediments that are now allowed to impede us?'[60]

In 1853 Lord John Russell produced a bill designed to assist the existing voluntary schools that accepted a government grant. Cobden described it as 'really little better than an abortion'.[61] It showed, he felt, that no strong lead could be expected from the coalition government in resolving the deadlock created by sectarian prejudice. For the time being, he told George Combe on 15 April, 1853, there was nothing to be done for educational reform. 'Therefore I raise my voice for the removal of the taxes on knowledge.'[62]

A cheap press was not of course an alternative to education, but in Cobden's mind the two were closely linked. 'Is it not enough to make one's blood boil over to think that the hypocrites ... who uphold this [newspaper] stamp pretend to be favourable to education?'[63] The two issues were also closely linked to political reform. An educated and knowledgeable working class which could be trusted to use its votes responsibly was an essential goal for radical reformers. Cobden was scathing about those who defended the newspaper stamp while opposing an extension of the franchise on the grounds of the people's ignorance. 'The stamp lies at the bottom of the great mound of ignorance and helplessness which bars the path of political and social progress in this country.'*[64]

Only a minority could afford a daily newspaper. Others who were interested either hired one for a small fee, read one in a newsroom or public house, or subscribed to a copy sent the rounds through the post (postage was free for stamped papers). In the early 1830s, during the agitation over the Reform Bill, hundreds of unstamped penny papers sprang up.[65] They leavened their political news and comment with literary, theatrical and humorous items, and most were neither blasphemous nor seditious. But they were illegal, and hundreds of those involved in producing and selling them were prosecuted. In 1836 the newspaper stamp was reduced from fourpence to one penny and new regulations were introduced for controlling the press. The net effect of the changes was to reduce the illegal 'pauper press' and strengthen the position of the established papers, such as *The Times*, which was why they stoutly opposed the removal of the taxes on knowledge. But newspapers were still too costly for the working class and many of the middle class.† As Cobden wrote in September 1850:

> So long as *the penny* lasts, there can be no daily press for the middle or working class. *Who* below the rank of merchant or wholesale dealer can afford to take in a daily paper at 5d? Clearly it is beyond the reach of the mechanic and the shopkeeper ... the great public cannot have its organs of the daily press because it cannot pay for them ... The governing class of this country will resist the removal of the penny stamp, not on account of the loss of revenue ... but because they know that the stamp makes the daily press the instrument and servant of the oligarchy.[66]

Cobden felt no sympathy for those who feared the effect of a cheap and uncontrolled press on the country's institutions. Nor had he any use for those who pointed to the cheap trash so popular with the working class and argued that they were not interested in anything better. He conceded that there was little popular demand for cheap newspapers, but pointed out that the majority had never acquired the habit of regular newspaper-reading because they could not afford them. During a debate on the taxes on knowledge in April 1853, he regaled the Commons with a list of the cheap publications sold by a

---

* A modern historian has estimated that in the 1840s between two thirds and three quarters of the working classes could read, although many rarely did so. (R. K. Webb. EHR (1950) Vol. LXV, 349)

† In 1853 an Arundel printer started a monthly penny periodical. It was unstamped and he was fined £5. When he produced it stamped, and charged twopence, he sold three copies in three villages where he had sold nearly thirty penny papers. (Cobden to Bright, B.L. Add. Mss. 43,650 22 Nov., 1853).

well-known retailer – *Black Monk, Hangman's Daughter, Love and Mystery, Blighted Heart* and so on. Would it not be preferable, he asked, to let people have better intellectual nourishment than this – the important news of the day and, for example, an item on Prince Albert laying the foundation-stone of a model cottage. Cobden maintained that if the working man could afford one or the other, he would reject the trash in favour of a publication that could give him knowledge and intellectual stimulus.*[67] For Cobden (if not for all those involved) the campaign against the taxes on knowledge was primarily part of the struggle for the education of the masses.

Cobden did not place himself at the head of the campaign. He spoke up for it whenever occasion offered and, from behind the scenes, gave constant guidance and encouragement. In Parliament the lead was taken by Milner Gibson whom Cobden had so mistakenly underrated when the Manchester reformers first chose him as their candidate in 1840. Outside Parliament a pressure group, originally organised by some moderate Chartists in 1848, had by 1851 evolved into a society with the cumbersome title of the Association for Promoting the Repeal of the Taxes on Knowledge, with Milner Gibson as chairman and Cobden and Bright among the members of the committee.

The financial penalties inflicted on those prosecuted for producing or selling unstamped papers could be very heavy, and the reformers hammered away at the hardship and unfairness caused by the vagueness of the law and the arbitrary and inconsistent way in which it was applied. No one could be sure what was news and what was not. A government lawyer and officials of the Inland Revenue gave Cobden the ridiculous ruling that the Queen's Speech was news, but the Chancellor of the Exchequer's budget statement was not.[68] In short, the stamp amounted to censorship because, as C. D. Collet, the indefatigable secretary of the APRTK, told a Commons Select Committee, 'the amount of news or political comment that we are allowed to write depends entirely upon the pleasure of the officer at the Stamp Office, and not upon the law of the land'.†[69]

Characteristically, Cobden's advice to the APRTK was always in

---

* A more prevalent view was probably represented by W. H. Smith, who told the Select Committee on the Newspaper Stamp in May 1851, in answer to a direct question from Cobden, that he did not think a newspaper could be published for a penny or twopence 'without pandering to a very immoral taste'. (Parliamentary Papers, 1851, Vol. XVII, 424)

† *Household Narrative*, a monthly chronology of facts and figures, was published as a supplement to Charles Dickens's *Household Words*. It was prosecuted for being unstamped, but was eventually acquitted on the grounds that it was not a newspaper under the terms of the 1712 Act, being published at intervals of more than 26 days.

favour of a moderate and conciliatory approach. Embarrass the
Inland Revenue officials with their contradictions and inconsisten-
cies, but do not indulge in vindictive personal attacks, do not adopt a
defiant or threatening tone, and do not forget that the great British
public does not seem to care nearly so much about the matter as you
do. When Collet sent him the draft of an address to Gladstone,
during the early stages of the popular anti-Russian clamour in 1853,
Cobden replied

> ... if you could only have the support of one such spontaneous
> meeting as we have seen supporting the Grand Turk ... you
> might then fling saucy phrases at the head of a Chancellor of the
> Exchequer with consistency. But cast your eye over the subscrip-
> tion list of the 'Association', and you will see how exclusively,
> almost, we comprise steady, sober, middle-class reformers – free-
> trade, temperance, education, peace advocates – who will stand
> by you from year to year ... provided you handle them judi-
> ciously, and do not place them in a position in which they think
> they are committed to a *tone* of agitation which does not represent
> their feelings. As an old master in that line, who served my seven
> years' apprenticeship, I must use the privilege of speaking
> frankly.[70]

To these sober, middle-class reformers Cobden was a great catch
as a public speaker and, by his own account, he was never before
'half so much persecuted' by them as in the autumn of 1853 – peace,
the ballot, education, the taxes on knowledge, juvenile delinquency
and mechanics' institutions were the movements he was asked to
support – 'and the screw is put on me in all directions to make me
go'.[71]

But at least he was able to fit in a visit to Dick at his school at
Worksop. Cobden's own dreadful experience of boarding school had
not stopped him from sending his son to one at an equally tender
age, but he took very good care that it was nothing like Bowes Hall.
The school belonged to a Dr and Mrs Heldenmaier and was run,
according to Cobden, 'on the Pestalozzi plan, combining the training
of a home with good practical and modern tuition'.[72] Dick had
settled down happily and had now been there nearly three years. His
father used to visit him when he was in the North and have earnest
conversations with Dr Heldenmaier about his son's progress. In
October 1853, Dick had been ill and was therefore allowed a couple
of days holiday, staying with his father in a hotel. One morning they
went over to Clumber to call on the Duke of Newcastle. They just
missed the duke, but his son showed them round the house which, in
Cobden's opinion, contained some good paintings. In the evening
some half a dozen old Manchester friends came to tea at Cobden's

hotel. It was a truly northern high tea, with every sort of cold meat and pastry – everything, in fact, except plain bread and butter.[73]

For Dick, however, the visit ended in tears because his father felt obliged to lecture him on his financial extravagance and the virtues of economy. Mrs Heldenmaier was asked not to give him any more money unless it was for a joint expedition of an educational nature with the other boys, and his mother was told not to provide him with so many postage stamps that they were worth bartering for something else. Dick spent a good deal of his money on his collection of birds' eggs, which his master – rather discouragingly for Cobden's economy campaign – said was a good thing because it showed that the boy could apply himself continuously to *something*. For Dick did not apparently much enjoy his lessons. He complained to his father that he was made to work too hard. Cobden backed up the masters but, since Dick was doing quite well with his French and German, he advised them privately not to drive the boy to desperation over his Latin. He attended a rehearsal of a school concert and was delighted to discover that Dick had quite a talent for singing. 'It has a most humanising tendency', he told Kate, 'and is just what Dick's rugged nature wants.' He suggested that in her next letter to Dick she should mention his father's praise of his singing and say how nice it would be for Dick to join the girls in a chorus round the piano on winter evenings at Dunford. Whether this would have appealed to Dick may be doubted, but it was typical of the close, loving and imaginative interest that Cobden took in his son's upbringing. Later, in the middle of a hectic and exhausting peace congress in Edinburgh, he wrote a long letter to Dr Heldenmaier, simply in order 'to keep alive his interest in the boy's progress'.[74]

The peace movement had met in Manchester in January 1853 in an attempt to dispel the anti-French hysteria then sweeping the country. When it next met the following October in Edinburgh the British press and public had replaced the French Emperor with a new bogyman: the Tsar of Russia. By now the principal actors in the long-drawn-out drama that culminated in the outbreak of the Crimean war had probably reached the point of no return, however much they – or most of them – hoped otherwise. In May 1853 a Russian demand for what seemed to be a Russian protectorate over the Orthodox Christian subjects of the Sultan had been rejected by the Turks. To the British and French governments the Russian demands seemed menacing and unreasonable and in June they ordered their fleets to Besika Bay, outside the Dardanelles. In July the Russians occupied Moldavia and Wallachia, autonomous principalities within the Ottoman Empire. In August a four-point peace formula was drawn up in Vienna by British, French, Prussian and Austrian representatives. It was accepted by the Tsar, but the Porte insisted on amendments. The Turkish attitude seemed justified when Count Nesselrode, the Russian foreign minister, publicly claimed that the Vienna Note was much more favourable to Russian pretensions than those who drafted it had intended. The war party in Constantinople was greatly strengthened and the British Cabinet became ineradicably suspicious of Russian intentions. The Tsar, who did not really want to go to war, tried to repair the damage. But on 4 October the 'beastly Turks' (as the foreign secretary, Lord Clarendon, called them) declared war on Russia, and a few days later the British Cabinet decided to ignore the Tsar's olive branch and order the fleet to sail through the Dardenelles to Constantinople. This broke an international convention and committed Britain (and the French, who also sent their fleet) to the defence of the Turks. 'In view of the state of public feeling' Clarendon wrote, 'we could not well do less'; but – he added – the idea of war 'for such a cause as two sets of Barbarians quarrelling over a form of words . . . is not only shocking but incredible'.[75]

That was not how the British public saw it. Tsar Nicholas had already trampled on the national aspirations of Poles, Hungarians, Circassians and others; he had invaded the Ottoman empire; he would occupy Constantinople, and doubtless he had designs on Western Europe as well. He had clearly tricked the British government over his plans for Turkey, and if it did not join forces with its French ally – now enthusiastically acclaimed – to protect the Turks, then the national honour would be irretrievably besmirched. All over the country there were crowded and enthusiastic meetings at which Lord Aberdeen was condemned as weakly pro-Russian, the Tsar denounced as a wicked despot and the Sultan hailed as a champion of religious equality and a bulwark against Russian aggression. As yet, probably most of those who enjoyed listening to the exciting rhetoric of platform orators or reading the exhilarating bombast in the popular press did not really want it all to end in war; and the more thoughtful papers, like *The Times* and the *Manchester Guardian*, still argued that a peaceful way out of the crisis could and should be found.

Cobden, holidaying with his family at Bognor, watched the mounting hysteria with profound disgust – 'at such gatherings as the Cutlers' Feast in Sheffield', he complained, 'every speaker is primed with gunpowder and belches nothing but defiance at some imaginary foe'[76] – and he wrote round to his friends urging them to go to the peace congress in Edinburgh. Peace could still be preserved, he felt, through the good sense of the people, if not through the efforts of the government.

'The great mass of the population' – he assured his old League friend J. B. Smith – 'is always ready to hear the truth . . . They have no interest in wrong-doing. Let us then by our great meetings in Edinburgh and elsewhere show that we are not afraid to appeal to the people against those who from ignorance, prejudice and sinister motives are trying to mislead them. We may roll back the tide of military enthusiasm whilst at its height if we will now make one great effort on behalf of the right.'[77]

When Cobden arrived in Edinburgh on the eve of the congress he found the members of the organising committee splitting hairs over the resolutions to be put to the congress; some of them, he commented impatiently, were 'very sharp theologians.'[78] It was not the best way to catch the popular attention, and there was nothing hairsplitting about his own speeches. They were robust, down-to-earth appeals to the common sense of his audience: Turkey was in a state of irreversible decay; Russia should not have invaded it but it was no business of ours; we were under no treaty obligations to defend Turkey; we had no moral right, in view of our conquests in Asia, to condemn Russian aggression; the Christian population of Turkey would much prefer Russian rule; and Russia, defensively strong but offensively weak, was no threat to Britain, and would not be even if it did overrun Turkey.[79]

After his major speech at a big public meeting, Cobden told Kate (with whom he dispensed with any false modesty) that he had made a '*telling*' speech. He professed himself very well satisfied with the whole congress, although, by his own account, its message may not have penetrated very far among 'the people'. He spoke of 'influential' deputations, and 'leading' local men, and described the public meeting, with characteristic underlining, as 'a great *intellectual* gathering'.[80] Nor did *The Times*'s correspondent's rather tongue-in-cheek description of the soirée which wound up the proceedings suggest that it was a very plebeian occasion. It was held in Edinburgh's Music Hall, very tastefully decorated; an arch at one end was inscribed 'Peace and Plenty', tables laden with fruit, ices and pastries were ranged along the other three sides, and in the centre

> 400 to 500 ladies and gentlemen intermingled in the greatest good humour, chatting over the cause of peace and interchanging civilities with each other while the organ boomed forth appropriate music. Messrs Cobden and Bright were the great lions of the evening. Wherever they moved they encountered groups of admirers; there was no end to the compliments and congratulations which they received, and the shaking of hands which they had to endure for fully two hours must have been attended with no small physical suffering.[81]

Mr Delane, the Editor of *The Times*, did not take such a bland view of the congress. He was outraged by the pacifist sentiments expressed by many of the speakers, and said as much in his editorial columns so trenchantly that he almost seemed to have joined the war party. Lord Aberdeen was moved to remonstrate. He did not, he told Delane, wish to support the absurdities of the peace conference, but 'I think that both the principal speakers [Cobden and Bright] uttered so much truth as to deserve a different treatment, by which the cause of peace might have been further advanced'.[82]

Early in December, the cause of peace received a setback from which it never recovered. News arrived in England that on 30 November a dozen Turkish ships at anchor in the harbour of Sinope had been attacked by a Russian naval force, with great loss of life. Since the Turks had already begun land operations against them, the Russians were perfectly entitled to attack the Turkish navy. The incident provided a sharp focus, however, for the British public's intense, but hitherto vague, animosity against the Tsar. It also placed the British and French governments, who had so spectacularly failed in their professed intention to protect the Turks, in an extremely unflattering, even ridiculous light. Cobden was expressing the universal sense of outraged indignation when he wrote in a private letter that

> ... I could not justify myself in sending an enormous naval force to the Bosphorus, thus encouraging the Turks to resist their powerful neighbours, and then to suffer their fleet to be destroyed and their crews slaughtered almost within hearing of our admiral, who is all the while banqueting and toasting with champagne his French colleagues, who I must say cut just as sorry and shabby a figure as ourselves.[83]

But he did not draw the bellicose conclusions expressed at public meetings up and down the country and in the columns of newspapers from which the voices of moderation and caution now died away. The resignation of Lord Palmerston, popularly believed to be the only politician capable of standing up to the Tsar, was an added goad to the public's exasperation with an allegedly weak and vacillating government.* But the Cabinet, divided though it was, did not need either the British public or the French Emperor to point out how false was its position. By the new year of 1854, the British and French fleets had been ordered into the Black Sea to protect the Turks, and the Russian fleet had been required to withdraw into its bases and stay there. The drift to war seemed unstoppable.

Cobden, however, doggedly refused to believe that war would break out until, he said, he had read the bulletin on the first battle.

---

* Palmerston actually resigned over Russell's reform bill, but the real reason was popularly supposed to be the government's handling of the Turkish crisis.

Instead, he tried to revive interest in primary education and, at the other end of the educational spectrum, spent a few days in Oxford. The university was girding itself (unsuccessfully, as it turned out) to resist reform, but Cobden seems to have gone there simply out of interest, to find 'a new field of observation'[84] – which perhaps was what he needed just then. 'Instead of a monastery' – he reported to his brother – 'the University is rather a great nest of clubs, where everybody knows everybody, and all are anxious to have a stranger of any note to break the monotony of their lives. I might have lived at free quarters for weeks amongst them. The best of fare, plenty of old port and sherry, and huge fires, seem the chief characteristics of all the colleges.'[85]

It turned out to be a very agreeable visit, unclouded, apparently, by Oxford's looming controversy with Westminster, or any other crisis of wider import.

When Parliament reassembled at the end of January 1854, the Turkish crisis was reaching a climax. Austrian diplomacy had failed to avert war and Russia was about to break off diplomatic relations with Britain and France. Although Lord Aberdeen still desperately hoped for peace, his Cabinet was closing ranks and preparing for war with varying degrees of reluctance. To confound its critics, it published two voluminous blue books on the development of the crisis. According to Charles Greville, they 'relieved the Government from a vast amount of prejudice and suspicion'.[86] Not, however, so far as Cobden was concerned. Always a dedicated student of blue books, he dug deep and found plenty of critical material. He supplemented it with information about Russia and Turkey obtained during visits to City merchants, and on 20 February made a long and closely-argued plea for peace in the House of Commons.[87] It was all wasted effort. A few days later the vanguard of an expeditionary force for the Dardanelles sailed from Southampton, and a despatch was sent to St Petersburg informing the Russian government that there would be war unless it undertook to evacuate the Principalities by the end of April. No reply was received to this ultimatum and war was formally declared on 27 March.

As late as the previous 23 December Cobden had claimed that the middle classes were still 'fanatically devoted to peace'.[88] He was wrong, just as in September he had been mistaken in hoping that a great popular movement could be mobilised against the war fever. There was to be no repetition of the triumphs of the anti-Corn law campaign. It is difficult to see why Cobden thought there might be, since he never ceased to deplore and condemn John Bull's pugnacious, arrogant, dictatorial, interfering character. He must have dulled his perceptions with large doses of wishful thinking. The British people were in an ebullient, expansive mood. They felt themselves to be destined to play a leading role on the world stage, and they found Lord Palmerston's high-handed, bombastic, assertive style much more attractive than the gradual, low-key, peaceful accumulation of influence through commerce and the wonders of British technology that Cobden advocated.

Thoughtful people were uncomfortably aware that Britain was going to war to defend a decadent Mahomedan regime against a Christian power which shared the concern of the rest of Europe about the fate of the Christians under Turkish rule. But to the ordinary Englishman the crisis at Constantinople was primarily an opportunity to cut the Tsar down to size and get him off the backs of the Poles, Hungarians and other oppressed nationalities. It was only a few years since Russia had snuffed out a briefly independent Hungary, and Kossuth's triumphant visit to England was still fresh in people's minds. (He came again in the summer of 1854 and spent several months touring the country, calling for the liberation of Europe from the menace of Russian despotism.) As Prince Albert explained to the King of the Belgians, the masses felt, but did not think. 'In the present instance their feeling is something of this sort: "The Emperor of Russia is a tyrant, and the enemy of all liberty on the Continent, the oppressor of Poland. He wanted to coerce the poor Turk. The Turk is a fine fellow; he has braved the rascal, let us rush to his assistance." '[89]

Cobden fully shared the common antipathy to the Russian Emperor whom he once described as 'the incarnation of military power and brute force'.[90] But Nicholas was only mortal, and Cobden maintained, as he had always done, that whatever the aggressive ambitions of its rulers, Russia would never be a serious threat to Europe because of its immense size, its geographical remoteness and the backwardness of its economy and people. And even supposing it were a threat, it was for the powers most directly menaced – Germany and Austria – to repel it. As for liberating the oppressed nationalities of Europe, Cobden had nothing but scorn for the radical newspapers and politicians who stirred up such vague and delusive hopes. 'They would have us set fire to our house for the chance of enabling the Poles, Hungarians and Italians to burn their fetters in the flames.'[91]

There were individuals, some of them influential, who were privately opposed to the war. According to Bright, even the editor of *The Times*, Delane, agreed with him that the war was not necessary,[92] although at the time his paper was publishing the most bellicose articles. But apart from Earl Grey, a solitary but persistent dissident in the Lords, and the Quakers, whom no one listened to, none thought it worth while to stand up publicly and put his finger in the dyke in an attempt to stem the flood of popular passion. Cobden and Bright did so simply because they believed it was their duty.

Unfortunately, they were as little likely to be listened to as were the Quakers. The historian of the Crimean war, A. W. Kinglake, commenting on their plight, wrote: 'A man cannot have weight as an opponent of any particular war if he is one who is known to be against almost all war.'[93] Cobden was always aware of this danger and tried to guard against it. 'The soul of the peace movement' (he wrote shortly before the Edinburgh peace conference) 'is the Quaker sentiment against all war. Without the stubborn zeal of the Friends, there would be no Peace Society and no Peace Conference. But the enemy takes good care to turn us all into Quakers, because the 'non-resistance' principle puts us out of court as practical politicians of the present day.'[94] But as he would not refuse to appear on the same platforms as his Quaker friends, inevitably Cobden failed to distance himself from them in the public mind.* ' "The Peace Movement", as it is called,' pronounced *The Times*, during the Edinburgh conference, 'has been from the first the ruin of Mr Cobden's reputation as a statesman, and remains so still. Every time he touches it, he complicates his position, and brings himself into still greater discredit.'[95] In any case, even if there had been no peace movement, Cobden's persistent pleas over a period of six years for a non-interventionist foreign policy and deep cuts in defence spending would have closed men's minds to his arguments when war actually threatened. During a debate on the Militia Bill in 1852 a Whig member observed that Cobden 'was never more provoking or aggressive than when he talked about peace'. He added that this was regrettable because 'the services of a highly-gifted and intelligent man were placed in abeyance by the unfortunate monomania to which he was subject'.[96]

With the Tsar's withdrawal from the Principalities during the early summer – for fear of adding Austria to his enemies – the immediate threat to Turkey was lifted. But the British government and people, having gone to war, were determined to fight, and in September an Anglo-French army landed in the Crimea with the aim of capturing the great Russian naval base of Sebastopol. Senior British and French officers had serious doubts about the feasibility of the enterprise, but the British public and press confidently expected a walkover. They did not get it. Instead they had news of a series of hard-fought and costly battles – Alma, Balaclava, Inkerman – at the end of which the Allies were firmly established outside Sebastopol but as far as ever from taking the place. A winter of stalemate was bad enough, but with weatherproof accommodation, warm clothing and adequate food, it would have been tolerable. The British army got none of

---

* Bright, although a Quaker, did not believe in the extreme principle of passive non-resistance in all circumstances.

these things. Instead, a combination of poor leadership, incompetent administration, lack of transport and atrocious weather condemned troops to months of indescribable hardship and suffering in their bare, wind-swept camp outside Sebastopol. By the end of November, the tragedy was becoming known in England through the private letters and official reports of officers at the front. By the middle of December the magnitude of the disaster was being revealed in W. H. Russell's harrowing reports from the Crimea in *The Times*, and shortly before Christmas, the newspaper, with its usual adroitness at catching the popular mood, began a series of thundering broadsides against the mismanagement of the war.

Throughout the autumn Cobden observed the unfolding tragedy from his rural retreat at Dunford. For once in his life he felt he had nothing to contribute. He could only stand aside and hope that, in due course, the war itself would make people understand the value of peace, In the meantime he tried to keep his mind off public affairs by unpacking, sorting and arranging his books and papers in his new library. But he was profoundly depressed by his isolation. Not only the uneducated, unthinking masses, but most of his own friends, who had worked so stoutly with him in the old League days, and most of his fellow MPs, had succumbed to the 'war mania'. Even the clergy, nonconformist as well as Anglican, preached martial sermons, and Cobden found 'something indescribably shocking' in invoking Heaven's blessing for the sanguinary battles in the Crimea.[97] In his more depressed moments he was tempted to give up public life altogether.

> So what can I do – he asked an old friend – more rational than bury myself here and study agriculture, whose laws are constant and invariable, and whose processes are not subject to those periodical panics and aberrations which in the moral and political world baffle all calculations and foresight? Or how can I better escape from the humbling spectacle of a nation given up to the dominion of its fiercest animal passions, *whilst flattering itself that it is wielding the sceptre of justice*, than in taking refuge in my nursery, where the children, if not more logical, are at least less hypocritical than those of a larger growth whose 'fe, fa, fi, fo, fum' is now resounding from our streets, theatres, churches and chapels? To confess the truth, I am afraid I am growing cynical, and I am half disposed to take to my tub, let my beard grow, and pass a vote of want of confidence in mankind.[98]

In fact, he was incapable of withdrawing, either mentally or physically, into an ivory tower. 'I can think or dream of nothing but this Sebastopol business', he wrote in mid-November. The Crimean expedition seemed to him such a hopelessly impractical way of subduing the mighty Russian empire that he felt he would no longer be

able to 'consider a balloon attack on the moon as *quite* impossible'.[99]
He went up to Manchester for a few days in the hope of making
others understand how he felt, but the war spirit there – much more
pervasive than he had realised – had spread to many from whom he
had expected better things. 'There is nothing for it', he told his
brother, 'but to let the moral epidemic take its course and run itself
out, keeping out of the way of those who are infected, just as one
would a cholera epidemic.'[100]

But he could not stand aside altogether. He had to demand an early
peace and he had to tell the people how much they were to blame for
the war; '. . . it is better', he told Bright, 'to face any neglect or
hostility than allow them to persuade themselves that anybody but
themselves are responsible for the war'.[101] During the winter of
1854–55 he made two attempts to persuade the country to end the
war. The first was in the House of Commons on 22 December.[102]
He left the oratory to Bright as he had done during the anti-Corn law
campaign and concentrated on the practicalities. He had been dismissed as an impractical dreamer, but he now strove to instil some
'homely common sense' into those who were conducting or supporting the war. Diplomatic efforts to end it had not ceased and
seemed to be making progress. What, therefore, asked Cobden, was
the justification for continuing the war? What was the point of destroying Sebastopol? After demolishing all the pro-war arguments, he
concluded that neither honour nor interest compelled the government to continue a war that was, as they all knew, causing such
shocking suffering and tragic loss of precious lives in the Crimea.

In the House of Commons, where enthusiasm for the war was less
than in the country, Cobden and Bright could be sure of a fair hearing. Not so, however, on public platforms outside. At a meeting in
Manchester, called by Bright's constituents to condemn his conduct,
neither he nor his accusers could make themselves heard amidst the
pandemonium. The Mancunians went so far as to burn their MP in
effigy, and a Whig peer whom he met on the train to London offered
his congratulations that his constituents had been satisfied with burning only his effigy.[103] But Cobden felt he would be 'shrinking from
an obvious act of duty' if he did not give the people of the West
Riding a chance to hear and criticise his opinions face to face.[104] The
leading reformers in Leeds cold-shouldered him, but he went ahead
all the same, confident that if his audience was deaf to his message,
it would at any rate reach the outside world through the report in
The Times. When he faced his constituents on 17 January, 1855, he
denied that he was for peace at any price, agreed that Turkey had
been justified in declaring war on Russia, and set forth his arguments
against British intervention with simple force and clarity. After
asking his audience to listen to him with good humour, he assured
them that the British had 'an immense amount of insular pride,

vanity and conceit'; they had seized territory wherever they could get it and to the rest of the world they seemed ill-qualified to sit in judgment on others. He asked the people of Leeds to remember the sufferings of the men in the trenches before Sebastopol, and he appealed to them not to demand that the war should go on just when there seemed to be real prospects of a diplomatic settlement.[105] He was listened to patiently, but his appeal was ignored, and he did not make another.

But now the public euphoria over the war had given way to anger over its mismanagement. On 28 January a motion introduced by Roebuck for an inquiry into the conduct of the war was passed by a huge majority of 157. The following day Lord Aberdeen thankfully laid down a burden that he had found increasingly distasteful. After Lord Derby, the Whig elder statesman, Lord Lansdowne, and Lord John Russell, had all failed to form a government, the Queen perforce turned to Palmerston; as he himself complacently noted, he was 'for the moment, *l'inévitable*'.[106] At the age of seventy, he had at last achieved the premiership. Bright disgustedly dubbed him the 'aged charlatan',[107] and Cobden declared that he would certainly never accept him as his leader.[108] But the general public was delighted and confidently expected a more vigorous prosecution of the war.

The Russians, however, had just accepted four allied demands as a basis for peace, and in March 1855 negotiations began in Vienna. They broke down in June over the size of the Russian Black Sea fleet. On 5 June, Cobden opened a debate about the breakdown with an attack on the government's war aims, its conduct of the war and its failure to obtain peace.[109] His speech, according to Bright, was 'in his best style: close reasoning, apt illustrations, statemanlike views, and solemn warning'.[110] The House was packed and Cobden was pleased with his attentive reception. 'Not a breath of disapprobation', he reported to Kate, 'and a fair share of support in the way of cheers.'[111] Next day Bright went round to his friend's lodgings and received some 'very judicious hints' as to his own contribution to the debate. 'It is a great advantage', he noted in his diary, 'to have a man of such honesty and sagacity to consult with and to discuss with upon all public questions.'[112] Other powerful voices spoke up against the war, including Gladstone who, in his erratic but brilliant course through the political firmament, had come down very close to the 'peace party' in the Commons.* But they remained a tiny

---

* Gladstone and three other Peelites agreed to remain in office under Palmerston. But a fortnight later they all resigned after the Prime Minister had given way to a Commons' demand that Roebuck's committee of inquiry into the war should still be set up in spite of the change of government.

minority. Neither the government, Parliament nor the country as a whole was prepared to consider peace so long as Sebastopol continued to defy its besiegers.

But the outcry against the mismanagement of the war persisted. The middle classes, whose deference to their social superiors had always infuriated Cobden, suddenly demonstrated that they would not, as he had once scornfully commented, prefer to be ruined by lords than saved by commoners.[113] The armed services were a jealously-guarded preserve of the aristocracy; and in the Crimea the aristocracy had demonstrated, in a far greater glare of publicity than during any previous war, that it was incompetent to run the country's military machine. The attack on the aristocracy's monopoly of the army was led by Henry Layard, a middle-class Radical MP, who had made his name as the excavator of Nineveh. He had got himself to the Crimea as an observer at the beginning of the campaign, so his repeated denunciations in the Commons of military incompetence had the added weight of personal experience. Outside Parliament, he set up the Administrative Reform Association with the slogan 'The right man in the right place'. It did not stop at the service departments but aimed at modernising the whole machinery of government. To the members of the middle class who flocked to the association's meetings, it seemed obvious that the affairs of the nation, whether in peace or war, should be run with the same up-to-date efficiency as they ran their private businesses. During a rollicking speech to a crowded and enthusiastic audience at the Drury Lane theatre, Charles Dickens declared: 'The great, broad, true case that our public progress is far behind our private progress, and that we are not more remarkable for our private wisdom and success in matters of business than we are for our public folly and failure, I take to be as clearly established as the existence of the sun, moon and stars.'[114] The association organised crowded meetings throughout the country and was strongly supported by the press, notably *The Times* and *Punch*. For a few weeks it flourished in the warmth of public attention and support. But having briefly served as an outlet for public disquiet, it disappeared from view, a victim to divided aims and weak leadership.[115] In Parliament, the one success of the supporters of administrative reform was a committee of inquiry into aristocratic influence in the army and the purchase of commissions.*

The administrative reform movement has a place in the story of Cobden's life for the paradoxical reason that he would have nothing to do with it. He was as shocked as anyone by the gross mismanage-

---

* Palmerston gave evidence before the committee and opposed reform. The abolition of the purchase of commissions and other such reforms were not achieved until 1870.

ment in the Crimea; for nearly ten years he had been looking for a reform 'agitation' that would attract a substantial volume of public support; the overthrow of aristocratic privilege and monopoly had been one of his most cherished aims all his life; the movement which had sprung up with just this object lacked the organisational drive and inspiring leadership which he could give. But he would have nothing to do with a public outcry that tried to divert responsibility for what had gone wrong from those who had instead on having the war in the first place. '*The people are to blame for this*. But they will make the aristocracy or the Court or the Quakers or any body the scapegoats rather than take blame to themselves.' Nor would he co-operate with people who were still clamouring for impossible achievements. 'My voice shall be raised for peace and I will not be the partisan of any body who is not ready when the war is over to repudiate the very principle of sending armies to fight the battles of the Continent.'[116] In any case, Cobden felt that the administrative reformers had got their priorities wrong. Parliament would never demand the recall of Lord Raglan because of his aristocratic con-nections. 'If people want the administration reformed they must begin with the House of Commons and the first step must be vote by ballot.'[117]

If his attitude pushed him still further into the wilderness, so be it. In any case, he had little appetite for public affairs while the war lasted. The only important issue – apart from peace – in which he maintained an active interest during the two years of the war was education. In spite of recurrent bouts of pessimism he went on try-ing, through private discussions, to find a solution to the problem of religious teaching. In March 1855 he helped to introduce a 'Free Schools Bill' on behalf of the National Public Schools Association. Two other education bills were introduced in the same session, but all three were eventually withdrawn. 'Still I am far from seeing my way over the "religious difficulty"', wrote Cobden on 6 August. 'It is the Malakoff Tower of the struggle. The nearer we get to it the more impregnable it seems to be.'*[118]

As often as he could, he escaped to Dunford, where he could look after his little estate, ride on the Downs and go for a 'picknick' with his family. It was really too hot, Cobden told Bright one morning at the end of June, 1855; 'but there is no baulking the zeal of our young folks, who have been for the last two days busy packing up plates, knives, and every kind of article, useful or useless; and they are now tugging at my sleeve to be off'.[119]

Bright paid his first visit to Dunford that July, and noted in his

* The Malakov tower, or fortress, was part of the defences of Sebastopol. Its capture by the French in September led to the surrender of the town.

diary: 'A nice house, and a pleasant family. A charming prospect from the windows and the lawn.' He and Cobden rode up to the top of the Downs on ponies – 'We had a charming ride'.[120] But the pony expeditions that Cobden enjoyed most were with young Richard.

> Yesterday I rode with my boy over the Downs ten miles to see the Roman tesselate pavement at Bignor. The air was delightful, and the ponies got so frisky on the turf that mine race[d] off with me half a dozen times; and I am afraid I cut a figure like the celebrated Mr Jno Gilpin, with my hat, which I had tied to my button, flying after me at the full speed of the little beast. However, I could not help moralizing, in my walking intervals, upon our folly in wasting our precious health, and shortening our lives in the public arena at the present moment when no possible good can result from our martyrdom.[121]

Neither Cobden nor Bright, however, had suffered such a martyrdom in the public arena as Lord Aberdeen. Cobden called on him one day when he was staying with the Bishop of Oxford who had a house a few miles from Dunford. The ex-prime minister was full of bitter regrets at having let himself be dragged into the war. Cobden could not help feeling sorry for him. 'It would have been ludicrous', he told Bright, 'if it had not been so sad, to hear him dilate upon the folly and unreasonableness of this war, which he characterised as less justifiable than any other in our history – as if every word he uttered did not go to his own condemnation.'[122]

In September Sebastopol at last surrendered, but the war which weighed so heavily on Lord Aberdeen's conscience still dragged on. Cobden, paying a visit to Chichester early in October, could not find anyone, lay or clerical, who was not enthusiastically in favour of it.[123] But the agricultural labourers round Dunford were hard hit by the steep increase in the price of bread caused by the stoppage of Russian grain supplies. They were, reported Cobden, 'looking haggard and pale and ragged.'[124] Towards the end of that year he was moved to sit down and write a pamphlet in which he tried to demonstrate the futility of continuing with the war. 'My indictment against war is that it brutalizes the masses, and makes the rich richer and the poor poorer . . .'[125] He could see the evidence with his own eyes, and argued convincingly about the damage that a long war would inflict on the country's economy and consequently on the working class. But when he claimed that Russia was able to continue the war almost indefinitely, he could write only as an armchair commentator deprived of essential and up-to-date information. He was nearer the truth when he argued, as he frequently did, that Russia was too backward to be a threat to anyone. The short Crimean war demonstrated – to the Russians as well as to Western Europe – that behind the imposing facade of the Russian colossus lay tremendous military, economic, social and administrative weaknesses. The Allies had gone to war primarily to protect Turkey from Russian domination. They achieved this aim by preventing the Black Sea from becoming a Russian lake, and the Russians could do nothing about it. Although much of the British public would not have agreed, the war had become pointless because it had been successful, although not as successful as Palmerston and the public would have liked. But the war's success was not a reason for ending it that Cobden could bring himself to give.

He called his pamphlet *What Next – and Next?* and published it early in 1856.[126] Although he had tried to make it attractive by introducing 'typographical artifices' and personal anecdotes, he was convinced that no one would read it – 'I claim some merit for patriotic motives in having gone through the drudgery of writing it under such a discouraging conviction'.[127] It was enough that he had written it out of the fullness of his heart and to set his conscience at rest.

CHAPTER 12

Private Grief and Public Rejection (1856–59)

The Treaty of Paris which ended the Crimean war was signed on 30 March, 1856. Although many criticised the terms of the treaty – the heralds who proclaimed it at Temple Bar were hissed by the listening crowd – the British people were happy to celebrate peace in the traditional way with illuminations and the firing of cannon in the London parks. But Cobden, who had yearned for peace on almost any terms, was too crushed by personal cares to enjoy it when it came at last.

During the spring of 1856 John Bright suffered a physical and mental breakdown. Bright later ascribed his illness to the mental stress and anguish he had gone through during the Crimean war. Cobden had been able to protect himself to some extent by adopting a fatalistic and largely passive attitude to the course of events. Bright had not been able to do this. He had to go on telling his countrymen the truth about the war, as he saw it, whatever the cost to himself. His illness was marked by severe physical weakness, great mental lassitude and frequent blinding headaches. It was by no means apparent that he would ever be able to live a normal life again.

For more than 15 years Bright had been Cobden's closest personal and political friend. 'Perhaps', he wrote during Bright's illness, 'there never were two men who lived in such transparent intimacy of mind as Bright and myself.'[1] Like many close friends they had not always seen eye to eye. They had seriously disagreed more than once over whether or not to campaign for political reform. But although there may have been an occasional temporary coolness, Cobden had never felt in danger of permanently losing the support, the stimulus, the constant fruitful interchange of thoughts and ideas that only Bright could provide. Now it seemed more than likely that he would lose it all.

But to Bright himself Cobden wrote cheerfully, almost light-heartedly, giving his own – rather eccentric – diagnosis of his friend's complaint and assuring him that he knew how to cure him as well as all the doctors in the world.

You have sprained your brain, and as it is a far more delicate organ [than an ankle] and far more difficult to deal with and reach, it will require the more careful treatment. You must lay it on a cushion however and afterwards put it in a sling, just as you would your ancle (sic). There is no way of doing this but by leaving old haunts ... Go abroad where you speak the language not at all, as in Germany, or with difficulty, as in France or Switzerland. Go at once ... whatever the doctors may say ... Your physical sense has been in one sense too strong. You make too much blood. And now there is another thing you must do on my authority. Eat less meat. You don't seem to know it, but you are a very great meat eater – to twice the extent of myself. Take largely to fish or vege-tables. I am afraid you are not like me a good sleeper. You are often perorating in bed when you ought to be in a state of obli-vion. Now there is no rest for your brain like sleep, and for this you must take exercise in mountain regions. I have too a theory that sun and *light* promote sleep ... Now you will get twice as much clear sunlight on the continent as in England. This acts through the eye like a subtle mesmerism on the brain promoting sleep without fatiguing or straining it. Go abroad at once.[2]

Several letters followed urging Bright to be cupped – 'the safest and most harmless mode of bloodletting'; twelve ounces taken from the nape of the neck was recommended. Finally, Bright was instruc-ted how he should pass his days: 'I hope you devote your days in this wise – half your time strolling or lounging in the open air – a fourth at billiards or other amusements, and the rest in the bath, or talking or reading *nonsense*. Eschew politics, political economy, and peace and war.'[3] It seems unlikely that a billiard table was to be found in Bright's Quaker household or, for that matter, any nonsensical reading matter. Bright did not immediately follow his friend's advice to go abroad. Instead he went up to Scotland with his eldest daughter, and by the banks of Highland rivers settled down to recapturing his boyhood skill as a fisherman.

Meanwhile, Cobden was nearly overwhelmed by a tragedy in his own family. The previous September he had taken Dick to a board-ing school near Heidelberg recommended by Baron von Bunsen, who had been Prussian minister in London and now lived in the neighbourhood. Early in April 1856, Cobden suddenly received a letter from Bunsen announcing that Richard had died from scarlet fever after a very brief illness. Owing to a misunderstanding between

Bunsen and the headmaster, no warning telegram had been sent. Cobden received the news at his lodgings in London. He immediately set out for Dunford where he found Kate in the middle of reading out Dick's latest cheerful letter to the assembled family. She was – almost literally – stunned by the news. Cobden himself was at first, as he confessed, completely 'unmanned' by the blow. 'Fifteen years of hopes and dreams, all centred in him, to be thus in one day, cast into the grave',[4] he wrote despairingly to Bunsen, a few days after the news arrived. But the piteous condition of his wife forced him to pull himself together. She was a woman who, as Cobden said, lived entirely for her children, and her only son had been the apple of her eye. If only, he constantly lamented, she had been able to watch over Dick's sickbed herself. The blow would not then have been so shatteringly abrupt and, moreover, she would have been able to satisfy herself that everything had been done to save the boy. As it was, she went on struggling against a reality she could not accept – 'Every day, with "Graham's Domestic Medicine" in her hand, with the leaf turned down at "fever", she, poor soul, seems to be holding an argument with death, and to be trying to show that her boy could have been saved.'[5] Two months after Dick's death, Cobden told a friend that his wife 'is as helpless as one of her young children, and requires as much forbearance and kindness'.[6] He remembered how uncomplainingly she had always put his political engagements before her own or her household's convenience, and he determined now to put her claims before everything else, even if it meant giving up his seat in Parliament. She took no interest in her daughters. Her husband was the only person who could give her the slightest relief, and she could not bear to be parted from him for more than a few hours at a time. He tried to stimulate her into some activity – putting knitting needles into her hands or persuading her to do some weeding in the garden – but nothing could keep her brooding grief at bay for long. At night she could never sleep without a narcotic.

In mid-June Cobden persuaded Kate to spend a week at his lodgings in London. He took her for walks through the crowded streets and parks, and she admitted that the stream of strange faces did divert her thoughts a little.[7] A month later they stayed with old friends, Mr and Mrs J. B. Smith, in Westbourne Terrace, making excursions to Windsor, Ascot and Kew. They went on to friends at Guildford, where they took long drives over the Hog's Back to Farnham and Aldershot. On their return to Dunford there were more excursions, to Brighton, Chichester and so on. By the end of July Kate seemed to be slightly better, but she still could not sleep without a sedative and Cobden, afraid that she might become addicted, begged the local doctor – without success – to reduce her dose.[8]

At the end of September he suddenly decided to accept the offer of his old Manchester friend, Mrs Schwabe, to lend him a house – he told his brother it was a 'palace' – on Anglesey, overlooking the Menai Straits. He sent his eldest daughter to a boarding school in Brighton and got rid of the governess, in the hope that Kate, who had not been able to bring herself to read or write, would exert herself to teach the three younger children.[9] Whether she did so is not clear, but at any rate at Glyn Garth there was no lack of stimulus and diversion. The local landowner offered them the use of his yacht and the run of his grounds and castle. There was 'some good amiable female society, such indeed as is found in the middle and upper ranks in every corner of Britain', and Cobden tried 'all sorts of stratagems' to induce his wife to join it.[10] A ferry boat plied continuously to Bangor from near their house and for twopence a day one could make unlimited trips. Cobden sometimes took Kate on it. They would go backwards and forwards, while Kate talked in her native Welsh to the country people. He hoped it would help to wean her from herself, but nothing seemed of much use. She was, he told Frederick despondently, as well off where she was as anywhere. 'But it is to me an awful ordeal'.[11]

The only relief he had throughout that dreadful autumn came from the arrival of Bright on a visit to a house on the mainland near Bangor. He was greatly restored. In fact, after eight months' separation Cobden could find little change in him, except that he was 20 pounds thinner and more gentle and subdued in manner. Cobden's secret fear that his friend was 'falling into a state of mental imbecility' was dissipated for ever. They exchanged visits, went for long walks, fished and played billiards together, and did not entirely succeed in keeping clear of the forbidden field of politics.[12]

By now, Bright's doctors were also urging him to go abroad. Cobden was full of advice on his wardrobe and his destination; first he recommended Egypt, then decided Rome would be better. (Bright went first to Algiers, where he was homesick and unhappy, and later to Rome.) Cobden also reproved his friend for not getting the best possible medical advice, pointing out, with unanswerable logic, that if 'your watch or piano were out of order you would resort to Dent or Broadwood and leave the repairs entirely to their skill and experience'. He hardly dared to hope that Bright would be able to resume his political career, but felt he might take 'quite naturally' to the fine arts as a form of moderate mental exertion well within his reach. 'He has a good deal of poetry in his composition, and likes to read Milton aloud for hours together, and although the Quaker education smothered all taste for painting, he is not I think too old to acquire it.'[13] He may have sounded a trifle patronising, but Bright was probably grateful for the affectionate zeal with which his friend tried to speed his recovery.

About his wife's recovery Cobden could feel far less cheerful. When they left Glyn Garth just before Christmas 1856 he thought she was worse. She was taking less notice of the children, she shut herself up more often in her bedroom and she still could not sleep without a sedative.[14] She had always lacked the elasticity of spirit which Cobden used to possess but which he feared was now deserting him. 'I used to say', he wrote to a friend at this time, 'that nothing but an evil conscience could depress me for an hour or deprive me of an hour's sleep. But I confess I have been very unhappy and quite beaten of late.'[15]

Throughout this period Cobden's own grief over the death of his son had to take second place to his wife's. He would have liked to relieve it by plunging actively into public life, but Kate's condition denied him this solace. There was, however, one absorbing task which he could work on at home.

In June 1855 the newspaper stamp had finally been abolished and one of Cobden's most cherished projects – a daily penny newspaper – at last became possible. The popular enthusiasm for the Crimean war was a painful reminder of the urgent need to penetrate the prevailing 'dense ignorance' about foreign affairs, and Sturge, Bright, Cobden and other prominent members of the peace movement began to discuss the practicalities of launching an anti-war newspaper. But Cobden, conscious as always of the practical disadvantages of too close an association with the pacifists, stressed the importance of first establishing 'a thoroughly good *newspaper*', and not just an extension of the Peace Society's *Herald of Peace*.[16] In the current climate of opinion, incessant attacks on the war would only alienate potential subscribers. If the paper was to pay its way there would have to be 'a good deal of the wisdom of the serpent as well as the harmlessness of the dove'.[17]

In the event, the *Morning Star* did not appear until the war was over. The necessary funds (£4500) were slow in coming in and there were disagreements over editorial and managerial arrangements. The editorial office was based in London with W. T. Haly as editor (he only lasted a few months) and Henry Richard, who also apparently found time to edit the *Herald of Peace*, as the chief leader writer. The management, which included George Wilson, remained in Manchester where most of the money had been raised. Cobden did not contribute, believing that it was unsuitable for a public man to have a pecuniary interest in a London paper.[18] But he agreed to be editorial adviser, and it was this duty which provided him with a desperately-needed interest and outlet during the tragic months after his son's death.

When the first issue of the *Morning Star* appeared on 17 March,

1856, it was cordially, if condescendingly, welcomed by the *Saturday Review* as being free 'alike from the vulgarity of the *Daily News* and the imbecility of the *Morning Herald*'.[19] Cobden thought it was an 'astonishing pennyworth' and was philosophical about the typographical mistakes, although he hoped there would not be any more blunders like 'putting the deaths under the head of marriages and the marriages under the head of deaths'.[20] In an effort to boost circulation an evening edition, the *Evening Star*, quickly followed, and for Bright's benefit Cobden painted a euphoric picture of its reception. 'Crowds of City people including clerks rush for it at the Exchange newsvendors before they get into their omnibuses to go home, thus carrying the latest news home for their family circle during the evening for a penny.'[21] He was passionately committed to the success of the paper and his commitment made him hard to please. A steady flow of complaints, instructions and admonitions went forth from Dunford (or Glyn Garth) to the offices in London and Manchester. The paper's sales were at first very disappointing – 'a dead failure by comparison with our anticipations'[22] – and Cobden repeatedly declared that unless the paper was put on a proper business footing it would never prosper and did not deserve to. He constantly lamented the fact that the editorial and management sides were separated by 200 miles and that no single head had been appointed to pull the whole concern together.[23] He was also dissatisfied with Hamilton who succeeded Haly as editor. Cobden valued Hamilton for his estimable character and impeccably correct principles,[24] but found his work intolerably slapdash. He wrote to him, at first delicately and then not so delicately, to suggest that someone ought to look through his work to prevent errors. Hamilton, for his part, seems to have been less concerned with his errors than with his anomalous position vis-à-vis Henry Richard who was clearly far more in the confidence of the paper's proprietors in Manchester and of Cobden in Sussex than he was himself.

Between Cobden and Richard there was indeed a close *rapport* – which was just as well since Cobden was severe in his criticism (as well, less often, as warm in his praise) and instead of merely advising on the paper's line and contents, virtually dictated them. He also came down heavily on typographical errors and careless slips, such as the treaty of Venice instead of Vienna. He knew that a newspaper must contain news as well as views and complained bitterly when the *Star* carried only a quarter column of telegraphic news (from Liverpool) about American affairs compared with nearly two columns in *The Times*.[25] He understood that daily journalism is largely the art of repetition – 'If you write too long and exhaustive articles, it is difficult to return again and again to the same topic.'[26] Articles should be 'short, sharp and telling'.[27] Above all, they should be topical and not look like 'treasured-up essays'; it was no good printing an article, however good, on Spanish affairs when the topic of the day was Russian trickery over the terms of the Treaty of Paris.[28] He urged Richard to take the New York papers, the *Herald* or the *Tribune*, as his model. 'Your writing may if you please be more classical and in milder taste, but it must be equally *direct* and *apropos* to the business of the hour, and you must not get into the way of one formal article, but give sparkling little leaders as they do.[29] Many of the articles – sparkling or otherwise – were based on Cobden's voluminous letters, sometimes even being lifted from them verbatim. He was not altogether happy about this – 'for I can often give you rapid hints for an article without any trouble to myself if I know that my own language is not necessarily to be printed. When writing *for the press* I am beset with a fastidiousness that almost paralyses my fingers'.[30]

When the *Star* was first published, popular interest in foreign issues was high. But to Cobden its mission was to revive the pubic's interest in domestic concerns, to become the organ of moral reformers of every kind. He summarised his foreign policy principles as 'little more or less than trying to persuade people to mind their own business instead of their neighbour's – the hardest thing in the world to do though it seems so simple'.[31] But he urged Richard to demonstrate that non-intervention was more than a sterile principle.

> ... we must show that the intervention principle is against the interests of our people in a variety of ways, as in distracting attention from home politics, adding loads of debts and taxation which keep down by their presence the working class and prevent them from rising in the social scale and *therefore* from rising politically. This should be brought out – or otherwise we appear to be merely fighting for a sentiment.[32]

But however presented, it was not a sentiment that appealed greatly to the British public, even in its somewhat chastened post-Crimean mood.

Although Cobden urged Richard not to divulge his own close connection with the *Star*, his views, when reproduced in the paper, could not be given a popular gloss. During 1856, for instance, Britain's relations with the United States were more than usually cool. This arose partly from the involvement of Crampton, the British minister in Washington, in illegal attempts to enlist recruits to fight in the Crimea, and partly out of rivalry in Central America. The British press huffed and puffed over the Crampton affair and Palmerston refused to recall him. But although the British government did not retaliate when the Americans sent him home, Cobden comprehensively condemned its handling of the affair. He did not intend his views, as reflected in the *Star*, to seem either unpatriotic or careless of the national 'honour', but that nevertheless was the impression the paper made.[33] Similarly, although the British involvement in Central America was widely regarded as an embarrassment rather than an asset, Cobden's succinct advice to the government to clear out of 'that region of earthquakes and volcanoes' seemed unhelpful as well as unpatriotic.[34] Inevitably, the *Star* came to be regarded as the organ of the censorious peace-at-any-price 'Manchester School'. This did not help it to compete with the other two London penny papers, especially the *Daily Telegraph*, which was usually strongly pro-Palmerston. Cobden had hopes for a circulation of at least 30,000[35], but both editions together never sold more than 15,000 daily.*

But Cobden's enthusiasm for the penny press did not easily flag. He called it 'the greatest human instrument for forming public opinion',[36] and in the conditions of the mid-1850s political education seemed to him by far the most important – indeed the only – option open to a political reformer. Demonstrations were useless – 'merely beating the air' – without public backing, or any practical object that might attract support. Joseph Sturge, who, in Cobden's opinion, had 'a morbid craving for a demonstration', visited him at Glyn Garth and tried hard to obtain his support for a 'peace' demonstration.[37] But Cobden thought his friend was much too vague and advised him to start a penny paper in the West Riding instead.

The Radicals' support of the war had made him very bitter – they 'have cut their throats before Sebastopol' – and he would not support their demand for a slimmed-down peace-time defence establishment so long as the country refused to mind its own business; 'a nation which undertakes to sway the destinies of Europe by bullying one half and protecting the other must make up its mind to bear the expense of such an attitude'. And as for parliamentary reform, they might, he felt, as well call out for the millenium. He was, he admitted, 'desponding', but supposed that the world would come right in the end.[38]

His private life showed little sign of doing so. His hopes that domestic responsibilities would shake his wife out of her depression quickly faded, and by the beginning of February 1857 they were installed at a hydropathic institution near Richmond, Surrey. He did not

---

* By mid-1857 the paper was for a time paying its way. Samuel Lucas, Bright's brother-in-law, succeeded the unsatisfactory Hamilton as editor, and Henry Richard faded out. After various vicissitudes, the paper was finally wound up in 1869.

himself have much faith in the treatment but took what comfort he could from the beneficial effects of a simple diet and regular habits.[39] Moreover, he hoped that at Richmond he could give his wife some daily companionship while resuming his seat in the House of Commons. It was, as it turned out, to be only for a few weeks.

The previous October the Chinese police had boarded a small vessel (the *Arrow*) in the Canton River and seized 12 of its Chinese crew on the grounds that they included several notorious pirates. The vessel was Chinese-owned, but was commanded by a British subject, was registered at Hongkong and (allegedly) flew the British flag. The British consul at Canton, supported by the governor of Hongkong, Sir John Bowring, demanded the return of the crew and an apology. Eventually the Imperial Commissioner at Canton, Yeh Ming-chin, sent back all the crew but refused an apology. Bowring thereupon began to apply pressure through the guns and sailors of the Royal Navy. During the next few weeks, the Chinese forts along the river were captured, Chinese war junks destroyed, the city walls breached, Yeh's palace captured (to the accompaniment of considerable looting by Europeans), and other official residences bombarded. Yeh responded with anti-foreign diatribes and a reward for every English head. In the middle of December the foreign factories along the waterfront were burnt down by a Chinese mob.

When the news of these dramatic events reached London, the Cabinet, whatever the private misgivings of some of its members, felt it had no choice but to support the man on the spot, even though he had insisted on his full pound of flesh with intemperate precipitancy. Bowring was a man of wide interests and many intellectual pursuits. He had been on friendly terms with Cobden for some 20 years, had been a Radical MP during the anti-Corn Law struggle and a dedicated supporter of the League. He had also been a prominent member of the Peace Society. But nearly 10 years' experience of the ways of the Chinese, first as consul in Canton and then as governor of Hongkong, had convinced him that without uncompromising insistence, backed by force, on treaty rights, European commerce would never get a foothold in China. He saw the *Arrow* incident as a weapon with which to force Yeh to carry out the terms of the 1842 Treaty of Nanking which allowed foreign merchants to live inside the city of Canton instead of being restricted to the waterfront.*

---

* Lord Derby said in the Lords that Bowring had a 'perfect monomania about getting into Canton'. Cobden, in the Commons, agreed and added that it was a pointless demand anyway since the Cantonese were so turbulent and anti-foreign that no foreigner could or would want to live among them (Hansard, CXLIV, 1414–15, 26 Feb., 1857.)

On the subject of the European presence in China, Bowring and Cobden were irreconcilably at odds. To Cobden, commerce was a way of promoting peaceful collaboration between nations and any attempt to extend it by violence or coercion was a contradiction in terms. In the particular case of the *Arrow* at Canton, Bowring – in Cobden's opinion – had not the slightest shred of legal justification and his action had caused a lamentable loss of life and property. Moreover, the *Arrow's* Hongkong register had run out about 10 days before the incident, but in his despatches home Bowring had claimed that since the Chinese were not aware of this (and he did not enlighten them) he was justified in acting as if the register had still been valid. 'I never', wrote Cobden indignantly, 'met with a more atrocious suppression veri – in fact it is tantamount to lying – than in Bowring's despatch ... It seems to me that we have not a leg or toe to stand upon in this bloody outrage which let us hope will be too great even for the House of Commons.'*[40]

Many MPs did share Cobden's indignation, if not so wholeheartedly, and some who did not thought it politically expedient to behave as if they did. On 26 February Cobden introduced a hostile but moderately-worded motion in a speech which went beyond condemnation of Bowring into a wide-ranging critique of British commercial policy in China and of the English merchants who traded there. Some of his criticism was well-founded but his case was based on an interpretation of his beloved blue books that was unrealistically partial to the Chinese and dismissive of the practical difficulties of dealing with them. He went so far as to make the far-fetched claim that wherever the British had access in China, the authorities had manifested 'the most consistent and earnest desire to carry out the provisions of the Treaties'.[41] One Tory MP, who had been inclined to vote for the motion, changed his mind after listening to Cobden and other Radical speakers. 'They were so anti-English, so ingeniously unfair, against ourselves and in defence of the Chinese.'[42] Cobden's Radical friend, Sir Joshua Walmsley, voted against him because of his great regard for Bowring and because he thought the government should support a public servant in such a situation. But he was deeply impressed by the 'Brutus-like severity' with which Cobden, 'impelled by a sense of public duty' denounced his old friend.[43]

The debate went on for four nights, and most of the big names –

---

* The legal issues, including the effect of the irregularities in the *Arrow's* register, were complicated and controversial. A modern authority believes that Bowring was legally justified because of the extensive extra-territorial rights granted to Britain by treaty in 1842 and 1843. (W. C. Costin, *Great Britain and China 1833–1860*, p. 227)

THE GREAT CHINESE WARRIORS DAH-BEE AND COB-DEN.

11 *Punch*, 7 March, 1857.

Lord John Russell, Sir James Graham, Gladstone, Disraeli –
supported the motion. On the last night Gladstone delivered – in
Cobden's words – 'a marvellous specimen of persuasive and moving
eloquence'.[44] He was followed by Palmerston, barely recovered
from a sharp attack of gout and much below his best form. The
excitement was great and the outcome uncertain. Nobody, Cobden
assured Bright, was as surprised as he was when his motion was at
last carried by 16 votes.[45] Gladstone thought the division did more
honour to the House of Commons than any he could remember.[46]
The victors were cheered by a crowd in Westminster Hall as they
made their way home at half past two in the morning, and Cobden
was reminded of the old League days.[47] He caught a glimpse of his
lost popularity, but it was only a glimpse and it turned out to be a
mirage.*

* The British government showed its misgivings over Bowring's handling of the
  Arrow affair by sending Lord Elgin on a special mission to resolve the stalemate at
  Canton and to try to put Britain's relations with China on a more satisfactory
  footing.

Palmerston's defeat had been sufficiently narrow for him to take up Disraeli's rash challenge and appeal to the country against the verdict of the House of Commons. Cobden felt certain that Palmerston would try to avoid the China issue (on which, in Cobden's view, he was on such weak ground) during the election campaign. 'I am sure', he told Sir James Graham, 'there is no safer battleground than the Chinese business. Our opponents will try to escape the issue, but we must rub their noses in it.'[48] There was no need. Palmerston positively flaunted it. His election address, which was widely distributed all over the country, referred to 'an insolent barbarian' (Commissioner Yeh) who had violated the British flag, broken treaties and planned the destruction 'by murder, assassinations and poisons' of British subjects.[49] In his flamboyant appeal Palmerston managed to make his opponents, whether Tories, Peelites or Radicals, seem unpatriotic. They bitterly resented the slur, but were powerless to wipe it out. In the popular view in March 1857, you were either a Palmerstonian or a Yehite. *

Cobden's dislike of his West Riding seat had not lessened with the years, and after a good deal of doubt and dithering he decided to stand for Huddersfield instead. It had the incidental advantage of being barely 30 miles from Manchester so that, as Bright was still convalescing in Italy, Cobden could fight for his friend's seat as well as his own. His optimism soon vanished and the strain and effort became almost too much for him. Two days before polling he wrote to Kate from Huddersfield: 'I am dragged about all the day through mud and mire canvassing, and hardly know whether I can win. I don't think they are by any means safe at Manchester.'[50] The following day he was having giddy spells. He wondered whether he was going to suffer Bright's fate and almost decided to abandon the contest.

If he had, the outcome would have been the same. He was decisively beaten, and so, at Manchester, were Bright and Milner Gibson. So too were Edward Miall, Henry Layard, W. J. Fox and many others who refused to jump on to the Palmerstonian bandwagon. For the aged Prime Minister it was a spectacular landslide victory which bruised his political opponents, whether Conservative or Radical, and scattered the Manchester School. 'Was there ever', commented Macaulay, 'anything since the fall of the rebel angels, like the smash of the Anti-Corn Law League'.[51]

Cobden was philosophical about his own defeat which he ascribed to local factors. But Bright's rejection by the constituents whom he

---

* Yeh had in fact had an extremely bloodthirsty career and he made a splendid bogeyman for the British public. *Punch*, for example, wrote on 7 March: 'Mr Commissioner Yeh had tied up thousands of men and women at his place of execution, and had them flayed alive and cut into slices . . .'

had served for 10 years moved him deeply. It was 'the most atrocious specimen of political ingratitude I ever encountered'.[52] But Bright had always been a controversial figure in Manchester. He had never deferred to the views of his constituents and, as their prosperity increased and their social aspirations swelled, his outspoken advocacy of a more democratic system and his criticism of the aristocracy became increasingly uncongenial. 'They have become prosperous and rich, with Free Trade', commented Cobden bitterly, 'and are too genteel to tolerate the plain blunt Quaker who helped them out of their Protectionist adversity; and so they kick down the ladder by which they have reached their prosperity!'[53] Bright, writing in the relaxed atmosphere of Venice, was more philosophic. 'We have taught what was true in our "School", but the discipline was a little too severe for the scholars.'[54]

Inevitably, after more than 15 years at Westminster Cobden had mixed feelings about his involuntary retirement. On the whole, however, he was pleased. 'The dose is nauseous, but the medicine is good for me.'[55] Throughout the previous winter the triple blows of his friend's illness, his son's death and his wife's deep depression had left him with ambivalent feelings about public life which in any case appeared to have little to offer him. 'I seem', he had written in November, 'to be always feeling about in my mind for an excuse for quitting the public scene'.[56] Even if he had wanted to drown his personal worries in public work – and he sometimes did – his wife's dependence on him made it virtually impossible. Moreover during the summer his brother's increasingly serious illness reinforced the ties that bound him to Dunford. Frederick was suffering from what seems to have been a form of muscular dystrophy but which Richard described as 'a long ordeal of suffering in the nerves of his lower extremities' which had left him paralysed in both legs. The doctors had little to offer – 'about the nerves', wrote Cobden sadly, 'we seem to know as little as of the modus operandi of electricity. Perhaps they are one and the same thing.'[57]

Cobden had fought the general election almost as a matter of habit, but in the months that followed his defeat he steadfastly refused all offers of alternative seats. (He also turned down the many various projects that well-meaning people suggested he should undertake to fill up his unaccustomed leisure.) It happened to be a particularly hot summer and Palmerston kept the Commons sitting through most of August until he had worn down the fervent opposition, led by Gladstone, to his Matrimonial Causes Bill. Whenever Cobden read that the House had sat particularly late, he hugged himself 'and looked out on the South Downs with a keener relish'.[58] He was a real countryman and took an immense pleasure in managing his small farm. He was always planning improvements, like draining meadows, or experimenting with new strains of wheat and barley or different breeds of livestock. During the winter of 1857–58, he took in another 12 acres, thereby bringing his farm up to 112 acres, which he felt was as much as he could manage. *

But it was not only congenial country occupations and family ties that reconciled him to staying out of the political arena. He felt he had no place there. He preferred, he told a friend, to stay with his cows and pigs because 'there is not a constituency in the kingdom whose opinions as you call them – or whose prejudices, passions and errors as I call them – I could honestly represent at the present juncture'.[59] He found it difficult to rejoice in the country's material prosperity because, instead of improving – as he had rather naively assumed – the intellectual and moral 'tone' of the public mind, it had, he believed, increased its 'arrogance and pride and brutal combativeness,'[60] An accumulation of private grief and public disappointment filled him with despair. He could not see the way ahead either for himself or for the country, and for the time being he was indeed better off among his cows and pigs.

But no country pursuits, however much he genuinely enjoyed them, could really distract Cobden's mind from public affairs. The stream of exhortatory letters to Henry Richard flowed on, urging him to stir up the agitation against the opium trade, denouncing the bloody reprisals that Cobden assumed (in the event, wrongly), would follow from Lord Elgin's special mission to China,[†61] laying down the *Star*'s line on parliamentary reform, discussing an *exposé* of the alleged secret connection between the government and some newspapers. Above all, there was the news of the outbreak of the Indian Mutiny on 10 May at Meerut.

To Cobden, British rule in India was, and always had been, an unmitigated disaster. In 1850 he confessed to Bright that he felt incapable of giving any constructive thought to how 'that gigantic scheme of villany' could be improved and was glad to leave it to his friend who was turning himself into an expert on India.[††62] But he

---

* When he went to Algiers for a long holiday at the end of 1860, he let most of his land to a local farmer.
† After Yeh had rejected a moderately-worded ultimatum, Elgin and his French allies captured Canton (and Yeh) early in January 1858. Great care was taken to minimise the loss of life and destruction of property.
†† Cobden sat on a Commons Select Committee set up in 1852 to consider the operation of the 1833 India Act which was due to expire at the end of 1853. In June 1853 he spoke in support of an (unsuccessful) Conservative motion designed to delay a revised India Bill. The new Act contained some useful reforms, but was opposed by Cobden (and Bright) mainly because it did not abolish the East India Company's role in the government of India. The Act was superseded by the post-Mutiny settlement.

could not entirely contain his indignation at the steady expansion of British rule and in 1853 published *How Wars Are Got Up in India,* a severely critical account of the origins of the recently-concluded second Burmese war which had led to the annexation of a further large slice of Burma.[63]

The Mutiny was the 'chastisement' Cobden had long foreseen, but no less horrifying for that. Each fresh instalment of atrocity stories from India gave him 'the shudders', and the shrill demands in *The Times* and other middle-class journals for the destruction of Delhi and the indiscriminate massacre of prisoners filled him with angry despair.[64] He recognised that India would have to be recon-quered, if only to protect the peaceful population from the mutineers, but he deplored the self-confidence – he called it vain-gloriousness – with which his countrymen set out to do so, and he saw no hope of governing the country satisfactorily after it had been reconquered. Climate and distance had always been against the British in India and now there was also an irrevocable (in Cobden's view) breakdown of trust between the races.[65]* 'The worst part of this Indian mess is that we are undertaking to govern 150 millions of people without any possible benefit to ourselves, and have involved ourselves in risks and responsibilities of the most serious character in an attempt to achieve an impossibility'.[66] The idea, so dear to many of Cobden's middle-class contemporaries, that Britain had a mission to bring civilisation and Christianity to India, was to him utter nonsense. The British could not even manage their own affairs properly. 'If the Board of Works can't give us a common sewer for London, is it likely to cover India with canals for irrigation? If Catholic and Protestant can't live together in Belfast, under something like martial law, are we the people to teach Christian charity and tolerance to the Hindoos?'[67] Fortunately – and he was very thankful for it – Cobden was not obliged to destroy what was left of his influence and prestige by airing his views in the House of Commons. Nor did he have to produce any ideas on the reforms that should be made when the Mutiny was over. He had, indeed, none to offer.

Unable to reconcile himself to the British presence in India, Cobden washed his hands of the problems this had created. Bright, on the other hand, accepted the situation, believing that British had a duty to restore order and then rule the country well. In August 1857 he was given a chance to return to public life. While completing his convalescence with a fishing holiday in the Highlands, he was

---

* Cobden sent Hamilton at the *Star*, some details of the climate at Delhi, taken from an Indian travel book, to be woven into an article. He added that one could only imagine the situation of the army before Delhi 'by supposing ourselves in one of the tropical hot houses in Kew Gardens and being pumped upon by warm water from an engine.' (31 July, 1857. B. L. Add. Mss. 43,669)

offered a seat at Birmingham where one of the Liberal MPs had just
died. Birmingham was a town of many small manufacturers, each
employing only a few men and apprentices. For a politician who
wanted to campaign for a wider franchise, it was, Cobden felt, a
much better home than Manchester, where a few wealthy capitalists
each employed hundreds of workers and there was 'a great and
impassable gulf' between them. But he still worried about his
friend's health, and urged him not to 'indulge in correspondence
upon anything more exhausting than the quality of your bait and
fishing tackle'.[68]

His exhortations followed Bright to London when the 1858
parliamentary session opened in February. 'Let nothing tempt you to
systematic late hours in the House, and avoid the deleterious air and
politics of the Reform Club.' And a few weeks later – 'Take care of
yourself and don't irritate your brain with Reform Club gossip.[69]
(Cobden himself had just been elected to the Athenaeum, so he was
able to abandon the Reform Club which he described, presumably
because it was too Palmerstonian, as 'one of the most pernicious
organisations in London'.[70])

Although Cobden too would have had no difficulty in getting
back into Parliament, he still felt he could not leave Dunford, where
he summed up the situation in a bleak comment to Bright: 'You
know what a state of helplessness my household is in.'[71] He cultivated an enthusiasm for farming and an indifference to politics. But
he did wish he had been in the House of Commons on 19 February
when Milner Gibson and Bright quite unexpectedly brought about
Palmerston's downfall. The Prime Minister had introduced a bill to
increase the penalties for anyone found guilty of plotting in England
to assassinate anyone abroad. It was a not unreasonable attempt to
pacify the French who were outraged because an Italian republican
named Orsini, who a few weeks earlier had tried to assassinate the
Emperor in Paris, was found to have procured his bomb in Birmingham and to have links with other Italian refugees living in London.
But French indignation begat English indignation, and when Milner
Gibson moved a hostile amendment, accusing Palmerston – of all
people – of not standing up to the French, he was sure of a sympathetic reception. The Prime Minister lost his temper, but his cocky
arrogance since his election victory had lost him much political
goodwill, and Milner Gibson's amendment was passed by a majority
of 19 votes. Palmerston resigned next day.

For Bright, the man of peace who had always courageously
opposed his countrymen's nationalistic ardour, it was hardly a
creditable victory. But even the equally high-minded Gladstone
managed to persuade himself that Palmerston's defeat had been a
vote 'for honour', and praised God. And for Cobden, who had tried

so hard to argue the country out of its bouts of Gallophobia, it was an odd cause for rejoicing. But rejoice he did.* There were, he told Bright, smiles and joy in his 'sombre household' at the news of his victory. 'If it had not been Sunday we must have given three cheers for Gibson and his supporters.'[72] So great was Cobden's antipathy to 'that venerable political imposter' who led the Liberal party but seemed not to have a shred of liberalism in his make-up, that he preferred to have the Conservative Lord Derby at the head of affairs.[73] At least, he was more honest.

Domestic troubles continued to dominate Cobden's life. At the end of March he told Bright that if he could afford it – which he could not – he would like to bring his wife and brother to London for six months (leaving his daughters with a governess) so that Frederick could consult a first-rate doctor and Kate could find some distractions. Less than a fortnight later, after days of excruciating suffering, Frederick died. With his brother's cries and groans still sounding in his ears, Cobden sat down the same evening to write to Bright. He tried to reconcile himself to the justice of a God who allowed a harmless being to undergo such torments. The only way, he felt, was to believe 'in a future state – where all that we suffer here will be compensated to us in a manner which to our present faculties is quite incomprehensible. There is no other present refuge from doubt and despair but in the trust in God and the mistrust of our own powers.'[74] According to his brother, Frederick was a timid and shy man, and to outsiders he may have seemed a rather ineffective one. He certainly did not seem to have much aptitude for business in spite of his 'encyclopaedic memory'. But Richard was devoted to him. He called him his second self, his companion when he was at home and his *locum tenens* when he was away.[75] After Frederick's death, Richard's acquaintances wrote to tell him that *now* he could leave home and take to politics again. They did not realise, he commented, 'how necessary poor Fred was to enable me to give up my time to the public'.[76]

In May Cobden took Kate to London for a few weeks, staying with various friends. On his return to Dunford he occupied himself with translating a pamphlet by the French reformer and thinker, Michel Chevalier, on the economic and financial consequences of the recent discoveries of gold in California and Australia. He got more than he had bargained for because Chevalier doubled the length of the original pamphlet before sending it to Cobden. The task may have helped to keep gloomy thoughts at bay. But he was thoroughly

---

* Cobden argued that the Emperor should not have demanded that the British government take action against the activities of refugees in England. 'To assume that assassination had sympathisers in England, France or elsewhere, was an insult to humanity.' (to M. Chevalier, 13 July, 1858. Morley, p. 682).

pessimistic about the new reform movement which Bright, now
fully restored to health, launched in the late autumn at a series of
enthusiastic and packed meetings. His friend would not, Cobden
opined, get much support so long as wheat, cotton and money
remained cheap. He was at odds with his world, and he knew it.
'I feel myself' – he confessed to Bright – 'in such complete dis-
accord with every political party, and *with nearly all mankind*, that
unless I play the rogue and hold my tongue, or say what I don't
believe, I could not find a plank to stand upon on any "platform" in
the country. I consider that we as a nation are little better than
brigands, murderers and poisoners in our dealings at this moment
with half the population of the globe.'[77] To add to his other worries,
public and personal, there was also his lack of financial security. Of
the £70,000 raised for him in 1846, £40,000 had to go on paying off
his business debts. With the rest he had bought and developed the
Dunford estate. He had first extensively altered and then completely
rebuilt the house. He had to pay an annual ground rent of at least
£1000 on some property he had bought in Manchester and never
been able to sell; he described it as 'more than the old-man-of-the-
mountain astride my shoulders for more than twenty years and is so
still.'[78] While in Parliament he had to pay for lodgings near
Westminster, as well as incurring the expenses of a large family
home where he loved to dispense hospitality to friends and
acquaintances. He was sometimes short of ready money and had to
apply to friends for loans to tide him over. In 1854 he put £1000 into
the Safety Life Assurance Company. It was established in offices off
the Strand, and Bright and George Wilson were also involved.
Cobden was sure there was a lot of business to be tapped, especially
in and around Manchester, and 'with an effort it may be made a
valuable property for us, and more so for our children'.[79] The
difficulty was to get the firm properly launched and managed. This,
it seems, was never achieved, and Cobden and his friends presumably lost their money.

Far worse, however, were the difficulties he was landed in through
his imprudent purchases of American railway shares. The Illinois
Central line ran for 700 miles from Chicago down to Cairo, at the
junction of the Ohio and Mississippi rivers. The company set up to
build the line in 1851 was granted 2,500,000 acres of land as security
for the bond issues that were to finance the construction of the line.
Four previous attempts to finance the work had failed, and during
much of the 1850s the financial position of the new company
remained precarious. In spite of the security provided by the huge
grant of land, which would presumably rise greatly in value as the
line was built through it, the Illinois Central was considered a long-
term and fairly risky speculation for investors.[80]

Cobden did not lack for advice from prudent friends who assured him that the Illinois Central was not a suitable investment for someone who could not afford any financial losses and who needed an immediate and steady return on his money. But he remembered his ecstatic feelings some 20 years earlier, when he had stood on the summit of the Alleghanies and gazed westward across the great Mississippi plain – 'here will one day centre the civilisation, the wealth, the power of the entire world' – and he was determined to invest as much as he could in the new line. He began by buying bonds which were a reasonably safe investment, but early in 1857, when the company's finances seemed to be improving, he decided to go in for its shares as well, paying 25 to 30 per cent of their nominal value of $100 each. The shares were liable to further calls, but the directors claimed – wrongly as it turned out – that none would be necessary. Cobden sold all his other investments and borrowed as much as he could with the intention of accumulating 3000 shares which he hoped would some day be worth £60,000 for his children. (He actually bought 1641.)[81] There was, he claimed, 'nothing in the world like it [the Illinois Central] and never will be such another speculation'.[82] He was obviously attracted by the prospect of large profits, but he also saw the Illinois Central as something more than an ordinary speculation. It was 'the acquisition of a landed estate more than double the size of Lancashire on the very easy terms of making it accessible [through the railway] to eager purchasers and cultivators'.[83] And he felt sure that with the greatly improved means of communication there would be a flood of people from the old world anxious to make a better life for themselves in the new.

During the second half of 1857, however, the Illinois Central fell victim to the economic and financial crisis sweeping through the United States, and the company was only able to ride out the storm by making repeated calls on its shareholders. With very little spare cash to meet his calls Cobden had to resort to the dangerous expedient of raising loans which only the munificence of friends and well-wishers later allowed him to pay off.[84]* But although he was well aware of the financial risk he was running, his vision remained undimmed. 'Nothing but an earthquake or some other convulsion of nature can impair the value of 2,600,000 (sic) acres of the richest soil in the world, situated in the midst of the most intelligent and industrious population.'[85]

* After Cobden's death, Bright noted in his Diary that Charles Paget MP and the Speaker (Evelyn Denison) had each advanced £1000 to help Cobden pay the calls on the Illinois Central shares. Both sums were 'cancelled to' Mr Thomasson of Bolton, who helped Cobden very generously at this time. Bright says Cobden never knew about the Speaker's loan. (The Diaries of John Bright. ed. R. A. J. Walling. 291–2.)

There were no natural 'convulsions', but during 1858 and 1859 the vagaries of nature added poor harvests to economic depression. In Illinois, land values, land sales and income from rail traffic all dropped. British investors, who had found the Illinois Central such an attractive investment that by now they owned a majority of the shares, became worried about the management of the company and formed 'protective committees'. During 1858 at least 12 representatives of these committees went over to the United States to investigate the company's affairs. They did not find anything seriously amiss.

Early in 1859 Cobden decided to go too. He was apparently yielding to pressure from friends, but his journey can hardly have been really necessary in view of all the shareholders' representatives who had preceded him. A more compelling reason was probably his 'strong desire' to visit again his favourite country which he had not seen for nearly a quarter of a century.[86] His wife agreed to take the children to Paris to stay with an old Manchester friend who took in boarders. He hoped that his eldest daughter would have access to some good music masters and they could all learn to speak French correctly. Above all, he hoped that Kate would benefit from the complete change and from having to stand on her own feet. He may also have felt that he himself could do with a complete change.

On 12 February, 1859, Cobden sailed for the United States on the Cunard steamship *Canada*. He disembarked at Boston a fortnight later. Much had changed since his last visit, not least his own position. Instead of an obscure young businessman, he was an internationally famous politician. He was received as an honoured guest by Congress and two State Assemblies, as well as by the Canadian Legislative Assembly. He was presented with free passes by railway and steamboat companies, and sometimes had special trains laid on for him. Everyone wanted to call on him, invite him to dinner, have him to stay. Twice he was serenaded, once by a band at Springfield (Illinois) whose leader apologised for not knowing the tune of 'God Save the Queen',[87] and once at Yale by a group of Collegians who sang some 'excellent choruses' and did know how to sing 'God Save the Queen'.[88]

Cobden's main preoccupation was the Illinois Central. He had long talks with directors and officials of the company in New York – where he persuaded them to omit some passages from their annual report which he thought might upset British investors[89] – and in Chicago. He examined every mile of the Illinois Central line, some sections several times. He travelled in the directors' private carriage, sometimes spending the night in it in a siding. From time to time he made expeditions by wagon into the surrounding countryside, examining the land and visiting villages, farms and emigrant colonies. All down the line he was delighted to find land 'as fertile as the very best soil in England, without an acre of heath, rock, hill or bog offering any impediment to the progress of the plough'.[90] From Cairo he went on down the Mississippi by steamboat to Memphis in order to see for himself how the line which was to connect Cairo (and Chicago) with New Orleans was progressing.* He found that only about 60 miles were still to be laid, and wrote home enthusiastically about soon being able to travel in less than two days 'from the region of thick snow and ice into the midst of orange trees and alligators'.[91]

The long-term prospects of the Illinois Central were, Cobden was convinced, rosy. Moreover, there was nothing wrong with the management, which British investors had, in his opinion, been very foolishly doing their best to run down. But the reports of a disastrous crop failure in Illinois, which Cobden had tended to dismiss as excuses for poor freight traffic receipts, turned out to be only too well founded. The farmers had nothing to sell and the railway nothing to carry. It was, he confessed to Kate, as he steamed down the Mississippi, 'very embarrassing' for him.[92] By the time he got back to New York in the middle of April he was forced to admit, at least to himself and his wife, that he had made a very foolish investment. He still did not doubt the line's ultimate success. 'But it unfortunately don't suit me to wait, and nearly all I have is at stake – It is too late to regret having been tempted so deeply into a concern that only ought to have belonged to rich men.'†[93]

Cobden always prided himself on his 'natural buoyancy', and although his financial problems sometimes 'almost unnerved' him,[94] they did not seriously dampen his interest in his American travels, nor deter him from making them as extensive as possible He paid two separate visits to the Illinois Central. The first time he went from New York to Chicago by way of Albany, Niagara (where 'the great and glorious cataract' seemed just as awe-inspiring as on his first visit), Toronto and Detroit. On the round trip of 24 days he reckoned he had travelled nearly 4000 miles. Three weeks later he set out again for Chicago, travelling this time from Washington to Cincinnati and on to Lafayette whence a short journey by wagon across the prairie took him to a station on the Illinois Central Line.

---

* He later travelled by steam-boat on the upper Mississippi, from the northern terminus of the Illinois Central at Dunleith down to St Louis.
† The following year, 1859, there was another disastrous harvest. Cobden's faith in the long-term prospects of the Illinois Central were largely justified, but not till after his death.

During these and other subsidiary journeys, he was amazed at the moral as well as material progress that had been made since his last visit. He found the key to much of the improvement in the 'universal hope of rising in the social scale', which accounted for 'the orderly self respect which is the great characteristic of the masses in the United States'.[95] In England he was constantly irritated by the deferential attitude of the middle classes towards the aristocracy. In the United States there seemed to be no social distinctions or class feeling. In all the schools he visited, the sons of rich men and poor men, of judges and blacksmiths, of physicians and labourers were sitting side by side on a footing of complete equality, competing for the same honours and all equally eligible to become President of the United States. In the single-class railway carriage the mechanic or labourer travelled side by side with the rich merchant or state governor, and his manners were 'quite as sedate and orderly as are those of what we in England should call his "betters" '.[96] When Mr Chase, the governor of Ohio and a popular candidate for the Presidency, arrived by train at the state capital, Columbus, he picked up his carpet bag like everyone else and walked off without attracting any particular notice. Cobden later compared this very favourably with the grand reception, complete with royal salute, accorded to the governor-general of Canada when he stepped ashore at Quebec accompanied by his secretaries and aides-de-camp.[97] Similarly, when staying at the White House with President Buchanan (whom he had got to know when Buchanan was American minister in London), he was impressed by the President's unpretentious style of living without any 'retinue of servants in gay livery'.[98] On the journey from Albany to Newhaven he noted approvingly that a 'general appearance of thrift and comfort and equality of condition charac- terises the New England States – No very large mansions and no squalid hovels meet the eye'.[99]

It was, indeed, not easy for him to find anything to criticise. He had been warned before he left England that political corruption, especially during elections, was increasing in the United States, and that some of his own public comments on the progress of American democracy did not accord with reality.[100] He made a number of inquiries and received varying answers. They did not shake his oddly simplistic and naive belief that 'a country which is progressing most rapidly in every respect of its social life, and where the people are every year growing richer and younger and stronger, should at the same time become decrepit and worn out in its political character – I don't believe it.'[101] He could perceive no pitfalls in the future, nor could he find any mistakes in the past. In Chicago he was told that in 1833 about 5000 Indians had been encamped round the town; twelve years later virtually all of them had disappeared. He noted this in his diary without comment.[102] If he had been in a British colony he would most probably have assumed that the Indians had been massacred by British soldiers, sailors or settlers. America, by contrast, was the land of promise, untainted by the sins of the old world.* The outbreak of war between France and Austria over the future of Italy reached Cobden, by telegram from Chicago, at a little railway junction deep in the prairie. It put him into the 'most dismal spirits' and next day he told Kate that if he were a young man, he would settle in the West 'where life is easy and everything in the greatest abundance, and where at least people are exempt from the follies and crimes of the statesmen and rulers of the stupid and wicked *old* world'.[103] He seems to have had no suspicion that in two years the United States would be embroiled in the most tragic warfare of all – civil war.

On 18 June Cobden sailed for home from Quebec and, after a voyage made hazardous by huge icebergs, pack-ice and thick fog, arrived safely at Liverpool 11 days later. Before he had disembarked, to his immense surprise, he was faced with the most difficult decision of his political career.

While Cobden was in America, Lord Derby's Conservative government had called a general election after the defeat of Disraeli's bill to extend the parliamentary franchise. At Bright's instigation the Rochdale Liberal party adopted Cobden as its candidate. Cobden did not welcome the news. 'It is', he told Kate on 11 May, 'a most inconvenient step for me and I am praying that I may not be returned.'[104] His prayer was not answered; he was returned unopposed. This much Cobden knew, but when he left Quebec the news that the Derby government had resigned after being again defeated in the new Parliament had not yet crossed the Atlantic. The government's defeat had been preceded by a great demonstration of unity by the Liberal party during a meeting in Willis's rooms at which Palmerston, Lord John Russell and Bright had sat side by side on the platform. Palmerston, when asked to form a new government, wished to demonstrate the Liberals' new-found unity by including one or two members of the far left of the party in his Cabinet. Bright had ruled himself out – and he knew and accepted this – by his vigorous public onslaught on the House of Lords and the aristocracy during the previous winter. Cobden, with equally strong feelings, had been more discreet, but his discretion brought

---

* Cobden was told that in the non-slave states there was a growing estrangement between the white and black races. He attributed this to the sense of superiority of the first and the consciousness of inferiority of the second. (Cawley, *The American Diaries of Richard Cobden* 176)

him a most unwelcome reward. As soon as his ship docked, he was given two letters: one, from Palmerston, offered him a seat in the Cabinet as President of the Board of Trade; the other, from Russell, strongly urged him to accept it.[105] 'If you do not', admonished Lord John, 'I do not see a prospect of amalgamating the Liberal party in my life-time.'[106]

Cobden went straight to a hotel where he was confronted with more than 100 of the leading men of Liverpool, who presented him with highly complimentary addresses urging him to join the government. Cobden, his 'head still swimming with the motion of the sea', answered them as best he could and felt he was being killed with kindness. He went on to Manchester where a deputation from Rochdale and many personal friends all urged him to accept Palmerston's offer. The pressure on him was so great that if it had been Lord Granville or even Lord John at the head of the government, he felt that he must, however unwillingly, have given way.[107]

As it was, he felt they must all have gone mad. For more than 12 years he had constantly and consistently attacked Lord Palmerston's policies and public conduct in the most uncompromising terms. It was inconceivable that, without any change in his opinions, he should go straight from the deck of a transatlantic steamer into Palmerston's Cabinet. He would, rightly, in his own opinion, deserve the severest censure from the general public and – worst of all – would lose his self-respect, 'without which a man is good for nothing'.[108] So he listened in silence to all his friends said, but his mind was already made up.

Cobden called on Palmerston as soon as he reached London. After being 'most pleasantly welcomed', he told the Prime Minister with unequivocal frankness that, whether he had been right or wrong in denouncing him as 'warlike, intermeddling and quarrelsome', he could not possibly announce a change in his opinions while holding high office in his Cabinet. Palmerston clearly felt that Cobden was straining at a gnat and did his best to overcome his objections. His most effective argument was that since foreign policy questions which 'were now uppermost' were decided in Cabinet, not in Parliament, Cobden should join the Cabinet where alone he could effectively influence them. Cobden found this argument difficult to combat. He was less perplexed by the Prime Minister's suggestion that it could be difficult to carry on the government if 'the natural representatives of the Liberals' would not join it; he pointed out that Milner Gibson had agreed to take office and he himself would hope to support the government from outside. In the end, Palmerston gave up. The whole discussion had been civilised and good-humoured, with both men disclaiming any personal feelings. As he said goodbye to the Prime Minister, Cobden hoped that in future their personal and political relations might be the same as if he were in the government. Palmerston immediately endorsed that hope by saying: 'Lady Palmerston receives tomorrow evening at ten.' Cobden promptly replied: 'I shall be happy to be allowed to present myself to her.' To which Palmerston answered: 'I shall be very glad if you will.'[109]

The outcome of this little exchange cannot be better described than in Cobden's own words.

> The next evening I was at Cambridge House for the first time, and found myself among a crowd of fashionables and politicians, and was the lion or rather the *monster* of the party. The women came and stared with their glasses at me, and then brought their friends to stare also. As I came away, Jacob Omnium and I were squeezed into a corner together, and he remarked, 'You are the greatest political monster that ever was seen in this house. There never was before such a curiosity as a man who refused a Cabinet office from Lord Palmerston, and then came to visit him here. Why, there are not half-a-dozen men in all that crowd that would not jump at the offer, and believe themselves quite as fit as you to be President of the Board of Trade.[110]

Cobden could bear the amazed curiosity of the fashionable crowd at Lady Palmerston's with equanimity. He found it much harder to bear the surprised disappointment of his political associates and personal friends, almost all of whom – Bright was one of the few exceptions – assured him that it was his *duty* to join the government. It was 'a most painful ordeal' and made him feel physically ill.[111]

When Palmerston, nonplussed at his refusal to join the Cabinet, laughingly asked him why he was in the House of Commons, Cobden, also laughing, had to reply that he hardly knew. He was equally unable to explain why he had gone into public life at all. It had been, he told Palmerston, by mere accident and for a special purpose, and it would probably have been better if he had kept his private station. Palmerston, more nonplussed and amused than ever, threw up both his hands and exclaimed: "Well, but being in it, why not go on?'

Why not indeed? After 13 years of frustrating opposition, why not try to work for reform from inside the system? Cobden told Joseph Parkes that he had an 'insuperable reluctance' to taking office. 'I am 55 and not of a long-lived family. The change of habits, and the repugnance I feel to official forms, would shorten my days. But, besides, I have a horror of losing my individuality, which to me is very existence itself.'*[112] It does not seem a very satisfactory explanation, even after making allowance for Cobden's uncertain health. Gladstone, who greatly regretted Cobden's refusal to accept office, had attacked Palmerston savagely; he had even supported the Opposition in the vote of confidence that brought about his downfall. But he was still offered, and he still accepted, a seat as Chancellor of the Exchequer, in Palmerston's Cabinet. He braved the disapproval of his friends and the derision of his enemies because he wanted to be where the action was. His personal consistency came second to what he saw as an opportunity to contribute actively to the welfare of the country. Cobden, on the other hand, believed that his ability to do good would be fatally flawed by any personal inconsistency.

Paradoxically for someone who accepted that reform must come gradually, Cobden could not reconcile himself to the inevitable compromises of Cabinet government. He seems to have felt that he would lose all moral influence if he was so closely associated with those with whom he did not always agree. And behind this fear was the deep ideological antipathy to the existing aristocratic 'establishment' which he had acquired as a young man and which he never lost or even modified. It was not that he had any chip on his shoulder; socially, he got on well with individual members of the aristocracy. But as a class, he regarded them as 'the enemy', the cause of all the country's past misfortunes and the great obstacle to its present and future progress. The placid acquiescence of most of his countrymen in the aristocratic dominance of government never ceased to infuriate him. Of course, members of the middle class did make their way into office, but they usually took pains to assimilate themselves to their new background. Cobden never had changed his spots and he never would. He would not even make the harmless concession to current social conventions of donning court dress, although he was not anti-monarchist and greatly respected Prince Albert. He thereby debarred himself from going to the Palace or dining with the Speaker.

> not because I have any churlish feelings which keep me away, nor from any sour feelings of a democratic kind which make me disinclined to pay my respects to royalty. But I have never had the courage to put on a court dress, certainly the most ridiculous one in the civilised world ... But if any public object could be served,

---

* This letter was written in February 1860, after Cobden had negotiated the commercial treaty with France. He argued that he could not have done this if he had been in office because he could not have remained in Paris for so long and he could not, as a minister, have used arguments that were very powerful coming from an independent MP.

I would make myself ridiculous by donning a Bartholomew Fair dress, or standing on my head, or eating fire, or any other harlequin exploit. But I would not like to do so for mere idle ceremony.[113]

One of the ultra-Tory aristocratic ladies of Sussex once refused to meet Cobden because of his allegedly destructive and revolutionary opinions.[114] The solid, aspiring bourgeoisie of Lancashire would not have recognised this caricature of their esteemed friend and associate. One important reason why they wanted him to join the government was that he had remained, outwardly at any rate, one of them, and his presence in the Cabinet would have represented a notable breakthrough for their own class. But Cobden preferred to remain, as Walter Bagehot wrote, 'an outsider'.[115]

CHAPTER 13

Plenipotentiary in Paris (1859–61)

'We must do our best', wrote Cobden to his wife from New York in March 1859, 'to live economically for the next year with as little appearance of penury as possible.'[1] Kate had made some recovery from her deep depression, but Cobden was still sufficiently worried about her to decide that a prolonged absence from the painful memories at home would do her good. Everything thus pointed to letting Dunford for a year and keeping the family in Paris, where they could live economically in lodgings without neglecting the children's education. After some difficulty a suitable tenant was found for Dunford by the early summer of 1859. He was a retired colonel – a 'quiet, gentlemanly man, precise and conscientious in small matters' – whose only drawback seemed to be that he might run the place at a higher standard than its owner would be able to maintain.[2]

The plan for a temporary migration to Paris helps to explain Cobden's reluctance to return to the House of Commons. It was not strong enough for him to reject the voters of Rochdale who 'elected me most generously and honourably in my absence without solicitation or expense'.[3] But his failure to provide financial security for his wife and children troubled his conscience and pushed politics to the back of his mind. His Illinois investments were paying no interest and he did not even feel justified in contributing £50 towards a memorial fund for his old friend Joseph Sturge, who had died while he was in America.[4] In September he travelled to Manchester to attend to his much-neglected property and from there wrote to a Sussex neighbour to explain his temporary absence from Dunford: 'I suppose all politicians neglect their own affairs, but I don't think they are justified in doing so, for, in my opinion, duty, as well as charity, begins at home. So I must be a money-grubbing old hunks for the rest of my days, but I assure you I have no intention of turning my back on Dunford, and I hope to be there again next mid-summer.'[5] It was in fact nearly two mid-summers before Cobden again settled down at Dunford after an achievement which, if it did not improve his finances, rescued his political career from the disappointments and frustrations that had dogged it for so many years.

On 5 September Cobden wrote to Gladstone from Manchester suggesting that he should 'run over' to Hawarden the following week and have 'a little talk' about trade with France. 'My good friend M. Chevalier insists very pertinaciously that the Emperor cannot reduce his duties unless you help him by a corresponding movement. How you are to do so, and fulfill [the Secretary to the Admiralty] Lord Clarence Paget's promise to keep fifty line-of-battle ships, I don't know!' Cobden added that he intended to spend part of the coming winter in Paris with his family 'and if I can be of any use to you in the way of inquiry I shall be glad'.[6] Gladstone was on holiday at Penmaenmawr, but he immediately arranged to meet Cobden at Hawarden on 12 September. That evening he wrote to his wife: 'I have had a walk and a long talk with Cobden who I think pleases and is pleased.'[7]

Michel Chevalier, a distinguished writer and economist, much influenced in his early days by the ideas of Saint-Simon, had resigned his chair of political economy in Paris in 1852 when Napoleon III appointed him to his Council of State. Chevalier was an enthusiastic and articulate free trader in a country with a strongly-entrenched tradition of protectionism. He first met Cobden at a banquet given in the latter's honour in Paris in August 1846. Since then they had corresponded on the progress – or lack of it – of the free-trade cause in France. Eventually Chevalier realised that the only way forward was by means of a treaty of commerce with Britain, which the Emperor had power to conclude without reference to the hopelessly obstructive *Corps Législatif*. He made unofficial overtures to the British government in 1856, but Palmerston was not interested.

Three years later, in July 1859, when Napoleon's military adventure in Italy had set off a new wave of anti-French agitation, Bright suggested that a reduction in the remaining British tariffs would be a good way of reducing tension between the two countries. He said nothing about a treaty, but his speech encouraged Chevalier to reopen the subject in a letter to Cobden.[8] In principle, commercial treaties were anathema to free traders because they implied an exclusive relationship between the signatories, but Cobden was sufficiently impressed by Chevalier's arguments to want to talk the matter over with Gladstone, the only influential member of the Cabinet on whose sympathy he could count. As a convinced free trader, Gladstone fully shared Cobden's disapproval of commercial treaties, but he was more pragmatic in outlook and equally alarmed

about the state of Anglo-French relations. At Hawarden he welcomed Chevalier's initiative and encouraged Cobden to follow it up.

Cobden's feelings were still mixed. The day after he left Hawarden, he wrote a curiously ambivalent letter to Chevalier which made
no mention of a treaty, emphasised that British manufacturers were
not looking for more foreign markets because they already had as
much work as they could cope with, and admitted that it was already
'very difficult to manage matters with the working classes owing to
the great demand for their labour'. On the other hand, he assured
Chevalier that he saw no other way of counteracting the antagonism
of language and race between the French and English than by making
them mutually dependent through supplying each other's needs. 'It
is God's own method of producing an *entente cordiale* and no other
plan is worth a farthing.' He offered, without much enthusiasm, to
discuss these ideas with French ministers, but they must not think he
was coming as a travelling salesman for British fabrics.[9]

Chevalier, however, did not give up easily. He came over to
London and his personal persuasions convinced Cobden that a treaty
was really the only way to reduce French tariff barriers. And, having
come round, Cobden wanted to do the thing properly. The French,
he told Gladstone, must be urged to make a substantial reform in
their tariff: 'for anything like a delusive or unreal measure on their
part, whilst it would not mitigate the virulence of their protectionist
party, would have a bad moral effect in this country, and defeat the
main object you would have in view in entering on such an
exceptional arrangement.' He added that the French were greatly
alarmed about the supposed power of their protectionists; 'I will try
to give them courage.'[10] Gladstone, in reply, urged him to speak
strongly in Paris because the present arms rivalry was 'disgraceful to
both countries and the age in which we live'.[11]

No such encouragement came from Gladstone's colleagues,
Palmerston and the foreign secretary, Lord John Russell, when
Cobden called on them. But they acquiesced in his unofficial mission
and Lord John offered him the services of the British embassy in
Paris. Both were much more interested in Napoleon's intentions in
Italy than in his trade policy. Cobden was disgusted by their
suspicions of France and their ready acceptance of the current
'extravagant' defence expenditure. But he did not expect much from
the French ministers either. 'Governments', he remarked to Bright,
as he was setting out for Paris, 'seem as a rule standing conspiracies
to rob and bamboozle people, and why should Louis Napoleon's be
any exception?'[12]

This pessimistic and rather half-hearted frame of mind did not
persist. Although success was never a foregone conclusion, and
sometimes seemed remote, it was soon reasonably clear that he had
not come on a complete wild-goose chase and that with stamina,

patience and persistence he had a fair chance of success. But without the advice and indefatigable support of Michel Chevalier, his chances would have been immeasurably less. It was Chevalier, 'the excellent, able and sincere advocate of Free Trade',[13] who prepared the ground with the Emperor and his ministers and opened all the doors that mattered for Cobden. He was also fortunate in having the willing co-operation of the British ambassador in Paris. Cobden called on Lord Cowley soon after his arrival in Paris and told him frankly that as he was to be a poacher on his territory, he intended to do nothing without his approval. Cowley replied equally frankly that as Cobden knew far more than he did about commercial matters, he had no objection at all to letting him take the lead.[14] On this basis of mutual goodwill, the British ambassador and Cobden, the scourge of diplomats and all their ways, got on surprisingly well together.

The key figure in the negotiations was the Emperor Napoleon. He was genuinely committed to the economic development of France and he realised that, without foreign competition, it would be very difficult to make French manufacturers modernise their methods and lower their prices. But the opponents of tariff reform were not, as Cobden tended to assume, mere paper tigers. They had demonstrated their strength in 1856 when their well-organised and determined lobbying had intimidated the *Corps Législatif* into rejecting a measure to replace the complete prohibition of imports by high protective duties. Napoleon could not afford to generate too much hostility. He had gained his throne by force and he might lose it by the same means. In France, he told Cobden, they made revolutions, not reforms.[15]

Cobden's first interview with the Emperor was arranged by Chevalier on 27 October. He was received amidst the sentries, liveried servants, splendid rooms and gorgeous tapestries of the palace of St Cloud. (Privately, he made invidious comparisons with his reception a few months earlier by the President of the United States, 'a plain man in a black suit' without either sentries or servants in livery.) He talked to Napoleon for more than an hour on the parlous state of Anglo-French relations. The Emperor complained strongly about the English press attacks on him. Cobden told him he must learn to laugh at them as he himself had done. He pointed out that English people were instinctively alarmed by the Emperor's name, and that the sudden and secret way in which he had embarked on war in Italy against Austria had greatly stimulated fears that he intended to follow his uncle's example. When Napoleon asked him how he could improve relations between the two countries, Cobden told him he must choose between the policies of Napoleon I and those of Sir Robert Peel, and that a bold measure of commercial reform would be his best policy. He found the Emperor to be a good listener, ignorant of the details of tariff policy but capable of asking very pertinent questions. He feared that he himself might have talked too much, but the Emperor said afterwards that Cobden had given him a little courage.[16]

Two days later, after giving M. Fould, the minister of state and a well-known banker, 'the first lessons in political economy',[17] Cobden reported rather complacently to Gladstone: 'The French tariff is in a worse mess than ours was in 1820 – and where they are to find Deacon Humes, Huskissons and Peels to reform it, I can't imagine. I certainly have met none yet.' His unofficial status helped him to combat the rooted suspicion of the French that he was pursuing some selfish end for his country, but the only other category they would put him in was that of fanatic – 'to which I have no objection'.[18] He was indeed rapidly becoming possessed by a fanatical determination to persuade Napoleon to give all Europe some striking proof of his intention to follow the paths of peace, not war. 'It is this alone', he told Gladstone, 'that I am anxious about. I would not step across the street, just now, to increase our trade, for the mere sake of material gain. *We have about as much prosperity as we can bear*. But to improve the moral and political relations of France and England by bringing them into greater intercourse and increased commercial dependence, I would walk barefoot from Calais to Paris.'[19] In mid-November he had to tear himself away from his absorbing pursuit to attend to his private affairs in London, in particular, his ill-fated investments in the Illinois Central. But at least he was able to talk things over with Gladstone with whom a shared enthusiasm and goal had fostered a very cordial relationship. The Chancellor of the Exchequer's unwearying interest and firm support went far to offset the neutrality, or worse, of most of the Cabinet. A discussion on Anglo-French relations with Palmerston, on the other hand, was a depressing experience. The prime minister retailed stories of France's warlike preparations – flat-bottomed boats, iron-clad warships and so on – which in his view indubitably proved the need for more defence spending.[20]

After a week of being 'kept on the trot' with public and private engagements in England, Cobden landed at Dieppe in a state of collapse brought on by a severe London fog and a sudden frost. He was unable to walk the hundred yards from the ship to the hotel without assistance and had to stop three times to get his breath.[21] He arrived in Paris feeling 'very poorly'.[22] The eminent doctor summoned by Chevalier listened to his lungs with a stethoscope and announced that they 'whistled and groaned like the pipes of an organ'.[23] As Cobden suspected, the doctor thought he had 'a sort of asthma ... and that the chill and the fog and the neglect have brought on a sort of congestion of the lungs'. His prescription was quiet and a warm room.[24]

There was no difficulty about a warm room, but quiet was another matter. A few days after his return, M. Fould appeared at his bedside, accompanied by the minister of commerce, M. Rouher, They listened while Cobden explained what he thought they ought to do and what they might expect his government to do in return. In brief, he proposed that Britain should abolish all duties on French manufactures and greatly reduce its duties on French wines and spirits, while France would give up all complete bans on English exports and set a reasonable level of duty instead. He made it clear that while the French concessions would apply only to English exports, his own government, with its firm commitment to free trade, would have to extend to other countries the concessions made to France.

During the ensuing weeks the French mulled over these proposals while Chevalier kept them in touch with Cobden, who remained confined to his room. So great was the fear of protectionist hostility that the strictest possible secrecy was observed. Fould confided to Cobden that it was particularly important to exclude the foreign minister, Count Walewski, from the negotiations. 'Only imagine', wrote Cobden to Gladstone, 'Lord Palmerston telling a comparative stranger that he must not make a confidant of Lord John!'[25] Rouher, who had been instructed by the Emperor to prepare a new reformed French tariff, could not even trust his own clerks. So he shut himself up at home and got Chevalier to obtain from the Bureau of Commerce the reports and other material he needed as if for his own use. 'The poor man [Rouher] is almost knocked up', reported Cobden.[26] In the absence of all official help, Rouher, Chevalier and Cobden had to rely on their wives (and in Cobden's case, his eldest daughter, Katie) to help out with the clerical work.[27] It was an odd situation for Cobden, the fierce and lifelong critic of secret diplomacy, but he merely described it as 'droll'.[28]

He was even more amused when Chevalier apologetically explained that Rouher was most anxious that the official record of their negotiations should suggest that the English had had to make substantial concessions to the French. Cobden replied that all he cared about was a satisfactory result.[29] When Gladstone hinted that he might be going too far in conciliating the French,[30] Cobden promptly replied that the French treaty 'is more than, or less than, a simple question of internal taxation, and you must therefore let me go on in my own way trying by every honest means to sway the policy of this country, and not suspect, even if my arguments from your point of view are not always strictly scientific, that I have forgotten my sound principles of political economy.'[31] By this time – mid-December – Cobden was in better health and was beginning to feel that the French meant business. Chevalier had told him that the Emperor approved of Rouher's tariff reform and had agreed that the rest of his ministers should be told. A few days later Cobden had his first interview with the foreign minister, who indicated that his government was now ready to begin formal negotiations. He found Walewski better informed than he had expected, but obviously anxious to minimise the tariff changes on the French side by emphasising the importance of abolishing all prohibitions. Cobden replied that the English public were well instructed in such matters, and if prohibitions were replaced by prohibitive tariffs, they would say it was as bad to be drowned in seven feet of water as in seventy.[32]

At his second interview with the Emperor, on 21 December, Cobden explained that the Chancellor of the Exchequer wanted to prepare his budget and it would be convenient for him to know whether he would have to make allowances in it for a commercial treaty with France. Napoleon assured him that he had quite made up his mind to have the treaty but he would have to face very powerful opposition from the protectionist lobby, and he went on to repeat all the arguments against the treaty that had been instilled into him by his fiercely protectionist ministers, especially the finance minister, M. Magne. (Cobden called Magne 'a regular cannon ball', completely impervious to the lessons in political economy which he bestowed on him.[33]) When Napoleon repeated word for word Magne's argument that every foreign import would displace an article made in France, Cobden laughed, held up both hands and exclaimed what an old friend that argument was. During the Corn law controversy in England they had answered it a thousand times by showing that a quarter of the people were not properly fed. Now, although large quantities of corn were imported annually, English agriculture was more prosperous than ever. Similarly, French people were now poorly clothed; nearly a quarter of them did not wear stockings and yet the import of stockings was banned. When Cobden said that French workers were working 20 per cent longer for 20 per cent less wages and paid up to 10 per cent more for their clothes than a similar class in England, the Emperor, instead of querying the figures, seized a pen and begged Cobden to repeat them, exclaiming as he wrote them down: 'What an answer for those people'.[34] To Cobden, the arguments of 'those people' were 'the mere A. B. C. of monopoly'.*[35]

---

* Cobden bolstered Rouher's resolution by introducing him to John Platt of Oldham, who employed 4000 workers in the largest machine-making establishment in the world. Platt told the minister that France was at the bottom of the league of European machine manufacturers with regard to the quality of its machinery, much of which was 20 to 30 years old. He said it took three French cotton workers to produce the same output as in England. (B. L. Add. Mss. 44, 135 to Gladstone 30 Dec., 1859.)

DAME COBDEN'S NEW PUPIL.

12 *Punch*, 28 Jan. 1860.

Meanwhile in England rumours that Napoleon was about to send his armies across the Channel continued to alarm the public, and recruits flocked to join the Volunteer Rifle Corps which had been started the previous summer. From Paris Cobden observed the agitation with profound distaste and tried, without success, to cultivate a 'stoical apathy'.[36] The public mood penetrated the Cabinet room, and even with Lord John's cordial support, Gladstone did not find it easy to get his colleagues' formal approval of the proposed treaty. It was, he told his wife, 'no small thing to get a cabinet to give up one and a half or two millions of revenue at a time when all the public passion is for enormous expenditure . . .'[37] But Gladstone's colleagues did eventually give their reluctant consent, and by the end of the year Cobden had been transformed from a private citizen into a plenipotentiary. Lord Cowley, who was to act with him, told Russell that the merit of whatever was effected would rest solely with Cobden, 'and it is but fair that he should have the satisfaction of putting his name to the final arrangement'.[38]

Early in January 1860, the Emperor sent word that he wanted the negotiations completed as quickly as possible. He was anxious not to give his protectionist ministers time to organise opposition in the country. For the same reason, they did all they could to delay the treaty, most notably by successfully persuading the Emperor that he must honour a pledge he had given in 1856 not to reopen the prohibitions issue without holding an inquiry into the state of French industry. The inquiry, however, was limited to two days, and on the day it opened, Napoleon published a long letter to Fould, laying down an extensive programme of economic liberalisation and reform, including the substitution of protective duties for the complete prohibition of imports.[39] He had at last publicly committed himself to the commercial treaty with England.

The Emperor's letter – which had been approved, with two small additions, by Cobden[40] – was received with dismay by French industrialists throughout the country. Leading manufacturers rushed to Paris – the men of Rouen chartered a special train – and demanded meetings with the Emperor and his minister of commerce. When these were refused, petitions were drawn up, one of which threatened to 'destroy the treaty by cannon fire'. Finally, the textile manufacturers began to close down their factories, hoping to drive their unemployed workers to revolt. But the government let it be known that if there was violence, it would be the bosses, not the workers, who went to jail. Faced with the Emperor's refusal to be intimidated, the agitation gradually subsided.[41]

In England the Emperor's letter had, temporarily, a calming effect on public opinion. But the final stage of negotiating the treaty was still an anxious search for ways of making it acceptable to one country without dangerously alienating the other. The most important concession sought by the French – their *sine qua non* – was to have a substantial reduction in the British duties on their wines and spirits written into the treaty. They were strongly supported by Cobden, but although Gladstone agreed that the existing duties were far too high, he had to consider the effect of the immediate loss of revenue on his budget estimates*. Eventually he gave way because he realised that the alternative was to lose the treaty altogether.

It was equally important that the treaty should seem fair to the British. In the draft proposals Britain agreed to make all its tariff concessions at once, but France granted virtually no immediate concessions in return. Cobden was so anxious to bring the maximum French duty down (if possible to 20 per cent) that he could see no difficulty in conciliating the French by allowing them to take their time over implementing their concessions. Gladstone agreed that they had a formidable task, but he had to meet the Cabinet's criticisms and in any case the treaty would lose most of its point if it were not accepted ungrudgingly in Britain. He could hardly accept Cobden's blithe assurance that it was in their interest 'to allow it to appear that we have the worst of the bargain'.[42] It was imperative, he told Cobden, to get 'something in hand' as an earnest that the French meant what they said.[43] In the end, Lord Cowley, recently returned from a visit to London and therefore more in touch than Cobden with opinion there, managed, with Chevalier's support, to extract enough concessions from the French to make the treaty seem less one-sided.

After a flurry of eleventh-hour telegrams and agitated letters, the treaty was at last signed on 23 January, 1860.[†] In spite of all the anxiety to mollify public opinion on both sides, Cobden still believed that it was the only way to ensure peace between the two countries. 'It is a sad conclusion to have come to', he told Bright, 'that the merchants' ledger is to do more than the Bible to carry out the Christian precept of peace and good-will among the nations of the earth.'[44]

---

* In order to discover the most reliable method of measuring the alcoholic content of wine, Cobden and Chevalier experimented with an 'alcoholometer', using the wine provided by Cobden's landlady. He sent Gladstone one of these gadgets, but a few days later wrote that a 'pocket still' was more accurate with wine. (B. L. Add. Mss. 44, 135, 24, 28, Nov., 1859.)

† France agreed to abolish all prohibition of imports, and to admit British goods at a maximum duty of 30 per cent within two years, and at a maximum duty of 25 per cent within five years. On a small number of specified commodities the reductions were to take place during the current year. The exact rate of duty on each item in the new French tariff was to be laid down in a separate convention.

A holiday in the south of France was Cobden's immediate goal after signing the treaty. Gladstone had urged him to come back to London to help defend the treaty in Parliament. Bright, he delicately explained, was not an adequate substitute because he was received with a 'kind of adverse prepossession' which Cobden would not encounter.[45] But for weeks the doctor had been urging him to go south, and Cobden, who every year felt a greater sense of weakness in his lungs,[46] was not inclined to disregard his advice.

Unfortunately, the warm sunny weather which had greeted the Cobdens on their arrival in Cannes disappeared after a few days. 'We might certainly', wrote Cobden sadly, 'have been better off in England with a good fire, and carpeted rooms, and doors and windows that can be closed, none of which comforts can be had by temporary lodgers here.'[47] The lodgings were 'pinched' and in an unattractive situation opening straight on to the main street of the little town. But the great compensation for their drawbacks was that they were next door to the house where Baron von Bunsen was staying with his family. On his daily visits next door Cobden greatly enjoyed Bunsen's 'charming conversation', while the Baroness and her daughters were 'kind and friendly' to Kate.[48]

Being in Cannes also spared Cobden from having to attend the late-night sittings of the Commons which he had begun to dread during the winter months. That February Gladstone also succumbed to the London fog, and had to take to his bed when he should have been delivering his budget statement. When he did make it a few days later, 'aided by a great stock of egg and wine',[49] it turned out to be one of his most memorable and admired performances. Cobden had special reason to feel gratified, because Gladstone not only swept away most of the remaining British tariffs, but he also made the treaty with France an integral part of his budget and paid a glowing tribute to Cobden's role in negotiating it. Cobden, in his turn, congratulated the Chancellor. He shared, he told him, the world-wide admiration of his great speech; but he could not refrain from adding that the 'enormous' defence estimates had also made him weep.[50]

They made Gladstone almost equally miserable. But faced with the relentless pressure of the Prime Minister, backed by most of the Cabinet and public opinion, he had had to give way. After the Crimean war the Royal Navy had been allowed to decline in strength while the French had greatly expanded their navy. In 1858 they laid down the first sea-going, ironclad warship. Even without the unpredictable Emperor Napoleon on the throne of France, it was inevitable that the British would feel obliged to start building ironclad warships too. On the way to Cannes Cobden visited the dockyards at Toulon, and the sight of frigates being covered with iron plates five inches thick left him unmoved. He supposed, he told Bright, that the British would cover twice as many ships as the French with iron half as thick again. They would, he added sarcastically, be found to roll better than they steam. 'I hope this sort of Don Quixotism in naval armaments may by and by tend to make the whole system a little ridiculous. Our time will come yet, if we only give the other side rope enough.'[51]

But when it became known early in 1860 that Napoleon intended to annex Savoy and Nice, the British were confirmed in their belief that they were not tilting at windmills. Cobden regretted the annexation because it provoked a fresh anti-French outcry in England. But he had no use for those who were alarmed at the infringement of the 1815 Vienna settlement, or who still clung to the 'ancient superstition' that territorial enlargement necessarily made a state more wealthy and powerful when everyone now knew that correct economic and commercial policies were far more important.[52] The Savoyards, he argued, were more French than Italian and would benefit economically from being united to France. Napoleon was merely acting like a large landowner who rounds off his estate with an acquisition from a neighbour. (This was an odd argument from someone who strongly condemned the perpetuation of large estates, through inheritance, in England.) In any case the annexations could do the British no harm and were no business of theirs.[53]

Many in the British Parliament thought otherwise, and the outcry over Savoy in both Houses was energetically promoted by those who already had genuine misgivings about the Anglo-French treaty. But Gladstone stoutly defended it in the Commons, and outside Parliament, especially in the manufacturing districts, gallophobia was for once overshadowed by the prospect of greater commercial prosperity held out by Gladstone's budget and Cobden's treaty. Widespread approval of both was expressed at public meetings and in petitions to Parliament. By the middle of March 1860 both Houses had formally approved the treaty.

The treaty itself, however, was only a framework. The 'altogether unprecedented affair' of French and English commissioners sitting down to settle the details of the new French tariff still had to be accomplished,[54] and everyone concerned, not least Cobden himself, felt that he was by far the best person to represent the English side. 'The whole success of the treaty', he explained to Bright, 'depends on the details still to be settled; for between 10 and 30 per cent, which will be the range of the duties to be laid on, there is all the difference between free trade and prohibition. Nobody can have so much

weight with the French government as myself.'[55] It was all settled
when he went to London early in April. The Cabinet thought he
might find it '*infra dig.*' to be appointed a mere first commissioner
after having been a plenipotentiary. He assured them that he could
survive the demotion,[56] and it was agreed that when it came to
signing the supplementary conventions, he should be promoted to
minister plenipotentiary.

He assumed, far too optimistically, that the business would only
take two months, and before rejoining his family in Paris he went
down to Dunford to make arrangements for taking over the house
from the retired colonel. He found he had not been mistaken in his
choice of tenant. Everything remained unchanged; not even the
carpet was worn. While there, Cobden made arrangements to
improve the heating by running a hot water pipe from the boiler at
the back of the house under the floor to where a marble sideboard
stood under the stairs, where, he explained, 'a coil of piping will be
fixed which will fill a metal chest as large as the sideboard'. This, he
hoped, would heat the house and, if not, it would be easy and
inexpensive to add some more pipes.[57] He already foresaw that the
London fog would in future force him to hibernate at Dunford
through the worst of the winter.

It was during this visit to England that Cobden's finances were at
last put on a stable basis. Other men's generosity had preserved him
from defaulting on the calls on his Illinois Central investment, but
the shares had been paying no interest and he had been sinking
steadily into debt. He tried at first to keep his financial difficulties to
himself, and when Henry Ashworth and other friends more or less
forced the facts from him, he insisted that all he needed was a loan of
£20,000 to pay off his debts. But they thought they understood his
problem better than he did himself.[58] So apparently did his wife.
'Mrs Cobden', reported Ashworth, 'has expressed a very correct
conclusion in regard to her husband's unfitness to take charge of
money matters. It seems to belong to those who have a right
appreciation of Cobden's mission of peace and commerce to pardon
as far as possible his apparent delinquencies in respect of his own
finances and not allow his memory, like that of Pitt and others, to
rest under financial obloquy.'[59] So a group of friends, mostly from in
and around Manchester, agreed to raise privately about £40,000,
half to be used to pay off Cobden's debts and the rest to be put into a
fund, to be administered by trustees for the benefit of Cobden and
his family. It was not at all easy to persuade him to accept a plan
which he must have found humiliating, but eventually he swallowed
his pride and, when Ashworth saw him in London in April, he found
him overcome with joy and gratitude at the kindness of his friends.[60]

Cobden's success in negotiating the commercial treaty with France restored to him much of his old popularity. When he took the train to Folkestone on his return to Paris, the railway company insisted on giving him a whole carriage to himself – a compliment he would gladly have done without because he enjoyed talking to his travelling companions.[61] But there was notoriety as well as popularity. Rumours, more or less true, about his private financial troubles leaked out and inevitably gave rise to hostile or disparaging comments which Cobden could not always avoid hearing. In the hotel at Boulogne, for instance, an English traveller started chatting to him about the boxing champion, Sayers. He could not, he said, see any sense in a subscription for him any more than for the subscription 'which it is proposed to raise for Cobden, merely because he has lost the money which was subscribed for him before'. Cobden recorded this encounter in his diary without comment.[62] Presumably he tried to shrug it off philosophically, just as some months later he shrugged off a painfully snide article about his private finances in *The Times*.[63] It was the price he had to pay for his freedom to follow his chosen path.

Two assistant commissioners, one from the Board of Trade and the other from the Customs, were appointed to help Cobden to negotiate two supplementary conventions. Their first task was to help the French authorities to collect the facts and figures on which the negotiations proper would have to be based. The *Conseil Supérieur du Commerce* tackled each industry in turn, taking evidence on prices and production costs from both English and French manufacturers. Deputations from British Chambers of Commerce were sent over to Paris by the Board of Trade and briefed by Cobden and his colleagues before giving their evidence. Cobden urged his Manchester friends to come over and bring with them anyone who might know about the 'odds and ends' of the cotton industry so that nothing was left out. A trip to Paris, he pointed out, was no great sacrifice.[64]

The French manufacturers were still fighting a rearguard action against the treaty and, in order to deprive them of any excuse for claiming they had not had a fair hearing, the government allowed the proceedings to drag on until the end of August. By that time Kate had taken the three younger children back to Dunford and seen them satisfactorily settled before rejoining her husband. It was an exceptionally cold and wet summer in Paris. 'I have not parted with my flannel or worsted stockings', wrote Cobden early in August, 'and am frequently obliged to resort to a great coat.'[65] But at least he did not have to work through a sweltering heat wave. And there were diversions of all kinds. He went to private dinner parties as well

as public banquets and balls – where he was more impressed with
the dresses than with the beauty of those who wore them.[66] He
made an expedition to Versailles; attended a fete champêtre at the
American legation on 4 July; took his children to the circus – where
he was particularly impressed by the acrobat;[67] and called on the
composer Rossini at his villa at Passy – 'a stout old man of about 70,
with a lively manner and a clever conversation'.[68]

The actual tariff negotiations began on 20 August and the hard
bargaining continued for nearly two-and-a-half months. Every
article was considered separately, and on each the French tried to
push up the duty while the English insisted on keeping it low enough
to allow fair competition. For Cobden it was a labour of love. But it
was also tedious and exhausting. 'If', he told a friend, 'you are on the
look-out for the very toughest task in the world, undertake to make
yourself jointly responsible for reforming an entire tariff in a twelve-
month!'.[69] In September they were trying to price and classify
thousands of articles made in Birmingham and Sheffield 'of which I
am as ignorant as a horse – and so we have some *experts* here from
those places with whom I am studying night and day the value of
pots and pans, curry combs, needles, anvils, fish hooks, anchors, pen
knives, etc, etc, etc, etc'.[70] A few weeks later he put himself 'under
the tuition of experts from Belfast and Dundee to be made master of
all the mysteries of flax, jute, hemp and tow. We are sometimes at
this work till 11 at night. However,' – he added confidently – 'all will
be right'.[71]

In the end it was, but not before a temporary setback which
confirmed all Cobden's lifelong prejudices against what he furiously
dubbed 'the circumlocution office' – in other words, the Foreign
Office. The first convention, dealing with iron and steel, other
metals and machinery, was ready for signature by the scheduled date,
1 October. But Lord Cowley suddenly decided that he could not
sign it without the Foreign Office's approval, and nothing that
Cobden could say about the impossibility of renegotiating the treaty
in London would make him change his mind. The convention was
duly sent over to London where it became thoroughly entwined in
red tape, while in Paris Cobden fulminated, listened with chagrin to
the surprised comments of the French and finally lost his temper
with Lord Cowley. He told the ambassador that he felt humiliated;
he had possessed greater discretionary powers when he was a commercial traveller of twenty, and he suggested that 'nullipotentiary'
would be a more appropriate title than plenipotentiary.[72] Cowley,
the diplomat, successfully smoothed him down and the convention
was eventually signed twelve days late.

Cobden was all the more upset by the delay because he already
suspected that the majority of Cabinet members were not parti-

cularly interested in the success of his negotiation. In mid-June he had read a report in *The Times* that the government planned to spend £12 to £14 million (it should have been £11 million) on fortifying the ports and naval arsenals along the South Coast. This upset him for the whole day, 'to an extent which I can hardly describe. I am bewildered almost, and lost in all sorts of suspicions'.[73] He dashed off a series of agitated letters to Bright urging him to try to stop a project 'so shockingly out of joint with what I am doing here', or at least to get it delayed until the details of the conventions he was negotiating were known.[74] Lengthy, and more measured, appeals were sent to Palmerston and Lord John. To Gladstone, Cobden unburdened himself freely. 'The two questions of extended commerce and diminished warlike preparations are logically connected. They have never been separated in my mind, and from the first I have felt little interest in the prospect of opening up new markets for our manufacturers compared with that which I have taken in ameliorating the moral and political relations of the two countries.'[75] Gladstone had in fact been fighting against the fortifications plan for months past, firing off memoranda and threats of resignation. Palmerston told the Queen that it would be better, though a serious blow, to lose Mr Gladstone than to risk losing Portsmouth or Plymouth.[76] In the end none of them were lost. Gladstone accepted a face-saving compromise and Palmerston told the Commons that the first stage of the fortifications plan (Portsmouth and Plymouth) would be begun forthwith. Cobden was furious. He felt that the ground had been cut from under his feet, and he told Cowley that if his heart were not in his work, he would throw it up and return to the House of Commons where he would do his best to destroy the government that was turning all his labour to mockery and ridicule.*[77]

Evelyn Denison, Speaker of the House of Commons, who received one of Cobden's epistolary lamentations about the government's hostility to France, commented that the letter was written 'in rather a spirit of exaggeration'; and he added perceptively that it was 'the fault of Cobden's mind to see one object so strongly that his view cannot embrace another at the same time'.†[78] He sent Cobden a

---

* In February 1863 Cobden paid a visit of inspection to the fortifications being built above Portsmouth. He was particularly incensed that the line of forts was being built along the Downs above the port on the apparent assumption that the enemy would make a successful landing. 'Either we ought to abandon the whole scheme or cease for ever to sing "Rule Britannia" or "Ye Mariners of England".' (B. L. Add. Mss. 43665, to Col. Fitzmayer, 4 Feb., 1863.)

† Walter Bagehot was to make a similar remark when commenting on Cobden's row with the Editor of *The Times* in December 1863. 'The specialty of his mind is to seize on some one aspect of a subject, and work it out exclusively and to the omission of all others.' (*The Economist* 26 Dec., 1863)

soothing reply, assuring him that the country was 'sound' on the treaty and the fortifications were quite a different issue.[79] To Cobden they were not, and when the second supplementary convention was at last signed on 16 November, he very much doubted whether Palmerston's government would try to gain any *moral* benefits from the treaty by adopting a less warlike attitude towards France.

But at least he could rejoice over the material benefits. The new French tariff was far more liberal than he had dared to hope, and although the French concessions were bilateral only, Cobden believed that the treaty had 'virtually knocked on the head' the whole European protective system.[80] In the short term, he was largely right. During the next decade, tariffs were substantially reduced throughout most of Europe, and – fortunately for his peace of mind – he did not live to see the tariff walls being rebuilt in the 1870s.*

Before starting south for a holiday away from the English winter, Cobden had hoped to go back to England to see his children, his house and his friends. But since his disastrous visit to London the previous November he had developed a nervous dread of the London fog, and in the end he decided not to go back to England at all. By way of compensation, Bright paid a brief visit to Paris during which he and Cobden had an audience with the Emperor. They used the opportunity to try to persuade him to abolish passports for English visitors. Barely three weeks later, after Cobden had turned his formidable persuasive powers on to the minister of the interior, the passports were abolished. Cobden could not help wondering why the Foreign Office could not have achieved this reform.[81]

On 9 December, 1860 Cobden, with his wife and eldest daughter, Katie, set out for Algiers. This time he had no reason to regret the comforts of an English fireside in winter. The weather was warm, dry and sunny, there were green peas and strawberries to eat and the countryside round Algiers was both beautiful to look at and ideal for walking and riding.[82] At first the Cobdens stayed at the Hotel de l'Europe which was very comfortable but too expensive. After about five weeks they found a suitable house beautifully situated about a mile outside the town; it turned out to be the same house in which Bright had passed part of his convalescence four years earlier.[83]

Shortly after Cobden's arrival in Algiers, nearly 150 members of

---

* France made similar bilateral treaties with Belgium, Italy, Austria, the German Zollverein, Scandinavia and Switzerland, and these countries made further treaties among themselves. Russia and Spain also made a modest gesture towards free trade. But the United States remained firmly protectionist.

the local Chamber of Commerce waited on him and presented him with a complimentary address.[84] Algeria had been a French colony for thirty years and was in process of being turned into an extension of France itself. Cobden does not seem to have disapproved. He discussed France's colonial policy with the Governor and made friends with the officers of the garrison. There were also many other English visitors, including a young man who, in spite of working in the Foreign Office, claimed to have made 'immense friends' with Cobden. They had long teasing discussions in which whenever Cobden got the better of his companion on a question of political economy, young Bidwell came up with some obscure classical allusions of which Cobden had to confess his complete ignorance.[85]

The Cobdens were enthusiastic sightseers. They made excursions to the classical sights along the coast and joined a party of English visitors who were entertained by a local Arab chief with a boar hunt and a traditional breakfast of roasted sheep. In the intrepid manner of Victorian travellers they also made a ten-day round trip into the interior. There were eight in the party, four travelling by carriage and four on horseback. They inspected ancient ruins and modern agricultural developments. The country seemed safe and settled, but the French settlers who entertained them had harrowing stories to tell of the very recent past.[86]

In Algiers the English papers were supposed to arrive three times a week, but because of the weather they were often late. Cobden thought that this uncertainty 'weans one from that craving after news which becomes a habit when it reaches us periodically and with regularity'.[87] But it was not in his nature to relax completely. The Anglo-French naval rivalry continued to preoccupy him. He drafted an Address to the Queen in favour of a mutual reduction of naval armaments by England and France, sent it to Samuel Morley in London and urged him to whip up support and signatures for it in the City.[88] He wrote to an acquaintance in Paris, urging him to organise a similar petition to the Emperor from French merchants.[89] Nothing came of either initiative and Cobden continued to nurse his bitter resentment at the frivolous way in which – as he saw it – Palmerston had jeopardised the commercial treaty by his openly suspicious attitude towards the French. In April he received a letter from the Prime Minister offering, on behalf of the Queen, to make him either a baronet or a privy councillor, whichever was 'most agreeable' to him. Cobden politely declined both honours, adding that 'it would not be agreeable to me to accept a recompense in any form for my recent labours in Paris'.[90] He would have found it very difficult to accept an honour from anyone; to refuse one from Lord Palmerston was not difficult at all.

The dry warm climate of Algeria proved just as good a tonic as

Cobden had hoped. But the shadow of ill-health, the feeling that he must nurse his diminishing physical powers, the fear that he might permanently damage his voice, never left him for the rest of his life. He had always been almost obsessionally aware that he did not come from a long-lived family, and as he entered his 58th year he wondered what risks he would be justified in taking with his health. 'If', he wrote as he began his journey back to England, 'I could pass the remainder of my days with only the labour of an average person of my years, I could, I dare say, nurse myself into a good old age. The question is whether I ought rather to content myself with a briefer span and the satisfaction of trying to do something a little beyond my strength? It is a nice question for casuists, for the home duties affecting one's young children intrude.'[91]

CHAPTER 14

'As I could not talk, I must write'
(1861–65)

When he reappeared in the Commons on 27 May, 1861, Cobden had no reason to complain of his welcome – an 'infinite shaking of hands on all sides'. But the next morning he woke up feeling poorly with a headache. 'I doubt', he wrote to Kate, 'whether my parliamentary life will be prolonged many years. I find myself less and less equal to it. And I really see nothing at issue between the contending political factions which is worth the sacrifice of my life or the loss of my health.'[1] He had the satisfaction, however, of supporting Gladstone in his tussle with the Lords (and the Cabinet) over the repeal of the paper duties – the last of the 'taxes on knowledge' which had preoccupied Cobden so much ten years earlier.* But generally, domestic politics, both inside and outside Parliament, were indeed in the doldrums. During the previous session Lord John Russell had abandoned his reform bill in face of the marked lack of enthusiasm on both sides of the House, and there seemed no reason to suppose that the government would make any further attempts at electoral reform. Cobden told Bright, in a gloomy letter from Algiers, that it would be ten thousand times better for both of them to sit on the opposition benches than to be identified with a government that did the work of the court and aristocracy in their name.[2] Bright thoroughly agreed, and apparently sounded out Disraeli about a joint effort to overthrow the government.† For the time being, however, it did not suit the Tories to turn Palmerston out. So Bright raged

---

* In 1860 the Lords defeated Gladstone's bill to repeal the paper duties. In 1861 he included this measure in his finance bill which the Lords did not dare to throw out.
† Lord Malmesbury told Palmerston that the French ambassedor had brought a similar overture from Cobden in Paris. (Palmerston to the Queen, 27 January, 1861.) *Letters of Queen Victoria 1837–61* (ed Benson and Esher), III, 547–8

about the state of politics and declared, to Disraeli, that he was only anxious to retire. Lord Stanley, Derby's son, was under the impression that Cobden had already in effect retired from public life.[3]

He added to the impression that he was semi-retired by deciding not to 'make a martyr' of himself in the Commons and to forgo public meetings and banquets. The only exceptions were the ceremony at which he received the freedom of the City of London – 'a terrible ordeal'[4] – and a meeting with his constituents. In his speech at Rochdale he concentrated on the British people's chronic fears of the French and the deadlocked state of parliamentary politics in which the 'outs' and the 'ins' agreed to do nothing. He declared that Parliament would never reform itself, and appealed to the younger generation to organise 'some decided and effective movement out-of-doors' to reform the political system. He could not, he indicated, lead them himself but he would certainly cheer from the sidelines.[5] The effort of speaking to a huge audience left him very tired and hoarse, but he was compensated by the very 'affectionate' welcome he received from the people of Rochdale as he walked through the town. 'They really smiled as if they were my personal friends, and they crowded everywhere about me to shake hands and some of the women insisted on me taking their children by the hands.'[6]

The American Civil War, which broke out in April 1861, sadly overshadowed the last years of Cobden's life. It was for him a profound shock to find that the country he had believed to be largely free from the sins of the old world had succumbed to the one he abhorred most. He and Bright were such ardent champions of the United States (perhaps provoking more exasperation than making converts) that they had become known as 'the two members for the United States'. But during the Civil War it was Bright, together with W. E. Forster, who stood out as the public champions of the Federal government. Cobden was handicapped by his increasingly frail health, especially during the winter months. Moreover, the Crimean war had left him with the bitter conviction that once a war had broken out, it was futile to say anything about it in public. Finally, for once in his life, he was confronted with a situation about which he found it extraordinarily difficult to make up his mind. All that was clear to him was that behind the scenes he must exert himself to the utmost to prevent England from being drawn into a war with the Federal government.

He never had any doubt about where his sympathies lay. 'As for the separation of the states', he wrote on 25 February, 'if I were a citizen of a free state, I should vote with both hands for a dissolution of partnership with the slave states.'[7] But he abhorred war as much as slavery, and he was both shocked and confused when Lincoln decided to restore the partnership by force. He did not, in the circumstances, blame the President for resorting to force – it was after all a Southern battery that had fired the first shot against Fort Sumter – but like most people in Britain, especially after the ignominious rout of the Federal forces at Bull Run in July, he felt sure that the North could not decisively defeat and hold down the South, or only after a long and costly war which would leave both sides in ruins. As he contemplated the huge map of the United States, which he had hung on his dining room wall so that he could follow the course of the fighting, he was appalled by the 'stupendous task' confronting the Federal forces in reconquering the South over such a vast battlefield.[8] And even if they were ultimately successful, it seemed inconceivable that North and South could 'ever lie in the same bed' again.[9] Yet separation seemed to be ruled out for geographical reasons: the free states of the North and West would never allow the mouth of the Mississippi to be in potentially hostile hands.[10] Cobden clutched at the idea of some sort of compromise, but could not work out what it should be, and frankly confessed that he was flummoxed. 'For my part', he wrote in January 1862, 'I can't see my way out of the mess'.[11]

Few people in England shared Cobden's agonising over the conflict in America. The Americans had made themselves unpopular by their aggressive diplomacy in Central America. They seemed to pose a constant threat to the security of Canada. They were beginning to be perceived as serious rivals to the economic and commercial supremacy of Britain. Their democratic institutions were feared for their influence on reformers at home. The Northerners were protectionist, the Southerners were slave-owners. Altogether, for a variety of reasons which between them influenced most sections of society, there was not much regret in Britain about the break-up of the Union.

But when President Lincoln proclaimed a blockade of the South on 19 April, 1861, it became impossible for the British to ignore the conflict, much though they might have liked to. 'We have not', declared Lord John Russell in the Commons, 'been involved in any way in that contest . . . and, for God's sake, let us if possible keep out of it.'[12] Shortly afterwards the government proclaimed its strict neutrality, thus implying that it recognised the seceded states as legitimate belligerents, not rebels. This greatly angered the Union government. It disappointed the Confederates who had calculated that Britain's dependence on Southern cotton would force it to recognise them immediately and if necessary intervene on their side.

As much as four fifths of the raw material of the Lancashire cotton industry came from the American South. If the supply was cut off, or even seriously depleted, the industry would be ruined and the three to four million people who depended on it in one way or another would be faced with starvation. At first it was assumed that the North would never be able to make the blockade effective. Moreover, the existing stock of raw cotton in England was unusually high, and in recent years there had been so much over-production by the cotton mills that a temporary recession was in any case regarded as inevitable. The warnings of more serious long-term difficulties, which had appeared in some of the newspapers even before the blockade was announced, went unheeded.

When Cobden, in Algiers, heard of the Southern states' secession, the grave threat to Britain's cotton supply was among his first react-ions, and a few days after his return to London he was writing to Bright at his home in Rochdale about 'the great danger which impends over the industry and almost the lives of the population of your district'.[13] But he kept his fears to himself when he went up to Rochdale the following month to address his constituents. In a brief passing reference to the cotton crisis he merely foresaw good coming out of present difficulties in the shape of new sources of supply, in particular from India, which would end the industry's regrettable dependence on slave-grown cotton.[14]

This line of argument could hardly have much appeal once the mills had begun to go on to short time or even to close down altogether. As early as 29 September, *Reynolds's Newspaper* put the issue in stark and simple terms: 'England must break the Blockade, or Her Millions will starve.'[15] Since any attempt to break the blockade would certainly lead to war with the United States, neither alternative was remotely acceptable to Cobden. He could only clutch at straws, hoping that heavy taxation and the hardships of war would soon make the Northerners ready for a compromise peace, or that somehow the cotton would find its way to the capital and labour waiting for it. He admitted that he did not know how it would do so. 'But to keep it locked up is too great an outrage on the laws of commerce, which are the laws of nature, to be successful.'[16] In the meantime he was acutely aware of the danger of England and the United States sliding into war, either through an attempt to break the blockade, or through an incident arising out of it which would be exacerbated by the hostility of most of the press and public in both countries and the mutual dislike and suspicion of leading members of both governments.

Towards the end of November, Cobden's worst fears seemed likely to be realised when news arrived that two Confederate commissioners, James Mason and John Slidell, on their way to

Europe on the British mail steamer, the *Trent,* had been forcibly removed by a Federal warship commanded by a Captain Wilkes. The indignation at this insult to the British flag was great, and it became greater when reports arrived of Captain Wilkes's hero's welcome in Washington. The Cabinet decided that it must defend the 'national honour', however little it relished the idea of going to war. Fortified by the law officers' opinion that a serious breach of international law had been committed, it demanded an apology and the immediate return of the commissioners.

It was more than a month before the American reply became known in London. In the meantime Cobden and Bright did their best to soothe the excitable British public, while privately preaching restraint to the government and encouraging a movement in favour of settling the dispute by arbitration.[17] In addition, they sent off a cascade of letters to Charles Sumner, the influential chairman of the Senate Foreign Affairs Committee, urging the Americans not to make war inevitable by refusing to release Mason and Slidell. Sumner was a vigorous opponent of slavery and a strong sympathiser with the peace movement. He had first met Cobden in London some twelve years earlier. They had immediately liked each other, and although they seldom had a chance of meeting – Sumner visited Dunford at least once – they continued to keep in touch by letter. Cobden discussed the *Trent* affair with uninhibited frankness. He could not, he wrote, understand how the Americans, as belligerents, could now claim to exercise the right of search of a neutral vessel when they had always vigorously denied (to the point of war in fact) that right to the British when *they* were the belligerents. Moreover, from a purely practical point of view it was most unwise. The capture of Mason and Slidell would boost the morale of the Confederates by encouraging them to hope that Washington would get involved in hostilities with Britain. And he made it clear that the hope was not unfounded. 'Formerly England feared a war with the United States as much from the dependence on your cotton as from a dread of your power. *Now* the popular opinion (however erroneous) is that a war would give us cotton. And we, of course, consider your power weakened by your civil war. I speak as a friend of peace, and not as a partisan of my own country, in wishing you to bear this in mind.'[18] Throughout the crisis, Sumner conveyed the views of Cobden and Bright to his government, and he read out their latest letters when Lincoln and his ministers met on Christmas Day to consider their reply to the British demand. It is impossible to say what influence they had, especially as so much pointed towards the wisdom of avoiding a confrontation. The Americans knew from their own sources in London that the British were not bluffing; the French had given their moral support to Britain and would probably join in if there was war; to add a foreign war to a civil one was clearly a recipe for disaster; and since Captain Wilkes had acted without official authorisation, it would be feasible to back down without loss of face.

The news that Mason and Slidell were to be released arrived in London on 8 January, 1862. The *Morning Star* hailed it as a great victory for the American Republic. But to most of the British press and public it was a great victory for the British Lion.

Early in November 1861, Cobden was presented with a fifth daughter. His wife was nearly 46 and the birth was not completely straightforward. 'Some people will say', wrote Cobden afterwards, 'that it ought to have been a boy, but I confess I was so anxious about the mother that I did not care for the sex of the child . . . It is very odd in our old age to be surrounded again with baby linen, and cradle and all the nursery paraphernalia!'[19] Nearly three months later, he reported that his wife was looking younger than ever, 'and the baby is such a brobdignag that her socks are an inch longer than those of any child of her age'.[20] Perhaps, with the birth of Lucy Elizabeth Margaret, Kate Cobden was at last as reconciled as she ever would be to the death of her son.

Soon after the baby's safe arrival, Cobden, unable to resist the pull of the political world, went up to London. But after about a fortnight he found himself almost sufficated by a combination of fog and frost. He could not walk across a room without panting for breath and he found it very painful to talk.[21] He had to retreat to Sussex, and when, early in December in Rochdale, Bright made a stirring defence of the Federal government and its handling of the *Trent* affair, Cobden could only contribute a letter to his constituents to be read out at the meeting.[22] For the rest of the winter he took great care of himself, going out only in the middle of the day when it was fine and talking to nobody except his family, and to them – or so he claimed – only at meal-times. The rest of the day he spent in a south-facing room upstairs, reading and writing – 'as I could not talk', he explained to Bright, 'I must write'.[23]

He wrote mostly about Anglo-French relations which his concern over the American conflict could not drive far from the front of his mind. A few weeks earlier he had sent a memorandum to both Palmerston and the French government suggesting that Britain and France should agree to a simultaneous and proportionate reduction in their navies.[24] (He accepted that Britain, with its far-flung commitments, required a larger navy than France.) He found the French response encouraging; from Palmerston he got no response at all. 'Perhaps', he commented in disgust, 'he gave it to some Colonel of

Volunteers to light his pipe.'[25] So he settled down to compose an account of the three occasions – in 1847–48, 1852–53 and 1859–61 – on which the British had allowed themselves to be carried away by a largely irrational fear of an imminent French invasion. He combed the pages of Hansard for allusions to naval affairs, and sent off a stream of requests to the long-suffering Henry Richard for the facts and figures he needed. He even persuaded the Peace Society to send him an assistant 'with a legible hand' who was asked for a few days and proved so useful that he stayed for ten. Cobden's aim was to show how groundless these panics had been and also to demonstrate his privately expressed conviction that they were 'really the result of a tacit conspiracy on the part of our governing class to extort money out of the people's pockets through their fears'.[26]

The Three Panics was very long, but Cobden managed to complete it by the beginning of February 1862.[27] 'You never saw such an exposure', he wrote triumphantly to Henry Richard, and he foresaw with positive relish that it would lose him the renewed popularity which the French treaty had brought him. 'Everybody again is tending to tolerance and favour. But when this pamphlet comes out – how I shall be baited in the House and the Press! However, I have the rogues on the hip, and there is not one of the chief offenders . . . that I cannot fire a reserve shot into if they open on me in the House'.[28] In the event he was disappointed by the small response to the pamphlet. But he claimed not to be surprised because all those writers and politicians whom it irrefutably demonstrated to have been wrong would not want to acknowledge as much.[29] Perhaps another reason was that although Cobden devoted about three quarters of the pamphlet to the latest panic, he failed to tackle adequately the basic reason for it – the revolution in naval warfare caused by the development of the ironclad warship. The French had seized the initiative in 1858 when they laid down the armour-plated *Gloire*. The British responded by laying down the *Warrior* with an iron hull. *[30] But by 1861 the French seemed determined to maintain and increase their lead, and the pressure in England to modernise and strengthen the Royal Navy in response to what was perceived as a new threat from the unpredictable French Emperor was too strong for any politician – even Gladstone, the economy-minded Chancellor of the Exchequer – to withstand. Cobden was desperately anxious to stop England and France from beginning 'the race of folly in these novelties'.[31] But his efforts to minimise French naval ambitions, both in his pamphlet and in the House of Commons, were gravely handicapped by his having spent so much time in Paris

* The *Warrior* is now being restored with a view to being eventually docked at Portsmouth.

and being known to be on such good terms with the Emperor and his ministers. Inevitably, there was a feeling that he had been, as Charles Greville put it, 'so flattered and bamboozled in Paris' that he took for gospel all the Emperor said.[32] It is difficult not to suspect that there was at least a grain of truth in this judgment.

With the *Trent* incident safely defused, British interest in the American Civil War turned towards the blockade of the South and its increasingly distressing repercussions on the Lancashire cotton workers. To Cobden it was all part of the general issue of international maritime law – 'the barbarous International Code, more suited to the Middle Ages than to these free trade times'.[33] The current state of the law had been set out in 1856 by the Paris peace congress in a declaration which made blockades illegal unless they could be made effective; exempted from capture neutral goods (except 'contraband of war') carried in enemy ships and enemy goods carried in neutral ships; and abolished privateering. Cobden's aim was to establish the principle of *'Free trade in time of war'*.[34] 'Free trade, in the widest definition of the term, means only the division of labour, by which the productive powers of the whole earth are brought into mutual cooperation. If this scheme of universal dependence is to be liable to sudden dislocation whenever two governments decide to go to war, it converts a manufacturing industry, such as ours, into a lottery, in which the lives and fortunes of multitudes of men are at stake.'[35] The two most important reforms proposed by Cobden were the exemption of *all* private property, except 'contraband of war', from capture at sea, and the restriction of blockades to naval arsenals and towns under siege from the land. In other words, naval warfare would be restricted to engagements between warships. Cobden argued that no power stood to gain more from these reforms than Britain, which depended so heavily on imports of food and raw materials and on its ability to export its manufactures. He poured scorn on the argument that England, being primarily a naval power, could not surrender the right to impose a commercial blockade on its enemies; it was, he insisted, 'a two-edged sword, which cuts the hand that wields it – when that hand is England – more than the object which it strikes'.[36]

In the middle of March 1862 Cobden planned to make a major intervention in a debate on a motion to consider the present 'ill-defined and unsatisfactory' state of maritime law. He took special pains with his speech, which he intended should be a flag under which free traders could rally. But ever since he had arrived in London early in February his health had been precarious – 'I am like a gnat or a butterfly depending on the sunshine and weather'[37] – and on the night of the debate it let him down completely. He developed a sore throat from a cold and lost his voice. In frustrated silence he listened to the debate and regretted that it was 'kept to too narrow a basis'. (The motion was eventually withdrawn.) In all his political career Cobden had never had, he felt, 'a more vexatious disappointment'.[38]

His views on the reform of maritime law appeared in the press shortly afterwards in the form of a 'Letter to Mr Henry Ashworth',[39] and the following October he expounded them in a lucid and eloquent address to the Manchester Chamber of Commerce.[40] But his hope that public opinion could be aroused to force change on the government was far too optimistic. The weapon of blockade was too traditional and believed to be too valuable to be lightly thrown away. Moreover, in striving to confine war to the professionals, Cobden was going against the whole trend of an age in which not only technology but the whole concept of politics and diplomacy imposed by the French Revolution and developed by Napoleon were shortly to involve whole populations in any conflict.

Cobden's views on commercial blockades in general being what they were, his attitude towards the American blockade was uncompromising: the Washington government should raise it voluntarily, both for its own good and for humanitarian reasons. The French and other Europeans, as well as the British, were suffering from the effects of the blockade and he was convinced that unless the North itself removed 'this unnatural obstruction to the world's commerce', the European powers would retaliate by recognising the South and finding some excuse to break the blockade. As soon as the *Trent* crisis was over Cobden began to lobby influential Americans in London and to write urgently and repeatedly to Charles Sumner. '*It is the suffering and misery that your blockade is bringing on the masses in Europe that turns men against you*'.[41] If the Northerners raised the blockade, the Europeans would leave them alone to deal with 'the Slave States, either by fighting them at your leisure or by leaving the West to outgrow them or Slavery to undo them'.[42]

These pleas were not supported by Bright, who argued that the quickest way through the cotton crisis was for the North to win the war, not to lift the blockade. Like most people, Cobden very much doubted whether the North could do this, or at any rate not without a protracted and bloody struggle. 'It is one thing to wish well to the North', he told Bright, 'and another to believe in their speedy success'.[43] Bright was one of the few who did, and Cobden greatly admired his stout championship of a cause that was undoubtedly unpopular and probably forlorn as well, in spite of some Northern victories, including the capture of New Orleans, early in 1862.

Cobden's pleas to the Federal government to lift the blockade fell, as might have been expected, on deaf ears. So did his proposal that English cotton traders should be allowed to go up the Mississippi and buy cotton from Southern planters. (Lord John had already made a similar suggestion without success.) Among the Lancashire cotton operatives there was growing hostility to the North and a widespread, although mistaken, belief that if the independence of the South were recognised, the cotton supplies would somehow become unblocked. In the meantime, more and more mills were being forced to close down completely, and more and more workers who had come to the end of their savings were being forced to undergo what for them was the ultimate humiliation of asking for Poor Law relief.

On 9 May Charles Villiers, now President of the Poor Law Board, assured the House of Commons that the Poor Law authorities in the distressed districts had the situation well under control. Two months later it was so obvious that many of them could not cope that the government was reluctantly obliged to intervene. Villiers brought in a bill that would allow a board of guardians to request a rate in aid from other parishes in the Union to which it belonged if its own poor rate rose above 5/–; if this still proved inadequate, a further request could be made to other Unions in the county.[44]

The bill did not have an easy passage. Lancashire, with its opulent millowners and operatives earning above average wages, aroused envy in the rest of the country. Why could not the wealthy capitalists look after their own people instead of tampering with the Poor Law? Why could not the Lancashire parishes which usually paid a much smaller poor rate than most rural parishes, step up their poor rate? But the most telling criticism came from those who argued that the bill was inadequate and inappropriate to deal with the plight of the Lancastrians. Cobden intervened vigorously several times in support of the suggestion (originally made for less disinterested reasons) that the most effective way to deal with the distress in Lancashire would be to allow the Poor Law guardians to borrow money on the security of future rates. The cotton famine was only a temporary calamity and the guardians themselves believed that this was the best way to deal with it. Cobden explained (as indeed Villiers had already done) that in normal times the poor rate in most Lancashire parishes was low because so few people needed relief. But when the mills closed down or went on short time, everybody – shopkeepers, ware-housemen, professional people – suffered. The cotton operatives were like the mainspring of a watch; when they stopped the rest of the works stopped too. It was pointless to try to extract a rate of 5/– from those who could barely afford one of 2/–. He defended the millowners whose wealth was largely tied up in their mills and machinery and who as a whole had not failed in their duty to their own work-people. He denied that those now unemployed in the cotton towns were paupers and he urged them not to stint their families, but to collect the parish relief to which they were entitled without feeling degraded.[45]

Eventually the government very reluctantly agreed to add to the bill an authority to borrow when the poor rate rose above 3/–, as an alternative to a rate in aid. Considering the size of the problem, the measure did not amount to much, and, moreover, it was to expire in six months. It was perhaps chiefly notable as an illustration of the authorities' extreme reluctance to introduce any innovation into the established system of dealing with distress, even in a situation that was admitted to be exceptional and temporary.

Towards the end of the Poor Law debates, Palmerston let fall some derogatory remarks about the rich manufacturers' attitude to their 'starving' employees. Cobden was furious. As soon as he could, he jumped to his feet and castigated the Prime Minister for making unjust aspersions 'tainted with that habitual incorrectness and recklessness for which the noble Lord is so remarkable'.[46]* His outburst was all the more scathing because of his profound exasperation that Palmerston – reactionary, extravagant, interventionist, the author, in Cobden's view, of all that was wrong in the country's affairs – should continue, in his 78th year, as leader of the government and – still worse – of the Liberal party. For years he had been assuming that the infirmities of age would soon force Palmerston to retire. But the old Prime Minister soldiered on, apparently indestructible, and as Cobden's frustration grew, so did his determination to do his best to discredit Palmerston in the country and somehow bring about his downfall in Parliament.[47] It was all quite unrealistic; for the time being, both the country and the Tories were quite content to leave things as they were.

Only new sights and sounds, Cobden decided, could set his mind free from politics,[48] and on 20 August he travelled up to Edinburgh with his wife and eldest daughter to relax and recuperate among the mountains of Scotland. The journey took $10\frac{1}{2}$ hours, and the first class fare, including a meal at York, was 70/– each. Cobden remembered that in 1825 the same journey had taken him forty-five hours on the outside of a mail coach and had cost him four guineas

---

* It is hardly surprising that Palmerston should have twice rejected Russell's suggestion that Cobden should be offered a pension. Cobden and Bright, he wrote in February 1864, 'have run a muck against everything that the British nation respects and values . . .' But after Cobden's death, Palmerston did offer his widow a pension, which she refused. (Ridley. *Lord Palmerston*, 526)

plus the cost of four meals and tips for half a dozen coachmen and guards. 'It is something', he reflected, 'to have lived in the 37 years which have witnessed such a triumph of human ingenuity. Unless our children are shot four hundred miles in a pneumatic tube, I do not see how they can gain any material advantage in locomotion over their fathers.'[49] From Edinburgh the Cobdens continued to Pitnacree, south of Pitlochry, where their old Manchester friend, Thomas Potter, had a house with lovely views, high up on the left bank of the Tay. Their host believed in keeping his guests 'always on the trot', and every day there was a new excursion over the moors with the sportsmen, either on foot or on ponies.[50] After about a fortnight they moved on, presumably still encumbered by Kate's unwieldy baggage about which her husband had protested 'incessantly' at Pitnacree. 'There is no remedy', he told his next host, Henry Ashworth, 'to be hoped for this evil but in the chance that the Empress of the French will make crinolines unfashionable. If – he added somewhat ungallantly – she would at the same time shorten the length of ladies' skirts, it would promote economy and cleanliness.'[51] Ashworth had a house near Blairgowrie. He was a keen sportsman and a 'capital shot', and provided his guests with plenty of fresh air and exercise on the moors. Cobden indeed feared that his host's enthusiasm for sport might overtax his physical strength, and wrote to him afterwards to advise him to have 'a week or two of idle lounging existence in the open air before you return to Manchester anxieties'.[52]

His own programme for the next month can have included little 'idle lounging'. With Kate and Katie he travelled the length and breadth of the Highlands, staying with friends and acquaintances and seeking out the most beautiful scenery. They went up to Inverness by way of Aberdeen, and then down the Caledonian canal to Oban. From there they went to Inverary, where they were entertained by the Duke of Argyll, Lord Privy Seal in Palmerston's Cabinet, who shared Cobden's anxieties about the Lancashire cotton workers and was one of the few members of the aristocracy who hoped that the North would win the Civil War. On their way back to Edinburgh Cobden read 'The Lady of the Lake' by the side of Loch Katrine. He was struck by the 'tinsel and diluted character' of the rhymes and decided that Scott's fame must rest on his novels, not his poems.[53] Sir Walter came in for more criticism when Cobden visited Abbotsford and was made melancholy by the thought that so great a man should ruin himself by building such a 'poor Cockney imitation of a feudal residence'.[54] But as he was continually complaining about the remaining traces of feudalism which he perceived in aristocratic society, Cobden would probably have found fault with any imitation of a feudal residence.

While he was on holiday, Cobden did his best to forget about politics and Palmerston, and rarely saw the London press. 'But the bloody telegrams from America meet my eye in the local penny papers, and haunt me everywhere.'[55] When he arrived in Manchester on his way home, travelling through 'a forest of smokeless chimneys',[56] he saw for the first time with his own eyes the consequences of the American conflict for the cotton workers. He was appalled. 'Altogether the prospect is very bad. The great object of solicitude should be the working classes. They are not receiving sufficient to keep them in health and contentment . . . Nothing but a large national subscription or a Parliamentary grant will meet the case.'[57] By the end of October, 208,600 people were subsisting on poor relief and a further 143,800 were being supported out of charitable funds raised by voluntary subscription.[58] By now almost all the cotton towns had set up local relief committees, and a Central Executive Relief Committee had been formed in Manchester under the chairmanship of Lord Derby, the county's most important local magnate, who had already successfully appealed in London for funds to help the cotton workers. The Manchester Executive Committee was nominally subordinate to a largely ornamental General Committee on which Cobden, as a distinguished local MP, had been invited to sit. He attended a meeting of the committee while he was in Manchester and, as the assembled company were about to disperse, he astonished them by suddenly getting up and making an earnest and eloquent appeal for a nation-wide campaign on behalf of the distressed cotton workers. The poor, he said, normally looked after each other, but in this completely unprecedented disaster they were all in the same boat. The rest of the country must be made more aware of their plight and actively canvassed for funds. Anything less than a target of £1 million would, he insisted, be 'utterly insufficient', and he reminded his audience that the success of a public subscription for even the best cause 'depends very much upon the amount of activity in those who solicit it'. When he sat down there was a stunned silence,[59] but his speech had done the trick. It had helped to overcome the deeply ingrained contemporary feeling that charity ought to begin – and end – at home. It had given the initial shove to a movement which others – from Lord Derby down – successfully carried on through appeals, public meetings, newspaper publicity and organised grassroots canvassing.*

---

* The Central Executive Relief Committee was finally wound up in June 1865. The total recorded amount raised for the cotton famine victims from all sources was £1,773,647, including contributions in kind valued at £111,968. There were also many unrecorded gifts of food and clothing as well as donations sent direct to individual clergymen. (Longmate *The Hungry Mills*, 278–79)

Cobden stayed in Lancashire much longer than he had intended or than was good for him. 'The weather', he wrote, 'is rather unsuited to my breathing apparatus.'[60] But he remained in the hope of being of some use, writing exhortatory letters and visiting soup kitchens and the sewing classes that had been started for unemployed mill-girls. He was deeply moved and deeply pessimistic. 'Heroic men and still more heroic women are everywhere devoting themselves to the task of stemming the almost overwhelming pressure of destitution and suffering'.[61] But he could not join them. By the middle of November he was increasingly confined to his bedroom and before the end of the month he had fled south to Sussex.*

When Gladstone told a cheering Newcastle audience in October 1862 that the American South had 'made a nation', he was reflecting a widely-held view. But to Cobden it was such a monumental misjudgment that he began to suspect that Gladstone's 'quota of usefulness as a public man' had run out.[62] He himself had by now reached the conclusion that the North would never concede independence to the South and that while the two sides were fighting it out, European governments should remain neutral in word and deed.[63] Like most people, he feared that Lincoln's emancipation proclamation, issued in September 1862, might spark off a slave revolt with horrendous consequences. But no slave revolt material-ised, and in the early months of 1863 huge meetings were held in London and many provincial towns to demonstrate support for the side that had clearly declared its support for the cause of the slaves. Cobden was delighted and assured Sumner that he need no longer fear any 'unfriendly act' from any British government.[64]

The Americans, however, were already simmering about what seemed to them a very unfriendly act. In July 1862 the British government had failed to prevent a Confederate warship from escaping from Laird's shipyard at Birkenhead. Since then the *Alabama* had been wreaking havoc on the North's shipping and – even worse – more warships were being built for the South at Birkenhead. The trouble had arisen because of loopholes in the legislation that was supposed to prevent such breaches of Britain's neutrality. In the Commons, Cobden pointed out that in the past the United States had repeatedly enforced strict neutrality on its citizens when Britain was a belligerent and was entitled to expect reciprocal

* The Union Relief Aid Act was twice renewed during 1863, and in June Parliament empowered the government to lend money to local authorities to finance useful public works, like roads and sewers, so that the unemployed could be rescued from the demoralising effects of idleness. It was warmly supported by Cobden.

treatment now. He added that Britain, with £100 million of property afloat on the high seas, had a greater interest than any other power in clamping down effectively on armed commerce raiders.[65] It was a carefully prepared and effective speech. Privately, he acted as an unofficial conciliator, giving Lord John repeated warnings (not always well received) about the excited state of American opinion,[66] and – perhaps more usefully – sending soothing and reassuring letters to Sumner. Russell's despatches might not, he wrote, be 'very civil', but he was genuinely angry about the escape of the *Alabama* and determined that it should not happen again.[67] Cobden's assurances were not misplaced; no more armed vessels were allowed to leave Laird's shipyard to fight for the Confederates. As for the *Alabama,* she was eventually captured and sunk in June 1864.*

In the late autumn of each year, Cobden went up to Rochdale and made a report, as it were, to his constituents on the current domestic and foreign scene. In November 1863 he spoke confidently of the eventual success of the North in the American Civil War and proclaimed the rightness of its cause, both as the enemy of slavery and the champion of the Union. When he turned to the domestic scene and spoke of the need for a further instalment of parliamentary reform, he suggested that the landless English farm labourer would never be able to better himself until he had got the vote. He specifically disclaimed any wish to achieve change through 're-volution or agrarian outrage'.[68] A few days later Bright mentioned the same subject along similar lines. *The Times* chose to misinterpret their remarks as a proposal that the lands of the rich should be confiscated and divided among the poor. Cobden was really in no position to complain if *The Times* attacked him unfairly, since his mouthpiece, the *Morning Star* had published the most venomous attacks on Delane, the Editor of *The Times*.† But he sent him a furious denial, adding for good measure an equally damaging allegation that Delane and his staff were corruptly rewarded for their support of the government. There followed a lengthy exchange of letters which did little credit to either side.[69]

---

* The issue of how much compensation Britain should pay for the damage done by the *Alabama* poisoned Anglo-American relations for some years. Eventually, in Septmber 1872, an arbitration tribunal in Geneva awarded the Americans £3,250,000 in damages. Gladstone braved public disapproval and accepted the award. Cobden would have greatly approved both of the method of settling the dispute and of Gladstone's moral courage in accepting the award.

† Charles Villiers told Cobden that the *Star* was a 'very unsafe guide'. He had frequently seen attacks on Palmerston it which were 'all *perfectly unjust and unfounded'*,(Cobden Papers, 94, 30 Dec., 1861.)

'If', wrote Cobden with reference to his second letter to Delane, 'I have failed to say as many unpleasant things as could be crowded into the space, it has not been for want of will.'[70] *The Times* had become a steady supporter of Palmerston and tended to comment on Cobden and Bright in a maddeningly superior and dismissive way. As a result, Cobden had developed what almost amounted to a persecution complex about 'the ungodly gang of Printing House Square'.[71] He claimed privately that they had been bribed by Palmerston 'to knock me and Bright about on all occasions',[72] and he deliberately seized on the paper's aspersions on his and Bright's views on land reform 'to take it by the throat . . . and to launch the threat of exposure of the illicit intercourse that was going on between *The Times* and the dispensers of government patronage'. He claimed to have proof of this 'illicit intercourse', referred to a 'secret conspiracy', and clearly meant to continue his onslaught.[73] But no proof was produced and the whole affair faded away. Its only interest now is as an indication of the bitter frustration that must have festered under Cobden's equable and friendly exterior. It was a rare public manifestation of his profound sense of alienation from the Establishment of his day. Henry Adams, the son of the American minister in London, who saw Cobden and Bright in the congenial surroundings of the American legation, was left in no doubt about the strength of their alienation. It was still a vivid recollection when he wrote his autobiography years later.

> They were classed as enemies of order – anarchists – and anarchists they were if hatred of the so-called established orders made them so. About them was no sort of political timidity. They took bluntly the side of the Union against Palmerston whom they hated. Strangers to London society, they were at home in the American Legation, delightful dinner-company, talking always with reckless freedom. Cobden was the milder and more persuasive; Bright was the more dangerous to approach; . . .[74]

The 1864 session of Parliament was overshadowed by the crisis over Schleswig-Holstein, a bafflingly obscure problem made even more intractable by the growing strength of Danish and German nationalism.* In 1852 a conference in London, masterminded by Palmerston, had agreed on a compromise settlement designed to satisfy both the

---

* For centuries the Elbe duchies of Schleswig and Holstein had been linked with Denmark through their ruler, the Danish king, who was also duke of Schleswig and of Holstein. Schleswig was predominantly Danish but had a large German minority. Holstein was very largely German and was a member of the German Confederation.

COBDEN'S LOGIC.

13 *Punch*, 5 Dec. 1863.

Danes and the Germans. It satisfied neither, and persistent efforts by the Danes to circumvent it with the aim of annexing Schleswig altogether eventually provoked the German Confederation into sending troops into Holstein. A few weeks later, in February 1864, Prussian and Austrian troops marched into Schleswig, ostensibly to force the Danes to respect the treaty of London. Before the end of the month Prussian troops had also invaded Jutland.

Although the British government was under no legal obligation to defend the Danes, it had managed to give the impression that it would. But when the Danes appealed to Britain for aid after Bismarck had sent his troops into Schleswig, the Cabinet refused. For weeks it went on agonising over what it should do instead. Russell, the foreign secretary, insisted that diplomacy must be backed up with a genuine threat of force. The Queen, on the other hand, deployed all her considerable influence to prevent any risk of war. Most of the Cabinet, even Palmerston, while not sharing the Queen's strong pro-German sentiments, realised that to go to war on behalf of the Danes would be both impractical and politically unwise. A naval expedition to the Baltic could not by itself deter the Germans, and Britain lacked the military manpower to intervene effectively on the continent single-handed. It needed an ally with a large army, and neither France nor Russia were willing, for different reasons, to cooperate. Moreover, although there was much pro-Danish sentiment (just as there had been much sympathy for the Poles who the previous year had once again revolted unsuccessfully against Russia) it was clear that the country did not really want to get dragged into another continental war. The Crimea was still too vivid a memory.

On 25 June a conference organised by Russell in London to try to solve the crisis, finally broke down. On the same day the Cabinet unanimously decided to wash its hands of the problem. It went on to salve its conscience by agreeing (by a majority of one) to think again if the independence of Denmark or the safety of Copenhagen were threatened.[75] The Opposition cried Shame and tabled a motion of censure. In the Lords the motion was carried. In the Commons, after a four-day debate, it was defeated by 18 votes – a bigger majority than the Cabinet had dared to expect. The government was roundly attacked for handling the crisis in an inept, vacillating and inconsistent manner, for letting down the Danes and for discrediting Britain in the eyes of Europe. But as virtually nobody wanted to go to war, there was a hollow ring about the critics' complaints. A few weeks later the defeated Danes were forced to cede the two duchies to Prussia and Austria.

The outcome of the Schleswig-Holstein crisis was a victory for the non-interventionist foreign policy which Cobden had been preach-

14 Cobden in his last years.

ing for more than thirty years. His first reactions, however, were cautious. On the eve of the censure debate he pointed out to Bright that everyone seemed to be driven 'by the force of circumstances with very little aid from us' towards 'our principles on foreign policy'. Non-intervention as the *'rule'* still had to be established.*[76] He voted against the censure motion because the government had in the end opted for peace, but in his speech he claimed that the crisis had exposed the 'utter futility' of our foreign policy and completely dicredited the Foreign Office. The old system of diplomacy had broken down, he said, and must be changed.[77]

A few months later he wrote confidently to Michel Chevalier as if Britain's foreign policy had indeed been changed. 'Henceforth we shall observe an absolute abstention from foreign politics.'[78] But to Henry Richard, the trusted exponent of his views, he was notably cautious. There was, he assured him, much more to be done before the two great political parties had been brought 'to an honest recognition of the *principle* of non-intervention'.[79] And although he told his Rochdale constituents in November that there had been a complete revolution in foreign policy, he spent much of the rest of his speech urging them not to tolerate any backsliding into interventionist ways.[80]

He was right to be cautious. For the next fifty years, with one brief frenetic exception in 1877–78, Britain kept aloof from continental affairs. But its abstention was due more to pragmatic and emotional considerations and the 'force of circumstances' than to the conscious adoption of Cobdenite principles. The government had decided to retreat over Schleswig-Holstein when it became convinced that it could not intervene successfully or with popular approval, not because it felt that intervention in itself was wrong. Since the Crimean war the British public had been losing its taste for intervening in other people's affairs, and the country's discomfiture over Schleswig-Holstein accelerated this trend. But in due course the pendulum of popular emotion swung back, and Cobden's hope that understanding between peoples would replace secret diplomacy between governments was to remain unfulfilled.

The British still took a romantic interest in European fighters for freedom, especially Garibaldi. When he visited England in April

* Cobden urged Bright to avoid all personal or party arguments in the debate and stick to principles. In the event, Bright remained silent because he did not trust himself to refer to the government with sufficient moderation to be able to vote for it in the division. (Cobden to Bright, 4 July, 1864, B. L. Add. Mss. 43652; Cobden to Richard, 14 July, 1864, Hobson, *Richard Cobden the International Man,* 330)

1864, London society lionised him and the workers turned out in their thousands to see and applaud him. Bright gazed down from a window in Parliament Street at the huge crowd cheering the Italian hero, and said: 'If the people would only make a few such demonstrations for themselves we could do something for them'.[81] (Palmerston was afraid that they might.) Cobden also deplored the apparent apathy of the working class about their political rights.[82] Without a substantial extension of the franchise there was, he felt, no chance for other reforms, such as elementary education[83] for which he had worked all his life, and land reform which he saw as the great issue of the future.[84]

Cobden had never lost his uncompromising hostility towards the landed aristocracy, although he had learned to approve – and even like – individual members of it. He still claimed that their interests were directly opposed to those of the rest of the country. He still treated them as if they were parasites, like the pre-Revolution French aristocracy. He never conceded that they paid substantial taxes, or that many of them played an essential – and unpaid – role in local government and in many other fields of national life. He felt that the system of primogeniture and entail which allowed the concentration of so much land in so few hands was both an anachronism and a shameful injustice to the many thousands who cultivated the land but could never own any of it. But although the slogan 'free trade in land' had been current in radical circles for years, it had never really caught on – perhaps because it smacked too much of an attack on private property – and it is not clear why Cobden should have thought it would now. His brief mention of it at Rochdale in November 1863 had shown him what a tricky subject it was. A year later, however, he returned to it again at Rochdale and said that if he were 25 or 30 years younger he would take Adam Smith (who had condemned primogeniture and entail as relics of a feudal past) as his guide and have a League for free trade in land just as they had had a League for free trade in corn.[85] He never spelled out exactly what he had in mind, but even if it went no further than a measure to remove all restrictions on the bequeathing and sale of land it would have had no chance in a Parliament still dominated by landowners.

By this time Cobden had given up hope of the middle class being a force for political change. They were far too deferential to those above them in the social scale and they seemed to lack any wish to share power with those below. Those who were willing to do so offered too little to win the sympathy and support of the masses. And unless the workers were stirred up to demand their political rights loud and clear, nothing – Cobden felt – would be achieved.[86] They were not (as the next few years were to show) quite as quiescent as Cobden in his frustration felt, and it is perhaps surprising that he did not fan the glowing embers of working-class political discontent that he must have known existed, for example in Manchester and Leeds, in the early 1860s. Presumably he would have done so had he lived. The Reform League was set up in London to agitate for manhood suffrage and the ballot only two months before he died. According to the League's secretary, the London brick-layer George Howells, Cobden was 'favourable' to it,[87] and he was even apparently tipped to be its president.[88] Cobden's own comments on the Reform League have not survived, and it is not clear whether his support went beyond household suffrage, to which he was definitely committed.* In November 1864 he asked his Rochdale constituents whether 'you can permanently exclude the whole mass of working people from the franchise?' He clearly assumed the answer to be No, but he did not imply that *all* of them should at once be included, although he had always regarded manhood suffrage as the ultimate goal.

Cobden spent most of the summer and autumn of 1864 at Dunford, partly because he and Kate found it easier – and less expensive – to entertain visitors during the summer (the railway now reached to Midhurst), and partly because his doctor threatened to order him abroad for the worst of the winter and he did not want to be parted from his family for longer than necessary.[89] Towards the end of November he went up to Rochdale for what was to be his last public appearance. Next morning he reported to Kate that he had got through the meeting better than he had expected, but had now lost his voice. 'It was an enormous assemblage. I never saw so many people on one floor under a roof. The building was intended for holding machinery and is covered with sky lights ... Nothing could have surpassed the admirable attention of the meeting, especially of the working class who were *standing* in the outside alleys.'[90] That evening he attended a reception where he had to shake over a hundred hands, and the effort, coming on top of his previous evening's exertions, was too much for him.[91] After a few days in Manchester nursing his 'breathing apparatus' and a heavy cold, he managed to set off for home. He arrived 'completely upset in every way from top to toe'. It was more than a fortnight before he could leave his bedroom, very much better although 'weakened by

---

* On 1 February, 1865 Marx told Engels that the General Council of the International had been invited to a provisional committee meeting at the London Tavern. 'Object: Monster meeting for manhood suffrage. *President. Richard Cobden!*' It seems unlikely that Cobden knew his name was being used in this way. (Marx and Engels. 'Correspondence. 1846–1895', p. 179. London, 1934)

blistering and doctoring'. He embarked on a course of novel-reading, beginning with *Vanity Fair,* and settled down in his winter quarters. [92] It was more than two months before he dared venture out of doors, and the lack of fresh air and exercise made it more difficult for him to regain his strength.

He was not sorry to miss the beginning of the new parliamentary session; domestic politics, he felt, were still a 'hollow sham'. [93] In February Gladstone offered him the chance of a new career by proposing that he should become Chairman of the Board of Audit with an annual salary of £2000. Cobden refused on health grounds. He added, rather ungraciously, that in any case, with his views on the government's indefensible extravagance, he feared that the 'nauseous ordeal' of passively auditing its accounts would undermine his health and shorten his days. [94]

On the other side of the Atlantic the prospect was much more congenial. Before his illness he had become so absorbed by the American elections that he sometimes found himself walking half-way to Midhurst to meet the paper boy. [95] He did not think much of the capacity of most of Lincoln's colleagues, especially with regard to economic matters, [96] but his opinion of the President himself had become increasingly enthusiastic, and he described his orderly re-election while the country was in the throes of civil war as a 'very sublime spectacle'. [97] After Gettysburg he had felt sure of the North's eventual victory and only wished it could be achieved more quickly. Only the certainty that it would result in the emancipation of the slaves reconciled him to the American Civil War. It would, he felt, have more to show for all the blood and tears than any other war he knew of, [98] and in the last weeks of his life he had the satisfaction of realising that it could not go on for much longer. [99]

Early in March Bright went down to Dunford where he found Cobden 'pretty well in health but looking older'. They went for a pleasant walk and had one of their absorbing discussions about America, Canada and politics in general. [100] Soon after Bright left, the weather turned very cold again, and Cobden decided to wait until it was warmer before venturing up to London. He apparently changed his mind quite suddenly, unable to resist a forthcoming debate on grants to improve Canada's defences against a possible attack by the United States. It was an issue about which Cobden felt so strongly that he had already fired off a couple of protests to Gladstone. [101] He felt that the government should not accept any obligation to defend people who undertook no obligations in return; in any case the Canadian frontier was indefensible and the threat imaginary. His prescription was to break the political thread between Britain and Canada as quickly as possible. But to most of the Cabinet there was an 'intangible connection' (as the Duke of Argyll put it) between the two countries which the government could not destroy against the wishes of the Canadians and which obliged it to fight for Canada even if its frontier was indefensible.[102] To Cobden this sort of argument was still as unacceptable and incomprehensible as it had been when he wrote his first pamphlet 30 years earlier. He would have been astonished beyond measure if he could have known that in 50 years' time Canadians would be enlisting to fight for Britain on the continent of Europe.

Cobden went up to London on 21 March with Kate and their second daughter, Nelly. They stayed in lodgings in Suffolk Street, as close as possible to the House of Commons and the Athenaeum. But Cobden never went to either. Almost immediately he was seized with a severe attack of asthma, and about ten days later developed broncho-pneumonia. He died peacefully on the morning of 2 April, with his wife, his daughter Nelly and his best friend, John Bright, at his bedside.[103]

His body was taken back to his home at Dunford and five days later he was buried beside his son in West Lavington churchyard, close by his beloved Sussex Downs. A special train of more than twenty carriages brought the mourners from Waterloo station to Midhurst. There were several hundred of them, including many Members of Parliament and deputations from Manchester, Rochdale Stockport, Oldham, Blackburn and other manufacturing towns. A large deputation from Midhurst headed the funeral procession, and the lanes along which it passed were thickly lined with local people. When it reached the church, twelve of Cobden's closest personal and political friends, led by Bright and Gladstone, carried the coffin. It was the first fine warm spring day, and the sunshine – in Bright's words – 'seemed to fight against the sorrow in our hearts'.*[104]

Cobden's death took men's minds back to the repeal of the Corn laws which, although barely twenty years old, was now as unquestioningly accepted as once it had been bitterly contested. It was not an occasion for any exact apportionment of credit and the commentators did not try. As the *Daily Telegraph* put it, 'he taught political economy to the gentlemen of England, and he brought untaxed bread into the poor man's home. Of no other politician can so much be said.' Walter Bagehot, who had attended the great League rallies in London, recalled in *The Economist* those extraordinary occasions 'when excited masses of men and women hung on the words of one talking political economy'. The excitement was always much greater when Cobden was speaking. 'By a kind of

---

* Bright broke down at the graveside, but after being comforted by Gladstone, managed to comment: 'I doubt if he'd have liked the 6 parsons though'. (Gladstone, *Diaries*, Vol. V, 347.)

keenness of nerve, he said the exact word to touch, not the bare abstract understanding, but the quick individual perception of his hearers'.[105]

Punch's tribute to Cobden – a poem of sixteen stanzas – was entirely devoted to the repeal of the Corn laws,* and other commentators also found little to say about his subsequent career, apart from a mention of the commercial treaty with France. The *Daily Telegraph* remarked that his policy on national defence was based on too idealistic a view of the possibility of peace between nations, while the *Daily News* perceptively commented that he 'only wanted a certain elasticity' to have filled many positions with distinction. In the House of Commons Palmerston (who survived for only another six months) said that a great number of people, himself included, had differed from Cobden on many matters, but they had never doubted the sincerity of his convictions or that his objective was the good of his country.[106]

Cobden made his name as the inspiration behind a great and successful campaign for a major reform. Afterwards he found himself living in a political climate, both inside and outside Parliament, that was unenthusiastic about further change at home and so unsympathetic to, and uncomprehending about, his views on a non-interventionist foreign policy that he was all too often wrongly dismissed as an unpatriotic advocate of peace at any price. He had the satisfaction of observing John Bull and his government beginning to have a change of heart about foreign policy. But he died just before the passive political climate at home changed. Two years after his death a further substantial enlargement of the parliamentary franchise was introduced, and three years after that, one of his most cherished aims – a national system of elementary education within the reach of all, however poor – was established.

To his contemporaries, Cobden's personality was the most memorable thing about him – and the most difficult for posterity to recapture. Walter Bagehot wrote that Cobden left behind him 'the gift of a *unique* character'. Apart from his personal charm and his intellectual liveliness, what most impressed contemporaries was his single-mindedness, his simplicity, his complete disinterestedness and his ability to exclude bitterness and rancour from fierce political

---

* Others, ere him, had seen and proved the wrong,/But he the wrong determined to set right:/Weak in all else, in single purpose strong,/With Power, Wealth, Prejudice, he braved the fight.

And won it, and was famous, powerful, great:/But with the triumph lay the truncheon by,/And in the ranks was proud to serve the State,/Poor save in that which riches cannot buy.

Punch. 15 April, 1865.

controversy. 'Very rarely', wrote Bagehot, 'if even ever in history, has a man achieved so much by his words . . . and yet spoken so little evil as Mr Cobden!'[107]

Perhaps the last word should rest with Gladstone, who confided this spontaneons and moving tribute to his brother: 'What a sad, sad loss is this death of Cobden . . . ever since I really came to know him, I have held him in high esteem and regard as well as admiration; but till he died I did not know how high it was. I do not know that I have ever seen in public life a character more truly simple, noble and unselfish'.[108]

NOTES

Chapter 1

1. BL Add. Mss. 43649, to Bright, 2 Sept., 1851.
2. CP 302. (Manuscript account of Cobden's early life by his daughter Emma Jane.)
3. BL Add. Mss. 43660, to Combe, 1 August, 1846.
4. Pope-Hennessy, Una. *Charles Dickens* (1945) Pelican ed., 1970, 130/1.
5. WSRO Add. Mss. 6009.
6. CP 302.
7. Morley, John. *Richard Cobden*, 5.
8. CP 19, to W. Cobden, n/d.
9. *Ibid*, W. Cobden to F. Cobden, 10 May, 1822.
10. *Ibid*, to W. Cobden, 6 May, 1822.
11. WSRO Add. Mss. 6019, to W. and Millicent Cobden, 20 Nov., 1821.
12. WSRO Add. Mss. 2760, to W. Cobden, 18 Feb., 1823.
13. WSRO Add. Mss. 6019, to W. Cobden, 5 March, 1824.
14. WSRO Add. Mss. 6011, to F. Cobden, 20 August, 1824.
15. CP 19.
16. *Ibid* to F. Cobden, 26 August, 1825.
17. *Ibid* to F. Cobden, 4 Sept., 1825.
18. *Ibid* to F. Cobden, 26 August, 1825.
19. *Ibid*
20. *Ibid* to F. Cobden, 20 Sept., 1825.
21. *Ibid*
22. Morley, 8, 5 Feb., 1826.
23. MCL, Cobden Family Papers, 19 August, 1826.
24. WSRO Add. Mss. 2762, 18 Sept., 1827.
25. De Tocqueville, *Journeys to England and Ireland*, 107/8. (1958 ed.)
26. MCL, M87, Cobden Papers, to F. Cobden, 21 Sept., 1828.
27. CP 19, 20 May, 1829.
28. *Ibid* Jan. 1830.
29. WSRO Add. Mss. 2760, 11 August, 1831.
30. Turnbull, *A History of the Calico Printing Business of Great Britain*. 109/10.
31. Baines, *Lancashire and Cheshire Past and Present*. Vol.II, ccxlii.
32. WSRO Add. Mss. 2762, to F. Cobden, (Jan.) 1832.

33. WSRO Add. Mss. 6019, 4 Dec., 1824.
34. Morley, 17, 21 Sept., 1828.
35. MCL, Cobden Papers, 31 Oct., 1832.
36. WSRO Add. Mss. 2762 (Jan.) 1832.
37. *Ibid* 1833.
38. CP 19, 17 June, 1833.
39. WSRO 6011, 9 March, 1832.
40. Morley, 22 n2, Sept. 1832.
41. McGilchrist *Richard Cobden*, 16.
42. MCL, Cobden Papers, 4 March, 1832.
43. CP 19, to F. Cobden, 27 July, 1833.
44. Prentice *History of the Anti-Corn Law League*, Vol. 1, 47. (1968 ed.)
45. Morley, 25/6
46. *Ibid* 20, to F. Cobden, 30 Jan., 1832.
47. MCL, Cobden Papers, 31 Oct., 1832.
48. McGilchrist, *op. cit.* 17.

Chapter 2

1. CP 19 to F. Cobden, 31 March, 1835.
2. Cobden, *England, Ireland and America*. Political Writings, Vol. I, 30.
3. *Ibid* 42/3.
4. *Ibid* 95.
5. *Ibid* 70.
6. *Ibid* 121.
7. *Ibid* 130.
8. *Ibid* 130.
9. *Ibid* 45/6.
10. *Ibid* 140.
11. *Ibid* 145 and 149.
12. BL Add. Mss. 43665, to Tait, 12 April, 1836.
13. CP 19, 30 April, 1836.
14. Thistlethwaite, *The Anglo-American Connection in the Early Nineteenth Century*, 146.
15. Cawley, *The American Diaries of Richard Cobden*, 101.
16. Morley, 31, 18 June, 1835.
17. Cawley, *op. cit.* 102.
18. Morley, 35/7, to F. Cobden, 21 and 22 June, 1835.
19. *Ibid* 5 July, 1835.
20. Cawley, *op. cit.* 119.
21. Morley, 39, to F. Cobden, 5 July, 1835.
22. Cawley, *op. cit.* 119.
23. Morley, 33/4, to F. Cobden, 5 July, 1835.
24. Watkin, E. W. *Alderman Cobden*, 117.
25. Gibbon, *George Combe*, Vol. I, 284/5.
26. *Ibid*, Vol. II, 11.
27. BL Add. Mss. 43660, to Combe, 23 August, 1836.
28. BL Add. Mss. 43665.
29. *Ibid* 23 May, 1836.
30. *Ibid* 6 June, 1836.
31. *Ibid* 1, 4, 11, 26 July; 23 August; 3 Oct., 1836.
32. Cobden, *Russia*, Political Writings, Vol. I, 166.

33. *Ibid* 215.
34. *Ibid* 192.
35. *Ibid* 193/4.
36. *Ibid* 258.
37. *Ibid* 288/9.
38. *Ibid* 299.
39. Reid, *Lord Durham*, Vol. II, 31/7.
40. *Ibid* 92/3.
41. BL Add. Mss. 43665.
42. CP 24, 7 Feb., 1837.
43. Reid, *op. cit.* 93.
44. CP 23, 21 Oct., 1836.
45. BL Add. Mss. 43672A, (Diary) 27 Oct., 1836.
46. Morley, 43.
47. *Ibid* 45/6, to R. Cobden's sisters, 11 Nov., 1836.
48. BL Add. Mss. 43,672A, (Diary) 17/8 Nov., 1836.
49. Morley, 51.
50. BL Add. Mss. 43672A, (Diary) 28 Nov., 1836.
51. Morley, 52.
52. *Ibid* 58/9.
53. *Ibid* 64.
54. BL Add. Mss. 43672A, (Diary) 26 Dec., 1836.
55. Morley, 70/2.
56. BL Add. Mss. 43672B, (Diary) 10/15 March, 1837.
57. Morley, 80/1.
58. BL Add. Mss. 43672B, (Diary) 24 March, 1837. CP 42, to Hannay, 3 April, 1837.
59. Southgate, *The Most English Minister*, 113.

Chapter 3

1. CP 24 to F. Cobden.
2. Morley, 113, 11 Nov., 1836.
3. BL Add. Mss. 43665, 29 April, 1837.
4. Martineau, *History of England*, Vol. II, 352.
5. Buckley, *Joseph Parkes*, (London, 1926) 162.
6. Morley, 136/7, to F. Cobden, 12 June, 1837.
7. *Ibid* 137.
8. *Ibid* 137.
9. *Ibid* 138, to F. Cobden, 12 June, 1837.
10. WSRO Add. Mss. 2762, to F. Cobden, 12 June, 1837.
11. BL. Add. Mss. 43665, to Tait, 3 Oct., 1836.
12. Morley, 951/5.
13. Cobden, *England, Ireland and America, op. cit.* 149.
14. BL Add. Mss. 43665, 5 May, 1837.
15. CP 21, to Prentice, 25 May, 1837.
16. CP 20, to F. Cobden, 6 June, 1837.
17. Morley, 115/7. CP 43, to Norton, 3 August, 1837.
18. Morley, 117.
19. Watkin, A. *Extracts from his Journal*, 195.
20. Fawcett, *Sir William Molesworth*, 133.
21. Ziegler, *Melbourne*, 276.

22. Gash, *Politics in the Age of Peel*, 21. (1st ed.)
23. McCord, *The Anti-Corn Law League*, 20.
24. Axon, *Cobden as a Citizen*, 26.
25. CP 43, to Hannay, 6 Nov., 1837.
26. BL Add. Mss. 43665, to Tait, 15 August, 1837.
27. Gatrell, 'The Commercial Classes in Manchester 1820–1857', (unpublished PhD thesis) 246/7.
28. Morley, 127, to Tait, 17 August, 1838.
29. BL Add. Mss. 43665, to Tait, 5 May, 1837.
30. Gatrell, *op. cit.* 246.
31. Cawley, *op. cit.* 121.
32. Cobden, *Speeches*, Vol. II, 573. (22 Jan., 1851)
33. Maltby, *Manchester and the Movement for National Elementary Education*, 49.
34. CP 41, to Coppock, 4 Oct., 1837.
35. Maltby, *op. cit.* 50.
36. CP 44, 9 Oct., 1844.
37. Trevelyan, G. M. *John Bright*, 29/0.
38. BL Add. Mss. 43649, 14 Dec., 1837.
39. Martineau, *op. cit.* 186.
40. BL Add. Mss. 43665, to Tait, 18 Jan., 1838.
41. Axon, *op. cit.* 30/61.
42. *Ibid* 20.
43. *Ibid* 35.
44. Fraser, *Urban Politics in Victorian England*, 121.
45. Redford, *History of Local Government in Manchester*, Vol II, 9/10.
46. Love and Barton, *Manchester as it is*, 26.
47. Axon, *op. cit.* 64/5.
48. Axon, *Ibid*, 67/81.
49. Axon, *Ibid* 84/8.
50. Axon, *Ibid* 99.
51. MCL, Wilson Papers, to Wilson, 5 May, 1838.
52. Parliamentary Papers, Vol. XX, Part II, (1837/8), 46/63. (Select Committee on Postage, 2nd Report.)
53. Wallas. *Francis Place*, 386/7.
54. Parliamentary Papers, Vol. XX, *op. cit.*, 54.
55. BL Add. Mss. 43678, to R. Hill, 12 and 19 May, 1838.
56. *Ibid* Hill to Cobden, 16/7 May, 1838.
57. Martineau, *op. cit.* 429.
58. CP 48, 24 Jan., 1840.
59. Hill, R. & G., *Sir Rowland Hill*, Vol. II, 31. 30 May, 1846.
60. CP 48 to Hill, 31 March, 1841.
61. Hughes, 'The Development of Cobden's Economic Doctrines', Bulletin of the John Rylands Institute, Vol. XXII (1938), 409. (quoting Cobden to Neild, Sept. 30, 1838)
62. BL Add. Mss. 43673A (Diary), 3 and 13 Sept., 1838.
63. *Ibid* 2 Sept., 1838, and Morley, 132/4.
64. BL Add. Mss. 43673A (Diary) 10 Sept., 1838.
65. *Ibid* 14 Sept., 1838.
66. Hughes, *op. cit.* 412.
67. CP 24 to F. Cobden, 11 Sept., 1838.
68. *Ibid*
69. Hughes, *op. cit.* 411.
70. Morley, 127, to Tait, 17 August, 1838.
71. *Ibid* 126, 5 Oct., 1838.

Chapter 4

1. Fairlie, 'The Nineteenth Century Corn Law Reconsidered', Economic History Review, 2nd series, Vol. XVIII (1965), 562/73.
2. Barnes, *History of the English Corn Laws*, 147, quoting R. Torrens, *The External Corn Trade* (1815).
3. BL Add. Mss. 43677, to T. Dick, 17 Oct., 1836.
4. Ashworth, *Recollections of Richard Cobden MP*, 14/5.
5. CP 43, to Norton.
6. Read, *Chartist Studies* (ed. Briggs), 34.
7. Prentice, *op. cit.* Vol. I, 85/7.
8. MCL, J. B. Smith Corn Law Papers, Vol. II, to Smith, 3 Feb., 1839.
9. BL Add. Mss. 43649, 6 Feb., 1839.
10. Greville, *Memoirs* (ed. Strachey & Fulford), Vol. IV, 123.
11. Melbourne *Papers*, 389/0, Melbourne to Lord John Russell, 20 Jan., 1839.
12. McCord, *op. cit.* 44.
13. BL Add. Mss. 50131, to Sturge, 26 Feb. and 1 March, 1839.
14. BL Add. Mss. 43662, to Villiers, 3 March, 1839.
15. Prentice, *op. cit.* 119.
16. BL Add. Mss. 50131, to Sturge, 4 March, 1839.
17. Boyson, *The Ashworth Cotton Enterprise*, 202.
18. McCord, *op. cit.* 168.
19. Somerville, *The Whistler at the Plough*, 82.
20. BL Add. Mss. 50131, to Sturge, 20 Nov., 1840.
21. Kohl, *Ireland, Scotland and England*, 145.
22. BL Add. Mss. 43653, to Ashworth, 14. Sept., 1851.
23. Morley, 118/9. to F. Cobden, 26 Oct., 1838.
24. CP 55, to König, 25 Nov., 1839.
25. Morley, 333.
26. BL Add. Mss. 50131 to Sturge, 4 March, 1839.
27. *Ibid* 1 March, 1839.
28. Himmelfarb, *The Idea of Poverty*, 241.
29. Ward, *Chartism*, 115.
30. Napier, *Sir Charles Napier*, Vol. II, 75. 23 August, 1839.
31. Ward, *op. cit.* 153/4.
32. BL Add. Mss. 43665, to Tait, 2 April, 1839.
33. Napier, *op. cit.* 23. 27, April, 1839.
34. *Anti-Corn Law Circular*, 3 Sept., 1839.
35. CP 52, to H. Cole, 27 June, 1839.
36. McCord, *op. cit.* 66/7.
37. BL Add. Mss. 50131, to Sturge, 22 Oct., 1839.
38. Somerville, *Free Trade and the League*, Vol. II, 500/01.
39. BL Add. Mss. 43662, to Villiers, 4 Feb. 1840.
40. *Ibid* 7 Feb., 1840.
41. *Ibid* 16 Feb., 1840.
42. *Ibid* 7 Feb., 1840.
43. *Ibid* 4 Feb., 1840.
44. CP 56, 5 March, 1840.
45. McCord, *op. cit.* 126.
46. CP 56, 10 and 12 Feb., 1840.
47. BL Add. Mss. 43662, 4 Feb., 1840.
48. CP 56, to Beadon, 10 Feb., 1840.
49. Prentice, *op. cit.* 150/6.
50. CP 25, to F. Cobden, 11 April, 1840.

51. Parliamentary Papers, (1840) Vol. IV, 32. (Select Committee on Banks of Issue.)
52. CP 25, 15 April, 1840.
53. Wallas, *op. cit.* 395.
54. CP 56, to Beadon, 24 Dec., 1840.
55. BL Add. Mss. 35151, to Beadon, 5 Oct., 1840.

Chapter 5

1. WSRO Add. Mss. 6015, 22 April, 1840.
2. CP 55, to König, 3 May, 1840.
3. Gaskell, *Letters* (ed. Chapple & Pollard,) 47.
4. WSRO Add. Mss. 6015, 2 May, 1840.
5. CP 25, to F. Cobden, 25 May, 3, 20, 30 June, 1840.
6. *Ibid* to F. Cobden, 29 July, 1840.
7. MCL, Smith Corn Law Papers, Vol. II, 1 June, 1840.
8. CP 59, 10, 14 June, 1840.
9. MCL, Smith Corn Law papers, Vol. II, to Smith, 1 June, 1840.
10. CP 59, to Wilson, 14 June, 1840.
11. WSRO Add. Mss. 6012, 26 August, 1840.
12. WSRO Add. Mss. 6011, to F. Cobden, 31 August, 1840.
13. MCL, Smith Corn Law Papers, Vol. II, 3 Feb., 1840.
14. Prentice, *op. cit.* 177.
15. McCord, *op. cit.* 84.
16. CP 56, to Beadon, 24 Dec., 1840.
17. Longmate, *The Breadstealers*, 130.
18. McCord, *op. cit.* 85.
19. Longmate, *op. cit.* 131.
20. BL Add. Mss. 50131, to Sturge, 5 Jan., 1840.
21. Garnett, *W. J. Fox*, (London, 1910), 259, to P. Taylor, 4 May, 1840.
22. McCord, *op. cit.* 89/0.
23. CP 43, to Norton, 9 May, 1839.
24. CP 59, to Wilson, 14 June, 1840.
25. *Tait's Edinburgh Magazine*, Nov. 1840. 747.
26. BL. Add. Mss. 35151, 22 Sept., 1840.
27. *Ibid* 5 Oct., 1840.
28. *Ibid*
29. Smiles, *Autobiography*, 95. (1905 ed.)
30. *Ibid.* 96.
31. Hobhouse, *Joseph Sturge*, 69.
32. BL Add. Mss. 50131, 15 May, 1839.
33. *Ibid* 20 Feb., 1841.
34. Thistlethwaite, *op. cit.* 161/2. Prentice, *op. cit.* 231.
35. CP 55, to Beadon, 13 March, 1841.
36. *Anti-Corn Law Circular*, 11 Jan., 1841.
37. Prentice, *op. cit.* 217/8.
38. Ziegler, *op. cit.* 330.
39. BL Add. Mss. 43662, [c. 28 Feb.,] 1841.
40. Smiles, *op. cit.* 99.
41. Prentice, *op. cit.* 212.
42. MCL, Smith Corn Law Papers, Vol. III, 2 May, 1841.
43. CP 21, to F. Cobden, 15 May, 1841.
44. Morley, 175, 16 June, 1841.

45. *Ibid* 176, to F. Cobden, 3 July, 1841.
46. Trevelyan, G. O. *Lord Macaulay* 404 (1959 ed.)
47. BL Add. Mss. 43662, [July] 1841.
48. Hansard (3rd series), LIX, 233/45, 25 August, 1841.
49. Trevelyan, G. O. *op. cit.* 126.
50. Morley, 184, to F. Cobden, 27 Sept., 1841.
51. BL Add. Mss. 43663, Wilson to Cobden, 26 August, 1841.
52. Gash, *Sir Robert Peel*, 269.
53. BL Add, Mss. 43649, to Bright, [5 Sept.] 1841.
54. Morley, 184, to F. Cobden, 27 Sept., 1841.
55. Hansard, LIX, 576/82, 17 Sept., 1841.
56. *Ibid* 795/6, 24 Sept., 1841.
57. *Ibid* 942, 28 Sept., 1841.
58. BL Add. Mss. 43662, 6 Sept., 1841.
59. MCL, Smith Corn Law Papers, Vol. III, 4 Dec., 1841.
60. Trevelyan, G. M. *op. cit.* 43.
61. McCord *op. cit.* 103/7.
62. MCL, Smith Corn Law Papers, Vol. III, to Smith, 4 Dec., 1841.
63. CP 59, to Wilson, 9 Oct., 1841.
64. CP 70, to P. Taylor, 15 Oct., 1841.
65. BL Add. Mss. 43649, [5 Sept.] 1841.
66. CP 59, 25 Sept., 1841.
67. CP 41, to Coppock, Sept. 1841.
68. CP 70, to P. Taylor, 15 Oct., 1841
69. Cowherd, *Politics of English Dissent*, 112/3.
70. Hovell, *The Chartist Movement*, 247.
71. BL Add. Mss. 50131, [11 Dec.] 1841.
72. MCL, Wilson Papers, 16 Oct., 1841.
73. BL Add. Mss. 50131, to Sturge, [2 Nov.] 1841.
74. Watkin, E. W. *op. cit.* 81.
75. MCL, Smith Corn Law Papers, Vol. III, to Smith, 4 Dec., 1841.

Chapter 6

1. Prentice, *op. cit.* 310.
2. Gash, *Peel*, 315.
3. Greville, *op. cit.* Vol. V, 11, 11 Feb., 1842.
4. Hansard, LX, 235, 9 Feb., 1842.
5. *Ibid* 1042/57, 24 Feb., 1842.
6. *Ibid* 1957/67.
7. Morley, 227, to F. Cobden, 28 Feb., 1842.
8. Hansard, LXI, 47/50, 4 March, 1842.
9. Parliamentary Papers (1842) Vol IX, 80/5 (Select Committee on Payment of Wages.)
10. BL Add. Mss. 43653, to Ashworth, 13 May, 1842.
11. CP 59, 24 Feb., 1842.
12. Hansard, LXII, 23/7, 7 April, 1842.
13. *Ibid* 75, 7 April, 1842.
14. CP 43, to Norton, 4 April, 1842.
15. MCL, Smith Corn Law Papers, Vol. III, 4 Dec., 1841.
16. Greville, *op. cit.* Vol. V, 16, 13 March, 1842.
17. Martineau, *op. cit.* 538.
18. BL Add. Mss. 43653, to Ashworth, 7 April, 1842.

19. Hansard, LXII, 703, 18 April, 1842.
20. Morley, 240, to F. Cobden, 12 March, 1842.
21. CP 21, to F. Cobden, 12 March, 1842. MCL, Smith Corn Law Papers, Vol. III, to Smith, 28 April, 1842.
22. Gash, *Peel*, 327.
23. Prentice, *op. cit.* 363.
24. UCL Parkes Papers, Parkes to Stanley, 28 July, 1842.
25. Hansard, LXIV, 1357, 11 July, 1842.
26. *Ibid* 924, 1 July, 1842.
27. *Ibid* 1217/8, 8 July, 1842.
28. *Ibid* 1333, 11 July, 1842.
29. *Ibid* LXV, 566, 22 July, 1842.
30. CP 71, 4 March, 1842.
31. BL Add. Mss. 43649, 4 March, 1842.
32. Trevelyan, G. M. *op. cit.* 77/8.
33. BL Add. Mss. 43649, 12 March, 1842.
34. *Ibid* 21 June, 1842.
35. BL Place Collection of Cuttings & Pamphlets, Set 7, Vol. 6. 13 July, 1842.
36. Watkin, E. W. *op. cit.* 94.
37. CP 59, to Wilson, 14 August, 1842.
38. Watkin, A. *Extracts from his Journal*, 218.
39. Mather, 'The General Strike of 1842', Exeter Papers in Economic History, No. 6, (1972), 5.
40. Rose, 'The Plug Riots of 1842', Trans. Lancs & Cheshire Antiquarian Society, Vol. LXVII (1957), 84.
41. BL Add. Mss. 43663. (copy of resolution sent to Cobden)
42. *Ibid* 15 August, 1842.
43. McCord, *op. cit.* 128.
44. CP 71.
45. Prentice, *op. cit.* 385.
46. *Ibid* 386.
47. Gash, *Peel*, 355.
48. WSRO Add. Mss. 6011, 26 June, 1842.
49. CP 21.
50. *Ibid* 14 July, 1842.
51. *Ibid* 2 August, 1842.
52. BL Add. Mss. 50131, 25 July, 1842.
53. BL Add. Mss. 43662, 13 Nov., 1842.
54. CP 70, to P. Taylor, 6 Nov., 1842.
55. CP 43, to Norton, 14 Dec., 1842.
56. CP 70, to P. Taylor.
57. CP 41, to Coppock, 27 Nov., 1842.
58. CP 55. to Konig, 2 Dec., 1842.
59. BL Add. Mss. 43660, 31 Dec., 1842.
60. McCord, *op. cit.* 136.

Chapter 7

1. CP 71, 6 Jan., 1843.
2. WSRO Add. Mss. 6015, 18 Jan., 1843.
3. Robbins, *John Bright*, 40.
4. BL Add. Mss. 50748, to Mrs Cobden, 11 Jan., 1843.
5. Gash, *Peel*, 364/6.

6. WSRO Add. Mss. 6015, 13 Feb., 1843.
7. CP 26, to F. Cobden, 16 Feb., 1843.
8. Hansard, LXVI, 836/9, 17 Feb., 1843.
9. *Ibid* 880.
10. Prentice, *op. cit.* Vol. II, 46.
11. Morley, 263/4, to F. Cobden.
12. *Ibid* 267/8, 1 March, 1843.
13. *Ibid* 264, to F. Cobden.
14. CP 26, 11 March, 1843.
15. BL Add. Mss. 43664, to Baines, 5 March, 1843.
16. WSRO Add. Mss. 6015, 23 Feb., 1843.
17. *Ibid* 16 March, 1843.
18. Morley, 207/8, 29 Dec., 1845.
19. Prentice, *op. cit.* Vol. II, 81.
20. Hansard, LXIX, 392/3, 15 May, 1843.
21. Prentice, *op. cit.* Vol. II, 89/0.
22. WSRO Add. Mss. 6015, to Mrs Cobden, [18 May], 1843.
23. BL Add. Mss. 43662, 27 Jan., 1843.
24. CP 71.
25. UCL Parkes Papers, 5 March, 1843.
26. Gash, *Peel*, 392.
27. WSRO Add. Mss. 6015, [2 April] 1843.
28. *Norfolk Chronicle*, 8 April, 1843.
29. *Norwich Mercury*, 8 April, 1843.
30. Morley, 276, to F. Cobden, CP 27, to F. Cobden, 14 June, 1843.
31. WSRO Add. Mss. 6015, [15 Jan.] 1843.
32. *Ibid* 16 Feb., 1843.
33. *Ibid* 26 April, 1843.
34. BL Add. Mss. 50748, 18 March, 1843.
35. WSRO Add. Mss. 6015, 22 March, 1843.
36. Morley, 284, 17 August, 1843.
37. Cobden, *Speeches*, Vol. I, 66/8. (28 Sept., 1843, at Covent Garden.)
38. BL Add. Mss. 43662.
39. BL Add. Mss. 50748, to Mrs Cobden.
40. *The Times*, 18 Nov., 1843.
41. BL Add. Mss. 43649, 15 April, 1842.
42. MCL, Wilson Papers, Cobden to Bright, 21 June, 1843.
43. *Ibid* Cobden to Wilson, 22 June, 1843.
44. *Ibid* Cobden to Wilson, 24 August, 1843.
45. Morley, 286, 14 Jan., 1844.
46. CP 27.
47. Morley, 288, 26 Jan., 1844.
48. Hansard, LXXIII, 862/95. 12 March, 1844.
49. Shannon, *Gladstone*, Vol. I, 149/0.
50. Hodder, *Shaftesbury*, Vol. II, 23.
51. BL Add. Mss. 43653, 18 Dec., 1843.
52. Finlayson, *Shaftesbury*, 199.
53. Hodder, *op. cit.* Vol. I, 522.
54. Maxwell, *Clarendon*, Vol. I, 244.
55. McCord, *op. cit.* 191.
56. Hansard, LXVII, 1471, 23 March, 1843.
57. Greville, *op. cit.* Vol. V 169, 31 March, 1844.
58. Gash, *Peel*, 439/0.
59. Hansard, LXXIV, 330/3, 26 April, 1844.

60. Gash, *Peel*, 440/1.
61. Hansard, LXXXVI, 1077, 22 May, 1846.
62. Hodder, *op. cit.* Vol. I, 425.
63. MCL, Cobden Papers, Hyland to F. Cobden, 25 Feb., 1845.
64. Hansard, LXXVII, 662/3, 18 Feb., 1845.
65. Finlayson, *op. cit.* 227.
66. CP 27, 19 Feb., 1845.
67. Hodder, *op. cit.* Vol. II, 210.
68. Morley, 302, to F. Cobden, 23 March, 1844.
69. *Ibid* 951, to W.C. Hunt, 21 Oct., 1836.
70. Hansard, LXXXVI, 1076/7, 22 May, 1846.
71. MCL, Wilson Papers, Cobden to Wilson, 17 July, 1844.
72. McCord, *op. cit.* 156.
73. BL Add. Mss. 43677, to J. Brooks, 18 June, 1844.
74. Mackie, *Duncan McLaren*, Vol. I, 272/3
75. Morley, 295, 4 June, 1844.
76. BL Add. Mss. 50748, 10 August, 1843.
77. Crosby, *English Farmers & the Politics of Protection*, 134.
78. MCL, Wilson Papers, Cobden to Wilson, 2 April, 1844.
79. *Ibid*
80. *Ibid*
81. Prentice, *op. cit.* Vol. II, 253/4.
82. McCord, *op. cit.* 152/4.
83. Prest, *Politics in the Age of Cobden*, 86.
84. *Ibid* 94.
85. *Ibid* 96.

Chapter 8

1. McCord, *op. cit.* 189.
2. Parker, *Peel*, Vol. III, 180, Ashley to Peel, 26 Feb. 1845.
3. Prentice, *op. cit.* Vol. II, 275/6.
4. Greville, *op. cit.* Vol. V, 205, 25 Feb. 1845.
5. Morley, 316, to Wilson, 28 Feb., 1845.
6. Hansard, LXXVIII, 113/4, 27 Feb., 1845.
7. Morley, 317, 11 March, 1845.
8. Hansard, LXXVIII, 809/10, 13 March, 1845.
9. Gash, *Peel*, 470.
10. Hansard, LXXVIII, 1028, 17 March, 1845.
11. Gash, *Peel*, 472.
12. Greville, *op. cit.* Vol. V, 214, 22 April, 1845.
13. CP 41, to Coppock, 13 April, 1845.
14. Hughes, *op. cit.* 414, to Firnly, 10 April, 1845.
15. Hansard, LXXIX, 968, 18 April, 1845.
16. CP 41, to Coppock, 1 May, 1845.
17. McCord, *op. cit.* 191.
18. Gash, *Peel*, 477/8.
19. McCord, *op. cit.* 157/8.
20. Prentice, *op. cit.* Vol. II, 328/34.
21. WSRO Add. Mss. 6016, 23 May, 1845.
22. Morley, 331/2, to F. Cobden, 6 & 19 June, 1845.
23. *Ibid* 329, to Mrs Cobden, 24 June, 1845.
24. *Ibid* 328/9.

25. *Ibid* 330, to Mrs Cobden, 26 June, 1845.
26. *Ibid* 7 April, 1845.
27. *Ibid* 332/3.
28. *Ibid* 334/5, 20 Sept., 1845.
29. Gash, *Peel*, 539.
30. Prentice, *op. cit.* Vol. II, 383.
31. Gash, *Peel*, 538.
32. *Ibid* 555.
33. Prentice, *op. cit.* Vol. II, 399.
34. Morley, 342.
35. Trevelyan, G. M. *op. cit.* 139.
36. MCL, Wilson Papers.
37. Morley, 342/3, 5 Dec., 1845.
38. *The Times* 13 Dec., 1845.
39. CP 29, 17 Dec., 1845.
40. Cobden, *Speeches*, Vol. I, 341, 17 Dec., 1845.
41. *Ibid* 324, 13 Nov., 1845.
42. Morley, 352.
43. *Ibid* 353, 2 Feb., 1846.
44. Greville, *op. cit.* Vol. V, 265, 20 Dec., 1845.
45. Parker, *op. cit.* 289, to Heytesbury, 23 Dec., 1845.
46. Morley, 344, 20 Dec., 1845.
47. Benson & Esher, *Letters of Queen Victoria*, Vol. II, 77/8. (Memorandum by Prince Albert, 25 Dec., 1845.)
48. Prentice, *op. cit.* Vol. II, 415.
49. Morley, 374, to Mrs. Cobden, 26 Jan., 1846.
50. *Ibid* 374/5, to Mrs Cobden, 28 Jan., 1845.
51. McCord, *op. cit.* 201/2.
52. BL Add. Mss. 43656, to Sturge, 12 Feb., 1846.
53. Mackie, *op. cit.* Vol. I, 244, to McLaren, 2 Feb., 1846.
54. CP 27. 9 Feb., 1846.
55. Parker, *op. cit.* 331/3. 22, 23 Feb., 1846.
56. Martineau, *Autobiography*, Vol. II, 263.
57. *Ibid* 264.
58. Hansard, LXXXIV, 275/92, 27 Feb., 1846.
59. Greville, *op. cit.* Vol. V, 303, 1 March, 1846.
60. Parker, *op. cit.* 342/3, 1 March, 1846.
61. MCL, Wilson Papers, 4 March, 1846.
62. BL Add. Mss. 43667, to Mellor, 5 March, 1846.
63. Stewart, *The Politics of Protection,* 63.
64. Greville, *op. cit.* Vol. V, 321, 21 May, 1846.
65. Morley, 383, 18 May, 1846.
66. *Ibid* 387.
67. Blake, *Disraeli*, 241.
68. Hansard, LXXXVII, 1027, 25 June, 1846.
69. Morley, 390/7, 23 June, 1846.
70. *Ibid* 397/401, 24 June, 1845.
71. Hansard, LXXXVII, 1054, 29 June, 1846.
72. Benson & Esher, *op. cit.* 101, (Memorandum by Prince Albert, 6 July, 1846.)
73. Morley, *Gladstone*, Vol. I, 291.
74. Hansard, LXXXVII, 1055, 29 June, 1846.
75. Gash, *Peel*, 612.
76. Woodward, *The Age of Reform*, 340, n. 2; 341.
77. Cobden. *Speeches*, Vol. I, 392.

Chapter 9

1. BL Add. Mss. 43667, to Welford, 1 July, 1846.
2. Morley, 371, to Hunter, 12 March, 1846.
3. BL Add. Mss. 43664, 18 July, 1846.
4. Morley, 408/9, to Paulton & to Ashworth, 4 July, 1846.
5. Prentice, *op. cit.* Vol. II, 269/0, 8 Jan., 1845.
6. MCL, Wilson Papers, 3 August, 1846.
7. Read, *Cobden and Bright*, 102.
8. Dickens, *Letters*, (ed. K. Tillotson), Vol. IV, 635.
9. CP 27, 19 August, 1846.
10. *Ibid* to F. Cobden, 4 Sept., 1846.
11. *Ibid* to F. Cobden, 17 Oct., 1846. BL Add. Mss. 43649, to Bright, 18 Oct., 1846.
12. BL Add. Mss. 50751, to F. Cobden, 6 Nov. & 3 Dec., 1846.
13. BL Add. Mss. 43660, to Combe, 26 June, 1847.
14. BL Add. Mss. 50751, to F. Cobden, 25 March, 1847.
15. Morley, 426, (Diary) 18 Jan., 1847.
16. BL Add. Mss. 50751, to F. Cobden, 9 May, 1847.
17. Morley, 433/4, (Diary) 22 Feb., 1847. Schwabe, *Reminiscences of Richard Cobden*, 58, Cobden to Mrs – Schwabe, 24 Feb., 1847.
18. Morley, 436/7, (Diary) 6 March, 1847.
19. *Ibid* 428, (Diary) 23 Jan., 1847.
20. *Ibid* 433, (Diary) 22 Feb., 1847.
21. *Ibid* 428, (Diary) 25 Jan., 1847.
22. MCL Cobden Papers, to Potter, 28 March, 1847.
23. BL Add. Mss. 50751, to F. Cobden, 25 March & 9 May, 1847.
24. BL Add. Mss. 43674B, (Diary) 25 April, 1847.
25. *Ibid* 29 April, 1847.
26. Morley, 437/8, (Diary) 28 May, 1847.
27. BL Add. Mss. 43674B, (Diary) 4 June, 1847.
28. Morley, 439, (Diary) 3 June, 1847.
29. *Ibid* 7 June, 1847.
30. BL Add. Mss. 43674B, (Diary) 6 June, 1847.
31. Morley, 439/0, (Diary) 21 June, 1847.
32. Schwabe, *op. cit.* 70, Mrs Cobden to Mrs Schwabe, 16 July, 1847.
33. Morley, 442, (Diary) 10 July, 1847.
34. BL Add. Mss. 43674D, (Diary) 16 July, 1847.
35. Morley, 448, (Diary) 31 July, 1847.
36. Trautz, 'Richard Cobden's Associations with Germany', Bulletin of the John Rylands Institute, Vol. 34. (1951/2) 461/2.
37. MCL Cobden Papers, to Potter, 28 March, 1847.
38. Schwabe, *op. cit.* 75, Cobden to Mrs Schwabe, 19 August, 1847.
39. BL Add. Mss. 43674D, (Diary) 19 August, 1847.
40. Morley, 453, (Diary) 25 August, 1847.
41. *Ibid* 453/6, (Diary) 27, 28, 31 August, 1847.
42. BL Add. Mss. 43674D, (Diary) 8 Sept., 1847.
43. Morley, 460/1, (Diary) 15 Sept., 1847.
44. BL Add. Mss. 50749, to Mrs Cobden, 29 Sept., 1847.
45. *Ibid*
46. *Ibid* to Mrs Cobden, 5 Oct., 1847.
47. *The Times* 7 August, 1847.
48. Morley, 474.
49. *Ibid* 443, (Diary) 10 July, 1847.

50. BL Add. Mss. 43660, to Combe, 26 June, 1847.
51. BL Add. Mss. 43674A, (Diary) 12 Oct., 1846.
52. CP 44, to Bright, 18, Sept. 1847.
53. BL Add. Mss. 43649, to Bright, 16 Sept., 1847.
54. CP 28, 2 Sept., 1847.
55. BL Add. Mss. 50749, to Mrs Cobden, 19 August, 1847.
56. CP 41, to Coppock, 3 March, 1860.
57. BL Add. Mss. 43660, 13 Nov., 1847.
58. Benson & Esher, *op. cit.* 100, (Memorandum by Prince Albert, 30 June, 1846.)
59. Morley, 403/4, 2 July, 1846.
60. BL Add. Mss. 43649, to Bright, (July) 1846.
61. Benson & Esher, *op. cit.* 153/5, 14 Oct., 1847.
62. Morley, 487, to Combe, 23 July, 1848.
63. BL Add. Mss. 43649, to Bright, 1 Nov., 1848.
64. BL Add. Mss. 43660, 21 March, 1849.
65. Morley, 365, to Combe, 7 March, 1846.
66. Hansard, XCVIII, 859, 11 May, 1848.
67. Morley, 631/2, to Bright, 5 Jan. 1855.
68. BL Add. Mss. 50751, 25 March, 1847.
69. MCL, Wilson Papers, to Wilson, 24 Nov., 1847.
70. CP 55, to König, 3 Jan., 1848.
71. Morley, 522, to Livesey, 10 Oct., 1849.
72. *Ibid.*
73. BL Add. Mss. 50749, 2 April, 2, 11, 13 May, 1848.
74. WSRO Add. Mss. 6011, 6 June, 1848.
75. BL Add. Mss. 43653, to Ashworth, 8 Jan., 1848.
76. BL Add. Mss. 43656, to Sturge, 3 Jan., 1848.
77. CP 60, 17 Jan., 1848.
78. Trevelyan, G. M. *op. cit.* 181.
79. BL Add. Mss. 43656, 28 Jan., 1848.
80. Morley, 609, to McLaren, 19 Sept., 1853.
81. Gooch, *Later Correspondence of Lord John Russell*, Vol. I, 258/60.
82. Prest, *Lord John Russell*, 281.
83. BL Add. Mss. 43653, to Ashworth, 21 March, 1848.
84. BL Add. Mss. 50749, to Mrs Cobden, 24 March, 1848.
85. Hansard, XCVI, 1429, 28 Feb., 1848.
86. BL Add. Mss. 43653, to Ashworth, 21 March, 1848.
87. Morley, 485, to Mrs Cobden, 10 April, 1848.
88. *Ibid* 487/8, to Greg, 15 May, 1848.
89. CP 60, 8 May, 1848.
90. Hansard, XCVIII, 860, 11 May, 1848.
91. BL Add. Mss. 50749, to Mrs Cobden, 13 May, 1848.
92. Hansard, C, 181/95, 6 July, 1848.
93. BL Add. Mss. 43649, to Bright, 16 Sept. & 25 Oct., 1848.
94. Gibbon, *op. cit.* Vol. II, 269/70.
95. BL Add. Mss. 43660, 28 Sept., 1848.
96. Morley, 493, 28 Oct., 1848.
97. BL Add. Mss. 43656, 16 Sept., 1848.
98. *Ibid.*
99. *Ibid* 28 Sept., 1848.
100. Morley, 503, to Bright, 23 Dec., 1849.
101. Morley, 495/9.
102. Calkin, 'A Victorian Free Trade Lobby', Economic History Review, 2nd

series, XIII (1960/1) 100.)

103.   BL Add. Mss. 43649, 27 Dec., 1848.
104.   Edsall, 'A Failed National Movement', Bulletin of the Institute of Historical Research, XLIX, (May 1976) 115.
105.   Morley, 515, to Bright, 1 Oct., 1849.
106.   CP 88, to Lattimore,
107.   Bellman, *Bricks and Mortals*, 34.
108.   Cobden, *Speeches*, Vol. II, 489.
109.   *Ibid* 491/2.
110.   Bellman, *op. cit.* 40.
111.   Morley, 516/7, to Bright, 1 Oct., 1849.

Chapter 10

1.   Greville, *op. cit.* Vol. VI, 147/8, 19 Jan., 1849.
2.   Morley, 506, 5 Jan, 1849.
3.   Hansard, C11, 1218/54, 26 Feb., 1849.
4.   Morley, 506, to Combe, 8 Feb., 1849.
5.   Hansard, CVI, 53/68, 12 June, 1849. Morley, 508/9, to Combe 19 June, 1849.
6.   BL Add. Mss. 43674E, (Diary) 22 August, 1849.
7.   Morley, 512, to Mrs Cobden, 25 August, 1849.
8.   *Ibid* 513, to Mrs Cobden, 28 August, 1849.
9.   BL Add. Mss. 43674E, (Diary) 20, 27 August, 1849.
10.   BL Add. Mss. 43653, to Ashworth, 3 Sept., 1849.
11.   *Ibid.*
12.   Lyons, *Internationalism in Europe*, 316.
13.   for example, see Cobden, *Speeches*, Vol. II, 412, 14 Nov., 1850.
14.   BL Add. Mss. 43668, to Cassell, 4 Sept., 1849.
15.   Lane-Poole, *Stratford Canning*, Vol. II, 201.
16.   Morley, 569/0, to Bright, 13 Nov., 1851.
17.   Cobden, *Speeches*, Vol. II, 179/89, 8 Oct., 1849; 191/210, 18 Jan., 1850.
18.   *Ibid* 418, 14 Nov., 1850.
19.   CP 28, to F. Cobden, 16 Oct., 1849.
20.   BL Add. Mss. 43665, to Roberton, 16 Oct., 1849.
21.   Malmesbury, *Memoirs*, Vol. I, 257, 6 Jan., 1850.
22.   CP 43, to Norton, 2 Jan., 1850.
23.   Cobden, *Speeches*, Vol. I, 418, 18 Dec., 1849.
24.   CP 43, to Norton, 2 Jan., 1850.
25.   Morley, 542, 18 Dec., 1849.
26.   Cobden, *Speeches*, Vol. I, 421, 18 Dec., 1849.
27.   Morley, 542, to Mrs Cobden, 19 Dec., 1849. WSRO Add. Mss. 6011, 25 Dec., 1849.
28.   BL Add. Mss. 50749, to Mrs Cobden, 24 Jan., 1850.
29.   Parker, *Sir James Graham*, Vol. II, 94, G. C. Lewis to Graham, 24 Jan., 1850.
30.   Blake, *Disraeli*, 285.
31.   Greville, *op. cit.* Vol. VI, 196, 2 Feb., 1850.
32.   Morrell, *British Colonial Policy in the Age of Peel & Russell*, 518.
33.   *Ibid* 488.
34.   Morley, 542/3, to Mrs Cobden, 21 Dec., 1849.
35.   Hansard, CV, 1063, 1 June, 1849.
36.   *Ibid* CX, 45/6, 8 April, 1850.
37.   *Ibid* CXVIII, 663, 666, 14 July, 1851.
38.   *Ibid* CXIII, 37/40, 19 July, 1850.

39. *Ibid* CXV, 1437/44, 10 April, 1851.
40. Hobson, *Richard Cobden: the International Man*, 240, (1968 ed.) to H. Richard, 21 August, 1858.
41. Hansard, CXVII, 836, 20 March, 1848.
42. *Ibid* CVII, 523, 18 July, 1849.
43. Fox, *British Admirals and Chinese Pirates*, 110/1, 118.
44. Runciman, *The White Rajahs*, 95.
45. Morley, 520, to Bright, 6 Dec., 1849.
46. Hansard, CXI, 294/6, 23 May, 1850.
47. *Ibid* CVIII, 665, 11 Feb., 1850.
48. *Ibid* CXII, 1318/21, 12 July, 1850.
49. Pringle, *Rajahs and Rebels*, 49.
50. Runciman, *op. cit.* 90/1.
51. McCord, 'Cobden and Bright in Politics, 1846/57', in *Ideas and Institutions of Victorian Britain* (ed. Robson) 92.
52. Runciman, *op. cit.* 102/5.
53. Hansard, CXVIII, 494/9, 10 July, 1851.
54. Hobson, *op. cit.* 239/0, to H. Richard, 21 August, 1858.
55. Greville, *op. cit.* Vol. VI, 199/0, 14 Feb., 1850.
56. Prest, *Lord John Russell*, 314.
57. Southgate, *op. cit.* 269/0.
58. Ridley, *Lord Palmerston*, 387.
59. Stanley, *Disraeli, Derby and the Conservative Party*, (ed. Vincent) 22.
60. Hansard, CXII, 673/4, 28 June, 1850.
61. Morley, 545, to Mrs Cobden, 2 July, 1850.
62. Schwabe, *op. cit.* 234, Cobden at Leeds, 17 Jan., 1855.
63. BL Add. Mss. 43665, 6 July, 1850.
64. Morley, 545, to Mrs Cobden, 4 July, 1850.
65. *Ibid* 541, to Hadfield, 5 July, 1850.
66. BL Add. Mss. 43649, 18 Oct., 1850.
67. BL Add. Mss. 43660, to Simpson, 4 July, 1846.
68. Fraser, 'Edward Baines', in *Pressure from Without*, (ed. Hollis), 196/9.
69. CP 41, to Coppock, 15 June, 1847.
70. Morley, 505, to Combe, 5 Jan., 1849.
71. BL Add. Mss. 43668, to Jenkins, 1 May, 1850.
72. Schwabe, *op. cit.* 129/0, 30 Oct., 1850.
73. *Ibid* 147, 31 Oct., 1850.
74. Maltby, *op. cit.* 78/9.
75. Cobden, *Speeches*, Vol. II, 589, 22 May, 1851.
76. BL Add. Mss. 43665, to Roberton, 25 March, 1854.
77. BL Add. Mss. 43660, to Simpson, 4 July, 1846.
78. BL Add. Mss. 43653, to Ashworth, 7, 28 Dec., 1850.
79. BL Add. Mss. 43661, to Combe, 8 Jan., 1851.
80. CP 64, 17 March, 1851.
81. BL Add. Mss. 43649, to Bright, 6 March, 1851.
82. Cobden, *Speeches* Vol. II, 463/4, 23 Jan., 1851.
83. Edsall, *op. cit.* 118.
84. Hobson, *op. cit.* 66/7, to H. Richard, n/d.
85. BL Add. Mss. 43668, to Gardiner, 10 May, 1851.
86. CP 21, to Prentice, 8 August, 1851.
87. CP 64, to Sturge, 9 Oct., 1851.
88. CP 29, 11 Oct., 1851.
89. CP 29, to Thomasson, 27 Sept., 1852.
90. BL Add. Mss. 43668, to Sandford, 4 Nov., 1851.

91. Trevelyan, G. M. *op. cit.* 195, 4 Nov., 1851.
92. Schwabe, *op. cit.* 56/7, to Mrs Schwabe, 6 August, 1851.
93. Trevelyan, G. M., *op. cit.* 196, 26 Sept., 1851.
94. Morley, 559/0, 29 Sept., 1851.
95. Morley, 558, to Bright, 29 Sept., 1851.
96. BL Add. Mss. 43649, to Bright, 7 Nov., 1851.
97. Walmsley, *Sir Joshua Walmsley* 225, 10 Sept., 1851.
98. Trevelyan, G. M., *op. cit.* 196, 26 Sept., 1851.
99. BL Add. Mss. 50749, to Mrs Cobden, 4 Dec., 1851.
100. BL Add. Mss. 43649, to Bright, 7 Jan., 1852.
101. BL Add. Mss. 43657, to H. Richard, 13 Jan., 1852.
102. BL Add. Mss. 43649.
103. BL Add. Mss. 43657, to H. Richard, 15 March, 1852.
104. Ridley, *op. cit.* 401.
105. CP 29, 25 Feb., 1852.
106. Blake, *op. cit.* 316.
107. Morley, 575/6, 28 Feb., 1852.
108. BL Add. Mss. 43662, 5 March, 1852.
109. Morley, 580, to Wilson, 20 March, 1852.
110. CP 64, to Sturge, 19 April, 1 May, 9 June, 1852.
111. CP 29, to F. Cobden, 4 Dec., 1852.

Chapter 11

1. Morley, 467/9, to Ashworth, 7 Oct., 1850.
2. BL Add. Mss. 50749, to Mrs Cobden, 14 Oct., 1848.
3. Cobden, *Speeches*, Vol. I, 441, 9 Jan., 1850.
4. WSRO Add. Mss. 6011, to F. Cobden, 8, 13 Sept., 1849.
5. *Ibid.*
6. BL Add. Mss. 50751, [3 Nov.], 1850.
7. BL Add. Mss. 50749, 30 March, 1851.
8. CP 28, 24 April, 1851.
9. Morley, 555, 22 April, 1851.
10. BL Add. Mss. 50749, 3 August, 1851.
11. BL Add. Mss. 43653, to Ashworth, 29 July, 1851.
12. BL Add. Mss. 50749, 7 August, 1851.
13. BL Add. Mss. 50751.
14. WSRO Add. Mss. 6016, to Mrs Cobden, [Jan.] 1852.
15. MCL J. B. Smith Papers, to Smith.
16. WSRO Add. Mss. 6012, 1 Dec., 1852.
17. BL Add. Mss. 50749, 20 Feb., 1853.
18. WSRO Add. Mss. 6011, 2, 11, 13, 15, 28 April, 1853.
19. CP 119, to Moffatt, 12 Nov., 1853.
20. WSRO Add. Mss. 6011, to F. Cobden, 4 August, [16 Oct.], 21 Oct., 1853.
21. *Ibid* 28 Nov., 1853.
22. BL Add. Mss. 43655, to Hargreaves, 23 Dec., 1853.
23. CP 29, to F. Cobden, 7 Jan., 1854.
24. BL Add. Mss. 43655, to Hargreaves, 23 Dec., 1853.
25. Chamberlain, *Lord Aberdeen*, 431/2.
26. BL Add. Mss. 43662, 28 Dec., 1852.
27. Trevelyan, G. M. *op. cit.* 208/9.
28. BL Add. Mss. 43662, to Villiers, 28 Dec., 1852.
29. Bright, *Diaries* (ed. Walling), 137, 2 March, 1853.

30. Trevelyan, G. M., *op. cit.* 208.
31. Chamberlain, *op. cit.* 432.
32. MCL, Smith Papers, to Smith, 28 Dec., 1852.
33. Parker, *Graham*, Vol. II, 184, to Graham, 2 Nov., 1852.
34. BL Add. Mss. 43657, 30 August, 1852.
35. *Ibid*, to H. Richard, 14 Jan., 1853.
36. Cobden, *Political Writings*, Vol. I, 364.
37. Morley, 597, to Thomasson, 27 Sept., 1852.
38. Cobden, *Political Writings*, Vol. I, 452.
39. *Ibid* 489.
40. *Ibid* 494/5.
41. Bright, *op. cit.* 133, 26 Jan., 1853.
42. *The Times* 28, 29, 31 Jan., 1853.
43. Morley, 605/6, to Mrs Cobden, 31 Jan., 1853.
44. BL Add. Mss. 50749, 29 Jan. 1853.
45. Cobden, *Speeches*, Vol. II, 438.
46. Hansard, CXXIV, 290, 18 Feb., 1853.
47. BL Add. Mss. 50749, 4 Feb., 1853.
48. Walmsley, *op. cit.* 275, 25 Sept., 1852.
49. *Ibid* 270.
50. BL Add. Mss. 43668, to Jenkins, 23 Oct., 1852.
51. BL Add. Mss. 43650, 3 Jan., 1853.
52. *Ibid* 17 Jan., 1853.
53. Bright, *op. cit.* 133, 18 Jan., 1853.
54. BL Add. Mss. 43649, to Bright, 30 August, 1852.
55. MCL, Smith Papers, to Smith, 27 Oct., 1852.
56. BL Add. Mss. 43650, [18 March] 1854.
57. Gooch, *op. cit.* 134, to Russell, 28 Feb., 1854.
58. Hansard, CXXVI, 682, 28 April, 1853.
59. CP 29, 28 April, 1853.
60. Smiles, *op. cit.* 169, 171, 10 Oct., 23 Dec., 1851.
61. BL Add. Mss. 43668, to Lucas, 12 April, 1853.
62. BL Add. Mss. 43661, to Combe, 15 April, 1853.
63. BL Add. Mss. 43650, to Bright, 22 Nov., 1853.
64. *Ibid*.
65. see Hollis, P. *The Pauper Press* (1970)
66. BL Add. Mss. 43668, to Cassell, 6 Sept., 1850.
67. Hansard, CXXV, 1181/2, 14 April, 1853.
68. Hansard, CXXV, 162, 14 March, 1853.
69. Parliamentary Papers, Vol. XVII (1851), 118, (Select Committee on Newspaper Stamp.)
70. Collet, *History of the Taxes on Knowledge*, Vol. I, 207.
71. BL Add. Mss. 43657, to H. Richard, 18 Nov., 1853.
72. BL Add. Mss. 50751, to F. Cobden, 3 Jan., 1850.
73. BL Add. Mss. 50749, to Mrs Cobden, 7 Oct., 1853.
74. *Ibid* 8, 13 Oct., 1853.
75. Maxwell, *op. cit.* Vol. II, 26, to G.C. Lewis, 9, Oct., 1853.
76. BL Add. Mss. 43650, to Bright, 10 Sept., 1853.
77. MCL, Smith Papers, 5 Sept., 1853.
78. CP 29, to F. Cobden, 11 Oct., 1853.
79. Schwabe, *op. cit.* 192/207, 12 Oct., 1853.
80. BL Add. Mss. 50749, to Mrs Cobden, 13 Oct., 1853. CP 29, to F. Cobden, 16 Oct. 1853.
81. *The Times*, 17 Oct., 1853.

82. Martin, Kingsley, *The Triumph of Lord Palmerston*, 168.
83. BL Add. Mss. 43655, to Hargreaves, 23 Dec., 1853.
84. BL Add. Mss. 43650, to Bright, 12 Dec., 1853.
85. Morley, 611, 14 Dec., 1853.
86. Greville, *op. cit.* Vol. VII, 15, 9 Feb., 1854.
87. Hansard, CXXX, 917/44, 20 Feb., 1854.
88. BL Add. Mss. 43655, to Hargreaves.
89. Martin, *op. cit.* 197n.
90. BL Add. Mss. 43657, to H. Richard, 12 Jan., 1855.
91. BL Add. Mss. 43665, to Roberton, 10 Feb., 1854.
92. Trevelyan, G. M., *op. cit.* 233.
93. Kinglake, *The Invasion of the Crimea*, Vol. I, 430, (4th ed. 1863.)
94. Morley, 609. to McLaren, 19 Sept., 1853.
95. *The Times*, 14 Oct., 1853.
96. Hansard, CXIX, 591, 16 Feb., 1852. (Bernal Osborne)
97. BL Add. Mss. 43655, to Hargreaves, 7 Oct., 1854.
98. *Ibid.*
99. CP 29, to Lady Hatherton, 16 Nov., 1854.
100. CP 29, to F. Cobden, 30 Nov., 1854.
101. Morley, n.d. 630.
102. Hansard, CXXXVI, 801/18.
103. Mitford, *The Stanleys of Alderley*, 97. (1968 ed.)
104. CP 61, to Wilson, 1 Jan., 1855.
105. Schwabe, *op. cit.* 213/39.
106. Ridley, *op. cit.* 436.
107. Bright, *op. cit.* 184, 14 Jan., 1855.
108. Hobson, *op. cit.* 124, to H. Richard, 5 Feb., 1855.
109. Hansard, CXXXVIII, 1409/34, 5 June, 1855.
110. Bright, *op. cit.* 197, 5 June, 1855.
111. WSRO Add. Mss. 6016, 6 June, 1855.
112. Bright, *op. cit.* 197, 6 June, 1855.
113. Walmsley, *op. cit.* 209, to Walmsley, 17 Oct., 1848.
114. *Speeches of Charles Dickens*, ed. K. J. Fielding (Oxford, 1960), 206.
115. Anderson, *A Liberal State at War*, 122.
116. BL Add. Mss. 43665, to Col. Fitzmayer, 11 May, 1855.
117. *Ibid* to Roberton, 5 May, 1855.
118. *Ibid* to Roberton, 6 August, 1855.
119. BL Add. Mss. 43650, 28 June, 1855.
120. Bright, *op. cit.* 200, 1 July, 1855.
121. BL Add. Mss. 43650, to Bright, 26 June, 1855.
122. *Ibid* 15 August, 1855.
123. MCL, Smith Papers, to Smith, 3 Oct., 1855.
124. Morley, 643, to Ashworth, 19 Dec., 1855.
125. Cobden, *Political Writings*, Vol. II, 198.
126. *Ibid* 111/208.
127. BL Add. Mss. 43650, to Bright, 7 Jan., 1856.

Chapter 12

1. Morley, 648, to Parkes, 11 Nov., 1856.
2. BL Add. Mss. 43650, 8 March, 1856.
3. *Ibid* 17 March, 1856.
4. CP 120, 11 April, 1856.

5. CP 29, to Lady Hatherton, 26 May, 1856.
6. Morley, 647, to Parkes, 23 May, 4 June, 1856.
7. Schwabe, *op. cit.* 280, Cobden to Mrs Schwabe, 21 June, 1856.
8. CP 20, Cobden to Roberton, 26 July, 1856.
9. CP 57, to H. Williams, 25 Sept., 1856.
10. BL Add. Mss. 43664, to Parkes, 22 Oct., 1856.
11. BL Add. Mss. 50751, to F. Cobden, 15 Oct., 1856.
12. Hobson, *op. cit.* 172, to H. Richard, 19 Oct., 1856; BL Add. Mss. 43650, to Bright, 13 Oct., 1856.
13. BL Add. Mss. 43661, to Combe, 4 Nov., 1856.
14. BL Add. Mss. 50751, to F. Cobden, 8 Dec., 1856.
15. CP 119, to Moffatt, 22 Dec., 1856.
16. Hobson, *op. cit.* 130, to H. Richard, 29 Sept., 1855.
17. Morley, 637, to Bright, 30 Sept., 1855.
18. Hobson, *op. cit.* 173, to H. Richard, 19 Oct., 1856.
19. Koss, *The Rise and Fall of the Political Press in Britain*, Vol. I, 110.
20. BL Add. Mss. 43658, to H. Richard, 18 March, 1856.
21. BL Add. Mss. 43650, 3 April, 1856.
22. MCL, Wilson Papers, to Wilson, 27 August, 1856.
23. BL Add. Mss. 43650, to Bright, [8 August], 1856.
24. Hobson, *op. cit.* 165, to H. Richard, 31 July, 1856.
25. BL Add. Mss. 43658, to H. Richard, 6 June, 1856.
26. *Ibid* 5 June, 1856.
27. *Ibid* 16 Oct., 1856.
28. *Ibid* 13 Nov., 1856.
29. Hobson, *op. cit.* 176, to H. Richard, 4 Nov., 1856.
30. *Ibid* 163, 28 July, 1856.
31. BL Add. Mss. 43658, to H. Richard, 5 July, 1856.
32. Hobson, *op. cit.* 171, 15 Oct., 1856.
33. *Ibid* 156/60, to H. Richard, 17, 18 June, 1856.
34. *Ibid* 153, to H. Richard, June [5], 1856.
35. BL Add. Mss. 43650, to Bright, 23 Feb., 1856.
36. BL Add. Mss. 43664, to Parkes, 3 Nov., 1856.
37. MCL, Wilson Papers, to Wilson, 17, 19 Nov., 1856.
38. *Ibid* 23 Sept., 1856.
39. CP 20, to Parkes, 1 Feb., 1857.
40. BL Add. Mss. 43658, to H. Richard, [7 Jan.], 1856.
41. Hansard, CXLIV, 1391/1421.
42. Fortescue, Chichester, . . . *and Mr Fortescue*, 104.
43. Walmsley, *op. cit.* 324.
44. BL Add. Mss. 43650, to Bright, March 6, 1857.
45. *Ibid.*
46. Gladstone, *Diaries*, Vol. V, (Ed. H.C.G. Matthews, 1978) 202, March 3, 1857.
47. WSRO Add. Mss. 6011, to F. Cobden, 6 March, 1857.
48. Parker, *Graham*, Vol. II, 303, 16 March, 1857.
49. Southgate, *op. cit.* 425.
50. Morley, 657, 24 March, 1857.
51. Macaulay, G. O. *op. cit.* 652.
52. Morley, 661/2, to Moffatt, 7 April, 1857.
53. Schwabe, *op. cit.* 291/2, to Mrs Schwabe, 11 April, 1857.
54. Morley 660, to Cobden, 16 April, 1857.
55. BL Add. Mss. 43665, to Col. Fitzmayer, 2 April, 1857.
56. Morley, 649, to Parkes, 11 Nov., 1856.
57. BL Add. Mss. 43661, to Combe, 7 May, 1857.

58. Morley, 664, to Parkes, 28 July, 1857.
59. CP 119, to Moffatt, 16 Sept., 1857.
60. BL Add. Mss. 43650, to Bright, 20 Nov., 1857.
61. BL Add. Mss. 43650, to Bright, [20 Nov.], 1857.
62. BL Add. Mss. 43649, 18 Oct., 1850.
63. Cobden, *Political Works*, Vol. II, 23/106.
64. CP 20, to Leaf, 1 Sept., 1857; Morley, 676, to Bright, 22 Sept., 1857.
65. CP 122, to Lindsay, 27 Sept., 1857.
66. BL Add. Mss. 43661, to Combe, 17 July, 1857.
67. Morley, 677/8, to Col. Fitzmayer, 18 Oct., 1857.
68. BL Add. Mss. 43650, 11 August, 1857.
69. *Ibid* [11 Feb.], 20 Feb., 1858.
70. *Ibid* [11 Feb.] 1858.
71. *Ibid* 31 March, 1858.
72. *Ibid* 20 Feb., 1858.
73. Morley, 684, to Lindsay, 28 March, 1858.
74. BL Add. Mss. 43650, 10 April, 1858.
75. BL Add. Mss. 43662, to Paulton, 15 April, 1858.
76. MCL, Smith Papers, to Smith, 20 April, 1858.
77. BL Add. Mss. 43650, 17 Oct., 1858.
78. CP 119, to Moffatt, 20 May, 1857.
79. MCL, Wilson Papers, to Wilson, 25 Feb., 1855.
80. Gates, *The Illinois Central Railroad*, 74/5.
81. Fielden, 'Richard Cobden and America', 184, (unpub. Ph.D. thesis.)
82. CP 119, to Moffatt, 20 May, 1857.
83. *Ibid*, 16 Sept., 1857.
84. Fielden, *op. cit.* 182/3.
85. Cawley, *op. cit.* 48, to Walmsley, 18 Sept., 1857.
86. BL Add. Mss. 43653, to Ashworth, 3 Feb., 1859.
87. Cawley, *op. cit.* 189/90. (Diary).
88. *Ibid* 199. (Diary).
89. *Ibid* 144, 147 (Diary).
90. *Ibid* 53/4 to Gilpin, 10 April, 1859.
91. BL Add. Mss. 43669, to Sale, 26 March, 1859.
92. BL Add. Mss. 50749, 20 March, 1859.
93. *Ibid* 14 April, 1859.
94. *Ibid* 8 March, 1859.
95. BL Add. Mss. 43651, to Bright, 29 April, 1859.
96. Cawley, *op. cit.* 208. ('Observations')
97. *Ibid* 215. (Diary).
98. *Ibid* 180. (Diary).
99. *Ibid* 198. (Diary).
100. *Ibid* 68.
101. BL Add. Mss. 43651, to Bright, 29 April, 1859.
102. Cawley, *op. cit.* 191.
103. BL Add. Mss. 50749, 11 May, 1859.
104. *Ibid*
105. Morley, 692, to Mrs Cobden, 30 June, 1859.
106. *Ibid* 691/2.
107. Morley 692/3, to Mrs Cobden, 30 June, 1859.
108. BL Add. Mss. 43653, to Ashworth, 10 July, 1859.
109. Morley, 693/7, Cobden to Sale, 4 July, 1859.
110. *Ibid* 697.
111. *Ibid* 697.

112. BL Add. Mss. 43664, to Parkes, 11 Feb., 1860.
113. BL Add. Mss. 43665, to Col. Fitzmayer, 22 March, 1856.
114. Nevill, *Reminiscences*, 182/3.
115. *The Economist*, 26 Dec., 1863.

Chapter 13

1. BL Add. Mss. 50749, 8 March, 1859.
2. Nevill, *op. cit.* 188, to Lady D. Nevill, 17 Sept., 1859.
3. BL Add. Mss. 43676, to Sumner, 15 August, 1859.
4. Sturge Mss, to Charles Sturge, 6 Oct., 1859.
5. Nevill, *op cit.* 188.
6. BL Add. Mss. 44135.
7. Shannon, *op. cit.* 395.
8. Dunham, *The Anglo-French Treaty of Commerce of 1860*, 50.
9. *Ibid* 51/2.
10. BL Add. Mss. 44135, 11 Oct., 1859.
11. *Ibid* 12 Oct., 1859.
12. BL Add. Mss. 43651, 17 Oct., 1859.
13. BL Add. Mss. 43675A, (Diary) 24 Oct., 1859.
14. Morley, 766, (Diary), 10 June, 1860.
15. Morley, 711.
16. *Ibid*, 708/13.
17. BL Add. Mss. 43675A (Diary), 29 Oct., 1859.
18. BL Add. Mss. 44135, 29 Oct., 1859.
19. *Ibid* 11 Nov., 1859.
20. Morley, 717.
21. BL Add. Mss. 43651, to Bright, 20 Nov., 1859.
22. BL Add. Mss. 43675A (Diary), 17 Nov., 1859.
23. BL Add. Mss. 43651, to Bright, 16 Dec., 1859.
24. BL Add. Mss. 43655, to Hargreaves, 21 Nov., 1859.
25. BL Add. Mss. 44135, 23 Nov., 1859.
26. *Ibid*, 28 Nov., 1859.
27. BL Add. Mss. 43655, to Hargreaves, 11 Jan., 1860.
28. Morley, 717.
29. BL Add. Mss. 44135, to Gladstone, 28 Nov., 1859.
30. *Ibid* 17 Dec., 1859.
31. *Ibid* 19 Dec., 1859.
32. *Ibid*.
33. BL Add. Mss. 44135, to Gladstone, 16 Jan., 1859.
34. Morley, 720/4.
35. BL Add. Mss. 43654, to Ashworth, December 1859.
36. Morley, 813, to Bright, 29 Dec., 1859.
37. Morley, *Gladstone*, Vol. II, 22.
38. Dunham, *op. cit.* 72, n.15, 23 Dec., 1859.
39. *Ibid* 83/4.
40. BL Add. Mss. 43654, to Ashworth, 18 Jan., 1860.
41. Dunham, *op. cit.* 125/30.
42. BL Add. Mss. 44135, 13 Jan., 1860.
43. *Ibid* 17 Jan., 1860.
44. BL Add. Mss. 43651, 23 Jan., 1860.
45. BL Add. Mss. 44135, 19 Jan., 1860.
46. BL Add. Mss. 43651, to Bright, 16 Dec., 1859.

47. BL Add. Mss. 43655, to Hargreaves, 24 Feb., 1860.
48. Schwabe, *op. cit.* 313, Cobden to Mrs Schwabe, 26 March, 1860.
49. Gladstone, *Diaries*, Vol. V, (Ed. H.C.G. Matthews, 1978) 464, 10 Feb., 1860.
50. BL Add. Mss. 44135, 25 Feb., 1860.
51. BL Add. Mss. 43651, 10 Feb., 1860.
52. BL Add. Mss. 43664, to Parkes, 11 Feb., 1860.
53. BL Add. Mss. 43651, to Bright, 10 Feb., 1860.
54. BL Add. Mss. 43655, Cobden to Ashworth, 27 August, 1860.
55. BL Add. Mss. 43651, 13 April, 1860.
56. *Ibid.*
57. BL Add. Mss. 50749, to Mrs Cobden, [12 April], 1860.
58. Sturge Mss, Ashworth to Charles Sturge, 15 March, 1860.
59. *Ibid*, 10 March, 1860.
60. *Ibid* 8 May, 1860.
61. BL Add. Mss. 43675B, (Diary), 19 April, 1860.
62. *Ibid* 20 April, 1860.
63. *The Times*, 1 Feb., 1861.
64. BL Add. Mss. 43676, to Slagg, 9 July, 1860.
65. WSRO Add. Mss. 2761, to T. Potter, 6 August, 1860.
66. Morley, 760.
67. BL Add. Mss. 43675B, (Diary) 30 May, 1860.
68. BL Add. Mss. 43675C, (Diary) 25 August, 1860.
69. BL Add. Mss. 43676, to Slagg, 11 Sept., 1860.
70. *Ibid.*
71. BL Add. Mss. 43651, 2 Oct., 1860.
72. Morley, 785/6.
73. BL Add. Mss. 43651, to Bright, 16 June, 1860.
74. *Ibid* 22, 30 June, 1860.
75. BL Add. Mss. 44135, 18 June, 1860.
76. Magnus, *Gladstone*, (London 1954. 1978 ed), 148.
77. BL Add. Mss. 43651, to Bright, 25 July, 1860.
78. Greville, *op. cit.* Vol. VII 482, 11 August, 1860.
79. BL Add. Mss. 43670, 2 August, 1860.
80. BL Add. Mss. 43659, to H. Richard, 22 Nov., 1860.
81. Morley, 792.
82. WSRO Add. Mss. 2761, to T. Potter, 28 Dec., 1860; Morley, 828.
83. BL Add. Mss. 43675C, (Diary) 21 Jan., 1861.
84. *Ibid* 21 Dec., 1860.
85. Malmesbury, *Memoirs*, Vol. II, 245, Bidwell to Malmesbury, 28 Dec., 1860.
86. BL Add. Mss. 43675C, (Diary) 11 March, 1–10 April, 1861.
87. BL Add. Mss. 43651, to Bright, 10 Jan., 1861.
88. BL Add. Mss. 43670, to S. Morley, 29 Jan., 1861.
89. BL Add. Mss. 43675C, (Diary) 26 Jan., 1861.
90. Morley, 796/8.
91. BL Add. Mss. 43654, to Ashworth, 26 April, 1861.

Chapter 14

1. WSRO Add. Mss. 6017, 28 May, 1861.
2. BL Add. Mss. 43651, 10 Jan., 1861.
3. Stanley, Lord, *Disraeli, Derby and the Conservative Party* (ed. Vincent), 167.
4. WSRO Add. Mss. 6017, to Mrs Cobden, 18 July, 1861.
5. Cobden, *Speeches*, Vol. II, 250, 26 June, 1861.
6. WSRO Add. Mss. 6017, to Mrs Cobden, 28 June, 1861.

7. BL Add. Mss. 43655, to Hargreaves.
8. CP 134, to Lucas, 25 Sept., 1861.
9. BL Add. Mss. 43652, to Bright, 9 Jan., 1862.
10. CP 134, to Lucas, 2 Oct., 1861.
11. *Ibid* 16 Jan., 1862.
12. Hansard, CLXII, 1379, 2 May, 1861.
13. BL Add. Mss. 43651, 19 May, 1861.
14. Cobden, *Speeches*. Vol. II, 254/5, 26 June, 1861.
15. Jenkins, *Britain and the War for the Union*, Vol. I, 166.
16. BL Add. Mss. 43676, to Slagg, 18 Oct., 1861.
17. Hobson, *op. cit.* 294, Cobden to H. Richard, 18 Dec., 1861.
18. Morley, 854/6, 29 Nov., 1861.
19. UCL, Parkes Papers, to Parkes, 7 Nov., 1861.
20. CP 119, to Moffatt, 26 Jan., 1862.
21. BL Add. Mss. 43664, to Parkes, 4 Dec., 1861.
22. Jenkins, *op. cit.* 219.
23. BL Add. Mss. 43652, 23 Jan., 1862.
24. Hobson, *op. cit.* 292, to H. Richard, 26 Oct., 1861.
25. CP 33, to Lindsay, 5 Jan., 1862.
26. BL Add. Mss. 43659, to H. Richard, 6 Nov., 1861.
27. Cobden, *Political Writings* Vol. II, 215/435.
28. Hobson, *op. cit.* 302, 2 Feb., 1862.
29. *Ibid* 304, 26 April, 1862.
30. Baxter, *The Introduction of the Ironclad Warship*, 131, 157/8.
31. Hobson, *op. cit.* 288. to H. Richard, 17 April, 1861.
32. Greville, *op. cit.* Vol. VII, 482, 11 August, 1860.
33. Hodder, *Samuel Morley*, 151, to Morley, 8 Nov., 1861.
34. BL Add. Mss. 43676, to E. Alexander, 19 Nov., 1862.
35. Cobden, *Political Writings*, Vol II, 17, 'Letter to Henry Ashworth'.
36. Morley, 865, to Chevalier, 7 August, 1862.
37. BL Add. Mss. 43652, to Bright, [18 Feb.], 1862.
38. Morley, 862, to Chevalier, 17 March, 1862.
39. Cobden, *Political Writings*, Vol. II, 5/32.
40. Cobden, *Speeches*, Vol. II, 279/303, 25 Oct., 1862.
41. Hobson, *op. cit.* 357, 12 Dec., 1861.
42. *Ibid* 360, 19 Dec., 1861.
43. BL Add. Mss. 43652, 14 Jan., 1862.
44. Hansard, CLXVIII, 682/91, 22 July, 1862; 942, 944, 28 July, 1862.
45. *Ibid* 751/60, 24 July, 1862.
46. *Ibid* 1031, 30 July, 1862.
47. BL Add. Mss. 43652, to Bright, 7 August, 1862.
48. BL Add. Mss. 43655, to Hargreaves, 7 August, 1862.
49. CP 119, to Moffatt, 19 August, 1862.
50. BL Add. Mss. 43652, to Bright, 28 August, 1862.
51. BL Add. Mss. 43654, 28 August, 1862.
52. *Ibid* 10 Sept., 1862.
53. BL Add. Mss. 43662, to Paulton, 17 Oct., 1862.
54. *Ibid*
55. Hobson, *op. cit.* 306, to H. Richard, 15 Sept., 1862.
56. Cobden, *Speeches*, Vol. II, 308, 29 Oct., 1862.
57. CP 71, to McLaren, 21 Oct., 1862.
58. Longmate, *The Hungry Mills*, 135.
59. Watts, *The Facts of the Cotton Famine*, 173/7.
60. BL Add. Mss. 43662, to Villiers, 6 Nov., 1862.

61. BL Add. Mss. 43655, to Hargreaves, 21 Nov., 1862.
62. BL Add. Mss. 43652, to Bright, 7 Oct., 1862.
63. *Ibid* 29 Dec., 1862.
64. Morley, 869/0, to Sumner, 13 Feb., 1863.
65. Hansard, CLXX, 723/36, 24 April, 1863.
66. Morley, 872, to Sumner, 22 May, 1863.
67. *Ibid* 871/2, 2 May, 1863.
68. Cobden, *Speeches*, Vol. II, 117, 24 Nov., 1863.
69. Morley, 887/98.
70. CP 135, to Lucas, 10 Dec., 1863.
71. BL Add. Mss. 43664, to Parkes, 1 Feb., 1864.
72. MCL Smith Papers, to Smith, 20 Dec., 1863.
73. BL Add. Mss. 43676, to Slagg, 26 Dec., 1863.
74. Adams, *The Education of Henry Adams*, 125/6. (Massachusetts, 1918 ed.)
75. Sandiford, *Great Britain and the Schleswig-Holstein Question*, 111/2.
76. BL Add. Mss. 43652, 4 July, 1863.
77. Hansard, CLXXVI, 827/42, 5 July, 1864.
78. Morley, 914, 5 Nov., 1864.
79. Hobson, *op. cit.* 330, 10 Nov., 1864.
80. Cobden, *Speeches*, Vol. II, 339/74, 24 Nov., 1864.
81. WSRO Add. Mss. 2761, Cobden to T. Potter, 10 May, 1864.
82. *Ibid*
83. BL Add. Mss. 43665, to Roberton, 22 Jan., 1864.
84. BL Add. Mss. 43652, to Bright, 30 March, 1864.
85. Cobden, *Speeches*, Vol. II, 367, 23 Nov., 1864.
86. BL Add. Mss. 43652, to Bright, 7 Feb., 1865.
87. Leventhal, *Respectable Radical; George Howell and Victorian Working Class Politics*, 63.
88. Howell, George, *Labour Legislation, Labour Movements and Labour Leaders*, (London, 1902), 144.
89. MCL, Smith Papers, to Smith, 8 Sept., 1864.
90. BL Add. Mss. 50749, 24 Nov., 1864.
91. BL Add. Mss. 43676, to Slagg, 24 Dec., 1864.
92. BL Add. Mss. 43652, to Bright, 14 Dec., 1864.
93. Walmsley, *op. cit.* 349, to Walmsley, 18 March, 1865.
94. Morley, 928/9.
95. BL Add. Mss. 43652, to Bright, 17 Nov., 1864.
96. Hobson, *op. cit.* 369, to Sumner, 13 Feb., 1863.
97. WSRO Add. Mss. 6017, to Mrs Cobden, 23 Nov., 1864.
98. BL Add. Mss. 43654, to Ashworth, 11 Nov., 1863.
99. CP 85, to Col. Cole, 20 March, 1865.
100. Bright, *op. cit.* 284, 5 March, 1865.
101. BL Add. Mss. 44136, 14, 20 Feb., 1865.
102. BL Add. Mss. 43671, Duke of Argyll to Cobden, 24 Feb., 1865.
103. Bright, *op. cit.* 285/6.
104. *Ibid* 288.
105. *The Economist*, 8 April, 1865.
106. Hansard, CLXXVIII, 673/6, 3 April, 1865.
107. *The Economist*, 8 April, 1865.
108. Morley, *Gladstone*, Vol. II, 143.

SELECT BIBLIOGRAPHY

Manuscript Sources

British Library, Additional Manuscripts, Cobden, Peel, Gladstone, Bright, Sturge, Place Mss.

West Sussex Record Office, Chichester. Cobden Papers and Additional Manuscripts.

Manchester Central Library. Wilson, J. B. Smith, and Cobden Family Papers. Anti-Corn Law League Letterbooks.

University College, London. Parkes Papers.

Sturge Mss. (in the possession of Mrs Sylvia Lewin.)

Theses

Fielden, K. 'Richard Cobden and America'. (Cambridge Ph.D. 1966.)

Gatrell, V. A. C. 'The Commercial Middle Classes in Manchester c.1820–57'. (Cambridge Ph.D. 1972.)

Carter L. J. 'The development of Cobden's thought on international relations particularly with reference to his role in the mid-nineteenth century peace movement.' (Cambridge Ph.D. 1971).

Published Sources

This is not intended to be a comprehensive list of either the writings of modern authorities or contemporary biographies, memoirs and journals.

Adams, E. D. *Great Britain and the American Civil War*. 2 Vols. London 1925.

Adams, Henry. *The Education of Henry Adams. An Autobiography*. Cambridge, Mass. 1918.

Anderson, O. *A Liberal State at War*. London, 1967.

Ashworth, Henry. *Recollections of Richard Cobden, M.P. and the Anti-Corn Law League*. 2 Vols. London 1877.

Axon, W. E. A. *Cobden as a Citizen. A Chapter in Manchester History*.

(Including Cobden's pamphlet 'Incorporate Your Borough'.) London 1907.

Baines, T. *Lancashire and Cheshire, Past and Present.* Vol. II. London 1867.

Barnes, D. G. *A History of the English Corn Laws from 1660 to 1846.* London 1930.

Barrington, E. I. *The Servant of All.* 2 Vols. London 1927.

Bartlett, C. J. *Great Britain and Sea Power 1815–1853.* Oxford 1963. 'The Mid-Victorian Reappraisal of Naval Policy' in *Studies in International History*, Eds. K. Bourne and D. C. Watt, London 1967.

Baxter, J. P. *The Introduction of the Ironclad Warship.* Cambridge, Mass. 1933.

Beales, A. C. F. *The History of Peace.* London 1931.

Bellman, H. *Bricks and Mortals.* London 1949.

Benson, A. C. and Esher, Viscount, *The Letters of Queen Victoria 1837–61.* 3 Vols. London 1907.

Best, G. *Mid-Victorian Britain 1851–70.* London 1971.

Blake, R. *Disraeli* London 1966.

Boyson, Rhodes. *The Ashworth Cotton Enterprise.* Oxford 1970.

Briggs, A. (ed.) *Chartist Studies.* London 1962.

Bright, John. *The Diaries of John Bright*, (Ed. R. A. J. Walling.) London 1930.

Calkin, W. N. 'A Victorian Free Trade Lobby'. (*Economic History Review*, 2nd series, Vol. XIII, (1960/1) p. 90 ff.)

Cawley, E. H. *The American Diaries of Richard Cobden.* Princeton, 1952.

Chambers, J. D. and Mingay, G. E. *The Agricultural Revolution 1750–1880.* London 1966.

Chamberlain, M. *Lord Aberdeen.* London 1983.

Cobden, Richard. *Speeches.* 2 Vols. ed. J. Bright and E. Thorold Rogers London 1870. *Political Writings.* 2 Vols. London 1867.

Cole, G. D. H. *Chartist Portraits.* London 1941. (1965 ed.)

Collet, C. D. *The History of the Taxes on Knowledge.* 2 Vols. London 1899.

Conacher, J. B. *The Aberdeen Coalition 1852–1855.* Cambridge 1968. *The Peelites and the Party System 1846–52.* Newton Abbot 1972.

Costin W. C. *Great Britain and China 1883–1860.* Oxford 1937.

Cowherd, R. G. *The Politics of Religious Dissent.* New York 1956. (London 1959 ed.)

Grosby, Travis I. *English Farmers and the Politics of Protection 1815–52.* Hassocks, Sussex, 1977.

Dawson, W. H. *Richard Cobden and Foreign Policy.* London 1926.

Driver, C. *Tory Radical: The Life of Richard Oastler.* New York 1946.

Dunham, A. L. *The Anglo-French Treaty of Commerce of 1860 and the Progress of the Industrial Revolution in France.* Ann Arbor 1930.

Edsall, N. C. 'A Failed National Movement: the Parliamentary and Financial Reform Association, 1848–54.' (*Bulletin of Institute of Historical Research*, Vol. XLIX, (1976), p. 108ff.)

Fairlie, S. 'The Nineteenth Century Corn Law Reconsidered.' (*Economic History Review*, 2nd series, Vol. XVIII (1965). p. 562ff.)

Fawcett, Mrs *Sir William Molesworth.* London 1901.

Fay, C. R. *The Corn Laws and Social England.* Cambridge 1932.

Finlayson, G. B. A. M. *The Seventh Earl of Shaftesbury*. London 1981.

Fortescue, Chichester. *... and Mr Fortescue:* A Selection from the Diaries from 1851 to 1862 of Chichester Fortescue, Lord Carlingford. Ed. O. Wyndham Hewett. London 1958.

Fox, G. *British Admirals and Chinese Pirates (1832–1869)*. London 1940.

Fraser, D. *Urban Politics in Victorian England*. Leicester 1976. 'Voluntaryism and West Riding Politics in the mid-Nineteenth Century', (*Northern History*, Vol. XIII (1977), p. 199ff.) 'Edward Baines' in *Pressure from Without in Early Victorian England*, Ed. P. Hollis. London 1974.

Gash, N. *Sir Robert Peel*. London 1972. *Politics in the Age of Peel*. London 1953.

Gates, P. W. *The Illinois Central Railroad and its Colonization Work*. Harvard 1934.

Gibbon, C. *George Combe*. 2 Vols. London 1878.

Gleason, J. H. *The Genesis of Russophobia in Great Britain*. Harvard 1950.

Gooch, G. P. (Ed). *The Later Correspondence of Lord John Russell, 1840–1878*. 2 Vols. 1925.

Grampp, W. D. *The Manchester School of Economics*. Stanford/London 1960.

Grant, J. *The Newspaper Press*. 2 Vols. London 1871.

Greville, C. *The Greville Memoirs 1814–1860*. Ed. Lytton Strachey and R. Fulford, 8 Vols. London 1938.

Hansard. *Parliamentary Debates*, 3rd series, 1841–65.

Henderson, G. 'The Pacifists of the Fifties', (*Journal of Modern History*, Vol. IX, (1937), p. 314ff.)

Hill, R.& G. B. *Sir Rowland Hill*. 2 Vols. London 1880.

Himmelfarb, G. *The Idea of Poverty: England in the Early Industrial Age*. London 1984.

Hobhouse, S. *Joseph Sturge*. London 1919.

Hobson, J. A. *Richard Cobden; The International Man*. London 1919. (ed. 1968.)

Hodder, Edwin. *Seventh Earl of Shaftesbury*. 3 Vols. London 1886. *Samuel Morley*. London 1888.

Hollis, P. (Ed.) *Pressure from Without in Early Victorian England*. London 1974.

Hovell M. *The Chartist Movement*. Manchester 1918. (1966 ed.)

Howe, A. *The Cotton Masters 1830–1860*. Oxford 1984.

Hughes, E. 'The Development of Cobden's Economic Doctrines and his Methods of Propaganda.' (*Bulletin of John Rylands Institute*, Vol. XXII (1938), p. 405ff.)

Irwin, G. *Nineteenth-Century Borneo*. Leyden 1955. (Singapore, 1965 reprint.)

Jenkins, B. *Britain and the War for the Union*. 2 Vols. Montreal/London 1974 and 1980.

Jenkins, M. *The General Strike of 1842*. London 1980.

Jones, D. K. 'Lancashire, the American Common School, and the Religious Problem in British Education.' (*British Journal of Educational Studies*, Vol. XV (1967) p. 292ff)

Jordan, H. D. 'Richard Cobden and Penny Postage', (*Victorian Studies* Vol. VIII (1965) p. 355ff.)

Kitson Clark, G. S. R. *Peel and the Conservative Party*. London 1964. 'The Repeal of the Corn Laws and the Politics of the Forties', (*Economic History Review*, 2nd series, Vol. IV (1951) p. 1ff.) 'The Electorate and the Repeal of the Corn Laws', (*Transactions of the Royal Historical Society*, 5th series, Vol. I (1951) p. 109ff.) 'Hunger and Politics in 1842', (*Journal of Modern History*, Vol. XXV (1953) p. 355ff.)

Kohl, J. G. *Ireland, Scotland and England*. London 1844.

Koss, S. *The Rise and Fall of the Political Press in Britain*. Vol. I. London 1981.

Lane-Poole, S. *Stratford Canning, Viscount Stratford de Redcliffe*. 2 Vols. London 1888.

Lawson-Tancred, M. 'The Anti-League and the Corn Law Crisis of 1846.' (*Historical Journal*, Vol. III (1960) p. 162ff)

Lee A. J. *The Origins of the Popular Press 1855–1914*. London 1976.

Leventhal, F. M. *Respectable Radical: George Howell & Victorian Working Class Politics*. London 1971.

Longmate, N. *The Hungry Mills*. London 1978. *The Breadstealers*. London 1984.

Love, B. *Manchester as it is*. Manchester 1839. (reprint 1971, E. J. Morton, Didsbury, Manchester.)

Lyons, F. S. L. *Internationalism in Europe 1815–1914*. Leyden 1963.

Maccoby, S. *English Radicalism 1832–52*. London 1935. *English Radicalism 1853–86*. London 1938.

McCord, N. *The Anti-Corn Law League 1838–1846*. London 1958. (1968 ed.). 'Cobden and Bright in Politics 1846–1857', in *Ideas and Institutions of Victorian Britain*, Ed. R. Robson. London 1967.

McGilchrist, J. *Richard Cobden*. London 1865.

Mackie, J. B. *Duncan McLaren*. 2 Vols. London 1888.

Malmesbury, Earl of. *Memoirs of an Ex-Minister*. 2 Vols. London 1884.

Maltby, S. E. *Manchester and the Movement for National Elementary Education 1800–1870*. Manchester 1918.

Martin, Kingsley. *The Triumph of Lord Palmerston*. London 1924. (1963 ed.)

Martineau, H. *History of England during the Thirty Years Peace 1816–1846*. 2 Vols. London 1850. *Autobiography*. 2 Vols. London 1877. (3rd ed.)

Mather, F. C. 'The General Strike of 1842', (*Exeter Papers in Economic History*, No.6, 1972, p. 5ff.)

Maxwell, H. *Fourth Earl of Clarendon*. 2 Vols. London 1913.

Melbourne, Lord. *The Melbourne Papers*, Ed. Lloyd C. Sanders. London 1889.

Mitford, N. (ed.) *The Stanleys of Alderley*. London 1939. (1968 ed.)

Morley, John. *Richard Cobden* 2 Vols. London 1879. (1 Vol. 1903 ed.) *W. E. Gladstone* 3 Vols. London 1903.

Morrell, W. P. *British Colonial Policy in the Age of Peel and Russell*. Oxford 1930.

Mosse, G. L. 'The Anti-League, 1844–46', (*Economic History Review*, Vol. XVII (1947) p. 134ff.)

Murphy, J. *Church, State and Schools in Britain 1800–1970*. London 1971.

Napier, W. *General Sir Charles James Napier*. 4 Vols. London 1857.

Nevill, Lady Dorothy. *Reminiscences*. London 1906.

Parker, C. S. *Sir James Graham, 1792–1861. 2 Vols. London 1907. (Ed.) Sir*

Robert Peel from his private papers. 3 Vols. London 1899.

Parliamentary Papers, Select Committee Reports: 1837/8, XX, Pt 11, Postage Rates. 1840, IV, Banks of Issue. 1842, IX, Payment of Wages. 1846, VIII, System of Registration for County Voters. 1851, XVII, Newspaper Stamp.

Prentice, A. *History of the Anti-Corn Law League.* 2 Vols. London 1853. (1968 ed.)

Prest, J. *Politics in the Age of Cobden.* London 1977. *Lord John Russell.* London 1972.

Pringle, R. *Rajahs and Rebels: The Ibans of Sarawak under Brooke Rule, 1841–1941.* London 1970.

Read, D. *Cobden and Bright: A Victorian Political Partnership.* London 1967. *The English Provinces c.1760–1960.* London 1964.

Redford, A. *History of Local Government in Manchester.* 3 Vols. London 1940.

Reid, S. J. *Lord Durham.* 2 Vols. London 1906.

Ridley, J. *Lord Palmerston.* London 1970.

Robbins, K. *John Bright.* London 1979.

Rose, A. G. 'The Plug Riots of 1842 in Lancashire and Cheshire', (*Transactions of the Lancashire and Cheshire Antiquarian Society*, Vol. LXVII (1957) p. 75ff.)

Runciman, S. *The White Rajahs: A History of Sarawak from 1841 to 1946.* Cambridge, 1960.

Sandisford, K. A. P. *Great Britain and the Schleswig-Holstein Question 1848–64.* Toronto 1975.

Schwabe, Mrs Salis. *Reminiscences of Richard Cobden.* London 1895.

Schoyen, A. R. *The Chartist Challenge: A Portrait of George Julian Harney.* London 1958.

Schuyler R. L. *The Fall of the Old Colonial System: A Study in British Free Trade 1770–1870.* London 1945.

Shannon, R. *Gladstone.* Vol. I.1809–1865. London 1982.

Slugg, J. T. *Reminiscences of Manchester Fifty Years Ago.* Manchester 1881.

Smiles, S. *Autobiography.* London 1905.

Somerville, A. *Free Trade and the League.* 2 Vols. Manchester 1853. *The Whistler at the Plough.* Manchester 1852.

Southgate, D. *The Most English Minister ...': the policies and politics of Palmerston.* London 1966.

Stanley, Lord. *Disraeli, Derby and the Conservative Party.* Journals and Memoirs of Edward Henry, Lord Stanley, 1849–1869. Ed. J. Vincent. Hassocks, Sussex. 1978.

Stewart, R. *The Politics of Protection: Lord Derby and the Protectionist Party 1841–52.* Cambridge 1971.

Taylor, A. J. P. The Troublemakers; dissent over foreign policy 1792–1939. London 1957.

Thistlethwaite, F. *The Anglo-American Connection in the Early Nineteenth Century.* Philadelphia 1959.

Thompson, F. M. L. 'Whigs and Liberals in the West Riding, 1830–60.' (*English Historical Review*, Vol. LXXIV (1959) p. 214ff.)

de Tocqueville, A. *Journeys to England and Ireland.* Ed. J. P. Mayer, London 1958.

Trautz. F. 'Richard Cobden's Associations with Germany', (*Bulletin of John Rylands Institute*, Vol. 34, (1951/2) p. 459ff.)

Trevelyan, G. M. *John Bright*. London 1913.

Trevelyan, G. O. *Lord Macaulay*. London 1876. 2 Vols. (1 vol. 1959 ed.)

Turnbull, G. *History of the Calico Printing Industry of Great Britain*. Altrincham 1951.

Vincent, J. *The Formation of the British Liberal Party 1857–68*. London 1966.

Wallas, G. *Francis Place 1771–1854*. London 1898.

Walmsley, H. M. *Sir Joshua Walmsley*. London 1879.

Ward, J. T. *Chartism*. London 1973. *The Factory Movement 1830–1855*. 1962.

Watkin, A. *Extracts from his Journal 1814–1856*. London 1920.

Watkin, E. W. *Alderman Cobden*. London 1891.

Watts, J. *The Facts of the Cotton Famine*. London 1866.

Woodward, E. L. *The Age of Reform 1815–1870*. London 1838.

Ziegler, P. *Melbourne*, London 1976.

INDEX